INJURY TIME

David Goldblatt

INJURY TIME

FOOTBALL IN A STATE OF EMERGENCY

MUDLARK

Mudlark
An imprint of HarperCollins*Publishers*
1 London Bridge Street
London SE1 9GF

www.harpercollins.co.uk

HarperCollins*Publishers*
Macken House, 39/40 Mayor Street Upper
Dublin 1, D01 C9W8, Ireland

First published by Mudlark 2025

1 3 5 7 9 10 8 6 4 2

A catalogue record of this book is
available from the British Library

HB ISBN 978-0-00-869740-2
PB ISBN 978-0-00-869741-9

Printed and bound in the UK using 100%
renewable electricity at CPI Group (UK) Ltd

Contents

Preface   1

Introduction
'Let the Soap Opera Begin!'
Football as the National Allegory   5

Part I
Brexitball
Football after the Referendum, 2016–19

1. 'We're All Leaving Europe!'
   Football and the Referendum   23

2. Uneven Playing Fields
   Success, Failure and the Economics of Football   37

3. Football's Dirty Secret
   Brexit, Racism and British Football   50

4. Duty of Care
   Football's Treatment of Its Youth   66

5. 'You Must be Joking, Ref'
   Football, Officials and the Decline of Authority   79

6. Goodbye, Great Britain
   Football and the Politics of National Fragmentation   99

7. Which England Will Turn Up?
   English Nationalism and the 2018 World Cup   131

Part II
Sick as a Parrot
Football in the Time of Covid, 2020–21

8. From Lockdown to Meltdown
   Football, Covid and the Mental-Health Crisis   141

9. Taking the Knee
   Football and Black Lives Matter   156

10. The Silence of the Stands
    Football without Crowds   164

11. A Crisis of Confidence
    Football, Vaccines and Science   174

12. Football's Shock Doctrine
    The European Super League as Disaster Capitalism   185

13. 'Let's Go Fucking Mental!'
    Post-Covid Mania at Euro 2020   196

Part III
Injury Time
Football in a State of Emergency, 2022–24

14. Poetry in Motion
    Football, the Arts and the Polycrisis   213

15. The Fall of the Roman Empire
   *Ukraine, Russia and the New Geography of
   Football Club Ownership*   227

16. The Return of the Repressed
   *Football Crowds, Pitch Invasions and the
   New Disorder*   246

17. Alternative England
   *Euro 2021 and the Rise and Rise of
   Women's Football*   265

18. Playing for a Pittance
   Grassroots Football and the Cost of Living Crisis   283

19. When the Fun Stops
   Gambling and Cryptocurrency in British Football   299

20. The Queen Is Dead
   Football, the Monarch and Memorialisation   310

21. Qatar 2022 and All That
   Political Football on a Global Stage   328

22. Power Games
   English Football and the Middle East   344

23. Playing Against the Clock
   Football and the Climate Crisis   358

Conclusion
   'There's Always Next Season'
   Football and the Politics of Hope, 2024–25 377

Acknowledgements   396
Notes   397
Index   455

'The state of emergency in which we live
is not the exception but the norm.'
Walter Benjamin

'Behind every kick of the ball
there has to be a thought.'
Dennis Bergkamp

Preface

In the last decade a series of percussive blows has struck the UK. First, following the global economic crisis of 2008, there was a near decade of fiscal austerity which broke what little was left of the social contract and the welfare state, and which, alongside wage stagnation for the majority and the soaring wealth of the 0.1 per cent, left the country at is most unequal since the late nineteenth century. Second, the Brexit referendum of 2016 saw the departure of the UK from the European Union, and in addition to the massive economic and political dislocations this entailed, unleashed a wave of nativism and racism, poisoning and polarising the character of public debate in the country. Third, the Covid pandemic of 2020 brought normal life to a halt, killed almost a quarter of a million people, left over a million more with long-term health conditions, and sent the nation's mental health and economic prospects, already perilous, into tailspins. Finally, in the wake of the pandemic, Britain was engulfed in a series of interconnecting crises beginning with Russia's invasion of Ukraine in early 2022, followed by an unprecedented cost of living crisis, a political meltdown that would see off three prime ministers in six months, and extreme weather which announced that the climate crisis had actually arrived.

Intellectuals have struggled to weave together any kind of plausible story that might explain this concatenation of events. Serious contributions have been made to individual strands of our predicament – our imperial amnesia, democratic deficits and scandalous inequalities – but a popular narrative that describes their intersection has eluded us. The Leave campaign's story was one early attempt to do so, positing the European Union and migrants as the villains of the piece and offering the sunlit uplands of 'independence' as the final chapter, but fantasy will only get you so far. Having presided over a succession of calamities for which it refuses to take responsibility, the Conservative Party has been reduced to inventing conspiracy theories to explain the failures of its term in office. Meanwhile, the Labour Party under Keir Starmer appears to have abandoned storytelling altogether in favour of an almost ideology-free New Labour Lite. The arts, still capable of commenting on and capturing aspects of this polycrisis, have yet to offer the kind of state of the nation panorama that it deserves. It would be a tall order for any novel or play or film to tell these stories in their interrelated complexity. It is hard to imagine that any single cultural form could narrate this extraordinary turn of events and simultaneously illuminate the deep structures and conflicts that produced them. How much harder would it be to do so in a way that explores the differences between the four nations of the UK? It is the contention of this book that football, without ever intending to do so, has offered us precisely that.

Football's capacity to illuminate something profound about our whole society is not new. Certainly, in retrospect, if not always at the time, the game has offered a richly detailed tableau of the state of the nation, and a popular, comprehensible analogy of its transformations: England 3, Hungary 6 in 1953, the first defeat at home to a foreign power, was a game that prefigured the Suez crisis and its confirmation of post-imperial decline; holy of holies, winning the World Cup in 1966 was the last glorious global moment for the best of industrial England

and its post-war consensus; the long era of hooligans, firms and social disorder gave symbolic form to the sharp conflicts and anger of the 1970s and 80s; the commercial transformation of the game in the 1990s and 2000s has stood as an exemplar of the country's economic globalisation and its deepening inequalities, while retaining a romantic relationship to the communitarian and social-democratic values of the lost working-class worlds it sprang from. Today, in a hyper-mediated world, the gap between act and remembrance, between reality and the narrative, has shrunk. Football, and the stories we tell ourselves about it, have become a running commentary on our contemporary state of emergency.

Football is certainly well suited to that task, for it has long embraced the language of catastrophe. The use of 'Disaster' has rightly been reserved for real disasters – Burnden Park, Ibrox, Heysel and Hillsborough – but upsets and shocks are its stock in trade, and flailing defences are at 'panic stations' requiring 'all hands to the pump'. Since the 1960s, in parallel perhaps with the gyrations of Britain's faltering economy, individual clubs and the game as a whole have been, seemingly, in a perpetual state of disarray: strikers and dressing rooms suffering from a crisis of confidence, squads gripped by an injury crisis, clubs floored by a financial one. In recent years, drawing on the language of our intersecting and cumulative global problems, football teams have been caught in 'perfect storms', while clubs and coaches now enter downward spirals, death spirals and doom loops.[1] The disruptions and threats that the Covid pandemic brought ratcheted up the rhetoric, with Daniel Storey, for example, declaring 'sound the alarms, man the barricades and tell the fat lady to start practising her scales. English football is in a state of emergency.'[2]

Football, however, offers more than just familiarity with the hyperbole of catastrophe. Much more extraordinary is that the game is now not just a reflection of the wider world, but has become an active participant in its construction, capable, as football commentators and managers increasingly say, of 'changing the narrative'. In the last decade, football pundits have challenged the language of government ministers, football players have shifted government welfare policies, and the coach of the English men's team has been an instrumental factor in the reconfiguration of English national identity. Some football clubs have turned into urban developers, others have become the agents of foreign powers; football fans have taken to the streets and the social-media barricades to both challenge them and support them; while the explosive growth of the women's game has been rewriting the gender politics of the country. In this regard, the game tells a story not just about who we have been and what we are now, but on occasion who we would like to be.

It has been my deepest pleasure and perpetual curse to follow, play, watch and study this game. It has made me laugh and despair. It has distracted me and illuminated me. It has made me feel deeply at home and profoundly alienated. It has helped me make sense of the world, and left me utterly confounded. I worry that it is unwise for us to have invested so much of our collective storytelling capacity and political imagination in football, but given the paucity of the alternatives available to us, I think we are lucky to have it at all.

Introduction

'Let the Soap Opera Begin!'

Football as the National Allegory

'Let the soap opera begin!'
Richard Masters, Premier League CEO

I

That Richard Masters, chief executive of the Premier League, could invite the world to see the 2022–23 football season as a soap opera did not just signal the fusion of football with the entertainment industry, it marked a significant moment in football's wider cultural ascent.[1] Over the past three decades, the Premier League – indeed, professional football as a whole – has not only assumed the dramatic form and social functions of soap operas in British culture, it has eclipsed them all and become 'the' soap opera. This constitutes a remarkable reversal of cultural fortunes. For almost half a century, from the launch of *Coronation Street* in 1960, British soap operas and their actors have been the mainstay of television schedules, celebrity gossip columns, tabloid exposés and everyday small talk. They were one of the few places in the cultural landscape in which at least a version of working- and lower-middle-class life had been on show, and thus one of the very few cultural forms that could claim to take the temperature of the nation as a whole. No longer.

The soaps have not entirely disappeared from our TV schedules, but their significance has been radically diminished. At their zenith, the 1986 Christmas episode of *EastEnders* attracted an audience of 30 million for Dirty Den and his divorce papers; by Christmas 2022 that figure had dropped to just 2.9 million. In their place, football has become the last bastion of must-see, appointment television. At peak moments, England, Scotland and Wales games have produced bigger national audiences than any soap can now manage. England's defeat to Italy in the final of Euro 2020 was watched by 31 million on TV and 11 million online, making it the most viewed event in British television history. Given that the rest of live football is nearly all on subscription channels and the soaps are free to air, the game gives them episode by episode a run for their money. The biggest Premier League matches are watched by two to three million British subscribers, with another million or so watching in pubs and public spaces, and plenty more viewing illegal streams, not to mention the tens of millions watching from around the world. Meanwhile, *Match of the Day* and other highlights shows serve as the game's own omnibus editions – a luxury no longer afforded to the soaps on broadcast channels.

The soap opera had once attempted to swallow football whole. In the mid-1960s, in an effort to match ITV's *Coronation Street* – then by some way the most popular programme on British television – the BBC commissioned *United!* Centring on the fortunes of a fictional Second Division club in Greater Manchester, Brentwich United, the show ran twice a week for over 140 episodes between 1965 and 1967.[2] Despite the genre's usual scission from actual events in the world, fiction and reality were soon blurring. Match sequences were shot at real grounds, actors playing football were intercut with film of real live matches. The *Radio Times* published Brentwich's fictional league table each week. Wolverhampton Wanderers made an official complaint to the BBC when they felt that the club's relegation troubles were a deliberate and unwelcome comment on their own dismal season. Up to six million viewers were tuning in, but this was less than a third of *Coronation Street*'s audience. It seems that the gender divide of the era was too much to bridge; too much football for most women (and not enough women characters), and too much emotional drama for most men (and disappointingly produced football sequences). The show was cancelled and, as was standard practice at the BBC at the time, every last tape was recorded over or lost.

After this, football retreated to a small corner of *Coronation Street*'s universe, and *EastEnders*, which debuted in 1985, would follow the northern soap's lead. Both shows occasionally featured a fictional local non-league club, Weatherfield County and Walford Town respectively, and occasionally minor football plot lines would feature in the shows. However, the real world of football never made it into the scripts. By contrast, football would happily bring the soaps into its domain, most notably in 1983 when Manchester United, during a League Cup tie against Arsenal, put up on the big screen 'Ken 1 Mike 0' – a reference to the *Coronation Street* episode that was being broadcast at the same time in which Deirdre Barlow had chosen to return to her husband Ken rather than stay with her lover Mike Baldwin. It was met by rapturous applause.[3]

More recently, as the relative cultural weight of football has grown, the soaps are now referencing football. *Coronation Street* has featured James Bailey, a gay Black footballer wracked with worry that his sexuality would be exposed and his career imperilled. In *EastEnders*, where previously Arthur Fowler was a devoted follower of Walford Town, everyone on the square now appears to support West Ham United. England's defeat to Italy in the final of Euro 2020 was the subject of a scene in the next day's *EastEnders* between an inconsolable Billy Mitchell still wrapped in a St George's flag and the more phlegmatic Bobby Beale. The victory of the England women's team at the

European Championship in 2022 was celebrated the day after in the Queen Vic.

Not content with mere real-time references to the game, the soaps have made space for football cameos. *Emmerdale*'s pub team played a side coached by ex-player and excitable pundit Chris Kamara. Harry Redknapp made a trip to Albert Square to see his old mate Rocky, and lightly bantered with the star-struck West Ham-supporting landlord as he bought himself a pint at the Queen Vic. At the same time footballers have been no less in demand for the two other mainstays of what remains of mainstream British television: *Strictly Come Dancing* (featuring Tony Adams, Alex Scott, Robbie Savage, John Barnes, Peter Schmeichel and David James) and *I'm a Celebrity …* (boasting an entire starting eleven, including Jill Scott, Ian Wright, Dennis Wise and David Ginola). Harry Redknapp, once again, proved the cross-over hit, winning the show and being crowned 'King of the Jungle' in 2018.

The most telling indicator of the shift in power from soaps to football has been their relative heft in the scheduling battles. In 2001, *EastEnders* and the BBC carried enough weight that the corporation could successfully persuade UEFA to delay the kick-off of a Champions League game between Liverpool and Barcelona by ten minutes so that viewers could catch an extended forty-minute special in which the person who shot Phil Mitchell was due to be revealed.[4] By contrast, in 2020, *EastEnders* would lose its place on BBC One to a mere fifth-round FA cup tie between Liverpool and Chelsea, while ITV and BBC coverage of the Qatar 2022 World Cup saw *Coronation Street* and *EastEnders* banished from their usual slots to the periphery of the broadcasters' digital empires. The subordination of the soaps was complete when, at the end of the 2023 season, *EastEnders* reorganised its schedule around football, adding an additional Thursday night episode to include celebrations of West Ham's victory in Wednesday night's Europa Conference League final.

For decades the British tabloid press has created their own football soap opera by relentlessly pursuing the private lives of players, coaches and even FA administrators, using the same techniques they employed to ensnare pop stars and actors: intrusive photography; paying insiders to spill the beans; phone hacking. Infidelities were their favourite plot line, as England manager Sven-Göran Eriksson and captain John Terry found out, but mental illness, acts of conspicuous consumption, and personal rows and feuds would suffice. In the early 2000s, the crossover football/pop couples David and Victoria Beckham and Ashley and Cheryl Cole were an entire soap in themselves, with walk-on parts for what became known as the WAGs (Wives and Girlfriends), whose antics took centre stage at the 2006 World Cup. However, like the soaps, the tabloids are in terminal decline. Hard copy circulation has collapsed and their increasingly ageing readership is not being replaced, even online, by the young. In 2022 the very public court battle between Coleen Rooney and Rebekah Vardy – who had been accused of leaking private information about Rooney to the tabloids – was termed the 'Wagatha Christie' affair, and occupied plenty of media space, but it was a one-off revival of the old version of football soap rather than a whole new series. Football players have become much warier of the tabloids, much more protective of their privacy and 'brand', while social media has allowed them to evade and ignore the papers that their predecessors relied upon for coverage, should they choose to do so.

As the soaps have ceded space to the real football soap opera, so the last fictional efforts to combine the two have been abandoned. Sky's *Dream Team*, which ran for a decade until 2007, began as a biweekly soap before mutating into a Sunday night absurdist comedy in which the chairman of the club, on discovering that his player-manager had been sleeping with his wife, ordered his assassination during the FA Cup final, while a goalkeeper was driven by his gambling debts into taking the whole team hostage for a ransom. ITV's *Footballers' Wives*, which ran until 2006, was always more 'drama' than 'soap', but its real break with the genre was socio-economic, revolving, as it did, around lives of conspicuous consumption in expensive gated estates and unaffordable restaurants rather than on the field. Not that television drama as a whole has abandoned football: Netflix threw money at Julian Fellowes's late Victorian historical melodrama *The English Game*; Apple TV had an unlikely hit with their saccharine comedy drama *Ted Lasso*; but none of them can hit the beats that soap opera demands.

Documentary presented as soap or drama has been the other route explored by television, with mixed results. Amazon's *All or Nothing* multi-sport franchise made its own unique and expensive ersatz *vérité* at Manchester City, Arsenal and Spurs, managing to turn even José Mourinho's blustering, ugly term at Tottenham into a bland corporate video. The closest that the media industry has come to capturing something of the real football soap opera has been Netflix's *Sunderland 'Til I Die*, which followed the club's disastrous 2017–18 season. Rooted visually in the city's industrial past and post-industrial present, it featured working-class fans, obsessive taxi drivers and the club's catering staff and groundsmen alongside the usual selection of executives, coaches and players: locations and a cast closer to a classic soap. It also didn't shy from extreme, even improbable dramas and plot twists. Relegated from the Premier League the previous season, the club and the filmmakers thought they would be making a 'return to the Promised Land' promotion story. In fact, they got a disaster movie in which Sunderland headed for a humiliating relegation to League One. Hollywood was taking note. American actors Ryan Reynolds and Rob McElhenney bought Wrexham FC in 2020 and, even before they had sealed the deal, began to film what has now become *Welcome to Wrexham*, a virtually weekly commentary on the club's return to league football streaming globally on Disney+. Their sell-out game with Manchester United in San Diego in the summer of 2023 drew a crowd who had watched football as a real-time soap long before they actually saw Wrexham play. Yet in the end, good as any show might be, none of these formats can match the real deal.

II

So, what is it that makes football such good soap opera? First, football's basic dramatic unit – the match – offers guaranteed jeopardy, uncertainty and action in every episode. Favourites win most of the time, but less often than in other team sports. Games hinge on a small number of chances, anything can happen. You just never know with football. The teams win, lose or draw, their position in the league shifts, hopes and aspirations are recalibrated, and we are always left with the cliffhangers: what will happen next week, will we win or lose, will the team be any better or worse? As with the best soaps, football combines this relentless weekly microdrama with a sense of the long *durée*, referencing characters and plot lines that play out over months and years. The meaning of any match is created out of both memories of past encounters and its place in the current season's drama.

Like all good soaps, football has a fixed set, located in the real world, that evokes a range of memories and meanings to give it depth. *Coronation Street* has Lowry's working-class Manchester, *EastEnders* has Cockney – now super-diverse – East London, but football as a whole has the entire country, and a version of the country that – its rural blindspots aside – cleaves to the real economic geography and urban diversity of Britain. Within this imagined space, football has a multitude of physical local sets – the nation's stadiums – serving the more local soaps that rotate around each club and town. Football also shares with soap opera a sense of compression, of lives speeded up and filled to the brim with incident. Just as soap characters have more deaths, accidents, divorces and secret children than any of us, so the narrative arcs of individual games, club seasons and player careers have more twist and turns, more glory and despair, per unit of time than everyday life. Just as soap's plot lines turn on a merry-go-round of relationships, reinventions and reunions, so too the managers and players that are sacked, sold and rehired, and after retirement reappear in new guises as pundits, presenters and ambassadors.

Soap's appeal and its wider social significance derived, in part, from a sense of community, born of watching it and discussing it with others. Although some people watch games alone, most football is consumed communally, either in the stands at the match itself, at home or in pubs and bars, and it has become pervasive in everyday conversation, workplace banter and pub talk. A great deal of chat also goes on in the rapidly expanding podcast space, where football alone accounts for 10 per cent of the listenership. At the same time, football has colonised social media and chat groups, and is occupying a great deal more space than the soaps. While *EastEnders*, *Coronation Street* and *Emmerdale* have 2.4, 1.4 and 1.2 million Twitter followers respectively, Manchester United have 36 million followers, Liverpool and Arsenal more than 20 million, and the Premier League itself has almost 50 million. On Instagram the gap is even wider, with the soaps managing less than a million followers against Manchester United's 62 million and Liverpool's 43 million.[5] Consequently, soaps stars and their private lives now get far less media coverage than football players, whose fashion and accessory choices, housing and holidays, dietary preferences, and sexual and financial misdemeanours are matters of collective fascination and moral judgement.

Good as these kinds of soap-style storyline are, football offers more. No one cares how soaps are made, what happened in the rehearsal, who's up or down in the writers' room or who owns the rights and the residuals. By contrast, there is an insatiable demand for gossip, rumour and even news about what happened in training, the progress of players' injuries, the state of clubs' finances, and the decision-making processes of boards, sporting directors and coaches. Soap's producers and directors are entirely invisible, but owners and coaches, even club executives, have become another strand to football's story machine. The introduction of the technical area in the game and the proliferation of cameras trained upon them have given coaches the most fabulous space to emotionally express themselves, usually through the medium of mime, while the modern camera lens can capture the merest flicker of emotion on the face of a club director in their executive box.

Like the soaps before them, many of football's narratives are driven by love and hate, relationships and conflicts. Owners and coaches, once so close, will acrimoniously and suddenly divorce, and on occasion remarry. New arrivals in the dressing room upset the delicate balance of family life. The secret debts of clubs and their shameful pasts are revealed as they teeter on the verge of bankruptcy. Today during the soap opera of the transfer window, a spin-off show that occupies the summer months, clubs struggle over transfer targets like rival lovers, while club presidents woo players, agents serve as matchmakers and players either accept, shun or spurn their advances. In this regard nothing much has changed since the BBC broadcast *United!*, which featured plots that pitted owners against managers, owners fighting among themselves, managers in conflict with players, and fans who were apoplectic with all of them. Now this is all done in the real world and framed as if it were a drama for our entertainment. But football needs no writers' room to make this happen, nor does it depend on ever-escalating sensationalism to maintain its audience's interest. The game itself generates all the narrative that is needed, and we – the public and the media – do the work of making it mean something.

III

The narrative and social parallels between soap opera and football are strong, but in two crucial ways football is a very different cultural form, and it is these additional elements that have enabled it to eclipse every other form of popular storytelling. First, it is a game that almost everyone can play. After many years of decline, more and more people are playing it. In 2022 the English FA reported that 14 million people, 3.4 million of them female, played football – almost a quarter of the country – and although the game is still unbalanced, women's and girls' participation has been growing at an unprecedented rate. The FA haven't been counting them, but the numbers playing the digital game on *FIFA* must add another million or two. The game's presence in British everyday life, compared with almost every other cultural practice, is remarkable. Those who were playing on real pitches were served by 37,000 referees; just for comparison, that's double the number of judges and magistrates in the country. And they were trained by 243,000 coaches – about the same number as all the primary school teachers in the UK. Football as a whole could draw on a pool of 1.4 million volunteers, from under-7s coaches to stewards, car park attendants, fundraisers and tea makers; almost thirty times as many as the National Trust could muster and more than seven times as many as the entire Scout and Guide movement. Baden-Powell, who viewed the game and its supporters with distaste, must be turning in his grave. Not everyone who plays or volunteers in football follows the professional game, but, in parallel with music, where a vast hinterland of amateur practice sustains a small professional elite, the pool of people who see something of their own lives reflected in football's narratives, and the degree to which they are representative of the country, are bigger than ever.

Second, and unlike soaps, which are never filmed with a studio audience, football is watched in person. Football crowds have been increasing since their nadir in 1985, but in the seasons since Covid restrictions were lifted, English football has recorded match attendances on a scale not seen since their peak in the early 1950s. This is a rare and extraordinary reversal of what appeared to be a long, structural and irreversible decline. The Premier League sold 15 million tickets in 2022–23, a number seemingly only limited by the size of its stadiums, which were at 99 per cent capacity. The Football League was watched by 22 million fans across its three divisions. The Championship became the fifth-most watched league in Europe, while even League One was in the top 10. Add in the three National Leagues below League Two – now all largely professional – and that's another 3 million spectators, a historically unprecedented audience for non-league football, not to mention a million spectators at the Women's Super League – also a record number – and we are looking at the biggest crowds that English football has ever drawn. Whatever the size of the crowd watching football, match attendance continues to be a form of ritual, not merely a form of entertainment. We go to the game, in the same place at the same times, often with the same people, very rarely alone. We take the same routes, sit or stand with family and friends and our fellow fans, the half strangers with whom we are on nodding terms, year after year, and share the same narrative fate that our team delivers us. Little wonder, then, so many of us should find that football provides a meaningful spine to our lives, one that is intimate, emotional and profound, but one that binds our individual experience to a wider community of fate and a collective sense of identity.

The presence of an audience at a live performance also makes football a form of public theatre in which the crowd is participant, chorus and commentator. This has not escaped the attention of political actors and social movements, both of which have increased their presence in English football in the last decade, from the arrival of Middle Eastern royalty pursuing global diplomatic agendas to far-right agitators and anti-racist activists pursuing theirs, and from fossil-fuel companies laundering their reputations to climate campaigners trying to destroy them. Football has appeared then not just as theatre, but as political theatre, in a way that the soaps would never have dared contemplate and with an audience that purpose-made political theatre could never reach.

IV

Football – certainly the Premier League – might seem at first glance to be an odd oracle of our times. The global economic crisis of 2008, the greatest shaking of global capitalism since the Great Depression of the 1930s, barely seemed to touch it. A few club administrations and bankruptcies aside, the game's prospects looked good, as revenues and attendances continued to rise, and international media deals and sponsorship grew. In 2010 the Labour Party's thirteen years in power came to an end, and the Conservative–Liberal Democrat coalition that replaced it embarked on the biggest programme of welfare cuts the country had ever seen. While much of the nation endured the longest income squeeze since the nineteenth century, wages in football soared. Student protests over tuition fees turned into major confrontations, while in 2011 arson and riots tore through English cities, but the crowds in the stadiums were increasingly orderly, as incident and arrest rates fell every year. Anti-migrant voices were becoming steadily louder, and UKIP's anti-Europe support was rising, but in football a great wave of foreign players and coaches were welcomed and celebrated, while European success remained the lodestar of every big club's journey.

Was there, perhaps, a time lag at work? These enormous economic and political shifts would need some time to work their way into the cultural fabric of the nation, but they eventually arrived. Certainly, in 2012, Manchester City's first Premier League title under the ownership of the UAE suggested a changing of the guard; indeed, it was a harbinger of both the club's coming dominance of the league and what has become a much wider Middle Eastern presence in English football and the British economy. It was also a triumph of storytelling, a season-ending climax of unprecedented drama. City were 2–1 down at home to QPR with just injury time to play. Manchester United had won their away game against Sunderland and, as things stood, were set to be champions. Three minutes later, Edin Džeko having headed in an equaliser, Sergio Agüero scored the final goal with just seconds left to play, and City won the title, the TV directors switching their cameras between ecstasy at the Etihad and despair at Sunderland's Stadium of Light. Perhaps it is all mere coincidence, but for the next four years there was a step change in the dramatic intensity and social commentary offered by football.

The following season, 2012–13, was the season of the long goodbye, the end of an era and the drawing-together of many strands of the Premier League's narratives. Manchester United, managed by Sir Alex Ferguson, had commanded the league since its creation in 1992. The winners of the inaugural Premier League season, the club won twelve of the first twenty championships. Their treble-winning season in 1999 signalled English football's return to the summit of Europe and spurred the league's extraordinary global popularity. Their victory over Chelsea in the Champions League in 2008 – the first all-English final – confirmed the Premier League as the richest and most popular football league in the world, a position it has not relinquished. Through all this Ferguson had provided fabulous theatrical entertainment: throwing teacups, giving hairdryer rants, playing cryptic mind games, and conjuring up Fergie Time – bending the time–space continuum until United grabbed a last-minute goal. Above all, though, he was a link to the past, taking on the same role in English football that Deputy Prime Minister John Prescott had performed for the Labour Party in the Blair–Brown years. They were both representatives of industrial Britain, born and shaped by the post-war consensus and the welfare state, and of the working-class urban milieu that had made the Labour Party and English and Scottish football, but which had been decimated. A member of the Party, and occasional figurehead in its campaigns, Ferguson lasted longer in power than Labour, who left government in 2010. Ferguson managed to stay ahead of the club's rapacious owners – the Glazer family, busy extracting cash from the club rather than investing it – long enough to win one last time and go at a moment of his own choosing. It is a measure of the club's fall that, while the Labour Party has eventually managed to return to power, Manchester United have not.

The 2013–14 season offered many narrative pleasures. Manchester United's worst season for thirty years satisfied the football nation's need for *Schadenfreude*. Sunderland's late rally, and improbable escape from relegation, went down to the line. The rare presence of two Welsh teams in the league, Cardiff City and Swansea City, offered regional variation and enmity. In the end it was Manchester City's season, as they won their second Premier League title, but it was meant to be Liverpool's. Twenty-five years since the Hillsborough disaster, twenty-three since they had last won the league title, 2013–14 looked like the season to put the curse to bed. Fan protest and political organisation had managed to evict their pernicious American owners, Tom Hicks and George Gillett, helped pursue justice for the Hillsborough victims and their families and kept the Murdoch press out of Liverpool, and made it more of a left-wing stronghold than ever. Now it was time to get back to the top. Leading the league for much of the year, their victory over Manchester City away from home seemed likely to be the definitive moment of the contest. In the team huddle after the final whistle, Liverpool captain Steven Gerrard delivered the line of the season: 'This does not fucking slip now! This does not fucking slip! Listen: we go to Norwich, exactly the same! We go again!' Two weeks later, as Liverpool's form disintegrated and City went on an unbeaten run, Gerrard's calamitous slip on the pitch allowed Chelsea's Demba Ba to score the opening goal in what would be a 2–1 defeat and the end of their title hopes. You really couldn't make it up.

The main storyline of the 2014–15 Premier League season had been established two years beforehand with the return of José Mourinho to Chelsea. His acrimonious departure from the club in 2007, after winning two league titles, was followed by an operatic European tour: a glorious Machiavellian spell at Inter Milan, and a bombastic failure at Real Madrid. Now he was coming home. His comment on returning to Stamford Bridge could have been spoken by any drama's long-lost lover, wiser and older but ready for a second shot at love: 'I am the happy one. Time flies. It looks like it was a couple of days ago but it was nine years ago … I have the same heart, the same kind of emotions related to my passion … But of course I'm a different person.' As it turned out, he was the same old person. The same old paranoid conspiracy theorist claiming that: 'There is a campaign against Chelsea. I don't know why there is this campaign and I do not care.' He was the same old barbed and public critic of his players, too: 'Eden [Hazard] is the kind of player that is not so mentally ready to look back to his left-back and to leave his life for him.' The players didn't like it much, but the public and the pundits lapped it up.

Mourinho hogged screen time, but in the end it was another league title for Roman Abramovich, Chelsea's owner since 2003, and confirmation that, Russia's illegal occupation of Crimea notwithstanding, London remained open for business to the post-Soviet oligarchy. League titles, public school educations, ultra-expensive real estate, money-laundering services and access to the Conservative Party were all still available. This was also the season in which Chelsea fans were filmed on the Paris Metro preventing a Black Frenchman from entering the train while singing: 'We're racist, we're racist, and that's the way we like it.' One might have thought, after the club's condemnation of the fans and their subsequent arrest, that this was the end of the story; for the sharp-eyed who saw this strange alliance of working-class nativist anger and Russian influence as part of the populist wave about to engulf the country, it was just the beginning.

Through the spring of 2016 it became increasingly clear that the impossible would happen: Leicester City, 5,000–1 outsiders, would win the Premier League. When, in early May, Tottenham Hotspur, their last faltering challenger, drew with Chelsea, the title was Leicester's. At the time, some read the moment as a triumph for Britain's first majority-minority city (59.1 per cent of Leicester's population is from ethnic minorities), and a team with a visibly diverse fan base, a Thai billionaire owner and a squad of a dozen nationalities, led by an idiosyncratic and avuncular Italian coach, Claudio Ranieri. Inès Hassen-Dakhli of the University of Leicester thought that the city 'surprisingly, may have become a global model for multicultural cooperation. And what is certain is that the city can position itself confidently as a champion of globalisation: a medium-sized city that has the world at its feet.'[6] However, such enthusiasm for globalisation and cosmopolitanism was not shared by everyone. Seven weeks after Leicester clinched the title, in the best, and most unexpected plot twist to the soap opera yet, their achievement would be eclipsed by an even more improbable victory: that of the Leave campaign in the battle over whether Britain should stay in or leave the European Union.

Part I

Brexitball

Football after the Referendum, 2016–19

1.

'We're All Leaving Europe!'

Football and the Referendum

British football has had an ambivalent relationship with Europe for more than 150 years. In the late nineteenth and early twentieth century, British economic migrants, cosmopolitan émigrés, diplomats, schoolboys and travellers took the game to much of the continent: shipyard workers from Sunderland played the first game in Bilbao and triggered Basque football fever; factory owners in Moscow established teams for their workers in an effort to divert them from drinking. Britons founded now famous clubs – Scottish gardeners in Vienna formed the core of what became Rapid Wien, the English Lowe brothers created Boavista in Porto – and supplied Europe with a generation of coaches. This sporting diaspora left the English language embedded in the local football vernacular; thus, Genoa and AC Milan, rather than Genova and Milano, and 'the Mister' as the shorthand for a team's manager. On the other hand, as late as the 1920s, Charles Sutcliffe, a leading member of the Football League's management committee, thought FIFA and European football an affront: 'I don't care a brass farthing about the improvement of the game in France, Belgium, Austria or Germany ... if Central Europe or any other district want to govern football let them confine their power and authority to themselves and we can look after our own affairs.'[1]

Both of these dispositions found expression in Britain's ambivalent relationship with FIFA, founded in 1904 and then an entirely European organisation. In 1905, having initially refused, the English FA, followed by the other home nations, reluctantly joined FIFA; contempt for the newcomers was overcome by a fear that they might take control. In the 1920s Britain's football associations would leave the organisation not once, but twice: first, in 1920, in a dispute over the participation in international football of the defeated Central Powers; then, after rejoining in 1924, they would again depart in 1928 in a spat over broken time payments to amateurs. Consequently, no British team played at the first three World Cups staged by FIFA in the 1930s.

Through the 1930s isolationists remained in the ascendent, but internationalists, like the new FA general secretary Stanley Rous, sought to keep lines of communication open and the possibility of rejoining FIFA a realistic if distant prospect. In 1938 both agendas were served when the FA, to celebrate its seventy-fifth anniversary, invited a Rest of Europe team – primarily the Italian World Cup winners – to test themselves against England at Highbury. England won that game 3–0, and for the moment the superiority of English football and the wisdom of glorious isolation were confirmed. However, after the Second World War, as new global institutions – from the UN to the World Bank – were being constructed, and Britain's place in the international hierarchy of power declined, glorious isolation no longer appeared a plausible option. The British football associations rejoined FIFA in 1947 and secured themselves a privileged status within the organisation. Not quite permanent membership of the UN Security Council, perhaps, but the four home nations were the only jurisdictions that were sub-regions of a sovereign state allowed to field international teams, and the four were also guaranteed a vice presidency at FIFA between them. At the same time, the long-held presumption of British superiority on the pitch began to look increasingly precarious, not least after a very mediocre debut performance by England at the 1950 World Cup, including a hitherto inconceivable defeat by the USA. In 1953, marking the ninetieth anniversary of the FA, England again played the Rest of Europe, and this time they could only manage a 4–4 draw. A month later, the shift in power would be confirmed when Hungary beat England 6–3 at Wembley – the first defeat by a foreign team on home soil – with a display of modern football that was almost incomprehensible to the British game, and clearly superior.

In 1954, three years before the signing of the Treaty of Rome and the creation of the EEC, European football acquired an institutional dimension with the creation of UEFA. England and the other home nations enthusiastically joined the new organisation, and England's national champions – Chelsea – were invited to play in UEFA's first tournament, the European Cup. If the FA now harboured the Europhile faction in the English game, the Football League was home to the Europhobes. Indeed, Alan Hardaker, the secretary of the Football League at the time, argued in public that Chelsea should not play in the competition 'for fear of fixture congestion and a loss of prestige for our own competition'. Privately, he was contemptuous, arguing that the European Cup was 'something of a joke ... at best, a nine-day wonder', while European football was a place with 'too many wops and dagoes'.[2] Chelsea duly complied with Hardaker, but the following year's champions, Manchester United, and their manager Matt Busby had other ideas. Immediately recognising the sporting importance of the tournament, and the global prestige accorded to its first champions – Real Madrid – United's relationship with the Cup took the form of an epic quest in which European triumph would validate the club's special status. Their first tilt at the title showed great promise and saw them lose to Real Madrid in the semi-final, their second was halted by the Munich air disaster and the subsequent defeat of a much-depleted squad. It would take almost a decade for United to become competitive again, a journey that helped secure the status of the European Cup, in Britain, as the very pinnacle of success. Consequently, victories for Celtic in 1967 and then United in 1968 – the conclusion of their epic arc of redemption – were received as proof that British decline had, in this sphere at least, been temporarily halted.

Football was just one of the many areas of British life in the 1960s and early 1970s – not to mention food, cars, holidays and rates of economic growth – in which Europe appeared increasingly attractive, and in 1973 the Conservative government of Edward Heath took the country into the EEC. To celebrate the occasion the government staged 'Fanfare for Europe', a week-long cultural festival featuring European-themed concerts, art exhibitions and a game at Wembley between the Three (the UK, alongside Ireland and Denmark, who were also joining the EEC) and the Six (the founding members of the organisation). The Queen and Prime Minister opted to attend a concert by a Danish orchestra that evening, but in the programme Heath wrote: 'Tonight's match is unique in embracing the whole of the enlarged community, and we are very glad our European friends are able to take part. I am sure that, with us, they will look upon this evening as a major landmark in the history of European football.'[3] The players selected for the game, when asked by the press, reflected something of their nation's attitudes to accession: indifference from Northern Irish goalkeeper Pat Jennings, who was 'really not interested'; narrow economic calculation from Alan Ball, who wondered 'whether or not it will make my family's summer holidays cheaper'. Johnny Giles, by contrast, took a wider view: 'A small country like Ireland needs close business and trade links with other European nations, so I'm certainly in favour.' Helmut Schön, the German coach of the Six, was enthusiastic, the game for him 'heralding a new era for Europe', while Alf Ramsey, in charge of the Three, could barely bring himself to engage, dismissively saying, 'All big Wembley occasions should be cherished.' Anti-European protestors who gathered outside the stadium thought otherwise, one telling a reporter, 'It's an early sign that Britain no longer has control over its own affairs and that, in the end, belonging to a Common Market will cost us far more than we can possibly hope to make from it.'[4]

For the next decade football would give voice to both sides of the European question. On the one hand, Jock Stein and Matt Busby, winning coaches of the European Cup in the 1960s, were recruited to the successful Yes campaign in the 1975 referendum, called by the new and divided Labour government on whether the UK should remain a member of the EEC. British teams had a remarkable run of success in European tournaments, burnishing their reputations in a way that domestic competition alone could not. Liverpool would win the European Cup four times, Nottingham Forest twice and Aston Villa once. Leeds United and Celtic would both lose a final. There were Cup Winners' Cups for Rangers and Everton, and UEFA Cups for Liverpool, Ipswich and Spurs. On the other hand, English and Scottish supporters became notorious for their disorderly and violent behaviour on European away days. In 1974 Spurs fans rioted in Rotterdam as they lost the UEFA Cup final to Feyenoord, and the following year Leeds United fans did the same in Paris as their team lost the European Cup final to Bayern Munich. England fans put on similar performances in Luxembourg in 1977 and at the 1980 Euros in Belgium. It was a pattern of behaviour that led to the Heysel disaster in 1985, where, in a poorly policed and poorly maintained stadium, a terrace charge from Liverpool supporters at that year's European Cup final resulted in thirty-nine Juventus fans dying beneath a collapsed concrete wall in Brussels. UEFA were shaping up to ban British clubs from European competition, but the FA withdrew before it could be imposed.

On this occasion departure from Europe was almost universally lamented. Roy Evans, when he was Liverpool's manager, thought the club's season 'without European football is like a banquet without wine'. Bert Millichip, chair of the FA, speaking after the ban was lifted in 1990, announced: 'English football has stepped back into the sunshine. We've been in a dark tunnel for a long time and at times we couldn't see the light at the end of it.'[5] For more than two decades, from Thatcher's resignation in 1990 to the final years of New Labour, and despite continuing opposition from Conservative eurosceptics, Britain appeared irrevocably bound to Europe. Once again, Europe became a vital element of British football cultures. Euro 96, hosted by England, was a hugely successful return to the mainstream. Manchester United's long march through Europe culminated in their extraordinary last-minute victory over Bayern Munich in the 1999 Champions League final and signalled the new strength of the Premier League and its commercial dominance to come. In 2003 Celtic fans restaged the great exodus of 1967, when tens of thousands of fans had made the journey to Lisbon to see the team win the European Cup: in an age of cheap air travel they mustered near a hundred thousand in Seville as the team lost the UEFA Cup final to Porto. Liverpool made European success ever more central to their own mythos after claiming the Champions League in 2005, coming back from 3–0 down against Milan to win on penalties in the 'Miracle of Istanbul'. In 2008 Manchester United and Chelsea played the first all-English final in the competition, while in 2012 Chelsea would finally win it, albeit as a club now owned by a Russian, coached by an Italian and with a squad that included three Spaniards, two Portuguese, a Czech and a Frenchman. Britain's love affair with European football did not, however, translate in much of the country into any great affection for the continent's political institutions. The celebration of so many foreign players and coaches did not ease the disquiet about the large refugee and eastern European migrations of the first decade of the twenty-first century. Indeed, the rise of the UKIP vote and anti-migrant sentiments, and the increasingly aggressive stance of anti-European groups within the Tory Party, suggested the contrary. Ex-Prime Minister Gordon Brown, for one, was baffled: 'Why is playing football in Europe considered the pinnacle of our game, yet in other spheres of life, that same phrase – "being in Europe" – is dismissed with suspicion?'[6]

In truth, no amount of love for Thierry Henry or Gianfranco Zola was going to head off the Eurosceptics, and in 2015, in an effort to quell internal dissent in the Tory Party and see off the threat of UKIP on his right flank, Prime Minister David Cameron called a referendum on the UK's membership of the European Union. It was to be held on 23 June 2016, in the short gap between England's and Wales' last group games at Euro 2016 in France and, should they qualify, their round-of-sixteen matches. Politicians began to reach for footballing analogies. Mandy Boylett, the UKIP parliamentary candidate for Stockton North in 2015, reprised 'Football's Coming Home' as 'Britain's Coming Home' in a campaign video, singing, 'They want our prisoners to vote/They've taken all our fish/And money through the years.'[7] Ed Balls, previously shadow chancellor of the exchequer, but now as an ex-MP with more leisure time, wrote for the *Daily Mirror* from France, where he had flown to see England in the Euros: 'At least if a football manager gets it wrong with his starting XI, he has the chance to do something about it: a change of tactics, or some substitutions. We've got our own big decision to take next week, but unlike a football boss, we only get one chance to get it right.'[8]

However, unlike the Scottish independence referendum of 2014, which had seen a significant politicisation of Scotland's football crowds and fan organisations, English football, along with much of the rest of the country, sleepwalked its way into Brexit. In the stadiums in the long run-up to the referendum there were neither chants nor banners for either Remain or Leave. Until the very eve of the vote, almost no one in English football seemed to have an opinion on the matter.

Online, and initially out of sight, Vote Leave offered football fans a £50 million prize if they could predict every result at the European Championship to be held that June, and, as their campaign director, Dominic Cummings, made plain, 'gathered data from people who usually ignore politics'.[9] Karren Brady, Tory peer and vice chair of West Ham United, was a rarity in the football world, writing to every professional team in the United Kingdom to argue: 'Clubs and fans all benefit from European action, laws and funding. Leaving the EU would hurt our leagues, create uncertainty for European transfers and be a step back for the next generation of footballers.'[10] The Premier League, like many business organisations, quietly warned that the migration regime that would follow on from leaving the EU would make recruitment harder and long-term economic prospects poorer. Richard Scudamore, the chief executive, felt: 'There is an openness about the Premier League which I think it would be completely incongruous if we were to take the opposite position.'[11] Feelings are one thing, but there were also real footballing and economic interests at stake. In words almost identical to the Remain campaign, Scudamore argued: 'Ultimately you can't break away, you can't just pull out, you have to get in and negotiate and try and organise and try and influence.' Yet, wary of the populist fury sweeping the country, the Premier League and the big clubs kept their heads down and planned for the worst.

In the final days of the campaign both sides put out their strongest squads. Remain published an open letter signed by David Beckham, Rio Ferdinand and Norwich's owner, Delia Smith, arguing: 'In sport, the one thing that matters above all else is your team … the same is true for Britain in Europe: we are stronger working together with other countries with the ability to travel, work and play sport right across the continent.'[12]

Beckham argued that Manchester United 'were a better and more successful team because of a Danish goalkeeper, Peter

Schmeichel, the leadership of an Irishman Roy Keane and the skill of a Frenchman in Eric Cantona.'[13] Ferdinand, in the *Standard*, revealed that 'Thursday will be the first time I've ever been motivated to vote in an election. That's how seriously I'm taking this … Britain is an amazing country, but we'll achieve much more if we're a team player – working with others to get things done.'[14] For Leave, Steve Parish, chairman of Crystal Palace, claimed that Brexit would open up new opportunities for smaller clubs and British players. Sol Campbell argued in the *Daily Mail* that 'because of European rules on freedom of movement, it is virtually impossible for us to get a proper grip on the situation. If we want to see more English stars like Harry Kane rise through the ranks we should take back control.'[15]

David James made the case not only in terms of migration, but, like the rest of the more fanciful Brexiteers, by talking up the possibility of trade deals outside of Europe. 'I would vote to leave because I think we have opportunities to create trade links and from a football perspective as well. If you think of the likes of an Indian player, they would have a better chance of having an opportunity here [if there was less European immigration], which would then open up and develop Indian footballers … I don't see a downside.'[16] James wasn't alone in his wishful thinking.

With immaculate timing the final days of the referendum campaign coincided with the final group stage matches of Euro 2016. England, their campaign already disrupted by state-sanctioned Russian hooligan attacks on their fans both before and during their opening match in Marseille, limped their way through the tournament. On 20 June, England played an excruciating goalless draw with Slovakia and, by a thread, stayed in the European Championship. Three days later, by an equally narrow margin, Britain voted to leave the European Union. Harry Kane spoke for the 28 per cent of the country who didn't vote at all: 'I don't know enough about it to be concerned … and I don't think the other players do as well.' Michael O'Neill,

Northern Ireland's coach, like many, regretted not voting: 'I personally made an error because I didn't give myself an opportunity to vote by postal vote, so I'm disappointed with myself.' Jamie Carragher's angry tweet – 'Well done to the over 50s for thinking of the future! Feel ashamed of my generation' – was a rare intervention from either player or pundit in Britain.[17]

Europeans were, by contrast, more outspoken. Petr Cech, previously Chelsea's goalkeeper, was irate: 'It looks like the biggest decision in the history of this country was made based on fake campaign and lies.' German goalkeeper Manuel Neuer was disappointed: 'I grew up at a time when it was normal that the EU stood together ... I think it's sad that Britain and Europe no longer have that feeling of unity.' Italian defender Giorgio Chiellini saw trouble ahead. 'Yesterday we went to sleep thinking that Britain would remain in the EU. Unfortunately that didn't happen, and I think the biggest concern is the domino effect that this choice could cause ... a referendum in other states.'[18]

Four days after the referendum, England played Iceland in the round of sixteen and, in a uniquely calamitous performance, were beaten 2–1. The bellicose chants of a small minority in the crowd were the loudest voices: 'Stand up if you hate the French', 'We're all leaving Europe!' and 'Fuck off, Europe, we all voted out!' Thousands more sat in horrified silence, watching their team freeze, completely unable to react to what was going on around them. Prime Minister David Cameron had already resigned by this point, now Roy Hodgson followed, departing with a thought that the former would have recognised: 'I would have loved to stay on for another two years. However, I am pragmatic and I know we are in the results business.'[19] Both their replacements would now declare themselves for Leave: Prime Minister Theresa May coined the gnomic notion that 'Brexit means Brexit'; new England coach Sam Allardyce was more straightforward: 'I am out. My feeling is that the European Union isn't doing the United Kingdom any favours.'[20] Not that it helped them; both May and Allardyce would be forced from office much sooner than they planned.

For the next four years, British political conversation was consumed by Brexit: whether to trigger Article 50 and begin a countdown to departure; what kind of new relationship to strike with the EU – variants of soft, hard and no-deal Brexits; and a long and unsuccessful campaign to call a second referendum on whatever deal was struck. Not that one could really consider it much of a conversation. Football's tribalism and performative identity politics provided a template for the new tribes of Remain and Leave, who proved as intransigent and partisan as their footballing equivalents. Out of this emerged a political debate in which wind-ups and banter were preferred to critical reflection, where radicalised politicians were judged with the eye of the fan, not the citizen. Football certainly reflected the nation's anger. Neil Warnock, then manager of Cardiff City, raged, 'I can't wait to get out of it, if I'm honest. I think we'll be far better out of the bloody thing. In every aspect, football-wise as well, absolutely. To hell with the rest of the world.'[21] Graeme Souness, commentating for Sky Sports, digressed: 'I live down on the south coast of England and I went to watch Bournemouth play Swansea City three weeks ago. It was like watching a Dutch game of football, lots of nice little passes, pretty technique with little passes. There was no fire. There was nobody smashing into anyone. There was no real anger in the game.' The presenter then asked him if he voted for Brexit, and Souness, with an uncharacteristic grin, replied, 'I certainly did, yeah.'[22]

Theresa May's efforts to pass a deal through parliament saw a spike in football Twitter exchanges. Peter Shilton and Peter Reid crossed swords as the former lauded the arch Brexiteer Jacob Rees-Mogg and the latter derided him. Boreham Wood FC posted a letter on their website calling on MPs to do their duty and vote against Theresa May's proposed deal. Chris Waddle exclaimed on Twitter, when her proposals were voted down, 'Well done Theresa May. Now let's leave with no deal,' and was deluged with anger; just one of innumerable cases in which the debate was reduced to who had the right to speak for whom and on what subject. On the matter of a second referendum, Jürgen Klopp implored, 'Let's think about it again and let's vote again with the right information.' Jamie Carragher made the case in terms of his own punditry: 'I am used to looking back at things after the event. It's what I do on match day. I think that is what we should do with Brexit. Look back at what we have learnt since 2016 and be able to give an opinion on where we are now in 2019 before we potentially relegate ourselves as a country.'[23]

Later that year, as new Prime Minister Boris Johnson promised to 'get Brexit done', Ipswich Town fans, playing away at Luton, were just one example of the Brexit-themed chants and animosities that had begun to seep into English football stadiums. Referencing Luton's super-diverse population they sang, 'Boris Johnson – he's coming for you', 'Born in the UK/You'll never sing that', and 'Brexit means Brexit'.[24]

What Brexit actually did mean was, of course, a conundrum, for it soon became apparent that neither the Leave campaign, the Tory Party nor the Civil Service had a plan for what it would actually look like. For that, certainly in 2017, the best place to find out was the simulation game *Football Manager*.[25] Already so remarkably detailed that it had thought through the impact of Scotland's independence referendum on the transfer market, it was given a new set of code to mimic the various post-referendum options facing the United Kingdom. Depending on how the negotiations went inside the *Football Manager* universe, players could find themselves operating in one of three worlds: the first, in which the UK stayed inside the single market and labour migration rules remained unchanged; the second, a soft Brexit with a relatively easy visa regime for European players; and the third and most difficult prospect, a hard or even no-deal Brexit under which strict rules would be applied to migrant players,

allowing in only those with considerable international experience. The game was so carefully modelled that MPs and senior
civil servants called for a briefing from its makers. Some players
were shocked by the implications of Brexit for their quest to get
Preston North End to the Champions League: 'If I'd have known
about this before the vote I'd have voted in a different way.'[26]

Football, like every walk of British life, had become enmeshed
with the endless Brexit conversation, and its language and opinions were an indicator of how ugly the debate had become; but
if one wanted to actually understand Brexit's origins and consequences, football's deeper structures offered a better guide. In
the years leading up to the referendum, football's economy
paralleled the huge inequalities that were developing in British
society and had driven part of the Leave vote, inequalities that
became increasingly clear as one compared the economic and
sporting fortunes of globally connected cities and post-
industrial towns. At the same time it became apparent that football had been and would increasingly become a toxic environment
for three groups that were not aligned with the Leave coalition:
the young, people of colour, and experts and arbiters. The country's past disregard for the young was revealed by the shocking
wave of historic sexual-abuse cases in football that came to
court, while contemporary disregard could be found inside football's increasingly pressurised academy system. Racism and
racists, previously contained, perhaps even diminished, were
given a new lease of life in football and the wider society. Experts
and arbiters who stood in the way of the Brexiteers, by accurately assessing the consequences of their blunder or judging
their actions illegal, were dismissed and vilified, but none have
taken more stick than football referees. Finally, perhaps the
greatest irony was that Brexit, a project designed to secure the
sovereignty of the United Kingdom, made the Union weaker
than it had been in a century; and that would be played out in
the performances and narratives of its national football teams.
By 2020, in the world of *Football Manager*, the consequences

of Brexit on club finances and transfer deals were so onerous that a campaign was mounted to allow Brexit to be turned off inside the game.[27] In 2022 it finally became possible to just change the settings and remove the whole sorry episode from the game. But for the rest of us, stuck in reality, this was not an option.

2.

Uneven Playing Fields

Success, Failure and the Economics of Football

English professional league football began with just twelve clubs, six from the Midlands and six from Lancashire, a world small enough that Preston North End could bestride it, winning the first two championships in 1889 and 1890. As the league expanded at the turn of the century, bigger cities and clubs came to the fore. The great industrial zones of late-Victorian England – Birmingham, Liverpool, Sheffield, Sunderland and Newcastle – would supply almost every winner for the next twenty years and for much of the first half of the twentienth century. It was not until 1908 that a club from Manchester would win the title, and not until 1931 that Arsenal, a London club, would do so. In the 1920s and 1930s there was still room for titles for industrial towns like Burnley and Huddersfield. After the Second World War the older urban hierarchy was disrupted by Portsmouth in the 1940s, Wolverhampton Wanderers in the 1950s, and in the very early sixties by Ipswich Town and, again, Burnley. However, the end of the maximum wage in football in 1961, and the creeping low-key commercialisation of the wider game, shifted the competitive balance of English football towards London, Liverpool and Manchester. The gap between the bigger cities with bigger crowds and smaller-town teams grew. There was a final flourish for cities outside this trio, from the beleaguered Midlands of the mid-1970s and early 1980s, when Derby Country, Nottingham Forest and Aston Villa all won the league, and Leeds United in 1974 and 1992. But in the era of the Premier League the title has only left London, Liverpool and Manchester on two occasions, and between 1992 and 2020 their clubs occupied 95 per cent of the top four slots. At the same time, the FA Cup, which in the past had been more widely contested by other cities, has, since 1992, seen only two smaller-town victories – Portsmouth in 2008 and Wigan in 2013 – both of whom have since gone bankrupt. Small-town teams and old industrial clubs have had their time in the Premier League, from Barnsley to Blackpool to Bradford, but its geographical centre of gravity has been shifting south as clubs like Brentford, Brighton and Crystal Palace have made themselves regular members, and old perennials like Middlesbrough and Sunderland have fallen away. By the late 2010s, after more than twenty-five years of unregulated economic globalisation in the game, football appeared to be a more accurate map of the country's winner and losers, sporting and social, than ever before, one confirmed by the voting pattens of the Brexit referendum.

Looking at the census data for the ninety-two constituencies of the clubs in English football's top four divisions, *The Economist* found that the distribution of sporting success had come to parallel the geography of economic success and urban vitality, among the most important factors in shaping the Brexit vote. Premier League clubs, in particular, came from bigger and denser cities, with significantly more ethnically diverse communities, younger populations and higher levels of income and economic output than their lower-league counterparts. These kinds of urban areas and their demographic groups tended towards Remain, while smaller, older, poorer and less diverse towns tended towards Leave.[1] Consequently, as of 2020, data scientist Omar Chaudhuri found that only 30 per cent of Premier League clubs sat in Leave-voting constituencies, and only one of them – Burnley – was in a strongly Leave-voting town; the corresponding figure in the Championship was 58 per cent of clubs, and 75 per cent in League One and League Two. The average vote across the constituencies that host the four divisions showed a similar pattern: the Premier League voted Remain by 55–45; the Championship was a 50–50 score draw, with Europhile Fulham cancelled out by Eurosceptic Stoke and West Bromwich. League One mirrored the nation as a whole, voting Leave by 52 to 48, while League Two backed Brexit 54 to 46; both lower leagues would have been more strongly Leave but for the anomalous ultra-Remainer constituencies that host Bristol Rovers, Oxford United and Cambridge United.

Correlation is not causality. The Premier League didn't make its hosts significantly richer. This is not to say that there wasn't some spillover effect, as the new money funded more jobs, brought more tourists to town and afforded smaller urban areas a unique kind of global exposure. However, player wages, the bulk of the game's money, were more likely to be spent in sequestered commuter villages, Bentley dealerships outside of town, and foreign tourist destinations. Did the Premier League make fans more inclined to vote Remain? Perhaps one could argue that big clubs' European experiences and aspirations were significant in shaping attitudes to the European Union, but the few and unreliable surveys of supporter-voting preference suggest otherwise. Chelsea fans, for example, despite their cosmopolitan football existence, were decisively Leave voters, and in any case club fan bases, especially with the bigger clubs, are drawn from a much bigger geographical area than their parliamentary constituency. In short, being in the Premier League didn't make fans vote Remain, while being in League Two didn't make them vote Leave. However, football as a whole, and at the level of parable, did offer a powerful illustration of what an economy looked like when it favoured globally connected cities over the old industrial heartlands and their small towns. As one angry Bury supporter told *The Economist* after the club was liquidated in 2020: 'The system just continuously lets people down, and it always lets people down at the bottom of the system. It never lets down the people at the top. And that's why people are so angry. I think that's why you can't split this from what's happening in the UK at the moment.'[2] The genius of the Leave campaign was to persuade so many that the system was the European Union, rather than global capitalism and Britain's own defunded and deracinated state.

How did that system, in football at any rate, come into being? A case could be made that the Premier League, as a concept, was shaped by eleven years of Thatcherism, during which many of the institutions of the post-war consensus were dismantled, commercialised or – like football's avatars the great Victorian industrial sectors of coal, shipbuilding and steel – sold off. The founders of the Premier League certainly exemplified a new breed of more aggressive entrepreneur that Thatcher had extolled. By the time they had created the Premier League, Thatcher had been deposed and the competition was first played through the five long years of John Major's second Conservative administration. This was a transitional moment, rather than a decisive break with the old. Revolutionary as the creation of the breakaway league had been, its impact was not immediately obvious. Though relentlessly advertised by Sky as 'a whole new ball game', it was, in fact, a spectacle much closer to the world before 1992 than our own era today. Watching live televised football was not new – it had been around since the mid-1980s, with ITV broadcasting twenty games the previous season. Seemingly a financial bonanza, Sky were actually only paying the league around £60 million a year, less than £3 million per club. Consequently, the number of foreign players remained low – just thirteen in 1992 – and they were recruited from inexpensive markets like the Caribbean and Scandinavia. Similarly, foreign coaches remained the exception. George Graham, Brian Clough and Ron Atkinson were all still in business, and even the presence of Ossie Ardiles at Spurs felt like a throwback to the English game of the late 1970s rather than the herald of a new cosmopolitanism. It was not until 1996 and the appointment of Ruud Gullit at Chelsea and Arsène Wenger at Arsenal that European coaches and their methods would have a real foothold in the league. Foreign owners were equally thin on the ground, with just Mohamed Al-Fayed, who had bought Fulham in 1997, mixing it with the new English football entrepreneurs, like Sir John Hall at Newcastle, Alan Sugar at Spurs and David Dein at Arsenal, and the old-school local industrialists, such as Jack Walker at Blackburn.

The stadiums were, at best, in transition. Much of the first two seasons of the league was played in grounds where at least one stand had been demolished, and others were being rebuilt: new steel frames could be seen being assembled above old crumbling terraces, new sponsor logos sat next to advertising boards erected a decade beforehand and still bolted onto a corrugated iron roof. The pitches were certainly from an older epoch, mostly ragged by the spring, still turning to mud baths in the rain. Sky's introduction of dancers and cheerleaders, spattered by mud, generated less razzmatazz than perhaps their advocates had expected. Although seats had been installed and new executive boxes were popping up, the demographic and demeanour of the crowd was not so different from the late 1980s, still predominately working class and overwhelmingly male, with its concentrated knots of old-timers and voluble, boisterous youth.

However, by 1997 all of this would be disappearing into the past. The first phase of stadium redevelopment had been completed, the terraces were gone, and the phalanx of new suites and boxes had arrived. Sharply increased ticket prices were beginning to shift the economic demography and age profile of the crowd, which had now become wealthier and older. At the same time the league's second TV deal more than doubled its income, the presence of foreign players became commonplace, and the global popularity and reach of the league began to climb. Thus, the Premier League, economically and culturally, would assume its current form, under thirteen years of New Labour government between 1997 and 2010. Major, harking back to the less monocultural sporting world of the 1950s and 60s, had quietly supported Chelsea but was truly a devotee of cricket, leaving 10 Downing Street for the last time and heading for the Oval; New Labour was all football. Blair made his affiliation to Newcastle United public knowledge and traded headers with Kevin Keegan on television. Gordon Brown's quietly obsessive relationship with Raith Rovers paired Scottish working-class authenticity with Blair's ciphers of football gentrification. Junior members of the government and its array of special advisers, many future cabinet ministers, played five-a-side in a team named Demon Eyes, referencing the Tory scare campaign in which Blair was depicted with wild, monstrous eyes. Football served as a way of politically signalling New Labour's historical connection to what remained of the core of working-class life, at the same time that its wider economic project was shrinking it even further.

The Blair and Brown years oversaw the globalisation of the British economy. This included increasing levels of immigration by skilled workers that helped Britain's finance, tech and higher education sectors boom; a concentration of growth and income among these globally competitive service industries and the bigger cities that hosted them; and a wave of foreign purchases of domestic assets of all kinds. Foreign players by 2010 made up over 60 per cent of the Premier League's squads, were present in the lower leagues and came from more than sixty different countries. Virtually an afterthought in 1992, the cultivation of foreign markets and the sale of media rights outside the UK became increasingly important and lucrative. Regular foreign tours, relentless marketing, an internationally successful fantasy football league and exemplary broadcasting services, all amplified by the global reach of the English language, created a new and truly global market for live football for the league as a whole, and among the biggest clubs a new worldwide network of fans.

By the end of New Labour's time in office, the Premier League's international rights were worth more than £350 million a season, around 40 per cent of the total rights income, while sponsors and advertisers were increasingly global. Finally, Labour's Britain fell over itself to welcome the arrival of the world's super-rich and their purchase of trophy assets, from the town houses of Belgravia to the nation's leading football clubs. Roman Abramovich's acquisition of Chelsea in 2003, unproblematically waved through, began a process that would see half of the Premier League in foreign hands by 2008, and three-quarters by 2020.

Paradoxically, this hyper-globalised version of elite English football was sold to the world, with extraordinary success, on the basis of club identities and football cultures that were deeply parochial – and, like the mainstays of the heritage and tourist trade, remade and repackaged as theme-park versions of their original selves. England's tightly packed stadiums, which brought the crowd close to the pitch, were preferred to the empty bowls and athletics tracks of Italy's Serie A. English crowds' preference for relentless if sometimes incautious attack, and their relish for the robust and the physical, made for better television; and their spontaneity, sense of humour and imaginative recycling of pop culture proved far more comprehensible and globally appealing than the cryptic though spectacular *tifo* of Italian and Spanish ultras.

The quid pro quo for such obeisance to global economic forces was that New Labour promised tighter and more effective regulation and a modicum of redistribution. While this was pursued with a kind of vindictive fury in the case of schools and hospitals, by contrast global finance, new tech and the privatised utilities were treated with kid gloves. New Labour's initial ambition, to reform and regulate football, saw the government establish a wide-ranging football task force, charged with investigating the game's finances, the state of the grassroots game, ticket prices and systems of fan representation. However, plans for the creation of an independent football regulator with real power on which real reform hinged were diluted and then abandoned. Consequently, the only restraints placed on the Premier League were self-imposed and nugatory. The introduction of the homegrown players limit meant that just a third of a club's squad needed to be English or developed within their own academy system. The introduction of what was then known as the 'fit and proper person test' for club owners and directors proved so powerful that the purchase of Manchester City, first by an exiled Thai prime minister and then the royal house of Abu Dhabi, was deemed unproblematic. The only change to the distribution of income in the game, which was becoming more unequal with each season, was that the Premier League started paying relegated clubs parachute payments in 2006: three years of guaranteed additional income to clubs who took the drop to allow them to cope with Premier League wage contracts when they were receiving lower-league TV money. It was, in effect, a middle-class subsidy to a class of clubs too big for the Championship and too small for the Premier League that has totally unbalanced the second level. The widespread opposition to proposals to play competitive league fixtures in foreign locations, and the subsequent abandonment of the plan in 2007, was the single significant break on the league's globalisation.

In the absence of any greater regulation of the Premier League, and any renegotiation of its relationship with the rest of the game, the globalisation of football produced a league that, despite an extraordinary growth in revenue, managed to lose money while driving a remarkable rise in inequality. As the league and its owners failed to countenance a collective agreement over wage restraint until the mid-2010s, the competitive drive of football, its relentless over-optimism and the preference among club owners for sporting glory over dividends, saw squad costs and player wages rise even faster than income. The capacity of many owners, particularly at Chelsea and Manchester City, to accept and absorb giant losses spun the wheel ever faster. The gap between the Premier League and the rest, already wide in 1997, became a chasm. In 2007 the Premier League's combined club revenues were, at £2.3 billion, more than four times that of the rest of the English Football League combined. By 2018 the Premier League's £5.6 billion was eight times the revenue of the EFL. In 2024 its near £7 billion turnover was ten times that of the leagues below.

This is how the system was meant to work. The primary reason for the creation of the Premier League by the biggest clubs was, by *force majeure*, to keep a significantly bigger percentage of the broadcast deals than they had received as part of the Football League, when bound to the three lower divisions. Nothing that has happened in football since then has dented the inescapable logic of this system. By 2023, 88 per cent of broadcasting money went to the Premier League and 7.4 per cent on parachute payments for teams relegated to the Championship. This left 3.2 per cent for the rest of the Championship, while Leagues One and Two got 1 per cent between them.

That said, this was the era not of the 1 per cent, but the 0.1 per cent, and the Premier League itself became almost as unequal as the whole of the pyramid. The distribution of broadcasting money gave clubs higher up the table and those that were on television more money, but equal shares of half the domestic and all the international income ensured that even the smallest teams could field a reasonably competitive squad. Even so, this could not counter the other factors that drove the league's income inequality. The match-day income that clubs earned from selling tickets, food and drink still accounted for 15 to 20 per cent of turnover. Here, the bigger clubs, with bigger stadiums, more skyboxes and 'entertainment' facilities, and the more expensive ticket prices that a richer fan base could afford to pay, stretched their financial lead. More important, though, has been the rising value of club sponsorships, determined by the global reach of the club brand. In 2022 Manchester City could command £67.5 million from the UAE's airline Etihad to be its shirt sponsors and Liverpool £50 million from Standard Chartered. West Ham, by contrast, could only manage £10 million from bookmakers Betway and Aston Villa just £6 million from vehicle retailer Cazoo, less than Arsenal received from the Rwandan government for just their sleeve sponsorship slot. The gap between top and bottom widened again when European money was taken into account, with Champions League qualifiers earning another £50–100 million, depending on how far they progressed, while Europa League qualifiers received around a quarter of that. Consequently, teams playing in Europe had triple the average income of those that didn't.

The final parallel between New Labour and the Premier League was that the limits of the model – the failures of self-regulation and the problem of accumulating debts – would each be exposed by a global shock, albeit more than a decade apart. New Labour's lightly regulated economic boom would be undone by the global banking crisis of 2008, before a decade of Conservative austerity eradicated most of its gains. The Premier League, which managed to thrive while much of the country struggled, would be broken by the global pandemic in 2020. Covid meant that match-day income disappeared and broadcast income dropped by £600 million a year, given the poorer quality of the product, and the Premier League clubs were £700 million in the red. After a five-year period between 2014 and 2019 in which it had just about made some money (its income rose and the Premier League's new PSR – profit and sustainability rules – forced a modicum of restraint on the clubs), the Premier League would then lose money in every subsequent year.[3] As ever, it was not for want of revenue. Post-Covid crowds were bigger than ever, and paying more than ever. The latest TV deal was only delivering 6 per cent growth, but commercial income was 38 per cent up and now at record levels; however, in a reversion to type, every increase in revenue was matched or exceeded by increases in spending. The short-lived reduction of the league's income-to-wage ratio was reversed, from 60 per cent in 2019 to 67 per cent in 2023. At the same time, payments to directors and senior managers climbed; the sharp increase in the cost of energy after Russia's invasion of Ukraine in 2022 made stadiums more expensive to run; and interest payments at those clubs with real debt, nearly £200 million a year, ticked upwards. Consequently, the Premier League lost more than £590 million a year between 2020 and 2023. The Championship saw its income level out, perhaps even reduce in real terms, and under regulatory pressure from the EFL clubs were forced to tighten their finances. Even so, they were still losing nearly £300 million a year.

Almost all of these losses were absorbed by an escalating level of club debt. In the Premier League, total debts rose from £6 billion in 2019 to £7.4 billion in 2023. In the Championship they rose from £1.4 billion to £1.7 billion.[4] Much of this was accounted for by soft loans from club's owners, which have no interest payable on them. These loans could, by the alchemical magic of accountancy, be made to disappear by their conversion into equity, the debt in effect paid off by new shares created by the club. Clubs have also extended their credit by purchasing players on instalment plans, deferring the cost over three or four years. These debts almost doubled from £1.5 billion in 2020 to just over £3 billion in 2023.[5] According to Fair Game, an alliance of small clubs campaigning for change, that year's accounts revealed that fifty of the ninety-two clubs in the top four divisions were technically insolvent, nine of them in the Premier League.[6] Finally, the flimsy PSR rules established by the Premier League a decade beforehand, and suspended during Covid, came into effect in 2022 and 2023, with Nottingham Forest and Everton found in breach and punished with points deductions.

Clubs have sought to generate more revenue by building a new stadium (Arsenal, Spurs, Everton) or expanding their old one (Liverpool). Brighton and Brentford have tried to outrun their budget by using data-driven recruitment models and developing players whom they sell on for a considerable profit. An alternative, if yet unproven strategy for lowering the costs of developing players has been the creation of a global network of collaborating clubs. Manchester City, for example, are the flagship of a nine-club network that stretches from Japan and the USA to Uruguay and Spain. Clubs have also made widespread use of accounting tricks and wheezes. Chelsea, since Abramovich's departure, have sought to fund a giant transfer spend and stay within PSR rules by amortising the costs of buying a player over eight-year contracts, rather than the usual three or four. Clubs have also been engaging in the swap game, where they exchange players, often at surprisingly high values, in a move that is designed to improve their balance sheets rather than their squads.[7] Some have resorted to the sale of their stadium or other property, also generously valued, to commercial entities owned by the owners themselves.[8]

While all this frenzied activity has allowed a few clubs to do better than their budgets might normally allow, or at least not contravene PSR rules, it remains the fact that English football is losing money, accumulating debt, and is breathtakingly unequal and worryingly monopolistic. Leicester City's title win in 2016 provided a short-lived fig leaf. After much complaint that the competitive balance of the league, dominated first by Manchester United and Arsenal and then by Manchester United and Chelsea, was stifling, the league seemed to have opened up and the title was won over five successive seasons between 2012 and 2016 by four different clubs: Manchester City (twice), Manchester United, Chelsea and Leicester City. Since then, Leicester have been relegated and Manchester City have won six of the last eight Premier League titles (as of 2024). They have done so with record points scores, in a league where the points gap between top and bottom is getting bigger and newly promoted teams find it harder to stay up. Measured by the Gini coefficient, the standard statistical tool for measuring income inequality, the Premier League has been heading in this direction for more than a decade, and there is no end to the trend.[9] The football, not least from Manchester City, has been very good. The narratives of these seasons – the duels between City and Liverpool and City and Arsenal – have been compelling. Manchester United's long, painful decline and Chelsea's post-Abramovich problems have provided ample *Schadenfreude*, Tottenham's inconsistency has been near comedic, Aston Villa and Newcastle's qualification for Europe made for a welcome return for the left behind. Even so, however City managed their ascent and whether they broke any financial rules or not, no commercial league, no institution of any kind, can survive this level of monopolisation without some kind of decay and corruption.

However, the sporting fate of Premier League and Championship clubs and their very well remunerated players is a long way from the real consequences of Britain's rising tide of inequality. In the lower leagues, where many clubs lurch from crisis to crisis, often in the financial limbo of HMRC wind-up orders, it is closer. Bolton Wanderers and Wigan Athletic, for example, who were in the Premier League, came close to insolvency and dissolution until they were saved by new owners prepared to cover their debts. There are limits, though, to this kind of philanthropic safety net. In 2020, Bury FC, unable to pay its very considerable debts, was kicked out of the Football League, of which it had been a founder member in 1888, and was then liquidated by its administrators. More than a century and half of accumulated cultural capital was vaporised, the victim of the threadbare economics and cumulative debt of the lower leagues, and a very dodgy property deal done by the previous owner; a fate, in its own way, as representative of the country as the concentration of success in its few globally connected cities.

3.

Football's Dirty Secret

Brexit, Racism and British Football

The comforting story that England and English football told itself in the early twenty-first century was that its once over-whelming, audible racism had been silenced. Rather than baying crowds, anti-racism statements over the public address system and pitch-side adverts were now the norm at every club. The sports press were sufficiently self-righteous that, where the England team was concerned, they could angrily condemn the racism of Spanish and Slovakian crowds. In this regard John Terry, the Chelsea and England captain, did the cause a favour, making it transparently clear that racism was alive and well when, in 2011, he was captured on film saying 'you fucking black cunt' to QPR's Anton Ferdinand.[1] Just eight days earlier, Liverpool's Uruguayan forward Luis Suárez had racially abused Manchester United's Patrice Evra, but that was brushed off by many as South American ignorance.[2] This was John Terry, East London lad, captain of Chelsea and England. Terry has always maintained that he was merely enquiring as to whether Ferdinand had uttered the same phrase to him, and at a criminal trial he was found not guilty. The FA, to their credit, saw things differently, fined him £220,000 and banned him for four matches.[3] Terry lost the England captaincy, but retained it at

Chelsea, where he was deified as a hero and leader. The incident generated so much disquiet that Prime Minster David Cameron felt compelled to hold a summit on racism in football at Downing Street and announced that apparently he would be 'crushing' racism in the game.

If a 2014 online survey of match-going fans was anything to go by, there was plenty of 'crushing' still to do: more than half of all fans who took part had witnessed or experienced some form of racism in football. One respondent, acknowledging the decline in the most vocal forms of hate speech, still thought that 'anyone who attends football on a regular basis will confirm racist undertones are still there and very much alive'.[4] Those racist undertones also lived on inside the professional game, as Malky Mackay's phone made clear. The then manager of Cardiff City was sacked in 2014 after text messages between himself and Iain Moody, the club's chief scout, were made public. Of Phil Smith, a football agent who, not for the first time in his career, was the subject of antisemitic abuse, Mackay was contemptuous: 'Go on Fat Phil. Nothing like a jew that sees money slipping through his fingers.' On the arrival of a South Korean player and his representatives, Mackay texted: 'Fkn Chinkys', before reconsidering his position: 'Fk it. There's enough dogs in Cardiff for us all to go around.' Somehow, the FA, on reviewing the case for eleven months, absolved Mackay and Moody, on the technical grounds that they had a 'legitimate expectation of privacy' that had been breached by the release of the messages, and took no further action.[5]

Clearly, during the years before the Brexit referendum, Britain and its football culture were not enjoying a golden age of tolerance and understanding. In 2012, for example, the Conservative Home Secretary Theresa May launched the 'hostile environment' policy against illegal immigrants, but with consequences for every person of colour in the country, as 'immigrant' served as a cipher for Black, regardless of citizenship. In the aftermath of Brexit, and after a decade of steady decline, the incidence of hate crimes and ethically motivated attacks, in football and in society, rose. Across the UK there had been over 42,000 hate crimes recorded in 2013; 62,500 in the year of the referendum; and 103,000 in 2019, the vast majority of which were related to race.[6] Football went the same way. In England the number of recorded hate crimes in the game – no doubt just a fraction of what was actually going on – rose by more than 40 per cent in 2017, and again in 2018, while arrests for racist chants doubled between 2016 and 2019, and rose 150 per cent in the 2019–20 season, despite it being truncated by the pandemic.[7] It is hard to see how the combination of xenophobia, nativism and rage conjured up the Brexit referendum and the victory of the Leave campaign would not translate into the normalisation of acts of hatred.

Players were the most visible targets. In 2017 Manchester City's Raheem Sterling was physically attacked and racially abused by a Manchester United fan outside the Manchester City training ground. A year later Chelsea fans screamed abuse in his face on the touchline at Stamford Bridge. The same week, a Tottenham fan was arrested for throwing a banana skin at the feet of Arsenal's Pierre-Emerick Aubameyang. Anti-racist organisation Kick It Out reported another 11 per cent increase in incidents of hate speech in football, more than half of which were racist. Sterling, posting on Instagram after the encounter at Stamford Bridge, reflected the weary cynicism of most Black players: 'Regarding what was said at the Chelsea game, as you can see by my reaction I just had to laugh because I don't expect no better.'[8] Islamophobia and antisemitism were part of the mix, too. Chelsea fans were recorded in Prague singing about Liverpool's Egyptian striker, 'Salah is a bomber', while West Ham fans were caught on a phone camera singing antisemitic songs after losing to Manchester United in 2018, and again on a plane bound for Belgium in 2022.[9] Racism might have been primarily directed at the pitch, but it clearly suffused the stands of English football. In 2019 a Sky Sports survey of match-attending football supporters found that 86 per cent had witnessed racist acts at the game, rising to 93 per cent of BAME fans, of whom one in four saw racism at every match they attended. Most dismal of all the statistics was that 70 per cent of BAME fans said they had been directly abused themselves, but only 29 per cent thought it worth reporting.[10]

In 2019 reports of racist behaviour, from the professional game to the grassroots, in person and online, multiplied. On a single weekend in April, English football saw Crystal Palace's Wilfried Zaha called a 'Diving Monkey' on Instagram after their game with Newcastle; in the Championship a Brentford fan directly insulted Derby's Duane Holmes, who was sitting on the bench having been substituted; and Northampton Town reported that their Black players had been openly abused at Notts County, their Slovenian midfielder Timi Elšnik calling it 'the most disgusting thing I've seen and heard'. The levels of abuse on social media also rose. Poor form or, worse, missing a penalty, saw racist attacks on Watford's Troy Deeney and Manchester United's Ashley Young. In a single weekend in August three Black players that missed a penalty were subjected to racist abuse on Twitter – Chelsea's Tammy Abraham, Reading's Yakou Méïté and Manchester United's Paul Pogba – mostly by their club's own supporters. The lower leagues were not immune. Hartlepool United fans screamed so much abuse at Dover's Inih Effiong after he scored a penalty that the game was held up for ten minutes as both sides considered leaving the field. In a first for the professional women's game, Sheffield United's Sophie Jones was found guilty by the FA of racially abusing Tottenham's Renée Hector and banned for five games.[11] In Scotland, where the space for bigotry appeared already occupied by sectarianism, there was still room for racism. A survey by Show Racism the Red Card found that more than a third of young people in Scotland had witnessed or experienced racism while playing football in the previous year. Kevin Harper, then the only Black manager in Scottish football, thought 'it's more prevalent now than it was five years ago'. Alex Dyer, the Montserratian coach of Kilmarnock, received old-fashioned poisonous racist letters, while his departure in 2021 was marked by racist graffiti on the walls of the club's stadium, Rugby Park.[12]

Anyone who had read the report by Labour MP John Mann, published in 2010, on the state of Islamophobia and anti-semitism in grassroots football would not have been surprised by the outpouring of racist incidents in the game. A decade earlier Mann had identified widespread racist behaviours, rarely if ever actually reported to the FA: 'I was astonished how players getting abused every single week were not complaining and felt there was no purpose in complaining ... in any other part of British society that kind of abuse would not be accepted.'[13] He recommended a raft of reforms to the Football Association, none of which were implemented. In 2019, Kick It Out reported, again, a sharp rise in racist incidents in grassroots football. Chief Executive Troy Townsend said that 'it's like the wild west. It's a free-for-all out there ... We see some pretty horrendous stuff. We've seen actual bodily harm. Blood pouring out of a player's face, his shirt on the ground with blood all over it.'[14] Lutel James, a youth football coach based in Chapeltown in Leeds, reported three incidents in one week; his report to the FA said that his team experienced 'continuous racism'.[15] ITN published a survey of British Asian grassroots players and coaches which found that 79 per cent had suffered racist abuse by either another player, a coach or spectator during a game, and nearly half of them had experienced this over the previous year. Blackburn United reserves captain Danyal Osman said, 'To be honest it happens a lot, it's not just the odd occasion and it gets stamped out, it's more or less a weekly thing ... Most of the opposition we come up against tend to use language like that.'[16] A report from the BAME Football Forum in Leicester found that 70 per cent of BAME grassroots players had witnessed or experienced racism or discrimination in football in the previous year and more than half thought that the problem had got worse over the previous five years.[17] The situation in youth football could be breathtakingly unpleasant. One under-8 player said, 'At this game, instead of shaking our hands, the opposition players slapped them and said "banana" as they went down the line and made monkey noises.' The referee was present, but no follow-up and no FA investigation were mounted. Among many BAME players and coaches there was a pervasive sense that referees were at best uninterested in these issues, and at worst actively discriminatory.

While obvious forms of racial abuse were ignored, efforts to challenge it were punished. Wythenshawe Town's manager, James Kinsey, was fined and suspended by the football authorities for instructing his players to come off the pitch due to an alleged racist incident involving a match official.[18] Wallace Hermit, a veteran of the South London Black grassroots scene, thought the treatment of his players was so unfair that 'I ended up getting someone to come and film the games … You see away games where you're better than the home team but you lose because of a biased referee. You complain to the county FA but it's like going to the Police Complaints Commission. Why bother?' Colin King, founder with Hermit of the BAME Coaches Association, explained why grassroots football could be such an uncomfortable space for minorities: 'I'm a qualified referee and I wouldn't do it anymore. I've had white teams chase me out the ground looking to fight me … But it's not just about the n-word. It's about white teams not shaking your hand or exchanging shirts. They don't want to be in the same space. You can see the parents don't want to be around black players.'[19]

The situation was as bad at the top of the game. In 2017 it became public knowledge that England player Eni Aluko had accused Mark Sampson, the then manager of the England women's team, of making racist comments in 2014. She would go on to reveal that other members of the coaching staff would speak to Black and mixed-heritage players in mock Caribbean accents. An FA internal inquiry then absolved Sampson and themselves, on the extraordinary grounds that 'on two separate occasions [Sampson] made ill-judged attempts at humour, which, as a matter of law, were discriminatory on the grounds of race', but the investigating barrister thought 'it important to emphasise that I have not concluded that MS is a racist'.[20] It required a House of Commons Select Committee grilling of senior officials, including chief executive Martin Glenn, to lay bare the FA's refusal to take players' complaints seriously, their attempts to reframe racism as harmless banter, and the culture of secrecy and bullying it traded in.[21] In 2019 Peter Beardsley, then coach of Newcastle's under-23s, was banned from football for eight months after being found guilty of using 'obviously racist' and 'wholly unacceptable' language: telling young Black players before a team-building exercise at the Go Ape adventure park 'you should be used to that' when talking about climbing trees; and telling a Black player celebrating by playing head tennis that he was 'a monkey'. Beardsley denied he was a racist, told everyone he loved a laugh, changed his evidence a lot, and never really saw that there was a problem, and that, of course, was the bigger problem.[22]

Despite all the apparent changes of the previous decades, many white people in football still could not see that what they termed 'banter' was demeaning language in which racism was structurally embedded, and that it was their responsibility to do something about it rather than expecting Black people to put up with it. John Yems, coach at Crawley Town between 2019 and 2022, was certainly one of those white people. In 2023 his original seventeen-month suspension from football was increased to three years as the FA examined a gigantic roll call of racist asides, microaggressions and slurs, *inter alia*: a Muslim player was refused a bib in training because his 'people blow up stuff with vests'; two Black players having a game of darts were 'more used to blowpipes than a game of darts'. Nonetheless, the FA 'accepted that Mr Yems is not a conscious racist' – which makes one wonder what a conscious racist would sound like and, to be frank, what has been going on in Mr Yems's consciousness.[23]

Lord Alan Sugar, once owner of Tottenham Hotspur but now a TV reality gameshow host, suggested that however much money Black footballers made, and however high they might rise, they are, in some people's imagination, just street hustlers. In 2018 Sugar tweeted a Photoshopped picture of the Senegalese World Cup team in front of a pile of counterfeit goods, accompanied by the trademark matey snark of racists everywhere: 'I recognise some of these guys from the beach in Marbella. Multitasking, resourceful chaps.'[24] Norwich City's sporting director Stuart Webber thought his own Black players were, if not for the munificence of football, all heading to jail: 'Where [the players] come from, it had to work out for them in football because the alternative is potentially jail or something else.'[25] Needless to say, the families of his players vociferously disagreed. Craig Ramage, speaking on the BBC about Derby County, went with the 'all Black players have a bad attitude' line, and didn't even bother to disguise it. 'When I look at certain players … their body language, their stance, the way they act, you just feel, hold on a minute, he needs pulling down a peg or two. So I'd probably say that about all the young Black lads.'[26]

Perhaps the crudest of all the stereotypes that Black footballers have been subjected to are the songs about the size of their genitals.[27] The framing of Black men as hyper-masculine, hyper-sexual, bestial and dangerous is a racist trope more than four centuries in the making, and it is currently being reproduced in English football. Romelu Lukaku, newly arrived at Manchester United, was 'a Belgian scoring genius with a 24-inch penis'. William Gnonto, Leeds United's Black Italian striker, was 'Willy Gnonto, Willy Gnonto/He eats spaghetti/He drinks Moretti/His cock's fucking massive'. The same treatment was meted out to Bambo Diaby, Yerry Mina and Ivan Toney. Lukaku, and other players on the end of this kind of objectification and dehumanisation, released statements through their clubs or the press asking fans to stop, but the banter just rolled on.

Less crude, but perhaps more pernicious, is the encoded racism of football commentary. One survey of thirty hours of coverage of the 2018 World Cup logged every item of praise that each player received. Black players were overwhelmingly acknowledged for their physicality or their 'natural talents', while white players were primarily praised for their learnt attributes – their dedication and training. White players were also nearly three times more likely to be praised for the nature of their character and their 'footballing intelligence' than were Black players.[28] A report from Danish company RunRepeat, released in 2020, surveyed more than 2,000 English-language match commentaries and found much the same. Commentators were six times more likely to talk about the power of a darker-skinned player than his light-skinned peer and more than three times more likely to reference his pace. By the same token, almost two-thirds of criticisms of a player's intelligence were directed at darker-skinned players, who made up just a quarter of the players involved.[29] One factor in perpetuating this situation was the very small number of commentators and co-commentators of colour, just 5 per cent in this survey. A glance at the press box at any English football match would confirm this lack of diversity. A report by the Black Collective of Media in Sport (BCOMS) revealed that of the 338 journalists of the British press corps covering sports mega events in 2018, only 32 were of BAME heritage, and of those only 5 were not ex-sportspeople. The same racialised judgements of the sports media were insidiously reproduced in the digital codes of the world's most popular football video game. An examination of the scores allocated to players by race showed that *FIFA 20* systematically made Black players faster, more aggressive and more physical, while white players had better technical skills in shooting and passing. As the researchers chillingly observed: '*FIFA 2020* is a site for the potent experiential socialisation in racialised myth whereby the gamers come to know race, not only through the usual channels of representation and discourse, but also through feeling the racialised difference ... quite literally through their controllers.'[30]

Pervasive as racist sentiments are in English football, the far right has struggled to seriously mobilise them. The National Front's efforts of the late 1970s and 1980s were effectively challenged by the first wave of anti-fascist groups in English football. More recently, Casuals United were recruiting among football fans in the early 2000s, as did the English Defence League until their demise in 2014. However, the air of everyday xenophobia and rage that descended on England after the referendum created a permissive environment in which some of the EDL's coalition could be reassembled. In June 2017, in response to the jihadi-inspired terrorist attacks at London Bridge and the Manchester Arena, the Football Lads Alliance (FLA) took to the streets. Its first march, attended by thousands, drew a mix of football casuals and right-wing veterans, both enraged by Islamist terrorism and fearful of and aggressive towards the whole of Britain's Muslim population. With the fissiparousness characteristic of the English far right, the original leadership stood down just a year after the group's formation and the organisation collapsed, only for the network to be reborn under new management as the Democratic Football Lads Alliance (DFLA). The Premier League and Football League had long since banned any of these organisations and their insignia from the matches, but the DFLA was never really interested in the football anyway: their battleground was the street. In October 2018 their first march in London had a very visible football presence, including Mark Phillips, coach of West Ham United Under-18s, but so too did the anti-fascist groups reinforced by the newly formed network Football Lads and Lasses Against Fascism, who helped drive the DFLA from the streets and into obscurity.[31]

The official response to football's post-Brexit racism was rather less robust. The FA, moving at its usual glacial pace, had established a small programme of bursaries, internships, support for BAME coaches and an FA inclusion advisory board, and in 2018 it launched its diversity and inclusion plan, tepidly entitled 'In Pursuit of Progress'. Focused almost exclusively on its own role as an employer, it aimed for 13 per cent of the FA's coaching staff to come from a BAME background – the same proportion of its staff in general – and for 5 per cent of people in leadership roles to come from a Black or minority ethnic background; all fair enough, but hardly a concerted response to the outbreak of very visible racism since 2016 and the still simmering and unresolved issues of institutional racism in coach and referee development. In 2019 Mims Davies, Minister for Sport, thought the situation urgent enough to call yet another football and racism summit, and seemed both informed and reasonably genuine in her concerns, but in the great churn of Tory Party politics she was gone from the job a few months later, and all the fine words were filed away. The Premier League, independently of the rest of the football world, introduced its own bespoke campaign, 'No Room for Racism', which was slick but banal. The PFA (Professional Footballers' Association) was galvanised into action by the wave of social media racism facing its members, and organised a 24-hour social-media boycott by players and some clubs, while calling for the technology companies to more actively intervene in the policing of hate speech. Arsenal's Danielle Carter summed up the mood: 'We have a discontented generation of players who won't stand for racist abuse any longer. Enough is enough.'[32] The boycott went ahead, many Black players supporting the boycott still got abused, social-media companies did not significantly change the ways they handled racist postings, and the number of hate crimes continued to rise.

In this situation it was left, as ever, to Black fans and Black players to do all the hard work. The Punjabi Wolves were founded in the 1950s as a supporters' group whose core was Punjabi, but has always been open to all.[33] In a constituency represented by Enoch Powell for almost a quarter of a century, they have served as a beacon for BAME supporters all over the country and set the template for the other BAME fan groups that emerged in 2010s. Boasting more than 500 members today and embraced by the club, Punjabi Cultural Day has been celebrated at Wolves to the sound of the region's distinctive dhol drum, while kabaddi – the state sport of Punjab – has been played on the pitch at half time. The Punjabi Wolves have now been joined by a series of fan groups in the Midlands which include Punjabi Forest, Blues for All in Birmingham, and Punjabi Rams at Derby. Pride Park now boasts a permanent banner in Punjabi script: 'Chak de Phatte'. Literally 'pick up the logs' – a reference to Sikh warriors' need for wooden planks to build fortification in their wars with the Mughal Empire, and best translated as 'Get stuck in!' Small beer, perhaps, but as one of the founders of the Punjabi Rams made clear, the presence of migrant cultures and brown faces in England's stadiums should not be underestimated. 'I remember the first away game when we went as a group … and made T-shirts for everybody. Let me tell you: 50 brown guys sitting in a block in matching T-shirts was very striking.'[34]

Getting people into the stadium, though, is easier said than done. In 2015 Humayun Islan, a supporter of Bradford City, and retired player Anwar Uddin founded the Bangla Bantams.[35] Uddin explained the challenge they faced: 'It struck me how many kids on Saturday mornings were playing football in the streets around the stadium but as soon as fans came they disappeared indoors. They'd heard negative stories around racism from parents and didn't feel they could share that space with football fans. They could see the stadium outside their bedroom window but it was like a spaceship that they didn't want to go in.' Previously, the club, aware at least of how few BAME fans were coming to see them, had just sent tickets to mosques and community centres without any sense of these kinds of obstacles to attendance. The Bantams have done the harder work to persuade the sceptical that Valley Parade is a safe space and that a day out at the football is actually for them.

Black players, past and present, and with almost no public support from their white peers, have been the people giving the endless press interviews, doing the interminable TV appearances decrying the latest racist outrage, or speaking out to try to hold the authorities to account for their latest inadequate response to the problem. It has clearly been exhausting. From among the generation that played in the 1980s, the key voices included John Barnes, Brendon Batson, Garth Crooks and Howard Gayle, all of whom could have pursued coaching careers but have spent most of their post-playing careers in the media, or outside of football altogether. Barnes's short-lived managerial experience – eight months at Celtic, less than a year with Jamaica, and a very brief stay at Tranmere Rovers, followed by neither interview nor job – was just the tip of the iceberg of the limited opportunities afforded to Black coaches in comparison with white coaches, and the very low threshold for failure against which they were judged. Barnes, in particular, was relentless in reminding the nation that racism in football exists because racism is rife in society, and that, symbolically important as the game might be, the real issue was much bigger than just the racism he had experienced on the pitch. Reflecting on a banana skin thrown at him, he said, 'It didn't surprise me because black people go through invisible banana skins being thrown at them and unspoken racial abuse every day of their lives.' Gayle's most powerful public intervention came in 2016, when he refused the award of an MBE for services to football on the grounds that 'the empire is something that oppressed black people'.[36]

More recent players active in the media have included Stan Collymore, Ian Wright and Les Ferdinand. Collymore, with almost a million followers on Twitter and regular slots on radio, was an outspoken commentator on issues of race and took an enormous amount of flak for his troubles. After writing a column in which he compared Sol Campbell's long and fruitless struggle to break into coaching with the red carpet treatment accorded Steven Gerrard and Frank Lampard, he wrote: 'At the last count there were 609 comments under my tweet plugging that column and the majority, as far as I can tell from their profiles, are from white people telling me to stop banging on about racism.'[37] Ian Wright used his ascent to national treasure, an office sealed by his extraordinary emotional appearance on *Desert Island Discs*, to criticise the FA's sluggish response to these issues. Beyond the public gaze he was among the most active mentors and guardian angels of young Black players. Les Ferdinand, one of the very few Black players to have established an executive career post-retirement – as director of football at Newcastle United and QPR – spent much of it keeping the absence of Black coaches in the news and offering a very sharp understanding of how power was distributed in football: 'The people in power can solve this problem if they want to but they don't really want to solve it because it doesn't affect them.'[38]

Of the recent cohort of players, Rio Ferdinand has been among the most vocal. In 2012 he refused to wear a Kick It Out T-shirt that read 'One Game, One Community' prior to a Premier League match, considering it an insipid response to the problem of racism in the game. In 2015, rightly sensing the deep racist tendencies in the game that would be unleashed again, he said, 'I think a lot of people became a bit complacent with racism. Because we're not hearing it so much in stadiums in our country people believe we've done the job ... It's been simmering, it's there. We thought football was a tool to suppress it [racism]. It's a good vehicle but the bigger issue is society and education.' Danny Rose became, in effect, the spokesperson for all those Black players who had just simply had enough; who no longer, if they ever had, believed the anti-racism platitudes of football's governing bodies; who had abandoned any idea of a coaching career given the impossible obstacles in their way; and who were just doing their best to stay sane before they could get out. Perhaps the heaviest burden fell on the shoulders of Raheem Sterling.

After being on the end of racist abuse from Chelsea fans at Stamford Bridge, he put a post on Instagram demonstrating how the media framed white and Black players differently, contrasting the *Daily Mail*'s treatment of his Manchester City teammates Phil Foden and Tosin Adarabioyo when they bought their family a house; the former was a loving son, the latter was an undeserving spendthrift: 'I think this is unacceptable. Both innocent have not done a thing wrong but just by the way it has been worded this young black kid is looked at in a bad light, which helps fuel racism and aggressive behaviour.' The *Sun* had certainly not been listening, and later that year ran a story about the rifle tattoo on his calf, giving lots of space to an anti-gun campaigner who thought he should have it lasered off or be kicked out of the England squad. Change a few details and it could have been one of a hundred moral panic pieces, erroneously linking young Black men, especially musicians and rappers, to knife crime and violence. Once again, with remarkable poise and clarity, Sterling turned their racist tropes around: 'When I was two my father died from being gunned down to death. I made a promise to myself I would never touch a gun in my life time, I shoot with my right foot so it has a deeper meaning.'[39]

While the Football Association, the Premier League and the EFL dithered, and Kick it Out, whose funding came from all three, kept focused on incremental lobbying, Sterling wrote a column for *The Times* that made clear just how bad the situation really was: 'When I was a boy growing up in London, going to school and playing football, I didn't know what racist abuse was because I never suffered any. So it seems crazy that, in 2019 the racism problem in football is so bad, runs so deep and is nowhere near being sorted.'[40] Sterling also put out a manifesto for action that called for much more serious punishments, no sanctions for teams that walked off after racist abuse, and for senior management and sponsors to stop talking and start taking their responsibilities seriously. Once again, Black players and coaches came out in support, but their white peers, for the most part, were silent, and the institutions unmoved. Les Ferdinand, attending another House of Commons event on racism in football, expressed the mood of angry exasperation with this stasis: 'We've been talking about this for 15 years now, the only difference is the venues seem to be getting better. When I first started doing it, it was in a little classroom, then we moved on to a hotel room, and now we're at parliament. But the outcome's still the same because we've not moved on.'[41]

4.

Duty of Care

Football's Treatment of Its Youth

Football delights in its lexicon of 'talents coming through' and kids with 'the world at their feet'. Fans and pundits alike want a 'young team' and worry about the decline of those whose average age is creeping up. Supporters of every club treasure the debuts of players who have 'come up through the ranks' or who are 'one of our own', and almost nothing in the game's collective consciousness can match the buzz around a teenage sensation, as the English football nation's joy at the arrival of Wayne Rooney testified to. Of course, there is also a shared amnesia for the many prodigies who failed to fulfil their promise, and the considered preference of most is for a 'blend of youth and experience', the calming influence of older and wiser heads and the presence of the battle-hardened 'old warhorses'. Still, there are few instances in English football of the near universal *Schadenfreude* felt for Alan Hansen after his claim that 'you'll win nothing with kids' prefaced a title-winning season for a very youthful Manchester United in 1996. Fandom too has its own romance with youth; after all, one is a supporter 'man and boy', a reminder that all these idioms and experiences have been reserved for men alone. Narratives of both players and fans invariably invoke the influence of male relatives taking sons and nephews to the match, or giving them a ball or boots for their seventh birthday, the initiation rituals into this overwhelmingly masculine cult in which lives are measured out in seasons. Little wonder, then, that the promise of youth, the fearlessness of the innocent, the bravado of the inexperienced are treasured, and though the old – in football terms anyone playing in their mid-thirties – are venerated, it is an altogether more muted love.

It is strange, then, perhaps even perverse, that this cult of youth should exist alongside a football industry that has marginalised the young. Photographs of crowds as late as the 1970s make clear the special boys' sections created on many terraces and the widespread presence of teenagers in unaccompanied groups. Footage of terrace fights, the invasion of ends and the street scuffles of the era show kids mainly under twenty. As late as the early 1990s, more than a quarter of the crowd would be younger than twenty-five. However, since the advent of all-seater stadiums and the sharp increase in the cost of tickets, the average age of the crowd has risen. In 2009, when the Premier League was still releasing data on the subject, it had risen to forty-one. Today's infinitely more detailed crowd photography suggests – wrinkles, grey hair and all – that it is now significantly higher. The loss of boys' sections is not the only way in which youth has been squeezed out. The cost of taking kids, in addition to one's own ticket, not to mention the aggressively marketed trinkets and expensive food available, has priced many out of regular family attendance. Although some clubs have retained significantly cheaper tickets for the young, many have either raised their prices for kids or abandoned concessions altogether.

As an alternative, football has offered children the chance to be consumers, as the aggressive promotion of children's replica kits, unknown until the 1990s, demonstrates. More visibly, they have been recruited as mascots, known in official club circles as player escorts. Walking alongside the team and holding their hands, mascots first appeared in Brazilian football in the 1970s and in Europe in the 1990s. The 1999 FA Cup saw two boys in replica kit lead out Newcastle United and Manchester United. At Euro 2000 the following year, an entire squad of mascots accompanied the teams onto the pitch and stayed for the anthems. The 2003 FA Cup in England followed suit, and it became the norm in the Premier League and then across all nations and leagues. Some clubs continue to offer kids the moment for free, though increasingly, being in the ballot for places requires a signed-up and paid-for membership of the official supporters' club. Many others have been shamelessly milking this revenue stream for years.[1] At the upper end of the mascot package, including kit, player meet and greets and a nice match ticket, West Ham were charging £600 a go. Most clubs have been asking something in the region of £300, and, needless to say, that has excluded a very considerable number of kids and their families from taking part. Bournemouth, in an act of exquisite cruelty, offered a cut-price package for just £150 that didn't include a match ticket. One wonders if stewards were designated to walk those mascots and their guardians off the premises before kick-off.

In much of this, football is little different from the rest of British society. Politicians maintain the illusion that the nation's children are its future. Media companies, consumer brands and advertising agencies chase the youth market. However, the political economy of a rapidly ageing society, in which the old vote at significantly higher levels than the young, has seen the price of austerity paid disproportionately by youth. While, of course, stratified by class and privilege of different kinds, the young have experienced a disastrous decade and a half. Pensions have been protected while real wages have stagnated or fallen; conditions of work are increasingly perilous and precarious; and social mobility, already faltering, has gone into reverse. Spending on a broken and unimaginative education system has fallen, while student debt for ever thinner levels of undergraduate teaching has rocketed. At the same time, government support for the housing market has provided huge capital gains for the elderly, while those excluded, especially the under-forties, are surviving in an ever more expensive and decrepit private rental sector. The challenge on the street to the decade of cuts to come – the student protests and the urban riots of 2011 – was dealt with by a combination of massive policing and rapid, harsh and punitive sentencing from the judicial system. Having corralled and impoverished the young, England's older voters, and the puppeteers that had entranced them, delivered them a kidney punch. The vote to leave the European Union, while linked to class and geography, correlated more closely with age than any other demographic factor. The micro majority of the 52 per cent, who have been dying at more than twice the rate of Remain voters since the referendum, consigned the living to a world that would be dominated by their nostalgia for a sovereign state and secure society that had never existed.

One special irony of the Brexit process that followed was that, despite 'taking back control' of its borders and immigration policy, the UK's level of net migration continued to rise, while the country's capacity to educate and train its population was found to be sorely wanting. In sector after sector, high and low paid, Britain consistently failed to fill the rising number of vacancies. The cruel fury over the arrival of migrants and asylum seekers has been designed, at least in part, to try to obscure these facts. In a similar fashion in football, the debate over the import of elite footballers has obscured the responsibilities of the country's academy systems and their training methods, which have not only produced a small return in terms of elite players but have presided over an often bitter and cutthroat culture that commercialises talented children, and neglects their mental health.

Football, not surprisingly, retains a nostalgia for the old ways, for an era of apprenticeships and the YTS over the aspirational academy; for a world in which trainees cleaned boots, swept floors and lodged with trusted landladies. Like the skilled working-class culture of industrial work it was modelled on, there was within that world a laudable attention to technique and skill, of lifelong learning and the inculcation of high craft standards, passed down between the generations. At the same time football's mythology has long celebrated the 'school of hard knocks', a world in which youth is prepared for the fire of the professional game by a mixture of banter, punishments and humiliations that, in any other realm – the military aside – would now constitute bullying and abuse, but is celebrated in football as character-forming. Efforts to suggest otherwise have often been met by the retort that the modern world has gone soft and modern players have become too sensitive; arguments wielded by players and coaches who survived the old order but were, no doubt, traumatised themselves.

Not all of today's footballers and their families have been prepared to meekly accept their fate, and consequently over the last decade a steady trickle of claims and cases of bullying and sexual abuse in youth football – current and historic – has turned into a flood. In 2017 the Premier League deemed the environment at Aston Villa as 'toxic'. Academy coach Craig Bellamy stepped down from his role at Cardiff City in 2019 after facing accusations of bullying, as did Peter Beardsley at Newcastle United (accusations that he denied).[2] Cardiff found serious concerns with Bellamy's behaviour and he offered a fulsome apology. Beardsley was found guilty by the FA of using racist language.[3] Chelsea received many reports about the behaviour of Graham Rix and Gwyn Williams. According to the evidence seen by club and the FA, Rix, in just one of many similar events, is said to have humiliated one of his Black outfield players by substituting him with the reserve goalkeeper. As the player was showering afterwards, it is alleged Rix shouted that 'if his heart was as big as his cock, he would be a great player that ran more'.[4] Rix denied the accusations but Chelsea settled out of court with the players accusing him of bullying, paying six-figure sums in compensation.[5]

Established in their current form in 2012 under the Premier League's Elite Player Performance Plan (EPPP), the system as a whole is now responsible for a small but not insignificant element of the nation's education system – more than 13,000 children. Graded into four groups, the top tier of academies offer coaching and development from the under-9s age group up to 18, full-time education from 11 to 16, and from 16 to 18 further education, usually BTEC courses. At this level, clubs are spending anywhere between £2 and 5 million a year on their academy programme. Educational munificence was not the primary motivation for this. EPPP was a response to the declining number of English players in the Premier League, playing fewer minutes – for under-21s almost halving between 2007 and 2011 – and what was perceived to be the woeful underperformance of the England international team. In the years since, they have become an increasingly important component of a club's financial and sporting strategies. On these metrics EPPP has been a success. After years of decline, in 2024 young English players were getting more match time in the Premier League than in any year since 2007. The need for clubs to adhere to stricter profit and sustainability rules has made them more attractive squad players, and the rising tide of injuries has given them more opportunities. They are, after a decade of high-level coaching, technically exceptional. There are murmurings that there has been too much coaching in the academies, which now employ over three times the number of staff than they did when they started: 'Players are often coached to limit their skill and craft, not to maximise it. They are coached not to experiment, in order to avoid mistakes. Academies like the school system have become places of conformity – if you don't fit in with what's asked then you are released.'[6] Critics have also pointed to the academies focusing on physicality and strength too young, a choice that saw players of the calibre of Harry Kane and Declan Rice dropped from academy programmes for being too small. On the other hand, most of the England team that made the final of the Euros in 2024 came through the system.

The competition to get to the academies is intense, but it is as nothing to the pressure once there. The most important aspect of the system is that the likelihood of further progress is frighteningly small. In 2017 Michael Calvin found that 98 per cent of players awarded an academy scholarship at sixteen were not playing in the top five tiers of English football by the time they were eighteen. Marginally better, in 2022 the Premier League reported that of 4,109 former top-tier academy footballers, 70 per cent were never given a professional contract at a Premier League or English Football League club. Only one in ten has gone on to make more than twenty league appearances in the top four tiers of English football.[7] Yet such are the rewards for success that, from a very young age, children and their future become commodified. Some agents increasingly monitor younger and younger players. Illegal inducements, in kind and in cash, are offered by agents and sometimes requested by families. Clubs have attempted to poach players from each other without the slightest regard for the interest of the child. Peter Andrews, himself an academy reject, who went on to develop a support programme for Manchester United academy players and their families, noted: 'Agents are controlling players being responsible for moves. There's no education process for parents.' That said, parents were not all angels: 'There is a lot of parental bullying going on. I know this will sound very harsh, but the socio demographics are such that you've got parents living their failed existence through a son who is now a lifeline.'[8]

Along the way, the academy system has not been preparing the overwhelming majority of its charges for what awaits – being released by the club. The choreography of this process has often been brutal. The norm, at the end of the season, would be to gather the squad in the dressing room and for them to be called, one by one, to their contract meeting. Even at clubs which chose a less gruesome procedure, the meetings, for the most part, are short, sharp and definitive. One ex-player, speaking anonymously, said, 'I've been there for five years, you know like the kit man, all the lads, the coaches and you literally get told no, and it's within ten minutes you've got all your stuff and you're out and you never see them again … so it's just kind of like from everything to nothing in a split second.' Another remarked on how little support was available: 'The club kind of just leaves you to it … they give it the old token "oh if you need anything, give me a call", but you never would … It was just kind of off you go and that was it. Just sort yourself out.'[9]

Some do and some don't. A study in 2015 by Teesside University found that 55 per cent of players were suffering 'clinical levels of psychological distress' twenty-one days after being released from an academy. At the same time their immersion in football culture will have made responding to the problem that much harder.[10] As one twelve-year-old, already acculturated to the norms of emotional denial required, put it: 'I would not communicate my feelings with any coaches as I would not want them to feel sympathy, nobody does, I mean you just don't … it may be seen as mental weakness and as a footballer you have to be mentally tough.'[11] Further down the line, after the merry-go-round of last-chance trials, failed try-outs and lower-league football has ended, players struggle with a legacy of perceived failure, reduced status and squandered time. Some find their way to higher education, especially via US sports scholarships, or move into coaching and community work, but an alarming number find their way to criminal occupations and prison. Luton Town's academy was at least brutally honest about this. A series of posters entitled 'The Real World of Professional Football (or 11 Rules of Survival)', pinned up in its dressing-room, read: 'Football is not fair – get used to it'; 'School has done away with winners and losers, but football hasn't' and 'Football is competitive so make sure you are a winner'.[12] Admirable candour, but with it comes the fact that, but for a handful, 13,000 children are at schools which will institutionally fail them.

Whatever the ultimate balance sheet for today's football academies, one thing is for sure: there is no going back to the past. Football has failed and continues to fail in its duty of care to the young, but nothing compares to the game's failure to recognise the scale of child sexual abuse in its recent history. Football is not alone in this. The exposure, in 2012, of Jimmy Savile's lifelong predatory behaviour has only been the most public example over the last two decades of cases of sexual abuse, also exposed in the entertainment industry, the Church of England, the Catholic Church and the nation's public schools. Sport, as a whole, was a realm in which the child protection laws governing education and care settings did not apply. At an institutional level there was a complacent assumption that such things only happened in the private sphere of family and home, and a lamentable lack of concern for children's wellbeing, despite the fact, as one of the leading lawyers on the subject put it, 'anyone could have unrestricted access to young people in intimate settings; systems to identify potential abusers were rudimentary'.[13] Not that identification of an abuser was any guarantee of action. Frank Roper, a youth coach at Blackpool, was convicted of four cases of child sexual assault in the 1960s, but managed another twenty years in the game at the club, running his own youth teams. Consequently, stories about certain coaches, like Eddie Heath, chief scout at Chelsea in the late 1960s and 1970s, were widely circulated but wilfully ignored. Later, he was revealed to have systematically groomed and assaulted at least twenty players in his time. Heath was able to survive repeated complaints from parents, as club staff discounted them and failed to pass them on to the club's board. Russell Davy, abused by Heath when at Charlton Athletic, wrote directly to the FA about his behaviour and was ignored. Even as late as 2015 Chelsea settled a case with Gary Johnson, abused by Heath when at the club, by offering him £50,000 compensation in return for his continuing silence.[14]

Football was not the only sport around which such rumours swirled, and it was swimming that finally broke the collective silence. In 1995 Paul Hickson, who coached the British swimming teams at the 1984 and 1988 Olympics, was sentenced to seventeen years for multiple rapes and sexual assaults of his athletes. The following year the governing bodies of swimming, athletics and gymnastics, alongside the Sports Council (now Sport England) and the NSPCC, began the process of drafting new safeguarding legislation and policies. Football, despite mounting evidence of widespread abuse in the game, held back. In retrospect it is remarkable just how many indications of widespread sexual abuse could be aired without any significant response from the football authorities. In 1996 Channel 4 broadcast an hour-long documentary – *Soccer's Foul Play* – in which accusations of persistent sexual violence against Barry Bennell at Crewe and Bob Higgins at Southampton, among others, were made plain, and patterns of denial, obfuscation and cover-ups at clubs were obvious; but neither the clubs involved nor the FA saw this as an opportunity to act.[15] In 2001 a former director of Crewe, where coach Barry Bennell's predatory behaviour was well known before his departure in the late 1980s, wrote to Tony Pickering, the head of education and safeguarding at the FA, requesting that the FA look into Bennell's history, especially since he had recently been convicted of sexual abuse in the United States, where he had taken up a youth coaching position. The FA did reply to this letter, but only three lines to say that the matter was closed. George Ormond, who had worked at Newcastle United for decades, was described by a judge in 2002 as a 'predatory abuser' after he was convicted of twelve indecent assaults and one attempted indecent assault on seven boys, taking place between 1975 and 1999, but again, neither Newcastle nor the FA were galvanised into action. Scottish football was no different, with Jim Torbett, the founder of the Celtic Boys Club in Glasgow, convicted in 1998 of sexual abuse (and in 2018 he would return to court to be convicted of a great many more crimes), but neither the SFA nor Celtic, with which the Boys Club was closely associated, saw fit to take the matter any further.

Eventually, the Football Association began to take action, to secure the future if not to address the past, developing its own safeguarding policies and education programmes, beginning in 2003 with the introduction of criminal-record checks for those dealing with children. That said, it would be hard to suggest that it was operating with any sense of how pervasive the problem was, or with the moral urgency that was required. Football was not alone in this. More than a decade after the first efforts to reform safeguarding in sport, a 2011 NSPCC survey of young people's experience in sport found that 75 per cent had suffered emotional abuse, 29 per cent sexual harassment, 24 per cent physical abuse and 3 per cent sexual abuse.[16] Statistics and surveys only cut so much ice. What was required to really transform the situation was for someone who had survived sexual abuse in football to waive their anonymity and tell their story. In 2016 Andy Woodward, a survivor of abuse at the hands of Barry Bennell at Crewe Alexandra in the 1980s, did so in the *Guardian*. It broke the dam of shame and silence, and released a wave of accusations in English and Scottish football, most notably from ex-Spurs and England player Paul Stewart. An NSPCC helpline was established, which took anonymous calls at a rate that exceeded even that of the line set up after the Savile affair. Investigations were launched by the English and Scottish football associations, some of the clubs most centrally involved, like Manchester City, Southampton and Chelsea, and more than twenty police forces. By mid-2018 more than 800 alleged victims had reported over 2,800 incidents at 340 different clubs, and identified 300 suspects, after which a number of the most egregious perpetrators were brought to court and tried.

Barry Bennell was found guilty of fifty offences against twelve boys and sentenced to thirty-one years in prison. Bob Higgins, who had worked at Southampton as a youth coach and run his own football academy, was found guilty of forty-five charges of indecent assault against teenage boys and sentenced to twenty-four years and three months. In Scotland, among almost a dozen other abusers in football, three men with connections to the Celtic Boys Club were put on trial. Jim McCafferty, a youth coach there and at other clubs in the west of Scotland, was found guilty of a dozen counts of abuse and was sentenced to nine years in prison, where he died. Gerald King, once chairman of the club, was put on the sex offender register for taking indecent pictures of children at football matches, while Frank Cairney, a former manager of the team, was on trial for eleven counts of sexual assault of children and saved from jail only by his advanced dementia. Unable to wait for his own decline to rescue him, Michael 'Kit' Carson, who had worked at Norwich City in the 1980s and had run Peterborough United's academy in the 1990s, was put on trial for eleven counts of sexual abuse, but chose to drive his car into a tree.

What emerged from these trials and the official inquires that followed them was that football had monumentally, repeatedly and unforgivably failed in its duty of care. As the Barnardo's report on Southampton and its relationship with Bob Higgins made clear, 'adults in Southampton Football Club during the time Higgins worked for them or on their behalf did not consider the welfare and wellbeing of the boys involved with the club as their prime consideration'.[17] Much the same could be said of all the clubs involved in these cases. Indifference and ignorance were compounded by the failure to take victims seriously, and, when their claims became unignorable, to minimise and marginalise them. At best, clubs found other grounds on which to sack perpetrators, but allowed them to move on and repeat their abuse elsewhere in the game. The Football Association and the clubs have all issued the most fulsome apologies, though the aggressive legal tactics of Crewe, Celtic and Newcastle United towards survivors and their claims for compensation suggest this might have been more performative than heartfelt.

Nonetheless, reforms have been made. Premier League clubs must now employ a full-time head of safeguarding, an academy safeguarding officer, a community safeguarding officer, and appoint a board member who is responsible for overseeing this. The Football League's policies and practices are similar. Grassroots clubs' arrangements are now annually reviewed by the FA and spot checks are carried out. Above all, like the entertainment industry, the Church and almost every institution in our society, football has been forced to come to terms with the fact that predatory sexual behaviour and violence is a real and enduring presence, overwhelmingly conducted by ostensibly heterosexual white men in positions of privilege and power.

What remains, despite all the apologies and compensation, is a terrible landscape of hurt, despair and trauma. Survivors have spoken of a lifetime of destructive addictions, uncontrollable anger, bleak and suicidal depression – the flight, fight and freeze reactions with which victims of trauma, violence and abuse everywhere must contend. Andy Woodward confided that his life had been 'a mess, spiralling to the point where I wasn't going to be here any more. I've parked in my garage with a pipe. I've been to the woods with a rope. I've had tablets, ready to go. I took it to the point where I couldn't be here any more.'[18] Even those that had managed to make a life and tasted the best that a career in football can offer, have been robbed of their due. Paul Stewart, who bravely spoke out about the abuse he suffered at the hands of Frank Roper, had played for England and won the FA Cup with Spurs, but could not feel the glory; 'I had some highs in my career, but I never enjoyed them like everybody else did, because I had this empty soul … Alone, I was dying. I was just dying inside.'[19] It took more than twenty years for British football to begin to respond with any seriousness to this, another decade for it to make a truly public reckoning with the scale of hurt and trauma caused. One wonders how long it will take for the shortcomings of the academy system – and the mental-health crisis among its rejects – to receive similar treatment.

5.

'You Must be Joking, Ref'

Football, Officials and the Decline of Authority

As Frank Lampard, then Chelsea's caretaker manager, ruefully noted in 2022, football's always limited capacity for consensus and balance had collapsed: 'It's a bit like politics: you either hate something or you love it, you're not allowed to be in between, and that feeds into football.'[1] The Brexit referendum and its consequences had changed the character and temperament of Britain's public conversations about politics, and football – always prone to crude binaries and emotive tribalism – followed suit. The rhetoric and conduct of the Leave campaign had delivered a sharp blow to the status of expert knowledge, while also undermining the very notion of independent trusted judgement. In this context, arbiters of all kinds – from the Supreme Court to vaccine regulators – faced a more febrile press and a more suspicious, divided public.

Football referees, who had long endured this kind of opprobrium, came under more pressure than ever. Since 2016, in the professional game, the level of dissent among both players and coaches has risen. Simultaneously, an already widespread breakdown in the authority of grassroots referees became considerably worse. Then, with the introduction of VAR to the Premier League in 2019, the already thin skein of trust that held together officials and the football public appeared to disintegrate. Referees, at best, were being recast as incompetents and killjoys; the pundit Jermaine Jenas, for example, complained on Twitter: 'Complete shithouse of a referee! They're all ruining our game.'[2] At worst, they were depicted as corruptible and, among the conspiracy theorists, as systematically biased.

Why is it that football, of all sports, has such a vituperative relationship with its arbiters? It is certainly a longstanding phenomenon. English crowds have been letting referees know what they think of their decisions since the Victorian era. William Pickford, one of the leading referees and administrators of the early twentieth century, wrote in his 1906 guide *How to Referee*: 'Don't worry your head about the noise spectators kick up. Free Britons have queer ways of enjoying themselves,' and, 'Don't let criticism hurt you, some people rejoice to see a referee writhe under it.' His peer, John Lewis, in an essay, 'The Much Abused Referee', took the spleen of players and fans alike as the inevitable norm, indeed as part of the game's attraction: 'For myself, I would take no objection to hooting or groaning by the spectators at decisions with which they disagree. The referee should remember that football is a game that warms the blood of player and looker-on alike, and that unless they can give free vent to their delight or anger, as the case may be, the great crowds we now witness will dwindle rapidly away.'[3] There was, on occasion, more than just barracking to worry about. In 1928, for example, the *Yorkshire Post* reported that a Northampton Town fan had struck a referee with a half-pound tobacco can. Cartoons depicted referees in disguise escaping angry crowds, and by the 1920s, whipped up by an increasing media focus on contentious decisions, they were being sent threatening letters. Percy Harper received accusations of corruption in the post after he allowed a goal for Newcastle in the 1932 FA Cup final against Arsenal, when almost everybody else at Wembley thought the cross that made it was from behind the goal line.[4]

The emotional temperature of football, the speed of play, and the large subjective grey areas created by its ambiguous rules of permissible contact and aggression laid the ground for these kinds of attacks; but there was a more everyday scepticism about authority that pervaded the game, a form of resistance born of the class divide between referees, players and supporters. The latter two were overwhelmingly working class. The former were effectively unpaid amateurs who needed considerable flexibility in their employment to take on refereeing, and were almost entirely middle class. The leading Victorian officials were Segar Bastard, a solicitor, William Pickford, a journalist, and John Lewis, who had a coach-building company. Alongside them, teachers were a major source of referees, comprising perhaps 20 per cent of officials in the late nineteenth century. Their presence in the twentieth century was even greater. Stanley Rous, the leading referee of the interwar era and subsequently the FA's general secretary and FIFA's president, was a grammar-school PE teacher. In the 1960s and 1970s senior referees like Ken Aston, Sandy Griffiths and Gordon Hill all taught in schools, while David Elleray, the leading official from the late 1980s through the 1990s, was a Harrow School housemaster and spoke to the players accordingly. Many of their contemporaries ran their own businesses. Jack Taylor still worked in his family butchers when he took charge of the 1974 World Cup final, Pat Partridge was a farmer, Clive Thomas had a variety of business interests, and Norman Burtenshaw had a chain of newsagents.

Given this social gulf, the relationship between referees and the players and crowd paralleled the industrial and educational culture of the times. In the world of work, authority lay with middle-class managers, but their working-class staff never accepted their rule as entirely legitimate or fairly earned. Indeed, there was often a quiet contempt for managers and generalists from the skilled craftsmen who actually ran the factory floor, but there was, even so, no sustained challenge to their authority.

In the same vein, working-class kids, policed at school with the cane, rejected the academic book knowledge of teachers, fighting back with misbehaviour and secret disdain. This was matched in football by professional players' grudging acceptance of referees' decisions, and the theatrical grumbling and complaints of the crowd.

In the 1960s, alongside a wider decline in social deference, players became more ready to talk back to officials and contest their authority. Jack Taylor, looking back to the 1950s from the mid-1970s, thought 'decisions were accepted much more readily than they are today ... players in those days usually had a feeling of responsibility. They were more concerned about doing the right thing. Not any more.' The crowds were less forgiving too, adding 'The Referees a Bastard' and 'You Don't Know What You're Doing' to the game's common songbook. Even so, serious dissent and confrontation on the pitch between players and officials was very rare, though given enough cause and alcohol the crowd could turn into a mob. In 1965, after Manchester City's game against Norwich had been abandoned due to a waterlogged pitch, the disappointed home fans surrounded a man they believed to be the referee, though it was actually Edward Cavanagh, the mayor of Stretford. He claimed that about 300 people confronted and kicked him as he headed for his car. Two years later referee Norman Burtenshaw was knocked unconscious by a pitch invasion of Millwall fans at the end of their game against Aston Villa.

In the last few decades, the class composition of officials, players and the crowd has changed. The crowd, under conditions of hyper-commercialisation and social change, has become considerably more middle class. Players have become immeasurably richer, while referees, since the advent of professionalisation in 2001, have become more working class. There were still recognisably middle-class routes to the job: Graham Poll started out in sales and marketing, Mike Riley was an accountant, and Uriah Rennie a barrister. The police and penal system, always a strong recruiting ground for referees, has been well represented too; Howard Webb, Alan Wiley and Chris Foy were all ex-police, while Anthony Taylor had been a probation officer before he went full time as a football official. However, along-side these more traditional referee backgrounds, the professionalisation of the role has opened up the possibility of a career to more working-class aspirants: Jeff Winter had run with the Middlesbrough hooligans and taken a grim job in banking before his refereeing days, Andre Marriner had been a postman, Mark Clattenburg an electrician, and Mike Dean had worked in a giant chicken factory in the Wirral.

This new social mix has not been matched by other forms of diversity. Between Uriah Rennie's retirement in 2008 and Sam Allison's first game in the Premier League in 2023, not a single referee of colour had taken charge of a match. In the game as a whole, BAME referees made 8 per cent of the total, but the further up the pyramid you went the fewer there were; during the 2020–21 season there were just 4 out of 200 in the top seven divisions, and none in the Championship or Premier League. Reuben Simon, a Black grassroots referee, argued, 'There are lots of black referees at the grassroots level, but they are not getting through the system. It's possible that every single black referee is rubbish, but if that's absurd, what's the other conclusion? They are being blocked because of racial bias.'[5]

The problems, as usual, began at the top. At the apex of the FA's system the referee committee was entirely white, and until 2021 chaired by David Elleray, who had been reprimanded by the FA in 2014 for telling a Black refereeing coach that he was looking 'rather tanned' and asking him, 'Have you been down a coal mine?' Elleray was sent on a diversity and inclusion course, but the committee and indeed all of the senior referee assessors in England, the people who decide whether other referees are promoted or demoted, remained uniformly white. Here, stereotyping, microaggressions and ingrained unreflective racism appeared widespread. In a report published in 2023 by the BAME Referee Support Group, one Black official recalled being told by his assessor, 'You lot can all run fast, but that's all you are good for,' while another recollected being told, 'If you want to progress, you need to cut your dreadlocks.'[6]

While the new breed of referees have shed the patrician hauteur and schoolmasterly tones that served their predecessors – and have increasingly understood their role as one of management of the game and players, rather than as punitive and punctilious disciplinarians – they have not been able to reestablish older forms of legitimacy and accepted authority. Over the last decade or so, levels of dissent in professional football escalated while the threshold for punishment appeared to rise. After Sunderland's Lee Cattermole was sent off for swearing at a referee in 2012, not a single red card was issued to a player for this transgression for eleven years. A combination of slow-motion replays, lip reading and YouTube suggests that there was no shortage of cursing during the interregnum. Similar levels of abuse began to be heard from coaches and their assistants, while fourth officials became the butt of endless carping and, on occasion, explosive rants and violent threats. In 2016, for example, John Sheridan, manager of Notts County, on a run of eight straight defeats and losing to Wycombe Wanderers, screamed at the entirely blameless fourth official: 'You're a fucking disgrace, you're fucking useless, you've not fucking got anything right today, you should be fucking ashamed, you're fucking shit, my kids aren't going to get any fucking Christmas presents because of fucking you.'[7] He was sacked, but this kind of behaviour was no barrier to him almost immediately walking into a new job with Oldham Athletic.

The FA considered the situation so out of hand that from 2018 it introduced red and yellow cards for what is quaintly called technical area misconduct. Perhaps most alarming of all was the prevalence and rising aggression of groups of players crowding the referee to contest a decision. In the 2014–15 season in the top five divisions of the English game, the number of these incidents where cards were issued for this tripled, but they seemed to be merely the cost of doing business. Defending his and Chelsea's aggressive behaviour in a Champions League match that year, captain John Terry described it as just 'part of the game'.[8] Abusive comments on referees have become ten a penny on social media and threats of violence have begun to appear. In early 2021 Mike Dean and his family received death threats that referenced his decision to send off West Ham's Tomáš Souček in the final seconds of their game against Fulham. The following season, Jon Moss got the same treatment after he refereed the Nottingham Forest–Huddersfield Town promotion play-off, and had his record store in Leeds vandalised for good measure. Kevin Clancy took charge of an Old Firm game, disallowed a Rangers goal, and in addition to death threats had all of his contact details published online.

It is hard to establish quite why this decline in behaviour has occurred, not least because the participants are rarely candid or public in explaining their motivation and actions, but part of the answer lies in the fact that so much of football is governed by norms rather than hard and fast rules. Consider the throw-in, for example, which should, according to the rules, be taken from the spot where the ball crossed the line, but is invariably taken further up the pitch as players attempt to steal territory. It is a practice rarely stopped and almost never punished. Similar leeway has always existed around the expression of dissent on the pitch, verbal abuse and even aggressive behaviour towards officials. Howard Webb, for example, has argued that the refereeing fraternity let new and more lenient norms evolve. Another factor perhaps is that the players at the top of the game have become part of the 1 per cent, economically if not culturally, stratospherically higher in the class system than any referee. The systems of authority and deference encoded in the British class system and reproduced on the pitch until the 1990s have dissolved as, first, players have ascended the social scale and, second, have been increasingly drawn from cultures and countries entirely unfamiliar with this historic legacy. At the same time there has been the malign influence of a new generation of coaches who actively encouraged confrontation with officials, and set the tone for their players by publicly berating them on the touchline and in the press – first among equals being Alex Ferguson, Arsène Wenger and José Mourinho. The fines imposed by the authorities for such tirades have, given everyone's income, been just another small business expense, while banishment from the technical area has been circumvented by the mobile phone.

The decline in the authority and standing of referees in the professional game has been unedifying, but in amateur football it has become a crisis. In 2008, responding to growing reports over the previous decade of referee abuse in grassroots football, the FA introduced its Respect campaign. This sought to modify the behaviour of fans, players and coaches towards officials in grassroots football, mainly through educational work and internal communications. By 2016, only 54 per cent of referees surveyed thought the campaign was helping, and even then, not by very much. As one referee put it: 'If the Respect programme is having a positive effect, I dread to think how bad respect was ten years ago.'[9] The same survey found that 60 per cent were on the receiving end of verbal abuse every couple of games, and almost a fifth reported being physically abused. Age was no barrier to this. Emily Dyke, then just fourteen, put an open letter on Facebook calling for change after she was verbally abused by parents when in charge of an under-8s game in Cleveland.[10] By the same token, a 74-year-old referee from Leamington Spa told the BBC, 'I have been stopped from driving my car by players lying in front of my car and jumping on the bonnet.'[11] Later that year, Graham Ekins, the chair of the Surrey Youth League, wrote an open letter to all its clubs imploring them to tackle the problem after a single weekend had seen an official being head-butted, two parents fighting on the touchline, and a referee threatened with a stabbing by a parent.[12]

In the years since, the problem has got worse. At first, in the wake of the Brexit referendum, levels of abuse merely crept up. Then, in summer 2020, when grassroots football returned after the first Covid lockdown, they became visibly more unpleasant – a situation that was highlighted by an attack in West London on referee Satyam Toki, who, having sent a player off for the use of foul language, was then punched and cut above his eye. His assailant received a ten-year ban from the FA, reduced on appeal to just five, and no more than a warning from the police. The following season, and another long Covid lockdown later, the FA reported that it had banned a record 380 people from football for attacks on officials, who had, among other things, been kicked, punched, strangled, spat upon, head-butted and threatened by players, club officials and spectators.[13] One official commented, 'I have been a referee for three years and I have never hated the role like I have this season.'[14] Dave Bradshaw, who refereed a match between South Lancashire Counties Football League amateurs Platt Bridge and Wigan Rose, might well have felt the same. He finished that game with broken ribs, concussion and a broken nose. Merseyside FA cancelled an entire weekend of games in its youth league to protest over the unrelenting verbal abuse and intimidation of its officials, many of whom were themselves children. In 2023 the Northumberland Youth League spoke in the exasperated disbelieving voice of administrators everywhere when they told their clubs and parents, 'This is children's football – there is no place for abuse of any type – if you cannot watch a group of children playing football without feeling the need to abuse/shout at a child … then please ask yourself if you have chosen the correct way to spend your weekends.'[15]

So how did we get to this? Within the grassroots game, opinions differ but circle around two notions. First, that the decline in standards of behaviour among professional players and coaches, broadcast in great detail on television, has given permission, in effect, for the same behaviours in lower-level football. Lee Warren, secretary of Brentford Youth AFC, thought the situation had become irretrievable: 'It's out of control and we can't get it back under control. People think they can do exactly what they want. I never used to believe in the idea that they do what they see on the telly, but it's so true.'[16] Second, the financial rewards available to young players, now significantly greater than ever before, have raised the stakes for young people, but above all for their parents. In an era of considerably reduced social mobility, football, perhaps more than ever, offers a way out for poorer families. The active presence of unscrupulous scouts and agents in youth football has fuelled these hopes and aspirations. At the same time, as we've seen, the number who will actually make it to academies, let alone the Premier League, is minuscule.

Toxic as this brew might be, it is still not entirely clear why it should nurture such extremes of anger. No one, as yet, has assaulted a seller of lottery tickets when they do not win, though the odds are hardly much worse. Perhaps, as some participants have sensed, something wider and deeper has been at work: a fraying of the social fabric combined with a heightened sense of individual entitlement; a withdrawal from collective norms combined with a decline in the legitimacy of the authorities that define and police them. Richard Trinder, a long-standing official in Sheffield youth football, remarking on another weekend of atrocious behaviour, located the problem in a wider decline of civility: 'Patience has gone, goodwill has gone, being nice to each other has gone.' Wilful hypocrisy and self-serving double standards – the default of much of the political class in this era – were a factor too. Referees are held to a standard that parents, players and coaches are never subjected to. As one long-suffering official wrote, 'Any hint of an error is an invitation for a dozen people to inform you of their disagreement, often loudly and aggressively, while a wild shot by a centre-back is laughed off.'[17]

All the time more and more referees have been getting out. For almost two decades the FA has been reporting that from a cohort of just under 30,000, some 7,000 referees leave the game every year, and replacing them is proving increasingly difficult. Everyone in youth football, and even the semi-professional leagues, has been struggling to find enough officials for their games. In 2022 Kent FA, for example, reported a 24 per cent drop in numbers due to 'an unacceptable level of physical and verbal abuse'. One young departing official said, 'A player under a false name head-butted an opponent, then told me if I dared send him off I was next. Match abandoned, I quit the next day.' Another recalled, 'I used to referee for a local under-12s league. I quit after I got spat at, punched and had my car keyed by parents, all in the same month.' Rhys Baldwin gave a penalty in a six-a-side game, part of a weight-loss programme for men over fifty, and quit after eleven years of officiating: 'The team captain ran up to me screaming in my face, called me a bunch of names, so I gave him a red card because of what he said. He went off the pitch, went into his bag, pulled out one of the Stanley box-cutter knives … stormed onto the pitch … and was walking towards me.'[18]

Things did not appear to be improving in 2023. A BBC Radio 5 Live survey of over 900 grassroots referees found that more than 90 per cent reported being verbally abused, more than a quarter had been physically assaulted, and a quarter had received threats of violence, of which 10 per cent came in the form of death threats.[19] Martin Cassidy, the chief executive of the charity Ref Support UK, said, 'The only thing that hasn't happened yet is a referee getting murdered and I'm not sure you'd bet against that.'[20] Not surprisingly, 40 per cent of those surveyed reported mental-health problems associated with refereeing.

The FA responded with a new slogan – the imploring 'Enough is Enough' – and promised more mentoring for referees, better and simpler reporting systems, and harsher sanctions. Nonetheless, in their survey of grassroots football for 2022–23, the FA reported that they had received 3,636 allegations of serious misconduct, a 9 per cent increase on the previous year, while 42 proven cases of assault were recorded alongside a 10 per cent increase in allegations of discriminatory abuse. The FA claimed that just 0.01 per cent of the 850,000 grassroots matches on which they received reports saw allegations of assault, but many officials thought this betrayed a massive underreporting of events. The sheer scale of local news items on problems at games suggested the FA's estimate might well have been much too low. Somerset FA, for example, reported a 66 per cent increase in the number of games abandoned due to serious misconduct in 2023–24. Referees also claimed that censured players gave fake names to officials, while clubs that had been punished and even disbanded would reappear under a new name but with the same old problems. Education and sanctions were proving inadequate, so the FA cast about for other instruments of control. Blue cards and sin bins had been introduced on a trial basis in 2019, giving referees the option of punishing dissent and other misconduct by sending players off the pitch for ten minutes. Internal FA reports suggested that this had had a positive cooling-down effect on volatile games and had begun to exert a deterrent effect as well; but the scale of the problem facing grassroots football demanded something more radical. In 2023 and 2024 referee body cams were trialled in eight FA county associations and their leagues. Whether this will be enough to deal with the terrible cocktail of ambition, anger, selfishness and entitlement that grassroots football can nurture remains to be seen. Technological fixes, as Britain's trade negotiators with the EU found out, are rarely a solution to deeper social and political problems.

Video technology has been shaping professional sport since the 1950s and early 1960s, when American broadcasters first pioneered instant replays and then slow motion. In the case of American football it proved hugely beneficial, making the almost incomprehensible melees of the game, especially on black and white television, understandable for viewers. The video-tracking technology of the Hawk-Eye system in tennis and its variants in cricket have been successfully incorporated into those sports, while rugby union has been using a television match official in contact with the on-pitch referee for more than two decades. In the United States all the major leagues use video refereeing in certain circumstances. And while there have been teething problems and complaints with the technology along the way, nothing compares to the controversy and anger that have followed its introduction into football. This should not surprise anyone, for a harbinger of contemporary responses to VAR can be seen in Italy, in the 1970s, where the introduction of slow-motion replays became the basis for an entirely new genre of football programming. Partisan and theatrical pundits furiously dissected a weekend's worth of controversial refereeing decisions, all of which could then be played out in the print media for the following week and selectively stored in the memory bank of fans, who became convinced that referees were not merely incompetent, but systematically biased – a corrosion of trust that has never been repaired. Social media has unquestionably amplified this tendency in football, but the game's combination of subjective grey areas and tribalism that these shows exposed suggests that the introduction of video refereeing had plenty of tinder to ignite.

In the twenty-first century, the increasingly detailed multi-angle coverage of televised football, and the sharply increased speed at which the game was played, made egregious refereeing errors more obvious. Despite the professionalisation of referees, their greatly improved athleticism and their stringent training and assessment regimes, it was widely thought that they were not up to the job. The use of Hawk-Eye-style technology for goal-line incidents was widely explored, and in 2010, building on the video-refereeing experiments in other sports, the Dutch football federation conducted major trials of video refereeing in support of an on-field referee that were deemed very successful. The president of FIFA, Sepp Blatter, criticised as a technophobe, was a cautious opponent of its wider introduction, but facing a rising tide of complaint over missed goals at World Cups, he allowed the introduction of goal-line technology in 2014. His successor, Gianni Infantino, was far less reticent, and FIFA introduced video refereeing at the 2018 World Cup. In England, goal-line technology proved accurate and popular, and helped build a demand from fans and pundits for the introduction of video technology to rule on more incidents in the game. In a 2017 survey by the FSA, three-quarters of English football fans wanted to see the introduction of the technology, and in 2019 the Premier League adopted it.[21] Be careful what you wish for.

VAR was originally the designation for a single official – a Video Assistant Referee – but quickly came to refer to the system as a whole. In the Premier League it consists of three people in a darkened room in Stockley Park – a business estate near Heathrow Airport – with a lot of screens and an audio link to the mic'd-up on-field referee. The rules governing their role are, at first glance, unambiguous. VAR should only intervene in four circumstances: sequences of play that result in a goal or penalty, straight red cards, and cases of mistaken identity when awards of any kind of card are made. Even then, VAR should only do so when there is a clear and obvious error by the on-pitch referee, or there has been a serious missed incident. VAR checks occur while play continues and are then communicated to the referee when the ball goes dead. If there is no problem, play continues; if there is an issue, VAR can ask the referee to take a second look at the incident on a pitch-side monitor. They in turn can either endorse or overturn the original decision. The maxim of VAR's advocates was 'minimum interference, maximum benefit'. It hasn't quite worked out that way.

Cases of mistaken identity were always rare, though staggeringly embarrassing, and VAR has yet to intervene much on this front. A handful of straight red-card decisions each season have been downgraded to yellow cards, but no one seems terribly bothered about these. However, decisions regarding penalties and goals, which turn on decisions about offsides, handballs and fouls, have proved more problematic. Perhaps the most immediate and unexpected shock for crowds was the impact of VAR on the experience of the game itself. Goal celebrations, the most ecstatic moment of any football match, were suddenly and incomprehensibly being curtailed by VAR checks. The breaks in the game after VAR intervened could last up to two or three minutes, destroying the game's sense of flow and dynamism. Worse, while those watching on television could see replays of the disputed action, those in the stadium were shown nothing. Two new chants began to be heard in Premier League stadiums, the direct, 'VAR is fucking shit', and the descriptive, 'It's not football anymore'.

Under new levels of scrutiny, handball and offsides became increasingly controversial. Handball problems stemmed from the difficulty of determining whether a player's arm was in an unnatural position – but first *define the arm*. It became clear that there is no acceptable definition of where arms ended and shoulders – which can be used to 'handle' the ball – began. This required a rewriting of the game's laws, stating that the shoulder begins at a line level with the bottom of the armpit, though determining where the armpit begins and ends, especially as players are in motion, has proved equally challenging. Offside lines, and player positions relative to them, have also proved harder to get right than imagined. Technical difficulties in drawing the lines have been part of the problem, but the margins involved have been so small that critics have challenged whether we can actually know the precise moment when a ball is passed and an offside line can be drawn.

Issues of definition aside, it has been errors of omission that have most exercised coaches and fans. In 2022, Tottenham's Cristian Romero had viciously yanked the luxuriant hair of defender Marc Cucurella in the Chelsea penalty area. VAR let this act of violent conduct – surely a serious missed incident – pass, and from the corner that was then awarded to Spurs,

Harry Kane scored a late equaliser. Chelsea's fans were apoplectic, collecting 160,000 signatures on a petition that read: '[Anthony] Taylor has an agenda against Chelsea and should not be allowed to referee a game involving the club again.'[22] Similarly, in a match between Arsenal and Brentford, VAR failed to spot that Brentford's Christian Norgaard was in an offside position before he crossed to Ivan Toney to score an equaliser. But perhaps worst of all was the goal scored by Liverpool's Luis Díaz in a game against Tottenham which was disallowed for offside by referee Simon Hooper. The VAR video operator immediately recognised that Díaz was in fact onside, but in a sequence of mistakes and miscommunications, the chief VAR official Darren England, thinking that Hooper had actually given the goal rather than disallowed it, failed to communicate that the goal actually was good before the game restarted. An exasperated Jürgen Klopp called for the match to be replayed. The following week Spurs fans were singing, 'There's only one Darren England,' while Brighton fans, dismayed by the referee's failure to give a handball against Liverpool's Virgil van Dijk, spontaneously broke into a chorus of, 'We want a replay.' In the audio recordings of the key moments, released by PGMOL (Professional Game Match Officials Limited) to try to calm the waters, Simon Hooper can be heard congratulating the VAR team with the words 'Well done, boys, good process' – now the favoured sarcastic meme for VAR disasters.

In 2019, its first year of operation, the Premier League said that VAR had increased the proportion of correct decisions from 82 to 94 per cent, and by 2024 it was 96 per cent. David Elleray claimed that not only was VAR helping accuracy, but it was acting as a deterrent to diving and off-the-ball acts of aggression. Yet popular disquiet was widespread enough that in early 2020 a parliamentary debate was held in Westminster Hall on the subject of VAR. In 2021 a fan survey reported that 95 per cent thought the technology had made the game less enjoyable, and by 2023 less than a third believed VAR to have been a success.[23] What explains this dissonance? Why, long pauses and a small number of inevitable human errors aside, should fans and coaches find this new and much more accurate form of refereeing a problem? Isn't this what we all asked for?

Perhaps referee errors are, compared with other sports, judged more harshly because football matches turn on a small number of chances and even fewer goals. A single point in tennis, or even a wicket in cricket, is far less consequential than scoring an equalising goal or not. Even so, there has been a serious problem of unrealistic expectations. VAR, it was popularly assumed, would simply eradicate errors from the game. Decades of listening to pundits claim that a single replay of an incident would resolve a disputed decision, or listening to an echo chamber of fans claiming that they had just witnessed a stonewall penalty denied, proved very inadequate preparation for the reality of detailed video scrutiny. What was, in the past, barely seen and soon passed over is now endlessly accessible, replayed and dissected. Common sense, the cry of critics everywhere, has proven vanishingly hard to actually define and locate. Video evidence simply does not speak for itself, as definitive accounts of malicious intent, intensity of challenges and degree of contact simply cannot be gleaned from the pictures alone.

Despite this now being obvious to everyone watching the game, referees are not being cut any slack. Indeed, it is remarkable how high a standard referees are held to. Players make innumerable mistakes and misjudgements, but for all the scrutiny they receive, it is only in the most extreme of cases that fans recall their misdemeanours. By contrast, referee performances are examined with a thoroughness and ruthlessness that no one else in the game receives. Referees are required to reveal any club allegiances, as well as those of close family, and are then unable to officiate in any game involving those teams. They also undergo regular and demanding physiological tests. After each game an assessor reviews every single decision and non-decision that they have made. These, in turn, are reviewed by a five-person panel – three ex-players or coaches, and a PGMOL and Premier League representative – who grade each of those decisions, allowing for complexity, and issue an overall mark. That mark then determines the official's place in a league table of referees, which is the basis on which games are allocated. Go up the table and you are taking charge of the Manchester derby, fall down the table and it's back to the Championship and cold Tuesday nights at Stoke.

In this gap between impossible promise and messy reality, conspiracy theories about referees, implied by coaches and nurtured on social media by fans, have flourished. Chelsea fans thought Anthony Taylor was out to get them, but then so did Manchester City and Everton. Liverpool coach Jürgen Klopp and many of the club's fans came to believe that Paul Tierney had treated them unfairly. In Scotland, Rangers' very long streak of playing home games without conceding a penalty was taken as prima facie evidence of a conspiracy in their favour – though the fact that Celtic had enjoyed similar and even longer runs in the previous decade was overlooked. Paranoid and deluded as all of these claims were, English football experienced a psychotic step change in the spring of 2024 after Nottingham Forest lost their crucial relegation-battle game with Everton 2–0. The club released an ominous statement on Twitter that read, 'Three extremely poor decisions – three penalties not given – which we simply cannot accept. We warned the PGMOL that the VAR is a Luton fan before the game but they didn't change him. Our patience has been tested multiple times. NFFC will now consider its options.'

On reviewing all the evidence, PGMOL concluded that only one of those penalty decisions was incorrect. Forest would have lost whatever, but the damage had been done. The club had implied deliberate refereeing bias, on the basis of Stuart Atwell's – the VAR for the game – connection to Luton, Forest's main competitor for the last safe slot in the league. It unleashed a torrent of similar accusations on social media. The declared club allegiances of PGMOL referees were shared and endlessly scrutinised, spawning another wave of new conspiracies.

PGMOL responded to the distrust of the system as a whole by going public. Whereas in the past referees did not disclose their thoughts to the press, Howard Webb, the senior referee at PGMOL, took to the airwaves, appearing regularly on *Mic'd Up with Michael Owen* to discuss the week's contentious decisions. In cases where this provided insufficient balm, and where significant mistakes have been made, PGMOL and Webb have issued official apologies to clubs, and *in extremis* audio recordings of VAR decision-making have been released. Despite the calls for more information and more explanation, there is a residual uneasiness with this. There was, among referees and the public, a consensus that the best referees should be virtually invisible, on and off the pitch. Half a century ago, Jack Taylor disapproved of the media's new obsession with referees as personalities: 'In 1958 the referee was no more than a line of small type in the programme. Nowadays his appointment makes headlines in the national newspapers and he gets a pen picture as big as the players.'[24] A handful of officials, like Taylor, Gordon Hill and Ken Aston, had enough of a profile to warrant ghostwritten memoirs. David Elleray, the best-known referee of his era, was mic'd up during a game between Arsenal and Millwall in 1989 for a TV documentary. But otherwise the officials were largely anonymous to most football fans, let alone the wider public. However, in recent years the press and the febrile chat rooms of the internet have taken a lot more interest in referees on and off the pitch, boosting their profiles and simultaneously taking them down for it. Mark Clattenburg was considered suspect for his love of fast cars, ostentatious tattoos and generously applied hair gel. Mike Dean, the most visible of modern referees – notorious for his no-look yellow cards, stepovers and celebrations of his own decisions – had crowds contemptuously singing, 'It's all about you/It's all about you/

Mike Dean/It's all about you.' Consequently, Webb's public appearances have not been considered a welcome democratisation of the debate, but often as PR flummery and a politician's weasel words.

That English football should have placed its leading referees in such an impossible position, damned whatever they do, is testament to the toxicity of the country's public conversations. The very people who actually know the rules of the game – still just seventeen of them, but now so complex they need a hundred pages to describe them – are censured by those who know almost nothing. Their extraordinary craft and robust athleticism are dismissed by the crudest of epithets and for the crudest of reasons. The possibility that referees could be acting in good faith, that every mistake is not a deliberate act of harm, is decried by the people – fans, coaches and owners – whose own judgements are the most systematically biased, and who are never asked to account for their own poor interpretations of events. Where pressure and abuse will not work there is now the threat, on and off the pitch, of violence. Were referees' critics to turn their performative hatred into action and actually remove referees from the game, they would soon discover that football simply does not work without them, indeed it would impoverish us all. One might think, after experiencing the reality of Brexit, there would be a little more caution in English football, a little more respect for expert knowledge, a common understanding of the need for trust and just a little more humility from those who thought VAR was an oven-ready solution. But there is, for the most part, just anger, blame and cynicism.

6.

Goodbye, Great Britain

Football and the Politics of National Fragmentation

In November 2014, two months after Scotland's referendum on independence in which the public voted 55–45 to stay in the union, the national team played a friendly against England at Celtic Park. The SNP's Alex Salmond, who had just stepped down as First Minister in the wake of this defeat, was in attendance. Both anthems, 'Flower of Scotland' and 'God Save the Queen', were drowned by booing, and the atmosphere was raucous, but as England took control of the game the dominant tone was struck by their fans. First, they drew on their usual unionist repertoire of 'Rule, Britannia!' and 'God Save the Queen', but they also offered new, if perplexing taunts too. On the one hand they ribbed the Scottish nationalists with the chant, 'You're British till you die.' On the other hand, they expressed their desire to be rid of the Scots altogether, laughing along to a rousing chorus of 'We all voted yes!' England, it seemed, still had a space for a triumphant British unionism, but it also harboured a new and contemptuous English separatism. At least there was no ambiguity about their position on the Irish question. The official England band struck up 'Follow England Away', to which the refrain, aimed as much at Celtic as at Scotland, was 'Fuck the IRA'. Just for good measure, a 'No

Surrender' banner was unveiled, followed by endless choruses of, 'No surrender, no surrender, no surrender to the IRA scum'.

There was, of course, a longstanding history of political subtexts to games between the four home nations. In 1977, alongside a surge in support for the SNP at home, the Scots beat England at Wembley. The crowd invaded the pitch, started tearing up the turf, and sang, 'Give us an assembly and we'll give you back Wembley.' Two years later, and just a couple of months after Scotland had voted yes to devolution in the 1979 referendum, only for the total number of yes votes to fall below the legal threshold required for creating a Scottish assembly, they were back. This time England won, but a frenzy of drinking and trouble-making all over London saw more than 300 Scottish fans arrested. In 1972, in the aftermath of Bloody Sunday, republican groups issued threats to the visiting mainland teams of sufficient seriousness that Northern Ireland moved its home games to Liverpool. The Home Championship was actually abandoned in 1981 when England and Wales refused to travel to Belfast, then engulfed in the social disorder and threats of violence generated by the Maze hunger strikes. In the end, the increasing demands of the global football calendar, pitiful attendance at many games, and English uninterest saw the tournament abandoned for good in 1984. Subsequent encounters between the nations were rare, just a few qualifying games for World Cups and European Championships, a tiny handful of friendlies, an England–Scotland group game at Euro 96; the England–Scotland game in 2013 was the first time that the two sides had met this millennium. However, the energies and antipathies of these encounters have not disappeared. In fact, during their long hibernation they have both intensified and mutated.

In the decade since Scotland's independence referendum, these energies were released by the impact of the EU referendum and the new politics of nationhood it unleashed within the United Kingdom. In Wales the decade saw the development of an increasingly confident modern Welsh nationalism, with a small shift towards support for independence; in Northern Ireland, Brexit and its aftermath brought a serious challenge to the fragile entente between its two national traditions, while the quiet demographic shift in the country finally saw the balance tilt in favour of the nationalist community over unionists, and a Sinn Féin First Minister installed at Stormont; in Scotland, which had voted unambiguously to remain in the EU, Brexit invigorated the independence movement, without yet resolving the economic and political dilemmas that a sovereign Scotland might face; while in England, still hiding within the tattered carapace of the Union Jack, different versions of the nation – one progressive and anti-racist, one atavistic and nativist – contested the contours of an emergent Englishness. Football tracked, perhaps even shaped, these processes in all four of the home nations.

Wales, by a small majority, had voted Leave, but this did not signal a revival of Britishness. As the economic downsides of departure from the European Union became apparent, not least the disappearance of the considerable European structural funds that had paid for a lot of Wales' new infrastructure, support for Brexit diminished. At the same time, public opinion shifted towards calls for greater Welsh devolution, more powers for the Senedd, and even independence. All these views had become more prevalent among the nation's football supporters who, not coincidentally, had been backing the most successful Welsh national football team of all time. Indeed, so intense was the public's response to their extraordinary run to the semi-finals of Euro 2016 that football began to eclipse rugby union as the pre-eminent sporting arena in which contemporary Welshness was being imagined and performed.

The space in which football could begin to transform Wales' sense of itself was created by the relative decline of rugby union and invigorated by a new and vibrant Welsh popular-music culture. The wave of Welsh bands that emerged in the 1990s like

Catatonia, Manic Street Preachers and Super Furry Animals – a moment dubbed Cool Cymru – first made their mark on Welsh sport in 1999 when Catatonia's Cerys Matthews sang out 'I thank the Lord I'm Welsh' in Cardiff's Millennium Stadium at the opening ceremony of the Rugby World Cup. However, in the years since, rugby union has reverted to a more traditional musical groove, a standard match-day playlist consisting of Guns N' Roses and 1980s power ballads. The cost of attending Welsh games, more than triple the average for the football team, had soared to the point where many could not afford to attend, and the crowd became visibly older, more masculine and less ethnically diverse than that at football. What remained on show was the old and now ageing alliance of the anglophone professional classes of South Wales and the working-class mining and industrial communities, in their political incarnation as the Labour Party, who together had made the Welsh game and in effect administered the country. It was Wales, but a Wales that was receding into the past. Welsh-language communication was almost invisible, the WRU's (Welsh Rugby Union) social-media presence pitiful. Daffodils, leeks and Prince of Wales feathers remained its chosen totems. One regular attender at both codes wrote: 'If the FAW is your cool uncle at the bar buying a round of jäger bombs, the WRU is your grandpa in the corner complaining that the music is too loud.'[1] The domestic game clung on, but Wales' few professional rugby clubs had become makeweights in a wider Celtic league, while at the grassroots football has long proved the far more popular sport, especially in the north of the country, and with girls and young women.

Welsh football embraced Welsh pop, but first of all Welsh pop embraced football. Super Furry Animals established their football credentials as far back as 1997, when they appeared in an S4C documentary smiling ruefully in the away end in Eindhoven as Wales conceded a seventh goal against Holland, before going on to play a gig in the city centre. Manic Street Preachers had been playing Wales games since 2002. Goldie Lookin Chain –

Newport's comedy hip-hop troupe – sponsored Newport County's third strip with their very own Burberry casuals' check. In the run-up to Euro 2016 the relationship between football and music appeared to deepen. Manic Street Preachers were commissioned by the FAW to write the team's official tournament song 'Together Stronger (C'mon Wales)', and were invited to play before a qualifying game against Andorra. Not to be outdone, Super Furry Animals released their first new tune for almost seven years, the surreal football-themed 'Bing Bong'. On the eve of the tournament, BBC Wales aired, at primetime, *C'mon Wales: Our Euro 2016 Singalong*, featuring orchestrated versions of fan-favourite chants, like the Human League's 'Don't You Want Me Baby' sung as 'Aaron Ramsey, Baby'. All of this and more could be heard in the stadiums in France, but the relationship between these two cultural zones was consummated when Super Furry Animals headlined the Rio Loco Festival in Toulouse the night before Wales' decisive final group game against Russia. Normally a more restrained celebration of pan-Celtic folk, the Furries played their set in front of a red sea of ecstatic Welsh fans. One fan recalled, 'I just loved it. Them, us, altogether, being Welsh and happy and singing along with every song. At times it was very emotional ... there were the onstage adlibs, the brass playing "Push It" to start a mass Hal Robson-Kanu chant, and then, when it was all over, Cian coming back out to lead a brilliant, raucous rendition of "Hen Wlad Fy Nhadau".' The Furries were on fire, but Gruff Rhys, the band's singer, ceded primacy to the football nation. 'I think eventually the audience became the gig ... after we finished playing the crowd stayed and sang the entire red wall 2016 repertoire for another half hour at least.'[2]

Important as the musical context had proved to this renaissance, it ultimately rested on the transformation of the FAW and its teams. A succession of managers – John Toshack, Gary Speed and Chris Coleman – had helped raise the level of coaching and the expectations of their players. The FAW steadily improved the training, medical and media infrastructures that sustained the squad, and it also took the decision to use the Welsh language in official communications, with the team always referred to as Cymru. Players and coaches, many of whom did not speak a word of Welsh, were taught the words to the national anthem and were expected to sing it. Coleman embraced the team's slogan, 'Stronger Together', and though a little pedestrian, even cheesy, it struck a chord with both the Welsh players and the public, who endlessly repeated it as a hashtag on Twitter. Looking at the team's reception at games in Cardiff, where attendances had been steadily creeping up, there appeared to be real bonds of solidarity emerging between the players and the supporters, now known as 'the Red Wall'.

It was certainly a team that reflected the demographic contours of a changing Wales and the Welsh diaspora. Actively seeking out players with at least one Welsh grandparent brought a diversity to the side never seen before. Jazz Richards, Hal Robson-Kanu and Ashley Williams all had African and Caribbean roots. Neil Taylor's mother was born in Kolkata. Welsh-based and English-based, Welsh-speaking and English-speaking players were blended into a single unit. Add to this the then most expensive player in the world, Gareth Bale, who had gone to Real Madrid for £100 million, and Wales' ascent in the FIFA world rankings from its nadir of 117th in 2011 to 10th in 2015 became explicable. Bale was exceptional on the pitch, but he brought a level of publicly stated patriotism and commitment to the team that was unparalleled, and he established an effortless communion with the supporters. The love was returned by the fans, who flew a banner of his unofficial slogan and list of priorities: 'Wales, Golf, Madrid: In that order'. The small North Wales town of Bala renamed itself Bale for the duration of Euro 2016 and painted over all its road signs to that effect, while Ellis James claimed that Bale was 'box office in a way that makes Anthony Hopkins, Catherine Zeta-Jones or Richard Burton shrink by comparison'.[3]

More than 30,000 Welsh fans made the journey for Euro 2016. Carwyn Jones, the country's First Minister, and many members of his cabinet, cleared their schedules in order to attend. At the opening game against England a banner referencing two medieval princes of independent Welsh polities and an Arsenal midfielder flew in the stands: 'Llewelyn 1258, Glyndwr 1400, Ramsey 2016'. It wasn't quite a bid for succession, but the Welsh team went on an extraordinary run. Slovakia, Russia, Northern Ireland and Belgium were all dispatched by a masterclass of collective verve and purpose, before they were beaten 2–0 in the semi-final by eventual champions Portugal. Even a group-stage defeat to England was savoured for a sensational Gareth Bale free kick from thirty metres out that curved around the English wall and left Joe Hart for dead. A long-suffering Welsh football blogger exclaimed, 'Gareth Bale has just delivered my message. He's interrupted the Queen's Christmas day speech, snatched the microphone out of her hands, and told every man, woman and child in England to fuck off!' But he was an outlier.[4] The dominant emotional tones of the crowd were ecstasy, joy, generosity and awe, typified by the 'Crying Man': a clip of Jamie Collins, a primary school teacher from Wrexham, sobbing uncontrollably as Wales dismantled Russia 3–0 to ensure their progress to the knock-out stages, went viral and became the defining image of the tournament on social media.

If Welsh international football created a space in which a new kind of nation could be imagined, Welsh domestic football was an equally powerful reminder of the economic and cultural realities that any move towards greater devolution or independence would face. First and foremost, Wales' four leading professional clubs – Cardiff City, Newport County, Swansea City and Wrexham – all play within the English football pyramid, and for most of the last hundred years in its lower levels. Consequently, the FAW's League of Wales, later renamed – more in hope than expectation – the Welsh Premier League, was a very low-key affair, with crowds that hovered around 400. It was not intended as a commentary on peripherality, but the stadium of Total Network Solutions – later renamed the New Saints – the dominant team in the league, was actually located in England. For much of the previous couple of decades, the clubs that had thrown their lot in with the English had fared poorly. Swansea and Cardiff kept themselves in the Football League, but they rarely troubled its upper reaches. In fact, Swansea had almost been extinguished by financial problems in the late 1980s and early 2000s, and had saved themselves from both bankruptcy and relegation from the league by a whisker. Newport and Wrexham really did go bankrupt and were saved by their supporters' trusts, but both had spent much of their recent past even further down the pyramid.

Locked into English structures, there was little appetite or space in which separatist identities could be articulated in Welsh professional football, but there was plenty of anti-Englishness. The standard repertoire when playing English clubs was un-imaginative but unambiguous: 'England's full of shit' and 'We are the England haters.' Much of this was cartoonish, even performative, never more so than when Sam Hammam, the Lebanese-British businessman who bought Cardiff City in 2006, tried to make it a vehicle for a more explicit Welsh nationalism. His opening pitch was: 'Wales and Welsh people are not an appendage, and it is through football and specially Cardiff City FC that we are going to establish identity and pride.'[5] There were a lot of theatrics – 'Men of Harlech' played before Cardiff games, and a Welsh-flag away kit in lieu of the owner's prefer-ence for abandoning the club's traditional blue altogether for the red of the national team – but Hammam's carnival of ersatz nationalism was fatally undermined by his limited grasp of the country's football culture. His attempts to diminish the club's enmity with Swansea, and even enlist Swansea fans in his nationalist crusade, were poorly received. As one fan put it, 'We hate the Jacks more than we hate the English.' Hammam sold up to Chinese-Malaysian oligarch Vincent Tan, who by his own admission knew nothing about football. He too tried to change the shirt to red, but more because of the colour's popularity in Asia than for its local political connotations. After fierce fan protest, Cardiff went back to blue in 2015, by which time a small Welsh renaissance was under way. Swansea, then under fan ownership, had been promoted to the Premier League in 2011, stayed there for seven years and won the League Cup in 2013. Newport County returned to the English Football League in 2013, as would Wrexham after their Hollywood takeover in 2023. In 2013, and 2018 Cardiff climbed out of the Championship and into the Premier League, albeit for short stays. Yet despite the surge of money and interest that these successes brought, it was never enough to play catch-up with their English competitors. In 2017 Facebook data suggested that Manchester United and Liverpool could boast more online Welsh followers than any of the Welsh clubs, and Arsenal and Chelsea weren't far behind Cardiff and Swansea. When they cross the border, the fans still chant, 'We'll never be mastered by no English bastard,' but the league table says otherwise.

In late 2015, in the days before Northern Ireland's decisive game against Greece in the qualifying rounds for Euro 2016, BBC News asked Cathal Ó hOisín, a Sinn Féin member of Stormont's culture and sport committee, whether he would be supporting the team. He replied, 'I won't call myself a supporter, but I won't call myself a detractor either … I would have a passing interest in it but that would be about the height of it. It's not on my radar.'[6] In Northern Ireland even such calculated indifference from a republican politician constituted progress for a team that until recently had received nearly all of its support from the Protestant community and whose home stadium – Windsor Park in Belfast – was considered a no-go area for many nationalists who had long-since transferred their sporting allegiance to either Gaelic sports or the Republic of Ireland.

Almost two decades on from the signing of the Belfast Agreement, Northern Irish football appeared, cautiously, to be moving on from the Troubles. The IFA's 'Football for All' programme had made significant progress in diminishing the display of provocative flags and banners at Windsor Park, and with the support of the clubs they had clamped down on sectarian chanting in league and grassroots football. Significant funding, much of it from the European Union, poured into cross-community football schemes for urban youth, and at least opened up channels for face-to-face contact between otherwise segregated communities. Windsor Park had become home to a self-consciously non-sectarian fan group – the Green and White Army – who had been chanting and singing over the sectarian songs that had once dominated Northern Ireland's home games. The implacable aggression of 'No surrender to the IRA' had given way to the self-deprecatory 'It's just like watching Brazil.' Even so, nationalists were hardly flooding into Windsor Park, and active cross-community support was still limited, at least in part because the IFA still insisted on 'God Save the Queen' being played before games – a practice that many in the nationalist community still found insensitive at best, exclusionary at worst. Linfield, the club side most clearly associated with the politics of unionism and loyalism, and which had refused to play Catholics for much of the twentieth century, now fielded a cross-community squad. Indeed, across Northern Irish football the sectarian temperature had dropped, as acts of violence, threats of violence, and aggressive chants, although not absent, diminished. By the same token, the GAA (Gaelic Athletic Association) had revised its constitution, lifting the ban on members of the police and security service from participating in their teams, not that there were many takers from among the ranks of the Northern Irish Police Service. In a large-scale survey on sport and sectarianism since the Belfast Agreement, released on the eve of Euro 2016, 84 per cent of the public thought that sports had become more inclusive and open.[7]

Northern Ireland went on to beat Greece 3–1, qualifying for their first international tournament since 1986. Six months later, more than 30,000 supporters made their way to France, and in an unprecedented show of official cross-community co-operation, they were joined in the stadiums by unionist First Minister Peter Robinson and nationalist Deputy First Minister Martin McGuinness. Back in Belfast, a fan zone was set up in the newly built Titanic quarter, a post-conflict space that, for all its architectural banality, offered a modern non-sectarian enclave in the city, where both Northern Ireland's and the Republic of Ireland's games were shown on the big screen. Fans of both teams mixed in both Belfast and France, where Northern Ireland fans were among the loudest and most carnivalesque supporters; never more so than when shaking the stadiums with renditions of the dance anthem 'Freed from Desire' sung as 'Will Grigg's on Fire!', a reference to the Wigan striker, who, despite the chorus, did not play a single minute at the tournament. Thanks to a 2–0 victory over Ukraine, Northern Ireland made it to the knock-out rounds, by which time the UK had voted to leave the European Union; Northern Ireland, however, had voted to remain by 56 to 44. The Welsh, who had narrowly voted Leave, beat them 1–0, but this was just the start of the country's Brexit problems.

Well-argued warnings from Northern Irish, Irish and British politicians – including ex-prime ministers Blair and Major – of the consequences of Brexit and withdrawal from the European single market for the open border between Ireland and Northern Ireland had barely registered on the mainland. The depth of cross-border interaction on the island of Ireland, invisible to the public in Britain, was laid bare by the immediate post-referendum concerns of some football clubs. Warrenpoint Town, located close to the border in County Down, was a club that had been making steady progress based on a strategy of recruit-ing fans, suppliers, staff and players from the Republic, and feared this exchange would be much more inconvenient and expensive should a closed border be imposed.[8] Derry City, who had once played in Northern Ireland before persistent sectarian attacks saw them withdraw from the local league and join the League of Ireland south of the border, were equally concerned. Some thought there might be Brexit opportunities in the transfer market for Northern Irish football, as richer English clubs, denied access to the European talent pool, would have more money to spend on Northern Irish prospects; but, like most Brexit bonuses, it has yet to transpire.

What Brexit did bring to Northern Ireland was a heightened state of political uncertainty and mistrust. Unionists, who had been enthusiastic supporters of leaving the European Union, found that the Belfast Agreement and the open border would not be sacrificed by the UK government, which thereby left Northern Ireland in the single market and created the need for new trade borders, checks and regulations with mainland Britain. The issue consumed them. Nationalists, for whom the open border was an unequivocal red line, remained deeply suspicious of unionist intentions. The Stormont Assembly, whose functioning was legally and politically predicated on a degree of mutual trust and cooperation between the two blocs, could not survive unscathed and was suspended twice: first, between 2017 and 2020 when Sinn Féin refused to participate, citing the long-running and unresolved corruption case against the DUP over a renewable heating subsidy scheme; and between 2022 and 2024 when the DUP refused to participate as a protest over the Northern Irish Protocol, a deal between the EU and the UK government that attempted to resolve Northern Ireland's post-Brexit border issues. The fate of the national team may not have been directly affected by this era of both chaos and stasis, but its performances, failing to qualify for any major tournament since, have never come close to the heady days of Euro 2016.

Domestic football in Northern Ireland has long had to compete with the appeal of GAA and rugby, the former attract-ing significant nationalist support and at times actively antithetical to football, while rugby union captured the sporting affections of the large and growing non-sectarian middle classes. Even among the football constituency, Northern Irish clubs have had to compete with a large and growing support for English Premier League teams, while the sectarian symbolism and politics of Celtic and Rangers gave both Glasgow clubs a huge following in the province. Despite all of this, the Northern Irish Premier League has been showing real signs of life. A part-time football economy began to give way to full-time professionalism. The level of play picked up, competition was keen, crowds were steadily rising, and sectarian behaviour, though present, was not overwhelming. By 2018 Linfield were playing in a rebuilt Windsor Park and paying their professional squad with their considerable cut from the gate at Northern Irish international games. The minnows of Larne, a grim port town of fewer than 20,000 people, were transformed into contenders and then champions by the money of sentimental hometown millionaire Kenny Bruce, co-founder of the property website Purplebricks. The enigmatic Welsh-Iranian businessman Ali Pour, who made much of his money in nightclubs, thought the league sufficiently promising to buy and then spend money on Glentoran.

Perhaps the most hopeful moment in the local league came in 2017, when Linfield went to Cliftonville – the main team in Belfast, with a significant nationalist identity and following – with a chance to win the title and were allowed, for the first time in a decade, to take their fans with them. Linfield won the game and the championship without incident. Support for the IRA, however anodyne or performative, was cracked down upon by both clubs and the IFA. Portadown cancelled the signing of Joe Gorman when a tweet he'd posted as a nineteen-year-old – saying that he would 'love to open up' on 'orange men' – was made public. Larne and John Herron parted company over a photo of the striker wearing an 'Up the Ra' T-shirt, while Coalisland Athletic were fined when a video of the squad celebrating their Junior Cup final victory by singing 'Up the Ra' on the bus home became public.[9]

The national team's home games remained free of sectarian chanting, but beyond the confines of Windsor Park and the presence of the Green and White Army there were other voices. In 2019, for example, a group of fans, some in Northern Ireland shirts, drinking in a bar in Belfast before the national team's game with Belarus, were caught on video singing the Tommy James and the Shondells' 1960s hit 'I Think We're Alone Now' with the chorus changed to 'We hate Catholics. Everyone hates Catholics.'[10] Grassroots, youth and amateur football, all troubled by sectarian abuse and violent confrontations in the early 2000s, had seen a steady lowering of tensions following the Belfast Agreement, but here too street-level conflicts and barely suppressed sectarian rage could still be unleashed. In 2019 DUP councillor Dale Pankhurst claimed that the football pitches of the Girdwood Community Hub in North Belfast 'continue to be used as a site for attacks on Protestants'.[11] Certainly, witnesses to the game between Ballysillan Swifts and St Patrick's FC reported cries of 'Orange bastards' aimed at Ballysillan and a shower of bottles raining down on the pitch before the game was abandoned. The players of nationalist club Crumlin Star had, in 2011, been attacked in broad daylight by an armed loyalist mob on the street of Ardoyne, with two of their number seriously injured. There have been no repeats of such blatant sectarian violence in football, but in 2021 Crumlin's manager and his wife and daughter faced a tirade of in-your-face sectarian slurs and violent threats on the touchline after his team had scored the winning goal against Islandmagee FC.[12]

If these events pointed to a still simmering set of grassroots fears and resentments, the politics of playing Northern Ireland's national anthem – 'God Save the Queen' – at football matches suggested they were equally present at the apex too. In 2011 sports minister Carál Ní Chuilín was the first Sinn Féin MLA (Member of the Legislative Assembly) to officially attend a

Northern Ireland game at Windsor Park; but as she arrived after the anthem had been played, and left early in the second half, she also managed to miss all the goals as Northern Ireland beat the Faroe Islands 4–0. By the same token, Peter Robinson, then DUP First Minister, attended his first GAA game in 2012, but did not take his seat until the Irish national anthem had been played. In 2017, on police advice, the IFA cancelled the playing of both the Northern Irish and the Irish national anthems before a qualifying match for the Women's World Cup, fearing loyalist protests. While the politicians tiptoed around the issue, the animus that the anthem could arouse on the ground was made clear at the 2018 Irish Cup final between Cliftonville and Coleraine. Despite Cliftonville's request that the anthem not be played before the match as in 2009 and 2013, the IFA insisted on its inclusion. Cliftonville players bowed their heads and their fans booed the anthem. Coleraine went on to win 3–1 but that was not the end of it. Linfield players refused to shake hands with Cliftonville at their next game in a form of low-key sectarian tit-for-tat, and Cliftonville returned the favour later in the season.

Upper Bann DUP MLA Carla Lockhart gloated after the final whistle in the Irish Cup final, tweeting: 'They got what their disrespect deserved. Well done Coleraine.'[13] Further along the loyalist spectrum there was more anger. Jamie Bryson, one of the loyalist leaders of the 2012 flag protests triggered by Belfast City Council's decision to limit the number of days that the Union Jack would fly over the municipal offices, also took to Twitter: 'Cliftonville FC are a despicable, disgraceful and outright sectarian football club. Delighted that Coleraine have won the Irish Cup. Cliftonville can bury their heads in their sectarian huddle all night!'[14] It was only after new elections in 2024 in which Sinn Féin, for the first time, were the largest party in the assembly, that power sharing returned to Stormont and some minor accommodation was possible. Newly elected Sinn Féin First Minister Michelle O'Neill stood for the UK national anthem at Windsor Park before Northern Ireland's women played Montenegro, and she stayed for all of the goals.[15]

In the vacuum created by Stormont's suspension, sectarian tensions had made their way back into the domestic league. Some Linfield supporters, despite the progress made at the club, could not contain themselves when 300 Celtic fans visited Windsor Park in a 2017 qualifying round for the Champions League and were treated to sectarian chanting, while a bottle was thrown at Celtic striker Leigh Griffiths. In 2020 similar scenes at Linfield saw the IFA fine the club for sectarian chants aimed at the Catholic players of Larne and Glentoran, to whom they sang, 'The Glens have a chapel on the Newtownards Road for all you Fenian bastards.' After a visit from Linfield, Carrick Rangers wrote an angry letter to the IFA describing events at the away end: 'It is totally unacceptable for supporters to bring a megaphone to a football match with the sole aim of directing abuse at players.'[16] Similar incidents could be found at other clubs with a unionist tradition, alcohol often playing its part. One supporter at Larne was punished for shouting, 'You fucking Fenian bastards!' at opponents Crumlin Star. The official report described him as 'aggravated by hospitality'. The same could probably be said for those involved in the large brawl between fans of Portadown and Newry City in the club's car park in 2018.[17]

Unpleasant as these incidents were, they were not premeditated or organised. However, at Coleraine premeditated or organised was precisely the modus operandi of the Coleraine Casual Army and the Railway End Crew. Over the last decade visitors have been attacked by one or more of these groups in the town's loyalist zone of Harpur's Hill, at the railway station and around the club's stadium, the Showgrounds. To be fair to these new casuals, they were remarkably unsectarian in their attacks. Attacks on Cliftonville fans in 2017, 2019 and 2022 were to be expected, but Larne fans, hardly a hotbed of republicanism, were abused at an Irish Cup quarter-final in 2019;

Portadown supporters received similar treatment as they tried to get on their bus home from Coleraine, prompting their goalkeeper, Jethren Barr, to tweet: 'I can excuse poor decisions from referees, but really shocking to have beer bottles thrown at my car and the Portadown bus as I'm leaving Coleraine Showgrounds.'[18] The Railway End Crew also established links with right-wing casual groups from West Ham United and Hartlepool United, both of whom travelled to Northern Ireland to join them in sectarian chanting and trouble-making, including a march through nationalist neighbourhoods in Belfast singing 'The Sash' and a display of Nazi salutes at Linfield.[19]

The endurance of these sectarian attitudes, especially on the unionist side, was an expression of weakness rather than strength. A unionist-controlled Stormont had failed to deliver significant benefits to the working-class enclaves from which they had sprung, and both leadership and grassroots could sense the slow but steady drift of demographic and political power in the province towards nationalists in general, and Sinn Féin in particular. In the world of football, the saga of Casement Park was perhaps the best illustration of this. Football stadiums have been a small but important thread in the post-Agreement politics of Northern Ireland. Under New Labour, Westminster seriously investigated the possibility of building one in central Belfast that might have hosted a non-sectarian Premier League club. Moving on from fantasy to the merely impossibly controversial, there were well-established plans to build a huge national stadium, serving all sports, on what had been the Maze prison, which had held both loyalist and republican prisoners for over three decades before its closure. Finally, in 2011, agreement was reached that money would be available to upgrade Windsor Park for football (£26 million), Ravenhill Stadium for rugby union (£14.7 million), and for the GAA and Gaelic games a brand-new stadium at Casement Park in West Belfast (£61.4 million). Given the zero-sum model of public expenditure held by the Stormont parties, the gap between football and the GAA was made up by an additional £36 million for stadium redevelopment in the local football leagues. Windsor Park and Ravenhill were rebuilt and open for business by 2014, but plans for Casement Park lagged behind. Planning permission was given in 2013, but a local campaign, driven by worries about the scale of the new stadium and its impact on the neighbourhood, saw the original permission withdrawn in 2015. A redesign followed by a reapplication for planning was made in 2017, and at last, in 2021, construction was ready to go ahead. However, the suspension of Stormont meant that the funds for both Casement Park and the local football leagues could not legally be released. In any case, the cost of the development had now risen sharply to perhaps as much as £150 million and the GAA was refusing to put up more than the £16 million they had promised a decade earlier. Northern Ireland had another stadium stalemate on its hands. What appeared to save the new Casement Park, and provoked a considerable backlash, was the IFA's role in a successful UK and Ireland-wide bid for the 2028 European Football Championship. Windsor Park, the obvious choice for such an occasion, had a capacity of under 20,000 and was too small to meet UEFA's criteria, meaning that only the new Casement Park, planned to hold more than 30,000, was suitable. Consequently, both the UK and Irish governments made clear that there would be additional funding to ensure Northern Ireland could co-host the tournament, but there was no sign that similar additional matching funds would be made available to Northern Irish domestic football. The news was met by Northern Ireland supporters attending a game against San Marino at Windsor Park with the chant, 'You can shove your Casement Park up your arse.' Issues of economic parity aside, there were deeper historical reasons for this animus.

Casement Park was opened in 1953 and served as the ground for the Antrim GAA, who in line with the constitution of the organisation at the time, did not allow football to be played within its confines, nor members of the security forces to participate. It sits in Andersonstown, at the far end of the Falls Road in West Belfast, an area that is almost exclusively Catholic by demography and republican in its politics. For these reasons alone it is, even a quarter century on from the Belfast Agreement, a place that most unionists and Northern Ireland supporters would be wary of. However, its name and histories make it even more exclusionary. Roger Casement was a Dublin-born British diplomat. As the First World War approached, he sharply shifted his allegiance towards Irish nationalism and was central to negotiations with Germany to supply arms for an Irish uprising. Returning to Ireland from Germany on the eve of the 1916 Easter Rising, he was caught, arrested, found guilty of treason and hanged in Pentonville Prison. Perhaps even more troubling for unionist sensibilities was Casement Park's role in the murder of corporals Derek Howes and David Wood in 1988. For reasons that still remain unclear, the two British soldiers, in civilian clothes but armed with pistols, drove an unmarked car into an IRA funeral procession in West Belfast. The previous week, loyalist Michael Stone had attended an IRA funeral in the city and killed three people. Unsurprisingly, the corporals' car was surrounded by funeral marchers, and when Wood drew his pistol and fired, the soldiers were dragged out of their car and taken to nearby Casement Park, where they were stripped and beaten; later, they would be taken to a piece of waste ground and shot dead. AONISC (Amalgamation of Northern Ireland Supporters Clubs), recognising that Casement would, after the Euros, be overwhelmingly used for Gaelic games, objected to the lack of legacy for football, and in coded language of disdain stated that 'football tournaments should be hosted by football stadia'.[20] Their wish has been granted and Casement Park will not now host football matches, but that is because there will be no European football matches played in Northern Ireland in 2028. As so often in Northern Ireland, every victory comes at some other cost. In the summer of 2024 the new Labour government looked at the latest estimates for building the stadium, now delayed by local political conflicts for more than a decade, and concluded that £400 million was not tenable, even if the project could be completed in time. Northern Irish football lost out on the economic and cultural energies of hosting the tournament, but at least all sides can blame the British government for pulling the plug.

Scotland was the ghost at the Euro 2016 feast, the only one of the four home nations not to qualify. It had become a habit: Scotland had failed to qualify for any national tournament for almost two decades. Last time out, in 1998, just a year after the country had voted to re-establish the Scottish Parliament, Scotland played at the World Cup in France and the Tartan Army were in delirious, celebratory mode. The team didn't make it to the knock-out rounds, finishing bottom of their group with just a single point from a draw with Norway, but it really didn't matter. While the English were still fighting themselves, the locals and the police, the Scots were making friends with everyone and having the best party in the country. The analogies can be overstated, and Scots themselves have been cautious about drawing too sharp a conclusion from their footballing fate; but after an initial outburst of national optimism, the discontents of devolution and the limits of Scottish Labour's narrow programme of reform have been paralleled by the dismal underperformance of the national team and the relative decline of Scottish elite football by comparison not just with England, but comparable smaller European countries.

Those discontents, and the failure of successive Labour administrations to significantly repair Scotland's social fabric, had helped bring about a significant shift in support to the SNP, who took power at Holyrood for the first time in 2007. There was no comparable transfer of power in the world of football, but there was a near universal consensus that Scottish football was underperforming and that the organisation, funding and governance of the game were deeply problematic. In part, this was a function of Scotland's peripheral place in the emerging global football economy, as money and talent were relentlessly concentrated in bigger leagues and countries, but there were domestic factors at work too. Much of this conversation was conducted in the key of nostalgia. Some bemoaned the decline of street football and the urban geographies of poverty and restricted spaces that had produced the football stars of the early post-war era. In a similar vein, the decline of heavy industries, small engineering towns and old mining communities had diminished the instinctive solidarities and feel for collective action that had animated football in the past. Others fretted over the country's rising tide of childhood obesity and declining activity rates. In 2010 Henry McLeish, former Labour First Minister and sometime professional footballer with East Fife, was commissioned by the SFA to take a look.[21] Dismissing the usual tropes, the report berated the game's administrators for their conservatism and neglect. It chastised club owners for failing to engage with their supporters and the high price of tickets that was driving many away from the game; but it saved its greatest venom for the state of the country's grassroots infrastructure and its fragmented and neglected systems of talent identification and development. In this regard the McLeish Report was similar to innumerable New Labour economic policy documents. It recognised that low productivity and decline relative to international competitors was born of low levels of investment, inadequate vocational education and self-serving management; and it proposed a plethora of minor changes in governance, small amounts of state expenditure on infrastructure and upskilling the workforce. What the report, in true New Labour fashion, barely mentioned were structural issues, be they the massive power imbalance between capital and labour in the economy or, in the case of Scottish football, the enduring dominance of the Old Firm and its consequences for everybody else.

As of 2010, when the report was published, no one other than Celtic or Rangers had won the Scottish league title since

Aberdeen in 1985. As of 2025, the situation remains the same. The Scottish Cup and League Cup have been shared a little more widely, but even here, three-quarters of the trophies since the turn of the millennium had gone to the Old Firm. Annual attendance at the two Glasgow clubs was over 1.7 million, accounting for almost 60 per cent of the Scottish Premier League's total. In terms of turnover, market valuation, transfer-market spending and wage rates, the gap between Celtic and Rangers and the rest of the league was even greater. Unlike the other clubs, both could draw on a global diaspora of followers as well as local support and top up their domestic earnings with regular European competition; income from the group stages of the Champions League alone would bring in more than the total income of the smaller clubs combined. Through the 1990s and into the 2000s, the two clubs had explored alternative options: joining the English pyramid, or playing in a trans-European Atlantic league made up of the big clubs from smaller nations, like Portugal and the Netherlands. Neither option was deemed feasible. So the Old Firm was stuck with Scotland, and Scotland was stuck with the Old Firm. In a refracted image of the way much of Scotland felt about England, this kind of hegemony was wearily accepted; but the way in which the Old Firm sucked up all the media space was deeply resented, as was the enduring and ugly spectacle of sectarianism and violence that accompanied their rivalry.

Sectarian singing and chanting was hardly new at either club, nor was it universal among their crowds, but there was a sustained and serious presence at both. Rangers were singing 'The Famine Song' and 'up to our knees in Fenian blood', Celtic praised the IRA. Union Jacks were put up against Irish tricolours, symbols of the monarchy were revered and reviled, but there was, under conditions of intense and expensive police surveillance, relatively little violence inside or immediately around the stadiums. Rather, the Old Firm cast its toxic shadow across the city. On the streets, fights over territory and urban space among the young and the drunk were widespread, occasionally homicidal. In 1995, sixteen-year-old Mark Scott had his throat slashed for wearing a Celtic shirt; most years since then, the derby has been accompanied by stabbings, attempted murders and the occasional death. Hospitals have proved dangerous zones on match day. One old hand from Glasgow's A&E departments described the scene on Old Firm derby day: 'Nurses wear blue, doctors wear green. This may not be the colour of choice of the individuals who need treatment. An injury that would take five minutes to stitch, ends up taking an hour with three staff trying to calm the guy down about the colour of someone's uniform.'[22] Above all, it was the everyday violence of all-day drinking that prevailed. In 2009, on the day of the Scottish Cup final between Celtic and Rangers, Strathclyde Police arrested more than 550 people, all of whom were drunk, as well as dealing with a sharp rise in the number of attempted murders, assaults and breaches of the peace. Incidents of domestic violence on the day rose by 88 per cent. Police statistics collated over the next couple of years revealed that when Old Firm matches were held on a Sunday, reported acts of violence and disorder more than doubled across the city. Saturday lunchtime kick-offs were even worse, and saw a 140 per cent increase in cases of domestic abuse.[23]

That this state of affairs should have persisted into the twenty-first century was perplexing. Scotland was an increasingly secular society and church attendance had plummeted, making, for most observers, the religious and theological dimensions of the Old Firm divide redundant. Rangers had long abandoned their policy of not signing Catholics; in fact, in 1998 the Italian Lorenzo Amoruso became the first Catholic to captain the team and literally no one blinked an eye. The signing of the Belfast Agreement in 1998, while not eradicating the divisions in Northern Ireland, had taken much of the heat out of the conflict in Belfast, yet it now seemed to burn more intensely in Glasgow. The collapse of heavy industry, where Protestants had often been privileged in the labour market, took another practical reason for sectarianism away. Glasgow City Council conducted its own review of sectarianism in the city in 2003 and found that most people thought its presence had greatly diminished, but for one thing: football. Successive public summits and campaigns designed to tackle this came and went. Labour First Minister Jack McConnell called a sectarian summit in 2005; UEFA regularly fined the clubs for their chants and banners; and both Rangers and Celtic launched anti-sectarian campaigns – 'Follow with Pride' and 'Bhoys against Bigotry', respectively. But all without much visible success.

Next up were the Scottish National Party, now in power at Holyrood, who approached the question rather differently, breaking with the hands-off volunteerism of their Labour predecessors in favour of something much more draconian and punitive. In March 2011 an admittedly very bad-tempered fifth-round Scottish Cup replay between Rangers and Celtic at Celtic Park saw scuffling between the players in the tunnel at half time, twelve yellow cards awarded and three Rangers players sent off. Most notably, at full time, there was enough aggression between the two coaches, Neil Lennon and Ally McCoist, that they had to be separated by their assistants. Despite this, there were remarkably few incidents in the crowd or between the two sets of fans on the streets afterwards; certainly, there had been more disorder and more violent encounters at many games over the previous decade. Nonetheless, the press christened it the 'Game of Shame'. SNP First Minster Alex Salmond and the chief constable of Strathclyde Police held an emergency summit on policing the Old Firm derby, which focused on its impact on the incidence of domestic violence rather than its sectarian character. Worried about the huge and escalating cost of policing the event in an era of shrinking budgets, they recommended stricter alcohol controls on match day.

Two months later, presumably emboldened by achieving a majority in the Scottish parliamentary elections that spring, the

SNP returned to the issue, and, deeply uncomfortable with identities – both unionist and republican – that stood outside their own version of civic Scotland, the SNP were now proposing to introduce a law that would, for football fans alone, outlaw sectarian chanting and abusive social media. Not only that, but they proposed to do so in indecent haste so as to be ready for the start of the new season, a timetable certainly insufficient for proper parliamentary scrutiny. The bill was delayed, but despite a wide range of critics from a wide range of Scottish society, from the Conservative Party to the Greens, the Offensive Behaviour and Threatening Communication Act was made law by the first vote in the Scottish parliament achieved without cross-party support.[24]

Perhaps the most important criticism of the bill was that there was already plenty of legislation for dealing with intimidating statements, slurs and acts. The main innovation of the law was to specifically target football fans, and in the process attempt to demonise them. In its first few months of operation, polls recorded considerable public support for the bill, but over the next few years this was eroded by the way in which it was policed. Police Scotland's strategy was primarily technological, relying on video evidence taken by fixed CCTV cameras in the stands, hand-held cameras carried by the police inside and outside the stadium, and body cameras carried by individual officers. Arrests and prosecutions were almost always made after games, with many reports of aggressive morning calls at people's homes. While the police were well aware that the majority of sectarian singing and post-match violence came from an older constituency among the fan bases, they invariably targeted younger working-class fans, especially those in the newly emerging ultra groups who were often raucous but very rarely violent or abusive. The police also increased their use of informers, many of them children, in a style of policing pioneered for infiltrating terrorist and radical environmental groups. Inside the stadiums the police actively withdrew from other forms of interaction with fans, leaving poorly paid and trained stewards to fend for themselves when dealing with any incidents of disorder or trouble. In the first year of its existence there were fewer than 300 arrests and a conviction rate of just over 40 per cent; a number that was never bettered, as reliance on police interpretations of what was and was not sectarian collapsed in court.

Fans Against Criminalisation was formed in 2011 to challenge police behaviour and call for the repeal of the bill. It attracted considerable support across Scottish football, and in 2013 was able to stage a 3,000-strong rally in central Glasgow. Human-rights lawyers and free-speech advocates who had already decried the bill for its illiberalism were appalled by the police's decision to use the law to arrest a man wearing a Free Palestine T-shirt at a game at Tynecastle. Meanwhile, the level of sectarianism in Scottish football remained precisely where it had been, and the already brittle relationship between the police and football fans had entirely disintegrated. Once the SNP had lost its majority in Holyrood at the 2015 election, the way was open for the bill to be repealed, and in 2018, despite a rearguard action from the SNP, the rest of the parties in the Scottish Parliament voted to do so. The standing of Police Scotland with football fans, already low, fell even further when crowd mismanagement at an Old Firm game at Celtic Park in autumn 2018 created a crush at the turnstiles so bad that five people were injured, while others only escaped by climbing high fences. A review of the policing of Scottish football was immediately commissioned from Britain's most senior police officer covering football, Deputy Chief Constable Mark Roberts, who quickly concluded that it was 'not fit for purpose'. In a consultation process designed to rebuild trust with football fans, Police Scotland asked whether they would like their officers to communicate with them more, but by now large majorities preferred them to just keep their counsel.

If the SNP's experiment with punitive legislation and Police Scotland's intrusive surveillance strategies in Scottish football offered a dystopian version of the nation, there was, alongside this, a utopian moment too. In 2012 the impossible happened: Rangers FC were declared bankrupt. It had been a long time coming. In 2009 the club announced that it owed the banks £18 million and HMRC almost £50 million for monies not paid, indeed illegally evaded, by paying players, in lieu of wages, in the form of offshore loans that would never be called in. Celtic, the bigger clubs and the League were all happy for the new Rangers that emerged from this process to carry on in the Scottish Premier League as if nothing had happened, maintaining the value of their TV rights. The rest of Scottish football, pressured especially by fans of smaller clubs, thought this kind of financial skullduggery should be punished and that Rangers should go down to the bottom of the league pyramid. Clubs that were almost entirely dependent on match-day income, given how pitiful the media income of the lower leagues had become, had no choice but to do their fans' bidding.

For a short period, a window was opened on what the Scottish game might look like without the suffocating presence of the Old Firm duopoly. In the first place, the presence of Rangers in the lower leagues, a grand odyssey of public humiliation, brought television coverage, huge attendances and welcome income to small-town Scottish football, as the club made their way back up from the fourth level to the Scottish Premier League. Even when they did return, they had been sufficiently weakened financially that the old order was not really re-established for a decade. Of course, in their absence, Celtic won the league at a canter, but this interregnum also made space for some of the bigger clubs to play in Europe and actually win something at home. The Scottish Cup was won by Hearts and Inverness Caledonian Thistle, by Hibernian for the first time in 114 years and St Johnstone for the first time ever in 2014, a feat exceeded in an extraordinary season in 2021 in which they won the Scottish Cup and the League Cup. Nonetheless, by 2016 Rangers had crawled their way back into the Scottish Premier

League, and with the arrival of Steven Gerrard as coach in 2018 began to look like serious contenders for the league title again. In 2021 they would, under Gerrard, win the title, and the stranglehold of the Old Firm was resumed.

In their absence another kind of Scottish football could breathe, and the now majority SNP Scottish government called a referendum on Scottish independence for September 2014. The campaign that followed was remarkable not so much for the outcome, but for the degree to which it politicised and mobilised Scottish civil society. On both sides of the argument a huge range of short-lived organisations emerged, rooted in locations and staffed by social groups normally absent from Scotland's political conversation. Football was no different. For most of its history, Scottish football kept formal politics at one remove. Of course, unionism was an important pillar of Rangers' tradition, and Scottish Conservatives could regularly be found on their board. Key figures from the Scottish Labour movement likewise sat on the board of Celtic, but neither group had sought to use the clubs in a directly political fashion. Scots Tory businessmen owned and ran many clubs in a primarily custodial fashion, while their fans, though not a homogeneous mass, were overwhelmingly working-class Labour voters who left their politics outside the gates. Scottish nationalists had despaired of the 'ninety minute patriots' that supported the national team with fervour and the constitutional status quo with apathy. The first sign of change was the formation of the Green Brigade, a European-style ultra group created by a core of young socialist and republican Celtic fans in 2006.[25] The group primarily coalesced around a dissatisfaction with the sanitised quality of support in the now much-enlarged but all-seater Celtic Park, and as promised the Green Brigade brought non-stop noise, banners and pyrotechnics. They also brought a new kind of politics, protesting in 2010 over the compulsory placing of Remembrance Day poppies on Celtic shirts, as well as founding and staffing a Celtic fans food bank. Then the revolt against

Rangers, and the emergence of Fans Against Criminalisation, confirmed that there was more of an appetite for politics in Scottish football than previously thought. The independence referendum ignited this tinder.

The more top-down, pro-union Better Together campaign drew on the support of many former Scottish football stars and coaches. Indeed, it was able to announce a first XI and substitutes bench that included Jim Leighton, David Moyes, Alan Hansen and Paddy Crerand, and both Rangers legends, like Barry Ferguson and Ally McCoist, and their Celtic peers, like Bertie Auld and Davie Provan. Anas Sarwar, Scottish Labour's deputy leader, argued: 'These men have played for the national team, have led for Scotland and are now saying what they believe is best for Scotland.'[26] Independence campaigners counted fewer footballing luminaries among their support – Steve Archibald and Michael Stewart being rare exceptions – but they were able to draw on the spontaneous emergence of supporters' groups for independence. In an act repeated many times over in Scottish football in 2014, about a thousand Celtic fans in the away end at Dundee United held up 'Yes!' placards in the eighteenth minute, a symbolic nod to the date of the vote on 18 September. By the same token, Rangers ultras, the Union Bears, unfurled a huge 'Vote No' banner at Ibrox. The campaign, especially in its final phases, aroused a level of emotion and on occasion animosity that had hitherto been absent from Scottish politics, though not, it should be said, from Scottish football. The venerable Archie Macpherson, campaigning for Better Together, faced a torrent of abuse in person and online: 'I was a commentator for umpteen Old Firm games and there was a level of vitriol associated with that, but nothing like what I got after the speech I made.'[27] Three members of Hearts Fans for Independence, handing out leaflets before a home game with Falkirk, were attacked by political opponents. A member of the Facebook group Heart of Midlothian Fans Against Scottish Independence posted: 'Well what did we say about 2 weeks ago about the yessers hassling the public outside Tynecastle?? We said it would end in trouble and it certainly did for them today … the No voters are starting to get pissed off with it.'[28]

Quite how much difference all this made to the result – a 55–45 victory for the No campaign – is hard to gauge.[29] Perhaps the example of Scottish football's incapacity to thrive as an independent entity in a global world helped bolster the No campaign's economic case against independence. Perhaps the weight of older football legends' support for the union carried some weight, but the impact of club-level identities and campaigns seems much more ambiguous. In a post-referendum survey, a majority of fans at Celtic, Kilmarnock, Motherwell, Partick Thistle and Rangers were in the Yes camp. A result one would expect at Celtic, but less so in Labour strongholds like Kilmarnock and not at all at Rangers, where so much unionist energy had been on display. Most supporters of Aberdeen, Dundee United, Hearts, Hibernian, Inverness, Ross County, St Johnstone and St Mirren were in the No camp, and again no surprises there by tradition for Hearts or Dundee, but Hibernian and Dundee United (given their Irish immigrant roots and republican leanings) might well have been expected to shift towards Yes. Looking at the voting patterns by the local areas in which the clubs are based suggested that football fans, broadly speaking, were voting like the rest of their neighbourhoods. Rangers fans might support a club with a strong unionist tradition, but at the ballot box they were Glaswegians rather than Gers. By the same token Hibs fans appeared to give less weight to their Irish antipathy to the union, and more to Edinburgh's support for it.

Despite the deep shade cast by the Old Firm, and in the absence of meaningful reforms, smaller gains are being made elsewhere.[30] Ann Budge, a businesswoman who made her money in IT, rescued Hearts from bankruptcy and brought a hitherto rare style of no-bullshit, high-competency club management to Scotland. Having stabilised the club, she is in the process of passing her shares to the supporters' trust and Hearts into fan ownership. Similar moments of financial crisis have opened the way for supporter ownership across Scottish football: notably Premier League perennials Motherwell, but also smaller clubs like Annan, Clyde Greenock Morton, Partick Thistle, St Mirren and Stirling Albion. The decision of many clubs to leave the hitherto entirely independent Junior football leagues and join the SFA's official pyramid was lamented by many, but it opened the door to a whole host of ambitious clubs like Edinburgh City, Kelty Hearts, Spartans, Bonnyrigg Rose and Cove Rangers, who have all invigorated the lower leagues, and Spartans have become a model of what a community-orientated football club can achieve in an area of high deprivation.

Cyprus aside, attendance at professional and amateur football remained, per capita, the highest in Europe. As with other sectors, the mainstream football press has been squeezed by the digital era, but a distinctive Scottish football conversation persists. *Off the Ball*, BBC Radio Scotland's iconoclastic and curmudgeonly football chat show, was approaching its silver jubilee and remained unmatched for its capacity to find the curious and the incredible in the game. *Nutmeg* magazine demonstrated the depth and quality of Scottish football writing, albeit with a bias towards nostalgia. *A View from the Terrace*, first aired on the BBC in 2018, brought refreshingly new voices and stories from every tiny corner of Scotland's football culture: a celebration of Gala Fairydean Rovers' remarkable brutalist concrete stand, the only listed building in Scottish football; the vivacious pre-teen ultras transforming the atmosphere at sleepy Dumbarton; and not least the news that Uri Geller, the spoon-bending Israeli illusionist, had bought tiny, uninhabited Lamb Island in the Firth of Forth, and on declaring it a sovereign micro nation had made mainland amateur side North Berwick FC – now nicknamed the Lambies – its national football team.[31] Small is beautiful, but in the meantime the level of inequality in global and Scottish football continues to rise inexorably; by 2022–23, Celtic and Rangers' combined income was over £200 million, individually less than any side in the English Premier League, but at home more than the rest of the Scottish Premier League put together. And Scotland was stuck with them.

7.

Which England Will Turn Up?

English Nationalism and the 2018 World Cup

In the wake of England's humiliating exit from Euro 2016 there was a changing of the guard. England manager Roy Hodgson tendered his resignation, and Greg Dyke, the chair of the FA, announced that he would be stepping down early. Their replacements did not, however, suggest a change of regime. Dyke, a Labour-supporting TV executive, was exchanged for Greg Clarke, previously CEO of Cable and Wireless, chair of the English Football League and Leicester City, who offered, above all, impeccable insider status. As to the manager, there was to be no reversion to foreign experiments like Sven-Göran Eriksson or Fabio Capello. The FA toyed with Eddie Howe and Steve Bruce, but opted for the most 'proper football man' they could find in England: Sam Allardyce. His public persona 'Big Sam' was all bluff, straight-talking Lancashire, a man from the rougher, tougher school of the pre-Premier League era. He had made his reputation with the most unglamorous of clubs – Bolton Wanderers – whom he had kept in the Premier League for a decade, before relatively unsuccessful spells with Newcastle, Blackburn and West Ham. By this time he had acquired a reputation for not only his antediluvian manner, but the style of football his teams played. West Ham fans, so infuriated by the team's dour and defensive quality, staged a protest during an away game at West Bromwich Albion, unveiling a banner that read: 'Fat Sam Out, killing WHU'. By the same token, José Mourinho claimed his teams played 'football from the nineteenth century'.[1] In fact, Allardyce was more thoughtful than he allowed himself to appear. In his time at Bolton he got the best out of flamboyant talents like the Nigerian Jay-Jay Okocha, and he was a pioneer in the use of data when most coaches were dismissive of what they saw as an irrelevant fad. One suspects that the FA weren't appointing him on the strength of either his record or his thinking, but as someone they thought looked like 'a real England manager'. What they got from his 67-day tenure was something else entirely.

Journalists from the *Daily Telegraph*, posing as Far Eastern football investors, invited Allardyce to a Chinese restaurant for an exploratory conversation and a meal, which, from the grainy video they would go on to release, was washed down with a great deal of alcohol.[2] The evidence is actually very poor, but football Twitter managed to convince itself that Allardyce had ordered a pint of white wine. Either way, his voice and demeanour suggests he was, at the very least, well-oiled. Certainly, it made for a loose tongue as he mocked Roy Hodgson's lisp, told his hosts that Hodgson's assistant Gary Neville just needed to 'sit down and shut up', and berated the FA over their redevelopment of Wembley. His career could have survived such indiscretions, but it was the conversation concerning third-party ownership of players that destroyed him. His musings, hovering in a grey area between describing the world of transfers and agents as it actually was and actively proffering advice on how to circumvent the 'ridiculous' FA and FIFA rules that regulated them, proved fatal. That he was being offered £400,000 for a few masterclasses on the topic in Singapore, albeit a gig he would have to 'run past the powers that be', when he was already on a £3.5 million annual salary, made him appear both shifty and greedy. The FA initially demurred, but in a flash he was gone. The following day the England players received post-cards from Allardyce celebrating their recent victory over Slovakia: 'Well done! Our journey has begun.'

Allardyce's replacement was Gareth Southgate, if not his polar opposite then certainly a very different kind of England manager. His playing credentials, including fifty-seven caps for England, were unimpeachable, but his coaching career and demeanour underwhelmed the press. Barney Ronay in the *Guardian* thought, 'So here we are. No bells will be rung, no flags fluttered ... Instead Southgate becomes England's 14th proper manager to a kind of anti-fanfare, a shared yawn of indifference.'[3] Southgate had served three years as manager at Middlesbrough before they were relegated, and then moved into the England set-up, coaching the under-21s. Despite some success there, and a serious track record of developing and nurturing young players, he was also bearded, softly spoken, thoughtful and from a middle-class background. For some he was clearly too nice, too soft, too middle England – though not too nice to drop an ageing Wayne Rooney before the World Cup – and he still bore the scars and the frailties of missing a penalty in England's defeat by Germany in the semi-finals of Euro 96. Ultimately, these things would be his strengths rather than weaknesses.

England qualified for the 2018 World Cup in Russia at a canter, but on the eve of the tournament expectations and engagement appeared lower than ever. Earlier in the year two Russian agents had poisoned Sergei Skripal, an exiled opponent of President Putin, in Salisbury. Prime Minister Theresa May had made it clear that neither the government nor the royal family would attend the tournament. Widespread fears about Russia's hosting and policing of the tournament meant that just a few thousand England fans took up the country's official ticket allocation, while at home many noted the absence of St George flags and other regalia on the nation's houses and cars.

The *Week* thought that 'England are a third-tier football nation, and to that end they should be congratulated on qualifying for the World Cup'.[4] Neither they nor anyone else gave the team much of chance, and many assumed that the usual England – an underperforming team and a disruptive, xenophobic following – would show up and depart early. FIFA were certainly worried enough about the allegiances of parts of the England crowd to warn them forcefully that pro-Brexit chants at the 2018 World Cup would be punished. In the end, a very different football nation showed up.

Prior to the tournament, Southgate made two significant breaks with tradition. First, he gave the squad a week's holiday before assembling for the tournament, where in the past they had been either dragooned into a training camp or had their passports confiscated to ensure no one disappeared for too much of a good time. Second, he invited the press to meet the players, giving journalists unfettered access to the team over a long afternoon of intimate conversation. The country began to warm to a squad that was, unlike their recent predecessors, open and accessible. Millionaires all, their life stories still spoke to some of their generation's difficulties. The country became familiar with Dele Alli's story of absent and alcohol-dependent parents. Danny Rose described his struggle with depression and Southgate's role in helping him out, saying, 'England has been my salvation and I can't thank the manager and the medical staff enough.'[5] Jamie Vardy's brushes with the law and his long journey, despite his talent, to the Premier League from the lower leagues became widely known. These were not inconsequential matters in England, where high levels of economic inequality had driven equally high levels of drug dependency and mental-health issues, especially among the young, and where the almost complete collapse of social mobility had seen the stifling and squandering of many of their peers' talents.

The public also warmed to Southgate himself. His claim that 'we're a team with our diversity and our youth that represent modern England' struck a powerful chord with many. The average age of the squad was just twenty-six (the third-youngest at the tournament), and eleven of the twenty-three players were Black or of mixed heritage, not to mention the Irish roots of Harry Kane and Declan Rice. There was something too about Southgate's tone: his clear-eyed view of what the team might achieve, his knowledge and respect for his opponents, and a notable humility. Small beer, perhaps, but it was a way of thinking and speaking that stood in sharp opposition to the bombastic tones of the nation's Brexiteers and the furious post-referendum debate that had engulfed the nation.

An equally popular, if unlikely dimension to Southgate's presence was his waistcoat. Part of a three-piece navy suit supplied by sponsors Marks & Spencer, it gave him an air that was both dapper and restrained, conservative yet a little iconoclastic. Certainly, it was a look that had never been seen on an England touchline. Searches for and sales of waistcoats on the internet exploded. The final ingredient required to ignite England's new love affair with its national team was for it to start winning games. England duly obliged with victories over Tunisia and Panama, enough to get them out of the group stage. In the round of sixteen England faced Colombia, and the game went to penalties. England's dismal record in these shoot-outs and Southgate's own tragic miss in Euro 96 hung heavily over the moment, but this England held their nerve and won. Southgate's delight in victory was matched by his compassionate embrace of Mateus Uribe, the unfortunate Colombian player who had missed his penalty.

In every round of post-match interviews Southgate now caught and energised the changing mood of the country. 'We are enjoying the journey. Everything we've done has been based on enjoyment.'[6] Blessed by a long, glorious, endless summer, the English football nation reassembled in unprecedented numbers, in public spaces and parks, stadiums, gardens and streets. The song 'Football's Coming Home' underwent a revival, chanted at every game and fan park. It was streamed and downloaded more than 2.5 million times, making it number one in the UK's Big Top 40 chart; but its currency was multiplied a thousand times over through hashtags and memes on social media that featured, inter alia, Vladimir Putin playing the song at a grand piano, and Colin Firth as King George VI finally blurting it out in an edited scene from the film *The King's Speech*.[7] The oleaginous Tory MP Rachel Maclean asked Theresa May: 'Mr Speaker, after last night I'm sure I don't need to ask the Prime Minister. Does she believe that football is coming home?' A second wave of memes with the hashtag GarethSouthgateWould depicted him as a paragon of kindness, empathy and self-effacement who would 'Pay an equal share of the restaurant bill, even though he didn't have a starter and only drank the tap water'.[8] In a real marker of his compassion, Southgate allowed midfielder Fabian Delph to go home in the middle of the tournament and attend the birth of his third child. He returned to the squad to let them know how the temperature at home was rising: 'Going back was incredible. The support was absolutely amazing. Even people who are not into football, stopping me, shouting and telling me "Make sure you bring it home." It was crazy, overwhelming.'[9] At Nottingham's Theatre Royal the final lifeboat scenes from *Titanic: The Musical* were interrupted by the cries of 'Yes!' from two women in the front row watching England's penalty shoot-out with Colombia on their mobile phones.[10]

Some of the celebrations that accompanied England's 2–0 quarter-final victory over Sweden showed a more troubling side. At the final whistle a large group of fans invaded IKEA in Stratford, riotously bouncing on the store's beds and sofas. Borough Market was brought to a halt by heaving crowds, and an ambulance was destroyed when fans climbed on its roof. One man in central London leapt off the top of a bus and onto the roof of a bus shelter, which promptly collapsed. Yet, just for once, a pacific and progressive England remained in the majority. The huge and peaceable crowds at the country's fan parks, young and diverse, looked much like the team. British Future's survey found that three-quarters of the country thought the team 'a symbol of England that belongs to people of every race and ethnic background', way ahead of any other totem of the nation.[11] Even the St George flag, almost invisible before the tournament began, was everywhere. Sunny Hundal wrote, 'There were mosques draped with the England flag. There were Hindu mothers and young Muslim boys doing faux-prayers in front of the TV. We shared memes, laughs and songs of "it's coming home" in countless multicultural settings. We showed that pride in England can be expressed in lots of different ways. We even got Harry Kane into a Bollywood song!'[12] In Russia the small but now growing band of England fans had dropped 'Rule, Britannia!' in favour of Earth, Wind & Fire's 'September', singing 'Woah, England are in Russia/Woah, drinking all the vodka/Woah, England's going all the way!' Perhaps more unusual, though, was the sound of the England crowd, not previously noted for its ease with sexual ambiguity, singing Atomic Kitten's 'Whole Again': 'Southgate, you're the one/You still turn me on/Football's coming home again.'

For a few idyllic days in July 2018 this other version of England dreamt and prepared to party. One survey conducted by an HR consultancy revealed that 'an England football game is the single biggest factor affecting absenteeism and lateness across the widest number and spread of industries', and business braced itself for the millions that were planning to pull a sickie the day after the semi-final against Croatia.[13] Southgate, once again catching the mood of the nation, said, 'We've spoken to the players about writing their own stories. Tonight they showed they don't have to conform to what's gone before. They have created their own history, and I don't want to go home yet.'[14]

When Kieran Trippier rifled a free kick into the opponent's net after just five minutes the dream looked like it might actually be for real, but Croatia – cannier and unyielding – woke them from their reveries with a second-half equaliser and an extra-time winner. Southgate station on the Piccadilly Line in North London stood proxy for the nation's reaction. Its signage and its roundels now read 'Gareth Southgate', and written on a notice board by the ticket barrier: 'Thanks Gareth for the incredible journey. Southgate is yours.' One woman made a pilgrimage to the station and said, 'I have friends who go mad if I even mention the word football and this year they've been sitting there watching it! The public have proper reconnected their love of football, and it's only because of this man!'[15]

Part II

Sick as a Parrot

Football in the Time of Covid, 2020–21

8.

From Lockdown to Meltdown

Football, Covid and the Mental-Health Crisis

As late as mid-February 2020, and despite the rigid lockdown in China, the overloaded hospitals of Italy and the advice of epidemiologists, most of Britain, football included, was not taking the coronavirus seriously. Prime Minister Boris Johnson was too busy to attend the Cabinet's emergency planning committee and Tottenham's Dele Alli was making Snapchat videos that ridiculed a mask-wearing man at an airport.[1] A fortnight later, the mood was changing. Sports organisations around the world began to announce the cancellation of their schedules, the Premier League banned pre-match handshakes and asked everyone to wash their hands for twenty seconds. Matters came to a head in the second week of March when Liverpool played Atlético Madrid in a Champions League tie at Anfield. Three thousand Atlético fans were due to travel from a city that was in partial lockdown, where Covid case rates were soaring and schools had already been closed. The day before the game, the Prime Minister, still in denial about the scale of risk the country was facing, suggested that the nation should be 'taking it on the chin … allowing the disease, as it were, to move through the population'. The match certainly facilitated that. Liverpool would lose the game 3–2 in extra time, and the UK's preliminary public inquiry into the pandemic would later conclude that the event caused thirty-seven preventable deaths.[2] A fortnight before, Arsenal had hosted Greek champions Olympiacos, whose owner Evangelos Marinakis, it transpired, had attended the game while infected. The day after the Liverpool game, Arsenal's head coach Mikel Arteta tested positive, the club went into lockdown and their game against Brighton was postponed. While the UK government dithered over whether to enforce a national lockdown, the Premier League, the Football League and the FA acted, announcing on 13 March that all football would be cancelled until at least late April. It would take the government another ten days to follow the same logic and call a national lockdown.

Football, like almost everything else, ground to a halt. Through the long weeks of spring 2020, the football nation struggled without its fix. Some dug out their old Subbuteo sets, for others *FIFA* and *Football Manager* remained a solace. One enthusiast recalled, '*Football Manager* became a beacon. It helped to quiet and settle my mind, not only when I was playing it but, more importantly, when I wasn't … when my mind would start to go to dark places.'[3] After their match with Cardiff City was postponed indefinitely, Leeds United broadcast a live stream of a digital duplicate of the fixture on *FIFA 20*. It finished 3–3. One fan, riffing on the usual chant 'All Leeds aren't we', tweeted: 'All avatars aren't we.'[4] Some took to watching old games on YouTube and organised watchalongs, which were complemented by blogging and tweeting as if they were live. Broadcasters and streamers filled the schedule with whatever football content they still had to offer. The European Championship, scheduled for June, was cancelled. Wales relived Euro 2016 as BBC Wales broadcast all of their games. England sat down to Euro 96 and the 1966 World Cup final, twice, wrapping the nation in the deep cocoon of football nostalgia. Players took to their gardens and smartphones. Clips of improvised training methods – like a young goalkeeper saving his own shots as they rebounded off the garden wall, and the kid who recreated a Paul Gascoigne free kick and celebration – went viral; but at every level people struggled without the routine, release and camaraderie the game had provided.

Politicians aside, no group were so closely policed for their fidelity to lockdown rules as football players and coaches, or reminded so often of their status as 'role models'. Consequently, over the next fifteen months, football players, and even coaches, were found to have persistently broken Covid regulations, though, in fact, probably no more than much of the population, and certainly less than the staff at 10 Downing Street. Early offenders included: Manchester City's Kyle Walker, caught hosting two sex workers at his home; Jack Grealish, who, just hours after tweeting out advice to stay home, was photographed in Birmingham city centre having crashed his car. At Spurs, José Mourinho was found holding a personal training session with Tanguy Ndombele, while Serge Aurier was repeatedly found to be breaking the rules as he sat for another haircut and posted the results to Instagram, although he pleaded that both he and his barber had tested negative. Over the summer of 2020, Paul Scholes was spoken to by the police for throwing a party for his son's birthday, five-a-side tournament and all.[5] It was a scene reprised in other households over the Christmas holidays, when Manchester City's Benjamin Mendy, West Ham's Manuel Lanzini and Spurs' Erik Lamela, Giovani Lo Celso and Sergio Reguilón were all also censured for throwing or attending parties.

Through the whole pandemic, as people searched for places to exercise, the inequality of access to green space and sports facilities was made plain; a fact made starker by the early return of middle-class pursuits like golf and tennis after the first national lockdown, and the much slower and more restricted return of grassroots football. Unable to bear it, youths took to midnight football, breaking Covid regulations to scale the fences of caged football pitches, playing five-a-side through the night.

In Glasgow this happened on an industrial scale, with players cutting fences and burning netting to access a multi-pitch complex, where an entire tournament featuring fifty teams took place.[6] Golf courses offered alternative and more secluded venues, and reports leaked out of teenagers playing on the greens of Musselburgh Links in May 2020, and a full eleven-a-side game staged at Belfairs golf course in Essex the following February.[7] With the partial lifting of lockdown in June 2020, and the return of the Premier League to empty stadiums, socially distanced drinking and communal watching of football became an option, but not for Leicester City fans, where worryingly high infection rates kept the city in lockdown as the rules in surrounding areas were relaxed. Consequently, a busload of Leicester fans went and watched the team in a pub in Nottingham, only to give themselves away when Jamie Vardy scored his hundredth goal for the club and the standard chant of 'Jamie Vardy's having a party!' alerted the neighbours. Similar unrestrained exuberance was the downfall of the landlord of a pub in Dewsbury where fans had illegally gathered to watch Leeds versus Crawley Town.[8] Towards the end of the long winter lockdown of 2020–21, players' restraint eventually snapped, and in February and March 2021 dozens of reports described illicit small-sided games played at shuttered sport centres, in Edinburgh, Glasgow, Leeds, London, Nottingham and Manchester.[9]

In retrospect it is amazing that there were actually so few incidents like this, and, the governing class aside, how closely the vast majority of the country, football players included, followed the rules. In fact, football appeared not only as law-abiding, but truly community-minded. Clubs, supporter groups and many players became involved in networks of mutual help that sprang up to support the isolated, the hungry and the disabled. Donations from supporter-led food-bank collections at games were replaced by donations from the clubs themselves, and by generous gifts from whole squads and individual players. Players and coaches, from Jürgen Klopp to Carlo Ancelotti, volunteered to call elderly and vulnerable season-ticket holders at home. Some, like Norwich goalkeeper Tim Krul, took milk and bread on a daily round to people shielding at home. David Moyes volunteered to deliver fruit and veg boxes. Club kitchens prepared food parcels and ready meals for food banks and emergency workers; club vehicles were used to deliver prescriptions and PPE. Kevin De Bruyne and Dele Alli live-streamed their games of *Fortnite* to raise money for charities. As medications became available, stadiums were used for mass testing and then mass vaccination.

Most remarkable of all was the contribution of 23-year-old Manchester United striker Marcus Rashford, whose brilliantly executed social-media campaign on child hunger forced the government to change policy and offer financial support to those families normally relying on free school meals. Rashford had long-established credentials in this realm, generously supporting the Homeless World Cup, working with FareShare to increase donations to food banks and telling his own stories of childhood hunger in a house where, however hard his mother worked, there sometimes just wasn't enough on the table. When the Tories came for him, he was more than ready. Ben Bradley, MP for Mansfield, tried to school him on the economic implications of feeding kids, only for Rashford to inform him that the current policy of hunger was, in terms of lost educational achievement, an even more expensive option. When Natalie Elphicke, MP for Dover, tweeted 'Rashford should have spent more time perfecting his game and less time playing politics', Rashford responded in the *Spectator*: 'Disappointingly for some, the "stick to football" advice doesn't cut it where I'm from. I'd be doing [my] community and my family a disservice if I did not use my platform to speak on behalf of the millions whose voices are not being heard.'[10] Later it would transpire that Elphicke herself had not been sticking to politics and had acquired a very lucrative second job.[11]

Football, in the language of Jonathan Van-Tam, Deputy Chief Medical Officer, also provided metaphors of hope. Describing the development of the Pfizer vaccine at a Downing Street press conference in the autumn of 2020, Dr Van-Tam thought 'this is like getting to the end of the play-off final. It's gone to penalties, the first player goes up and scores the goal. You haven't won the cup yet, but what it does, it tells you that the goalkeeper can be beaten.' The wider vaccine rollout that began later that year was going to change the narrative of the game: 'It's clear in the first half, the away team gave us an absolute battering, and what we've done now is it's the 70th minute, they got a goal, and in the 70th minute we've now got an equaliser. OK, we've got to hold our nerve now, see if we can get another goal and nick it.'[12]

Football was certainly able to reflect the best of the nation's response to the pandemic – generous, communitarian and hopeful – but the reality of those months for many was a terrible decline in their mental health, and football reflected this too. In fact, football had been tracking the wider mental-health crisis among the young in Britain for a decade before Covid. In keeping with the US, Canada and Scandinavia, Britain's Generation Z, born in the late 1990s and becoming teenagers around 2010, had experienced sharp increases in their rates of anxiety, depression, self-harm, loneliness, use of mental-health services and suicide. They were also the first generation to go through puberty in a truly digital world with almost universal access to smartphones and social media. Jonathan Haidt, the social psychologist, has argued that this generation were peculiarly ill-equipped to cope with this digital deluge, as they also experienced more restricted childhoods than their predecessors.[13] In societies where levels of trust were in decline, parents increasingly perceived the world in terms of risks and dangers, and were prone to moral panics about child safety. Consequently, these children experienced much less unsupervised play, and even then at a much later age, diminishing their sense of a secure and developing self. The shift to phone-based childhoods has brought in its wake widespread sleep deprivation, a catastrophic fragmentation of attention spans and, given the nature of social-media algorithms, deeply addictive behaviour patterns. When one adds to this, first, the rising levels of social inequality in these societies, long linked with rising rates of mental-health conditions, and, second, the collapse of mental-health services for young people in the UK under successive Conservative governments, then it is hardly surprising that Generation Z have experienced a mental-health crisis of unprecedented scale, and that Covid would make it demonstrably worse.

For the population as a whole, 10 per cent were experiencing mental-health problems prior to the pandemic, a figure that almost doubled over the first lockdown between March and June 2020, and had reached 23 per cent by March 2021. The end of the pandemic saw rates fall back to 16 per cent, but left the nation considerably more troubled than it had been before.[14] The story for the young was even worse. The NHS's main survey of young people's mental health found that in 2017, 12 per cent of children aged eight to sixteen had a mental illness in 2017, but by 2022 it was up to 20 per cent, and for seventeen- to nineteen-year-olds 23 per cent.[15] Across the world, football players' mental health went the same way. Surveys by the international player union FIFPRO in late 2019 found that 11 per cent of women players and 6 per cent of men were reporting symptoms of depression alone, while a similar survey conducted during the first month of the global lockdowns in 2020 saw those rates climb to 22 and 13 per cent, while almost one in five of both genders reported a state of severe anxiety.[16]

In October 2020, eighteen-year-old Jeremy Wisten was found hanged in his sister's bedroom. A year earlier he had been released by Manchester City's academy and, unable to find another club that would take him on, had withdrawn from the game and entered a depression so deep that it would see him take his own life.[17] The isolation and anxiety of the lockdowns had, no doubt, made his mental health even worse, but it is clear that football, in many ways, was a perfect environment for nurturing depression and anxiety, and a very poor one for dealing with it. Linguistically, at any rate, football culture has treated mental health as a comedic affliction, from the Scottish song 'Fitba Crazy' (written in 1900 but recorded innumerable times since) to the terrace chants of 'Let's go fucking mental!' It has celebrated its loose cannons, wild men and nutters, but it has rarely enquired into their wellbeing. Former England captain Tony Adams broke the silence in English football in his 1998 autobiography *Addicted*, which laid bare his struggle with alcoholism. In 2009 the suicide of Robert Enke, Germany's leading goalkeeper, shocked the whole of European football, but it would take events closer to home to truly shake the British game: the suicide of Gary Speed, manager of Wales, in 2011; and that of Josh Lyons in 2013. Speed was a victim of terrible depressions. Lyons never recovered from being released by Spurs at sixteen, and went on to struggle at Fulham and Crawley Town before walking in front of a train in 2013. That year, Clarke Carlisle, then with Northampton Town and chairman of the PFA, fronted the BBC documentary *Football's Suicide Secret*, revealing his and other players' deep struggles with depression and attempted suicide.[18] The issue was, at last, unignorable. Since then the PFA has taken annual surveys of the state of players' mental health and the results have been consistently troubling. In early 2020, for example, they found that 22 per cent of current or former players polled felt depressed or had considered self-harm. In 2023 they reported that one in five players said they had experienced severe anxiety. In the women's game almost a quarter of female professionals surveyed said that money and contractual issues were causing debilitating stress, while more than 40 per cent said they had experienced some form of online abuse.[19]

Why should mental-health problems be so prevalent among football players, even allowing for their age and the wider incidence of mental ill-health? They are, at least, financially comfortable, many are rich, and a good number are exceptionally wealthy. They appear to be doing something they are both very good at and that, in some sense, they love. Certainly, at the top of the professional game they enjoy a position of high status, basking in the game's reflected glory. All true, but they live the most peculiar and unbalanced lives. Like their peers, they are struggling with problems of sleep deprivation, attention fragmentation and addictive social media, and for those who come through the academy system, the long span of an over-policed, over-surveyed childhood continues into their late teens. The social inequality and struggle for shrinking resources (education, housing, employment) that are dragging down their peers are, in microcosm, even worse in football. Not that they are struggling to pay the rent, but they have to operate in an environment which is intensely competitive: on the pitch, of course, but above all within the dressing room, where every player wants to play but not all can. As one ex-pro put it: 'It's just so ruthless. You're constantly on trial really. If things go well on Saturday, and you play and you win, you just kind of dodge the bullet because it's coming round the corner next Saturday.'[20] In 2023 the PFA reported that almost half of players said that fears around being dropped were impacting their wellbeing. In the lower leagues, where there is far less financial security, these anxieties can take on a life and death dimension for some. One player recalled thinking of his encounter with opponents on the pitch: 'The outcome of it is either: I'm going to eat or you're going to eat, my family is going to eat or your family is going to eat.'[21]

If this kind of brutally competitive environment is difficult to handle for many players, then injuries present an even tougher problem. In 2017 FIFPRO reported that in a survey of professional footballers, mental-health problems became seven times more prevalent among the seriously injured than the physically healthy.[22] As one recently retired player put it, 'No one says, "How are you feeling?" They're not bothered how you're feeling ... being injured you realise you're a commodity really quickly, that they want you for what you can deliver. They don't want you because it's you.'[23] Physical discomforts aside, injury means that a player's normal schedules are disrupted, their social networks broken, while the fear that they might not recover or will have lost their place in the club's pecking order can turn into anxiety, depression and, sometimes, addictions. Manchester City's Fabian Delph, for example, said, 'Not being in the team and only being spoken about in terms of my injury was hard. Being injured massively affected my mental state – self-doubt crept in.'[24]

It is not just coaches and clinicians who relentlessly scrutinise football players, but the media and the public too. While footballers have long had to live with tirades from columnists, depressingly low match ratings in the papers and taunts from both home and away fans in the stadium, social media has made them targets all day, every day. If you are on your phone, and most younger footballers certainly are, it becomes impossible to avoid. X (formerly Twitter), in particular, has become a space in which highly personalised attacks, sometimes racist and sexist, are directed towards players and endlessly circulated on the platform. In 2022 the Alan Turing Institute reported that three-quarters of Premier League players had been abused online.[25] Marcus Rashford, who received much more than his fair share of this bile, tweeted back to a fan site that pointed this out: 'I appreciate your support! It is abuse and has been for months. Enough is enough.'[26] Of course, for the trolls and the cruel it has not been enough at all.

Players are coping with all of this while fulfilling a peculiarly demanding and disorientating work schedule. At first glance a couple of games a week and a few training sessions might not seem too much. Even allowing for other club work, and for most a daily trip to their personal gym, it doesn't appear too tough a timetable. However, the demands of both games and training are now so intense, and the season so long, that even this rate of activity is impacting on players' health and resilience. Above all, it is the highs and lows of the schedule that really bite. Most players describe just how hard it is, given the sense of anticipation, to sleep well before a game; and, given the euphoria or despair that the game can bring, how hard it is to sleep afterwards. Consequently, the use of sleeping pills is rife in professional football, and players like Dele Alli and Ryan Cresswell have revealed how dangerously addicted they had become to them as a way of regulating these intense fluctuations.[27] One might think that the collegiality of the dressing room would provide refuge from this, but some players experience it as a bull pit. Football banter – the exchange of jokes and put-downs, pranks and piss-taking – is assumed to be the essential lubricant of social interaction among players; and sometimes it is. However, it is equally clear that this discourse is deeply hierarchical and bound to other group dynamics: older players asserting their authority over younger players, 'in' groups excluding 'out' groups, rivals attempting to undermine each other. In most workplaces this kind of behaviour would now be considered bullying, and increasingly players are recognising that. A PFA survey of players in the Premier League and EFL found that 12 per cent reported bullying during their career, and 5 per cent reported suicidal thoughts as a consequence. Rising Baller, a charity working with young footballers, reported in their 'Next Wave' survey that '73% of players believe there is bullying between players'.[28]

In the late 2010s a new generation of prominent players began to make their own mental-health struggles public. In 2017, Aaron Lennon, then at Everton, revealed that he had been picked up on the verge of a dual carriageway by police in Salford and was then sectioned. In 2018, Danny Rose spoke with great eloquence about how a damaged knee, which had kept him out of the Tottenham squad for months, led to a terrible depression, much worse than the original injury. In the years since the pandemic, former West Bromwich Albion and Burnley player

Steven Reid recalled that he had experienced serious panic attacks in the middle of Premier League games. Marvin Sordell revealed that he had attempted suicide when he was at Bolton Wanderers, while former Tottenham centre-back Steven Caulker has told his story of a career dominated by gambling and alcohol addictions.[29] Yet for all this openness, it was clear that these players really were just the tip of an iceberg, and that most players who needed help were neither seeking it nor accepting it. The PFA, for example, found that only a third of male players and a quarter of female players said they would feel comfortable sharing concerns regarding their mental wellbeing with their clubs. West Ham's Michail Antonio, who had fallen out of love with football, was an exception: 'I started therapy because I was really struggling ... and how I grew up, it was never a thing, I thought therapy was for crazy people. But therapy changed my life.'[30] For all the talk, it remained the norm in football that mental ill-health was a sign of weakness and therapy was for losers.

Should players be lucky enough to come through their career in one piece emotionally, retirement poses an even bigger set of problems for their mental health. In the first place, their physical health may well be very precarious, which for people who have built their identity around athletic excellence can be a disturbing experience. A study from 2022 estimated that in Britain, 48,000 retired footballers were living with osteoarthritis and were diagnosed with the disease more than ten years earlier than the average man.[31] Despite this, it is still not recognised in law as an industrial injury. A second study – of 300 former players, over 60 per cent of whom had played in the Premier League – found that: more than a third had required surgery in retirement, mainly knee or hip replacement; 30 per cent were taking medications for conditions acquired while playing; 15 per cent were officially registered as disabled; and 3.5 per cent had neuropsychological problems like persistent dizziness and headaches.[32] In the case of Jeff Astle, West Bromwich Albion's star striker of the 1960s, headaches turned to dementia and death in 2002 at the age of fifty-nine. The coroner in his case recorded a verdict of 'death by industrial disease', arguing that a lifetime of heading sodden footballs and experiencing low-level concussions had been the main cause of his demise. In 2020 the same verdict was reached in the case of Hull City defender Alan Jarvis.[33] The FA has promised more research and recommended that heading in training should be sharply reduced. However, documentary evidence makes it clear that the organisation was well aware of the problem as early as 1983, and it now faces a lawsuit by players and families of players who over the last fifty years have suffered concussion injuries, dementia and early deaths.

Medical problems are often compounded by marital and financial problems. Emotional and personal issues, obscured by the demands of the game, become starkly apparent when training and playing stops. Retired players, already struggling with the loss of their central form of identity, find themselves strangers in their own homes, living in relationships that have not been sufficiently tended or have worn thin by the disruptions of a peripatetic life. Extraordinarily, one in three male footballers will get divorced in their first year after retiring from the game; and while the population as a whole has a divorce rate of around 40 per cent, for footballers it climbs, five years after retirement, to 70 per cent.[34] With divorce come expensive legal settlements, which have proved the financial and mental undoing of even the richest of players. Poor financial planning and unsustainable levels of consumption, often made worse by the demands of players' entourages and disastrous investment 'opportunities' finally going to the dogs, tip many more over the edge. The post-2008 property crash profoundly affected a number of players, such as Lee Hendrie, who was bankrupted in 2012 and attempted to take his own life, twice. Other players' finances disintegrated when HMRC decided that film industry investment schemes that many footballers had put millions into, and which had served as a form of tax relief, were actually ineligible.[35]

Players whose lifetime earnings were easily in the tens of millions have found themselves close to penniless. David James, who had a career income of more than £20 million, was reduced to selling off his memorabilia. In 2016 Paul Gascoigne was declared bankrupt for a second time as his already perilous physical and mental health collapsed. Since then, players have earnt considerably bigger salaries, but still the bankruptcies keep coming: Marcus Bent, who had succumbed to alcohol, depression and cocaine abuse, went under in 2019; while Wes Brown, Emile Heskey and Craig Bellamy are just the most high-profile figures who have followed him to the insolvency courts. Of course, some players hold on to their money, others find their way to new and lucrative careers in the media or in coaching, and some have managed to chart a course through higher education or a fresh career – like former Wigan Athletic defender Arjen de Zeeuw, who became a police detective in the Netherlands, or Everton's Thomas Gravesen, who became a professional poker player – but for those that don't have such exotic ambitions to pursue, serious mental-health problems and addictions are a likely alternative.

For those players that do manage to make the transition to coaching, the pressures on their mental health become even greater. Not merely concerned with their own performance, they must deal with an entire squad's worth, balance training and preparation with issues of recruitment, and handle the demands of their board and chief executive, their director of football, their own staff, the media and the club's supporters. At the same time as the complexity of the job has grown, the already tenuous level of job security has dropped. The average tenure of football managers in English football has declined in every decade since the 1950s, and in 2023 across the four leagues it fell as low as fifteen months.[36] When the data for the few coaches who have managed to retain their position for longer – like Guardiola and Klopp – are stripped out, the average tenure is even shorter. In the 2022–23 season alone, Premier League clubs employed, including caretakers, thirty-six coaches over the season. Stressful as this is, it is made worse by the fact that managers' fates are ultimately determined on the pitch by events and decisions beyond their control.

Even if coaches manage to avoid the sack, they are still operating in what has become an increasingly toxic environment. Sean Dyche, when at Burnley, said, 'This is angry Britain … There's a thirst for blame, everyone wants a reason. It's an undertone of life. Demand is instant. Managers' heads are on the block every single week.'[37] And there is no escape: Karl Robinson, then at Oxford United, recalled a Sunday morning walk in the park with his daughter, the day after a defeat. He made the mistake of laughing and relaxing with his child, only for a fan who encountered them to shout, 'You find losing funny, do you?'[38] Even more than players, managers are reluctant to reveal weakness or distress. Many feel it is their responsibility to maintain the mood of the club, and that means staying silent and sucking it up, but their body language often sends a different message. Richie Wellens, coach of Leyton Orient, knew the job had aged and weakened him, not just the usual mid-life problems of hair loss and putting on weight, but his facial hair too: 'I know it sounds mad, but I can't grow a beard anymore … I only get stubble around my mouth, like a goatee.' Worse, he said, 'I clench my jaw a lot at night … and sometimes I wake up in the morning with bleeding gums.'[39] Nathan Jones, when in charge at Stoke City, would bite his nails so severely that his fingers bled. Yet Martin Ling is perhaps the only manager, so far, to have publicly disclosed just how bad the mental-health problems of football coaches can get, revealing the depth of his depression and alcohol dependency while at Torquay and then again at Swindon Town, where he lasted just fifty-six days.[40] He is surely not alone. As with the rest of society, Covid forced football to look its own mental-health pandemic in the eye, but neither have yet truly absorbed the scale of the problem or found a way to manage it.

9.

Taking the Knee

Football and Black Lives Matter

In late May 2020, George Floyd was murdered by a police officer in Minneapolis. Caught on video and globally disseminated, this act ignited a wave of protest against systemic racism and police violence, first in the United States, loosely coordinated by the Black Lives Matter movement, and then across the rest of the world. Despite the Covid lockdowns, crowds gathered in England's bigger cities to join them. Unusually for such a moment of popular rebellion, footballers were present and vocal. Rio Ferdinand went to the protest in London and Aston Villa's captain Tyrone Mings did the same in central Birmingham. In Bristol the demonstration passed the statue of slave trader Edward Colston. It was pulled to the ground, rolled to the harbour and dumped in the water. Leroy Rosenior, who had grown up in Bristol and had played and coached for Bristol City, tweeted: 'I attended COLSTONS (slave owner and killer) primary school in order to receive my "education". Pardon me for enjoying this moment of irony. #BlackLivesMatterUK #BlackLivesMattters [sic].'[1]

A right-wing riposte to the protests coalesced around the nation's cenotaphs and war memorials that were supposedly under threat from a global movement against racism. Football firms and colours were a very visible part of the mix that attended these gatherings, especially in London, Grimsby and Bristol. They were, no doubt, the source of the chant heard in Whitehall 'There's only one Winston Churchill.'[2]

Players responded to the George Floyd protests in training, with Liverpool and Chelsea's squads posting pictures of the team taking the knee. A Zoom meeting of all the Premier League captains in early June was addressed by Watford's Troy Deeney, who argued that a collective response to the moment was required, and that taking the knee – as Colin Kaepernick had done in the NFL during the playing of the American national anthem – was a powerful option. When the Premier League resumed in late June, shirt names were, at the players' insistence, replaced with the words 'Black Lives Matter' and every player and official at every game took the knee. The Football League would do the same at its play-offs. The backlash began immediately when a Burnley supporter arranged for a plane to fly over their game against Manchester City trailing a 'White Lives Matter Burnley!' banner.[3] For the 2020–21 season the Premier League dropped the BLM branding and went with its own in-house slogan 'No Room for Racism'. Players continued to take the knee in the still-empty stadiums. When small crowds were permitted at games in early December 2020, some Millwall fans celebrated by booing their own players. Colchester fans did the same before their game with Grimsby.[4]

That November, when Greg Clarke, chair of the FA, was giving evidence in parliament to the DCMS (Department for Culture, Media and Sport) select committee about the Premier League's potential bailout of English Football League clubs, the conversation turned to matters of ethnicity. Given that when he took the job Clarke had described claims that the FA was institutionally racist as 'fluff', this did not bode well. Addressing the under-representation of British Asians in the game, he mused, 'If you look at top-level football the Afro-Caribbean community is over-represented compared to the south Asian community. If you go to the IT department of the FA there's a lot more south Asians than there are Afro-Caribbeans. They have different career interests.' It didn't help that he referred to Black players as 'coloured', and told an anecdote about how girls were afraid of being hit by the ball. Clarke resigned the following day.[5]

It was exactly these kinds of entrenched, unreflective stereotypes in football that left many Black players wary of tokenism. Crystal Palace's Wilfried Zaha argued, 'It's becoming something that we just do now and that's not enough for me. I'm not going to take the knee, I'm not going to wear Black Lives Matter on the back of my shirt, because it feels like it's a target.'[6] Brentford and Bournemouth's squads decided to stop taking the knee, arguing that the gesture had become ineffective. The England team, however, would continue to take the knee, and when crowds returned to football at the European Championship in June 2021, the symbolic battle over taking the knee in football would resume.

Three years on from the Black Lives Matter protests, Kick It Out announced that they had received a record 1,007 reports of discriminatory behaviour during the 2022–23 season – a 65 per cent increase on the previous year – while reports of online abuse had increased almost threefold and half of all of these incidents were race-related.[7] It was not merely the scale of abuse that was shocking, but also the degree to which individuals felt able to perform racist gestures and chants in public. In late 2022 David Ellis was caught on camera, seemingly untroubled by those around him, making ape gestures during Leeds' game against Aston Villa. At his trial the judge sentenced Ellis to sixteen weeks in prison and suggested: 'You definitely need to find a new hobby, Mr Ellis, you really won't be going to football again.'[8] Mr Ellis might have been absent for the rest of the season, but there were plenty more to take his place. They were certainly out in January and February 2024 when Coventry City's Kasey Palmer was confronted by a man making monkey gestures in his face, and two games were halted as players informed referees of the racist abuse they were receiving: Bradford supporters screamed 'Paki bastard' at AFC Wimbledon's Omar Bugiel, while West Bromwich Albion suspended the season ticket of a fan arrested on suspicion of racially abusing Birmingham's Juninho Bacuna.[9]

Some online abuse came from opposing teams' fans, like that directed at Brentford's Ivan Toney in October 2022 after he scored twice in their win over Brighton. The following day he posted on Twitter: 'I wasn't even going to post this but I woke up angry', alongside a screenshot of the message 'Black Cunt'.[10] The troll was subsequently banned from all football stadiums for three years, but the deterrent didn't seem to be working. Toney was again assailed by racist slurs, this time after Brentford's game against Arsenal in early 2023, as were Newcastle United's Bruno Guimarães and Joe Willock after a 1–0 win over Arsenal. On the other hand, Sheffield United's Mason Holgate, who got himself sent off as the team lost 5–0 to Brighton at home, was abused by his own fans on Instagram. Online racial abuse is not, however, limited to the players. A report from YouGov in 2021 found that a quarter of BAME football fans had been racially abused online in football conversations, and one in ten had been on the end of this kind of treatment multiple times. Among BAME match attenders, who were, one presumes, more deeply embedded in the cesspit of football Twitter, over 40 per cent had been directly racially abused.[11] British Asians appeared to attract special venom. Bhavs Kapoor, an Arsenal fan, said, 'Any tweet that I make talking purely about football, there will always be a quote or a comment regarding race, the fact that I'm Asian, or something like that,' while Davina Pindoria, a Spurs supporter, was blunt: 'Online, you're up against a firing squad of racist abuse.'[12]

All things considered, this should have been favourable territory for the right in British politics, but, the exchanges over the knee at the Euros aside, they have found it very hard to make political capital out of football. The Democratic Football Lads

Alliance has virtually disappeared. The footballing wing of the Cenotaph defence squads that appeared on Remembrance Sundays remained tiny, and were virtually absent from the various anti-migrant and anti-hostel demonstrations orchestrated over the next few years. In the absence of land forces, the far right was forced into an air war – its only significant football intervention in 2022 came when the neo-Nazi clique Patriotic Alternative flew a plane and the banner 'British to be a minority by 2066' over the Etihad while Manchester City and Liverpool drew 2–2.[13] For a man who has an unpleasant opinion on everything, it is noticeable that Nigel Farage, the England team aside, has kept a very low football profile. He told Matt Le Tissier on his online chat show that though cricket was his favourite sport, he had supported Crystal Palace since the early 1970s, but neither he nor Crystal Palace have said anything on the matter since. This might have been a wise strategy for his successor as UKIP leader, Paul Nuttall, who probably did like football a lot – enough for him to repeatedly claim that he was an ex-professional with Tranmere Rovers, until it was discovered that he was actually just in the youth team. His claims that he had lost close friends and family at the Hillsborough disaster were also, once questioned, retracted. UKIP's successors, the Brexit Party and Reform UK, have, apart from standing ex-chair of Southampton Rupert Lowe as a by-election candidate in 2023 and as a successful parliamentary candidate in 2024, been a largely football-free zone.

At the same time, and in record numbers, senior Tories have made their footballing affiliations public; few have been very convincing. Theresa May and Boris Johnson clearly had no interest or connection to football. May in that regard was the most authentic of them all, while Johnson inevitably cosplayed the fan when he needed to. When, after his resignation as Prime Minister, he was seen attending a Covid enquiry in a Grimsby Town FC bobble hat, setting football Twitter alight, it was clear he had no idea what he was wearing. Grimsby Town fans immediately started an online petition asking that he refrain from wearing the hat, which was 'shaming a community'.[14] In a truly surreal performance to celebrate England's victory in the semi-finals of Euro 2020, Jacob Rees-Mogg, then leader of the House of Commons, gave a painful reading of John Barnes's rap from the New Order 1990 World Cup song 'World in Motion'.[15] Liz Truss claimed Norwich City as her team, and as she moved into the premiership told the nation she would 'channel the spirit of Don Revie', without revealing whether that would be the cosy patriarchy of carpet bowls in the Cabinet Office, or systemic use of violence and trickery.[16] Rishi Sunak made sure he was seen in the stands of Southampton, perhaps finding something allegorically appealing about their story of relegation from the Premier League and fight to return that coincided with his own time in office. However, as with so much of his public persona, it was hard to read his presence at St Mary's as that of an actual human being, let alone a seasoned football supporter. Either way, when Sunak watched Southampton beat Plymouth 2–1 in December 2023, coach Russell Martin, an active environmentalist, said, 'He might have come down [to see the players], but I have no interest in saying hello ... because I'm a football manager. I'm not sure we're aligned on too much politically but I know he's a fan and I hope he enjoyed watching the team.'[17] Matters of authenticity and public demeanour aside, one wonders whether the right's difficulties with football are also ideological. Boris Johnson's populist antennae were sufficiently alert for the Tories to respond to fan protest over the European Super League in 2021 with the fan-led review and then the proposal of legislation that would establish an independent football regulator; but it would be hard, for example, to argue that the success of the Premier League would be possible without enormous levels of labour migration, or for Brexiteers to feel comfortable with a cultural form that prized its place in a wider European community.

Perhaps the best that could be said of football's sometimes performative anti-racism was that it made explicitly political racist and nativist football projects impossible to pursue and created an uncomfortable space even for the most proficient dog-whistling racism. Its deeper, institutionalised injustices, seen above all in the ethnic make-up of its many workforces, remained. In late summer 2020 the FA finally began to address this and launched its Diversity Code. It was, in effect, a voluntary agreement by the FA, the Premier League, the EFL and the clubs that signed up to it to radically increase the number of women and minorities in the game. Targets included having 15 per cent of new hires in senior leadership positions with a BAME background and 30 per cent being women. In coaching roles the BAME target was 25 per cent and for senior positions – in effect head coaches – 10 per cent. The following year, in adapted form, the FA called on clubs from the women's pyramid, the National League and the grassroots to sign up too. Needless to say, in its first couple of years in operation, only the FA – who had made many significant BAME hires in the England coaching set-up – was actually hitting its targets.

The scale of the problem was made stark in 2022 by the Black Footballers Partnership (BFP), a new network of players, ex-players and coaches that commissioned the Szymanski Report – the first comprehensive survey of ethnicity and employment in the English football industry.[18] Simply put, the further one went on the journey from player to coach to executive and owner, the more white football became. It found that 43 per cent of Premier League players were Black, as were 34 per cent of EFL players. However, only a quarter of the players who took their coaching badges were Black, and among those with the top coaching qualifications – a UEFA pro licence – it was down to 14 per cent. Of those occupying professional coaching roles, just 9 per cent were Black, and among head coaches in the professional game their presence was down to only 4 per cent. In the boardrooms, where all the hiring and firing was done, the numbers were white 98 per cent, Black 2 per cent. Bad as this was, Szymanski found that, as of 2023, there were no Black chief scouts or youth scouts in the Premier League, just one sporting director and only three of the more than sixty academy managers. As ever, Les Ferdinand nailed the problem with the FA's intervention: 'It's a voluntary code, so it's made no difference whatsoever, because there's no repercussions for anyone if you don't follow [it].'[19] Playing catch-up, the FA is now considering making reporting mandatory and introducing some kind of sanction for failure, but no one is holding their breath.

A follow-up report in 2023 found that in comparison with white coaches, Black coaches accumulated less than half as much experience over their career, and taking performance into account, were 41 per cent more likely to be fired.[20] Delroy Corinaldi, from the BFP, argued: 'A career in football management often looks like a game of Snakes and Ladders; but for black former players, it's pretty much all snakes and no ladders.'[21] Even when a Black coach did make it to the top, like Darren Moore at West Bromwich Albion, and was celebrated by the community, it created new problems. As Colin King, co-founder of the BAME Coaches Association, put it: 'Darren Moore is somebody who represents us. But he epitomised something that is really dangerous too. If he fails as a manager, he fails as a black manager, not on an individual level. Then it makes it harder for clubs like West Brom to employ black managers.'[22] This is not, of course, the case for white managers, who appear to represent no one but themselves, but are in actual fact bountifully endowed with white, collective privilege. Colin King demanded a different kind of conversation, not about snakes and ladders or targets and protocols: 'Let's talk about the politics of whiteness and the privilege that white managers have to lose a job and not be accountable to the white race. White managers mess up left, right and centre. They get another job.'[23] Until that conversation begins, code or no code, it is hard to see how this situation changes.

10.

The Silence of the Stands

Football without Crowds

Through the spring of 2020, every kind of social, recreational and cultural activity was cancelled – cinema, theatre, musical performances, restaurants and nightclubs – and all were in desperate economic straits. But nothing received the attention given to football, its absence, its finances and its possible return. As the country contemplated the implications of closing down much of the economy, professional football players were singled out by Matt Hancock, Secretary of State for Health, for particular scrutiny: 'I think everybody needs to play their part in this national effort and that means Premier League footballers, too. The first thing that Premier League footballers can do is make a contribution, take a pay cut.'[1] A similar request, needless to say, was not made of bankers, hedge-fund managers or ministers of state. In mid-March the FA and Premier League had cancelled all fixtures until further notice. The EFL, the National League and the Women's Super League took the decision to end the season prematurely, determining the league standings on a points per game basis. Just a month later, the government was encouraging football to think that under sufficiently strict Covid protocols, and in empty stadiums, it might return. The Prime Minister was eager, saying that football's reopening would be a 'much-needed boost to the national morale'. Danny Rose, then at Newcastle United, was angry – 'I don't give a fuck about the nation's morale, bro, people's lives are at risk' – and wearily cynical about the game's shift from folk devil to essential service: 'Matt Hancock was saying that footballers need to halve their wages, and then six weeks later, we're needed to try and entertain people.'[2]

It was now clear what a huge economic impact the pandemic would have on football clubs, as broadcasters stopped paying for games that weren't played and match-day income (especially important for smaller clubs) disappeared entirely. The Premier League saw annual revenues decline by £600 million, the Championship's dropped by £120 million, League One was £60 million down and League Two just under £20 million. Scottish football as a whole was another £100 million in the red. Consequently, forty-three of the eighty-five English league clubs who actually returned accounts that year were technically insolvent: seven in the Premier League, fourteen in the Championship, and eleven in each of League One and League Two. A few clubs' senior staff volunteered or agreed to accept small pay cuts, like Bournemouth's chief executive Richard Hughes and coach Eddie Howe, their peers Karren Brady and David Moyes at West Ham, and all of Brighton's senior management. Attempts by clubs to make use of the government furlough scheme, in which the state would pay 80 per cent of the wages of non-playing staff, were all rescinded when they were opposed by a wave of moralising protest from fans and media, a standard that was not applied to any other commercial sector. Nonetheless, clubs committed to paying their part-time and match-day staff. Plans by the leagues and individual clubs to impose across-the-board pay cuts on their squads were thwarted by the players' union, the PFA. Arsenal voluntarily accepted a 12.5 per cent cut in their wages, but most other reductions – like those at Sheffield United, Watford and West Ham – were really in the form of deferrals; a fact, perhaps, obscured by the noise around the

Premier League players' collective donations to the NHS (large for mere mortals, but less than 1 per cent of their salaries). Later, it would transpire that much of the money passed on to the NHS from clubs came from auctions of specially signed shirts, ultimately paid for by fans.

A combination of forces – the government's desperate desire for some modicum of normality, the broadcasters' need for some actual content, and the clubs' struggle to preserve some of their broadcasting income – underwrote the decision to allow the Premier League to return in mid-June 2020, the FA Cup to be played in July, and the EFL to conduct its play-off matches. Danny Rose, blunt as ever, spoke for many players: 'People are suggesting we should go back to football like we're guinea pigs or lab rats … I could be potentially risking my health for people's entertainment and that's not something I want to be involved in if I'm honest.' But he and the rest of the squads had little choice but to comply.[3]

Initially, players were allowed to train but had to maintain physical distancing. Widespread testing, controversial at a time when tests were in desperately short supply, was conducted at every club: when just 16 positive cases were discovered from almost 9,000 tests, contact training was allowed and clubs began to prepare their staff and stadiums for the new Covid protocols. Everyone, up to a maximum of 330 people at any one stadium, had to show evidence of Covid testing and be temperature checked. Staggered arrivals and departures were conducted through sterile routes to the dressing room. Journalists and camera crews were banished from anywhere but small demarcated areas around the pitch. Post-match interviews were awkwardly conducted across advertising boards. Players were instructed not to shake hands, spit or clear their nose (a euphemism for projecting a stream of snot from their nostrils onto the grass), to only drink from their named individual water bottle, and to abstain from celebratory hugging, crowding officials and mass confrontations. Ball boys were absent, leaving players to pick up a ball from the many left on small stands around the edge of the pitch. Mascots, mercifully, were cut from the roster. Medical staff were required to wear full PPE, and anyone not actually on the pitch had to wear a mask and socially distance, including the now nine permitted players on the bench from which five substitutions could be made. A frenetic schedule of games followed – three a week for most clubs – and every single one was broadcast somewhere. Sky and BT Sport took the lion's share, the former broadcasting a couple of dozen games for free, while the BBC, for the first time in more than thirty years, showed live league football too. Whatever the channel, the public was hungry for football of any kind, and subscription levels received a boost, while Sky itself was enjoying record audiences. The Premier League and its finance officers, despite agreeing a £330 million rebate to the TV companies given the diminished calibre of the product, breathed a collective sigh of relief.

Football without crowds was eerie. The new soundscape featured the thud of the ball against advertising boards and the cries of players and coaches, which normally went unheard, reverberating around empty stadiums. Club DJs still reported for work, played the same old playlists and offered the same old cries of encouragement to no one. While a few acquired a taste for the new minimalism, most found the game in this form almost unwatchable. Football tried to adapt to the new situation. In Spain, La Liga experimented with digital crowds, filling the lower stands of televised games with artificially generated people. Rejected in Britain, clubs instead filled the stands behind the goals with large cut-outs of individual fans, which they themselves had paid for. Some displayed great chequerboards of fans' flags and banners, most wrapped big blocks of seats in club colours and crests. Others had fans watching over Zoom who would appear on big screens during the match. Broadcasters responded by introducing crowd noise, which, in a weird act of cannibalism, was culled from the sound libraries of the video games industry, which had acquired it in the first place from TV broadcasts of the Premier League. There were teething troubles, for sure, as when a shot by Everton's Richarlison in the Merseyside derby was incorrectly signalled by the sound engineer as a goal, only to be replaced a few seconds later with the crowd sound of a missed goal when it became clear that he had fired the ball wide. The invective in the comments section on YouTube suggested just how closely people were listening.[4] However, broadcasters became steadily more adept at matching their synthetic hubbub with the action on the pitch. First, a layer of standard low-level crowd noise would be laid down. Then volume and direction controls could be adjusted to allow for the different intensity and location of home and away fans in a given stadium. To this, a range of individual sounds could be added as the game progressed: the roar for a goal hitting the back of the net; the ooooh! of a missed chance followed by a smattering of claps; whistles from the crowd contesting a referee's decision. With time, sound engineers came to vary the intensity and length of these, giving more weight, for example, to a last-minute missed equaliser than a half-chance in the first fifteen minutes. Club-specific chants were also added to the mix, and Sky's app allowed fans to vote on which ones they preferred to hear.

Innovative as all of these measures were, it was clear that nothing can replace a ground full of people, for the most significant impact of the absence of crowds was that home advantage disappeared. More than two-dozen statistical studies have been published on this topic on football alone, and though a small number found no or minimal change to the game, the vast majority were unequivocal.[5] In terms of points won, goals scored, penalties scored, chances made and even expected goals, the edge that hosts had formerly enjoyed was blunted. At the same time the tendency of referees to award more red and yellow cards to away teams evaporated in the absence of baying and partisan supporters. Yellow cards for foul play also declined in the Premier League as the usual levels of collective mania and aggression, transmitted from stand to pitch, were absent. That said, in the new silence, player backchat and protest were more easily heard and harder to ignore: yellow cards for dissent rose. Although not confirmed by any study in Britain, a survey of Italian football, which measured the pre-Covid and Covid-era match ratings of footballers, found that Black players appeared to be performing significantly better, while white players were slightly poorer.[6] It is hard to think of an explanation for this that does not involve the absence of the quotidian and vicious racism of Italian stadiums.

In late June 2020 Chelsea beat Manchester City at Stamford Bridge and Liverpool's lead at the top of the Premier League became unassailable. For the first time in thirty years, Liverpool were champions. Within the hour, crowds, unseen since the lockdown, spontaneously assembled at Anfield and in the city centre. Fireworks exploded across the night sky. Cavalcades of cars adorned with red-and-white scarves filled the roads. There were masks and there were some who maintained a semblance of social distancing, but beneath the canopy of red smoke bombs and gleaming flares, there was uncontrollable hugging and kissing and dancing. In July, after West Brom failed to beat Huddersfield Town, a thousand or so Leeds United fans gathered at Elland Road to celebrate Leeds' return to the Premier League after sixteen years, wreathed the stadium in blue-and-yellow smoke, and toasted the squad who stood at the windows of the main stand. The following weekend, after the club had won the Championship title, more than 7,000 made their way to Millennium Square in the centre of the city for a near twelve-hour revelry of alcohol and chanting, which on the fringes eventually mutated into violent confrontations with the police.[7] Even so, given the ruthlessness with which police had been charging students for sitting in each other's rooms, or prosecuting the small home gatherings that they uncovered, there were barely any serious efforts to enforce Covid protocols or arrest transgressors.

In the brief interlude between seasons, and encouraged by the Chancellor's VAT cut on restaurant prices – the glibly named and ill-advised campaign 'Eat Out to Help Out' – the country took its chances and went outside. The government, as ever overoptimistic about the course of the pandemic and its capacity to manage it, began to plan for a return to crowds at sporting venues for October. The Premier League, in particular, stung by the sight of crowds in cafes, cinemas and offices, albeit socially distanced, began to push harder for the return of spectators. A trial crowd was allowed in September in Doncaster at the St Leger horse-racing meeting, but the local spike in infections it produced and the worryingly rising tide of cases across the country saw such experiments cancelled. With the announcement of a second national lockdown at the end of October, football, like other sports, was resigned to playing behind closed doors. In November, with infection rates back under some measure of control, there was a second push for fans to return and the government announced that a further set of trial games, conducted under strict social-distancing protocols and with crowds of just 2,000 (up to 4,000 in the most capacious stadiums), would be played in December. Fans were to be temperature tested, subjected to spot checks of their testing status and required to wear masks. Official medical advice warned against overenthusiastic chanting: 'If singing is expected to take place, spectators should be reminded of the risks. The cumulative effect of aerosol transmission means the more people involved, the higher the risk of transmission.'[8] A further caveat was that these games would only be permitted in regions of the country designated tier one or tier two, where the rate of infection was at its lowest. In early December six EFL matches were played with small crowds, and for a brief few weeks the stands were thinly but gratefully populated across the country. However, once again, the government's lack of caution and its underestimation of the potency of Covid saw a huge winter spike in infections, and by Christmas only the Isles of Scilly were left in tier one or two. The Premier League played its last game on 27 December and the EFL closed its turnstiles two days later. A national lockdown was imposed for the third time, and a very long winter awaited.

It was only with the roll-out of the mass vaccination programme in the new year that the government could once again propose a path back to spectator sport. Again, in April 2021, experimental crowds were permitted, first at the World Snooker Championship and then at the semi-finals of the Carabao Cup. By now restrictions were being lifted more widely, as small outdoor gatherings and hugging were permitted, but the patience of a nation, cooped up in their own homes for the best part of a year, began to fray. In March 2021 the celebrations in Glasgow among Rangers fans, who had won the Scottish league for the first time in a decade, were just the most egregious example of the collapse of social distancing.[9] By May the government had made it clear, despite considerable warnings from the medical profession, that all restrictions would be lifted in the early summer, and again football stadiums were permitted to accept crowds, of up to 10,000 people in the biggest arenas. As the season came to its climax, each Premier League team was permitted a single home game to be played under these rules, as were the international friendlies played by England and Scotland. The opening rounds of Euro 2020 had around one-third capacity crowds and by the final rounds of the tournament were close to full.

In retrospect, this moment appears like a fever dream in the collective consciousness of the football nation. Intense, bizarre, nightmarish on occasion, and then, with wakefulness, dispelled in a moment, lingering only in the deepest recesses of memory. Yet linger it does. What, then, does this dreamworld tell us about ourselves? Certainly, politicians' relationship with football had changed. The only comparable national emergencies – the First and Second World War – had seen football banned or much diminished. In 1915 it was deemed unpatriotic for the game to continue and the league was abandoned until 1919. In 1939, recognising the importance of the game in maintaining morale, professional football was halted, but then reincarnated as an endless round of regional tournaments and local cups featuring all of the professionals now drafted into the armed forces. Such, though, was the game's popularity, power and financial heft in 2020 that the government went out of its way to ensure its continuation – a degree of political effort that was, by contrast, not available for the reopening of schools and universities.

For a few fans, the hiatus was so profound that they had tired of the game: 'I have not missed it nearly as much as I thought I would, especially the hype and endless coverage about very little. So much of it is exhausting and uninteresting.' For some, the romance was over: 'I've missed it much less than I thought I would … I've completely fallen out of love with the Premier League and its feelings of self-importance. I couldn't care whether the league comes back or not given that people are dying from a pandemic.'[10] The majority, however, were profoundly grateful. Indeed, on their return to the stadium, most fans were overwhelmed by emotion, resorting to football's limited but accurate lexicon to express this. A Luton Town fan said, 'I'll explain it as a football cliche – I'm over the moon – it is fantastic. It has been too long … I have been coming to football for 50 years and Luton for 45 and every other Saturday it has been like missing a tooth.'[11] A Leeds fan, speaking after his first game, recalled, 'Describing this is incredibly difficult. The rain drenched me as I walked to Elland Road and I was so emotional I barely noticed.'[12] More elegiac, a Blackpool fan reached for theology: 'The first time I stepped back into Bloomfield Road after the pandemic was very emotional and a few tears were shed. I'm 59 years old and have followed Blackpool for 51 years. Going there is like going to church on a Sunday – it's a religion; it's my sacred place that means the world to me.'[13] Another spoke for much of the football nation:

'Life may not be completely normal, but being back watching football live again is definitely bringing it back!'[14] True, but as with so many aspects of British society, what came back would not be the same as what had gone before.

11.

A Crisis of Confidence

Football, Vaccines and Science

In the late spring of 2021 the biggest crowds at football stadiums, many of which had been made into temporary vaccination centres, were now the long patient queues for the first rounds of Covid jabs. This process would culminate in June 2021, when the vaccine was made universally available and the country's stadiums served the millions of young people who had hitherto been unable to access a jab. Not everyone in football was entirely happy about this. Matt Le Tissier, the ex-Southampton and England striker, was the most prominent anti-vaccine voice in the game, though this was just one element in a social-media output that covered the full far-right bouquet of conspiracy theories, from the CIA planning 9/11 to Ukraine faking Russian war crimes. It was certainly all too far down the wormhole for his employers at Sky Sports, who announced his departure from *Soccer Saturday*, saying the programme was going 'in a different direction'. Rickie Lambert, another ex-Southampton striker and a supporter of Le Tissier, posted on Instagram a message for those who were vaccinating children: 'You are a CRIMINAL! The Nuremberg code has been broken!'[1] Many others shared in the conspiracy theory that Christian Eriksen's heart attack, when playing for Denmark in their opening game of Euro 2020, was caused by his vaccination, which was remarkable given that he hadn't been vaccinated.[2]

Le Tissier and his supporters stayed online, but offline there was a spate of anti-vaccine protest through 2021, including invasions of hospitals, schools and testing centres, and groups serving what they claimed to be 'legal papers' on pro-vaccine celebrities. Commentator and ex-England star Alan Shearer, who in a Premier League video had encouraged people to get a booster jab that winter, was a target. Protestors released a video of themselves supposedly standing by Shearer's front door, in which one of them can be heard saying, 'Everyone is going to get this, every celebrity, sick of you. That's the truth in that letterbox there, in Alan Shearer's fucking house.' A moment of menace, for sure, but one undercut by the fact that the papers had no legal standing and that they were delivered to the wrong house.[3] Liverpool manager Jürgen Klopp, whose mother had died of Covid earlier in the pandemic, was incandescent with the anti-vaxxers and the vaccine-resistant. 'I don't take the vaccination only to protect me, I take the vaccination to protect all the people around me. I don't understand why that is a limitation of freedom.'[4]

Liverpool had a 100 per cent vaccination record and, like a number of clubs, had made it clear that they would not sign unvaccinated players, but others were rather more relaxed on the matter. The *Daily Mail* reported that only seven Premier League clubs had vaccinated their entire squads, and that more than a quarter of players, it transpired, were not vaccinated – considerably fewer than in any other European elite league. As late as October 2021, almost a year after vaccinations had begun, the BBC noted that less than half the players in the EFL were fully vaccinated, a number considerably lower than that of their age group in the general population. Reports of many unvaccinated players in the England squad saw health secretary Sajid Javid play the role-model card, again: 'They should recognise that ... the difference that makes in terms of encouraging others.'[5] Deputy Chief Medical Officer Jonathan Van-Tam held a special briefing session with every Premier League captain. The PFA's chief executive implored them not to 'believe all the myths and lies', but to little avail. One club doctor said, 'The conspiracy theories have really taken hold in some dressing rooms ... We've got senior players, intelligent men, coming out with all sorts of nonsense and they won't be budged ... Players are saying that it will make them infertile, that it's part of a plot involving Bill Gates, the pandemic is just propaganda.'[6]

England manager Gareth Southgate wondered whether the amount of downtime players had spent alone with their phones during the pandemic had provided the space for them to go down some conspiracy-theory wormholes. They were not alone in making this journey, but their scepticism was reinforced by their perception of risk: as ultra-healthy young athletes they appeared the least likely of people to fall seriously ill with Covid. West Brom's Callum Robinson had two bouts of the disease and still refused vaccination. Certainly, a whole generation of athletes, near obsessed with controlling what went into their bodies and prey to the illusion of invincibility, constituted an enthusiastic audience for those preaching 'natural' cures and offering 'alternative' facts. The power dynamics of dressing rooms, in the absence of a manager openly committed to vaccination – like Klopp, but also Thomas Frank at Brentford and Guardiola, who had also lost his mother to Covid, in 2020 – favoured the voices of the respected but deluded. Rochdale's club doctor Wesley Tensel was blunter than most: 'Football changing rooms are different to most workplaces. They're all together, it's an echo chamber, so if one of the senior players ... has seen something on social media and that's passed to somebody else, they're not necessarily likely to critically appraise where that's come from and they can end up going down a rabbit hole.' Football players are hardly the only people to tread this path, but that there should be such scepticism about scientists and scientific evidence among footballers is particularly paradoxical, for over the last decade they have operated in an environment in which scientific knowledge and technology are more present than ever before, and where both had a significant impact on their bodies and performance. Consider just four examples: nutrition, data science, medicine, and the stadiums and pitches where they played.

The arrival of Arsène Wenger at Arsenal in 1996 is considered the seminal moment in the transformation of footballers' eating habits. In part, he just reflected the common-sense expectations of French culinary culture, but he also came out of a coaching world in which nutritional science had been taken seriously since before the Second World War. The greasy spoon was off limits, alcohol was frowned upon; poached chicken, pasta, fruit and broccoli – previously absent from club canteens – became the new norm. While this nouvelle cuisine was not immediately and universally adopted in English football, it is the case that Micky 'Sumo' Quinn, who retired in 1995, is the last Premier League player whose weight was individually and correctly celebrated in song: 'He's fat/He's round/He's worth a million pounds'. Frank Lampard was teased mercilessly his whole career with the soubriquet 'Fat Frank', but he was never anything other than lean. In the years since, one could still hear a substitute who had not been training as well as he might be greeted with, 'Who ate all the pies? Who ate all the pies?', but it is unquestionably rarer.

In 2009 Arsenal employed the first full-time nutritionist in English football. Pep Guardiola would soon do the same at Barcelona and has made it a priority ever since. Nutritionists are now at every Premier League club and at many lower down the league. Nor are they merely in the business of taming excess. As Matt Jones at West Ham put it: 'When I first started out I was there to help people lose weight. Now it's about fine tuning athletes.'[7] Jürgen Klopp considered the arrival of Mona Nemmer, who had previously worked at Bayern Munich, as 'one of my most important signings'.[8] Nemmer worked with a detailed nutritional profile of every player that, beyond obvious physio-logical data, noted and accommodated ethnicity, individual tastes and their playing position. To this was added the analysis of an endless stream of nutritional data derived from samples of players' saliva, blood, urine and stools, and all of this was used to create distinct menus for the squad's training days, travelling days, match days and recuperation days. High-fibre vegetables like Brussels sprouts, perfect for travelling days, were too gassy for match days. Carbohydrates of the right kind – brown rice and al dente pasta – were always available to players at Anfield on the day of a game, served in designated carb-loading stations. The half-time orange and a handful of jelly beans gave way to rehydration fluids and power gels. After the game, individual protein shakes, designed to feed the body's own muscle-repair system, became compulsory. The deep desire among players, post-match, for carbs and fat is no longer satisfied by the fish and chips that George Best, for one, relished, but by pizza; though even this may become off limits as the most spartan of coaches, Guardiola for example, have banned it. Liverpool has tried to steer its players towards oat and soy yoghurt boosters laced with granola and berries. On recovery days, especially for those with swollen muscles and joints, the recommendation at West Ham was anti-inflammatory treats like 'cumin and turmeric shots ... and polyphenols like berries, cherries, dark chocolate and pomegranates', a list of ingredients once more likely to be found in Yotam Ottolenghi's kitchen but now the snacks of choice at their Rush Green training complex in Dagenham.[9]

The current generation of players has, by and large, bought into the dietary advice being offered, if not necessarily followed it to the letter. Booze, for most, is a much smaller part of their lifestyle, end of season celebrations aside, while the increasing number of Muslim players has denormalised alcohol; for this reason the once ubiquitous bottle of champagne for the man of the match has been abandoned. There remained sceptics. Some players were just able to get away with it, eat what they liked and still perform, like Barcelona's fast-food aficionado Ousmane Dembélé, but even he was brought to book. Increasingly, there is no way for football players to hide what they eat, how their bodies are working and how they are really performing, and the reason for that is the wider data revolution in the game.

Whereas the sequential games of baseball and cricket have been collecting and examining statistics for almost 150 years, football – a game of flow – has been resistant to quantification. Although a number of pioneers devised systems of record-keeping reliant on eye, film, pen and paper, they were too time-consuming and generated too little data to make much difference to the way the game was played. With the arrival of unlimited video and computer power, however, every move of every player in every game could be measured, located and quantified a hundred times over. By the 2010s, players routinely trained and played wearing GPS sensors and other data-collecting technologies, all of which provided real-time analysis of their performance, position and physiology. Consequently, every club acquired a substantial analytics and data department, and they worked with a new generation of coaches who took that data seriously. Certainly, this avalanche of data has made it harder for players to mask a decline in individual physiological performance, but the extent to which it has truly transformed how clubs operate in the transfer market and how the game itself is actually played is much harder to discern.[10] Brentford and Brighton, who are known to use the new data in their recruitment policies, have performed considerably better than their wage bills would normally determine, and have made a lot of money in the transfer market; but neither is publicly explaining how they do it. Despite a now considerable literature on the data revolution, none of its practitioners have actually revealed how, on the ground, their work has altered a team's tactics or style of play. The key innovations in the Premier League over the last decade – possession-based positional play and aggressive counter-pressing – were popularised by Guardiola at

Manchester City and Klopp at Liverpool – and their adoption of these methods clearly predates the rise of data analysis.

Football's late embrace of data, given the technological limits of the pre-digital world, is no surprise. However, the glacial pace at which its relationship with sports medicine has developed is harder to explain.[11] In France and Germany it had emerged as a recognised specialism in the early twentieth century, was taught in medical schools and its research widely absorbed by coaching cultures. In Britain the first diploma in the subject was offered in 1981, and it was only in 1998 that the Royal Colleges developed specialised advanced programmes for doctors. As late as 1999, Manchester United had won the treble with a medical staff of just three people: two physios and a masseur. There was a club doctor, but that was a part-time appointment, more sine-cure than elite medical role. Even then, most club doctors were bereft of any specialist training in sports medicine and were recruited on the basis of who they knew, many of them serving as directors of the club as well as being its physician. The Football Association was as lackadaisical as the clubs; indeed, it managed 120 years without any forum for discussion of these matters, until 1983, when it established its first medical commit-tee. That said, for most of the first decade of its existence the committee did almost nothing, failing to meet entirely between 1989 and 1991. Things began to advance in 1997 when the FA commissioned its first study of football-related injuries, and in 2003 when it required club doctors to actually have a sports medicine qualification. Trainers, as today's physiotherapists were once known, have followed a similar course. Prior to the Second World War they were all ex-players, often given the job as a form of post-retirement grace and favour. After the war, as the medical value of massage and rehabilitative exercise was recognised in the treatment of veterans, a small body of know-ledge in treating muscle stress and fatigue developed. Much of this was still learnt on the job by football trainers and without the benefit of very much, if any, paramedical training. While their status might have been rising outside the game, physios were regularly overruled by managers on the grounds that players needed to just 'run off the knocks' and 'play through the pain'. Ian Adams, Leeds United's physio in the 1960s and 1970s, disagreed so vehemently with Don Revie over players' capacity to play that he resigned on four occasions. Laurie Brown, at Manchester United, would protect players from manager Tommy Docherty by putting them in plaster; medically unnecessary but enough to deter 'the Doc'. It was only in 2001 that football required its physios to have the basic professional qualification, and only in 2004 that they should have the FA's diploma in sports medicine.[12]

Since then, the Premier League – and to some extent the lower leagues, too – have transformed their attitude to sports medicine and sports science and hugely increased their investment in both. In today's game, no professional club can operate without a full-time club doctor with a sports science specialism. They are supported by teams of up to two dozen other full-time staff, adding dieticians, psychologists and rehab experts to the time-honoured physios and masseurs. Examinations, once mainly confined to transfer-related medicals and a cursory pre-season once-over, are now meticulous and relentless. Where once there was a hot communal bath and a rubdown, there are now medically prescribed cryo chambers, cold-water immersions and compression socks. Even the sleep patterns of players are monitored and the findings of sleep science applied to their habits. Similarly, whereas the pitch-side physio of the 1980s really didn't have much more to aid them than a bucket of water and the 'magic sponge', today's medical kit bags are closer to what you might expect on a battlefield, with a remarkable range of analgesics. In 2020 Manchester United spent millions acquiring their very own top-of-the-range MRI scanner, specially designed to catch the muscle tears that normal machines miss; given that football has an injury-at-work rate 2,000 times that of the rest of the economy, it was a bargain.

It is this – the economic cost of injuries to players – that has driven the new football medicine. Long-term data is unavailable, but certainly the number of injuries in the Premier League has been sharply rising: 15 per cent between 2020 and 2024 alone. In the first half of the 2023–24 season, Newcastle United lost sixteen players to injury, while fourteen other squads in the league were carrying at least six unavailable players.[13] On this matter there is a widespread consensus that the number of games being played, and the speed and intensity at which they are played, are the main culprits. In addition, some have argued that the decline in fitness during Covid, and the injuries accumulated afterwards, have not quite gone away, as past problems continue to recur for players. Others think that the sheer cognitive overload of today's football, demanding more mental energy and concentration, on and off the pitch, is a factor in exhausting players and making them vulnerable to injury. Knocks, muscle injuries and knee problems are widespread, but hamstring troubles, 118 across the league in 2023–24, are by far the most common and the fastest-growing problem; they are much more likely to occur under conditions of muscle fatigue. A basic estimate of the cost of injuries can be made from counting the number of days players were unavailable in a season (disciplinary and other matters excluded) and taking that as a ratio of their annual salary. By this measure, in 2023–24 injuries cost the league as a whole £280 million, Chelsea £46 million, Manchester United £35 million and Premier League clubs, on average, £14 million; not much for the biggest clubs, but Nottingham Forest were spending a quarter of their whole wage bill on injured players. Hamstrings alone were costing clubs more than £70 million.[14]

In the past, one cause of those injuries had been the poor quality of the pitches. As recently as the 1990s, players would have to negotiate poorly drained and uneven surfaces, and were prey to slips and turned ankles. However, Premier League football is now being played on the most immaculate pitches that world football has ever seen. England has become the Silicon Valley of turf science, as coaches have asked for better, faster, flatter pitches, broadcasters have demanded more aesthetically perfect swards, and a new generation of groundsmen, with budgets up to £10 million, have delivered.[15] Thus, the celebratory knee slide, an act of self-harm on many pitches before this era, has become the norm. Today's pitches are dependent on grass-seed varieties engineered to deal with drought and shade. The turf is grown on specialist farms and harvested with extraordinary mechanised cutters and rollers that can deliver the sods to the stadium within twenty-four hours. Once there, it is placed on a multilayered substrate within which both drainage pipes and heating elements have been inserted. This pitch is then blended with new artificial fibres, literally sewn into the surface, around which the natural grass roots entwine, hugely strengthening the turf. Despite heavy use, these pitches can be played on and regrown in a matter of days, trimmed with mowers that can cut with an accuracy of a single millimetre. Pep Guardiola insisted on ultra-short nineteen-millimetre pitches at Bayern Munich, but under the colder, cloudier Mancunian climate, where growth is slower, he had to settle for twenty-three millimetres. Beneath, they are criss-crossed by thousands of Bluetooth-enabled sensors that measure the temperature and moisture levels, directly affecting how much heat, light and water each square metre receives from the now automated robotic heating, watering and grow-light systems. And no one has, as yet, suggested that Bill Gates secretly controls them.

The pitch is not the only part of the football stadium in which digital technologies have been embedded. It is increasingly hard to purchase a ticket without access to the internet, which cuts out 6 per cent of the population and a fifth of all over-65s. Paper tickets are an endangered species, as a smartphone becomes increasingly essential for accessing stadiums and paying for anything; so much so that touts are now handing over phones with e-tickets on them to their customers, and reclaiming them inside the stadium. Cards are still accepted, but many clubs are now cashless. Phones are just one of the many, many screens that supporters must endure while inside, from the hundreds of televisions, showing Sky Sports News and betting prices on the concourses, to the endlessly rotating and piercingly bright LED advertising boards that line the pitch, in some cases in double lines. In new stadiums they are built into the very structure of the building, creating a 360-degree panorama of distraction. If that were not enough to fragment one's attention, there are the now enormous screens, hung high above the stands, all of which can, as one breathless manufacturer of this technology wrote, be combined into 'a single epic super-wide canvas either for atmospheric content or brand takeover'.[16] In a way, it is amazing that the crowd has the energy left to look at their own screens, but somehow we manage. Indeed, if the tech firms burrowing their way into football have their way, 'There will soon be a million things to do, from ordering food and drink from your phone to participating in polls, voting for player of the match, betting, content creation and in venue discussions.'[17] A million things other than watching the game as part of a collective experience, or speaking to the person next to you. Perhaps the only way that we will be tempted to look up and actually watch what is going on in front of us will be the augmented reality glasses that are being touted, which will superimpose players' names, statistics and no doubt adverts over our view of the action. In the emollient words of one company, 'the future of sports spectating is all about creating a more connected and immersive experience' – except that we will be connected to a corporate algorithm rather than other human beings, and we will be immersed in our own anomie.[18] Precisely the conditions, strangely enough, under which trust in science has declined and conspiracy theories have flourished.

12.

Football's Shock Doctrine

The European Super League as Disaster Capitalism

It might not have been quite the rapacious disaster capitalism that can emerge in the aftermath of environmental calamities and wars, the kind documented by Naomi Klein in her 2007 book *The Shock Doctrine*, but Project Big Picture – the plan to restructure English football proposed by the owners of Manchester United and Liverpool in October 2020 – was working from a similar playbook. As Klein put it, 'in moments of crisis, people are willing to hand over a great deal of power to anyone who claims to have a magic cure,' and the Glazer family and Fenway Sports appeared to offer precisely this to both their Premier League rivals and the beleaguered lower leagues.[1] In fact, what purported to be a structural transformation that would benefit the common good was a set of proposals that would further concentrate money and power in English football among a small elite, while offering a few baubles to the useful idiots that such deception requires.

The headline item was an offer to support the Covid-ravaged EFL and FA to the tune of £250 million and £50 million respectively. It was not, however, an act of solidarity or a gift. For the EFL it was, in effect, a payday loan to the desperate, with two years of future broadcast income set aside to pay the debt; while the FA was given the chance to sell its freehold and take the money in exchange for relinquishing its golden share in the Premier League's ownership structure. Similarly, the offer to share a quarter of broadcast revenues with the Championship, whose media rights would be sold in a bundle with those of the Premier League, was actually the offer of a quarter of the revenue from a much smaller number of collectively sold matches. Hidden in the small print, the plan was to allow clubs to sell eight of their own games globally – a huge source of revenue for a small number of global brands, but not much use to the likes of Wycombe Wanderers – the money from which would not be put in the collective pot. In fact, it was not much use to the lower half of the Premier League either, who were being asked to sign up to a new distribution of broadcasting money within the league that was even more heavily weighted against them. Worse, with so many games being made available through new streams, the main package was likely to shrink in size and value. The EFL was being offered, in effect, a bigger cut of something much smaller than that currently on offer. And just in case anyone thought the EFL might be getting back on level terms with the Premier League, the new world would see the Premier League reduced to just eighteen teams with two automatic promotions from the Championship as before, but the third-bottom team in the Premier League, previously relegated, would get a second chance and enter a lopsided promotion play-off with three Championship sides. Parachute payments to relegated teams were to be cut entirely, though they would reappear in a new form, as teams falling into the Championship would be given £25 million held back from broadcast monies earned while in the top division. League One and Two would, as usual, get a few crumbs from the table and were to be relieved of the burden of running academies so they could serve instead as feeder teams for the bigger clubs, and as a place to store, as loanees, more of their ever-increasing roster of players. The grassroots and the women's game were offered hush money too, though by the time one had taken out the money already being put into these areas by the Premier League and the FA, and the lack of clarity about quite where any new money was coming from, it looked like a poisoned chalice.

The plans to reduce the Premier League itself to eighteen teams from twenty did not, however, clear sufficient space in the schedule, and accordingly Project Big Picture proposed abandoning the League Cup and the Community Shield. With a nod to the equally disingenuous claims of the inventors of the Premier League in 1992, they cast their plans as a benefit to the often-exhausted national team. In fact, the clubs planned to fill the schedule with more lucrative overseas tours and, for the bigger clubs, more games in an expanded Champions League. Thus, for the marginal gain of an additional early August friendly in Adelaide and a Champions League game against Anderlecht, Project Big Picture were happy to dispense with more than a century of tradition for everybody else. The Community Shield, previously the Charity Shield, had opened the season since 1908. The League Cup, in all its many sponsored incarnations, was more than sixty years old. Perhaps, most careless of all, the reduction of the Premier League to 18 teams, while the three leagues below retained 24 clubs, would require two teams at the bottom of League Two to be ejected, and that meant the end of the 92 – the number of clubs in the Football League since 1950, and the most venerated digits in English football's obsessive numerology. If cabalistic sentiment wouldn't put EFL clubs off the deal, the finances of the League Cup might, given that the competition delivered over half the value of the EFL's current broadcast deals, and offered bumper payments to the teams good enough to progress beyond the early rounds and lucky enough to draw a big Premier League club. By the time these losses had been subtracted from the EFL's income, as well as the reduced size of the new parachute payments and the reduced scale of the proposed collective rights deal with the Premier League, they were looking at even less money than they started with.

Finally, and most importantly, the plan envisaged giving nine clubs in the Premier League preferential voting rights, which would allow just six of them (you know who they are) vetoes over any number of key policy decisions, while a further three – West Ham United, Everton and Southampton – were to be given enhanced voting powers on broadcasting rights and promotion and relegation issues, creating in effect an oligarchy with a managed three-tier system of suffrage. Amazingly, no one on the Project Big Picture team had done the electoral maths, or even bothered to inform any of the clubs whose support they would need to get the proposal past the Premier League's own board. The nine might have voted for it. Rick Parry at the EFL and Greg Clarke at the FA had been part of the conversation and had agreed to the changes (though they had not consulted their own constituencies), but the other eleven Premier League clubs were never going to sign their rights away.

Neither John W. Henry nor any of the Glazers attempted to defend the project publicly, effectively leaving Rick Parry as its sole spokesperson, attempting to fend off strong criticism from pundits, the Premier League itself, the FA, many individual clubs and the UK government. The Football Supporters' Association tartly responded with the thought that 'very few of our members have ever expressed the view that what football really needs is a greater concentration in power in the hands of the big six billionaire-owned clubs'.[2] Just four days after the report had first been leaked, the Premier League voted unanimously not to proceed with it and to pursue its own plans for reform. Richard Masters, the league's chief executive, was curiously emollient afterwards: 'I don't think it takes too much to put things back together … I don't think it's irreparably damaged the Premier League.'[3] But if he thought the league's elite were finished with this kind of opportunist, divisive and self-serving manoeuvre, he was wrong. Six months later the disaster capitalists were back.

Not that they had ever been away. In mid-April 2021, the formation of the European Super League (ESL) was simultaneously announced on the social-media feeds of twelve clubs, three from Spain (Real Madrid, Barcelona and Atlético Madrid), three from Italy (AC Milan, Juventus and Internazionale) and the six usual suspects from the Premier League. It was, in essence, the same old format that Silvio Berlusconi, then owner of AC Milan, had first argued for in the late 1980s, and which the big clubs had used to pressure UEFA to reform the format and finances of the Champions League in their favour. This time around, the driving forces were Real Madrid's president Florentino Pérez and Juventus' Andrea Agnelli. The consortium, backed by no more than a $3.5 billion loan from American bank JPMorgan Chase, proposed replacing the UEFA Champions League with their own twenty-team competition, fifteen of whom would be permanent members, plus a further five who, like supplicants, would be granted a place at the league's discretion each season. Founder members would receive a large injection of cash up front. Games would be held midweek, and clubs would continue to play in their domestic leagues. Beyond that, the details of the organisation's statutes, legal basis, internal regulations, TV rights and audience projections, not to mention a proposed calendar, were absent.

The political strategy was equally threadbare. The clubs sent a letter to UEFA informing them of their departure and then Florentino Pérez, who was their de facto spokesperson, went on Spanish television and was allowed, unchecked, to ramble. According to Pérez, the youth of the world wasn't watching football, the Champions League had become boring, and the Super League would save it: 'We don't want the rich to be richer and the poor poorer. We have to save football. Everything I do is for the good of football, which is in a critical moment.'[4] Perhaps, more accurately, the plan was intended to save Real Madrid, Barcelona and the other Mediterranean clubs, all now groaning with debt made worse by Covid and looking enviously on at the Premier League, whose revenues continued to exceed their own. Immediate cash-flow problems were uppermost for

Barcelona, for example, whose debt had climbed towards €1 billion. That said, not even the Premier League clubs could look comfortably at their balance sheets in the midst of the pandemic. All were motivated by the idea, still unproven, that the ESL would be as financially successful as the Champions League; and they warmed to the prospect of cutting out UEFA and its irksome financial regulations, medium-sized clubs who had the temerity to occasionally qualify for the Champions League, and all of those troublesome solidarity payments. Equally important was the question of financial security, for none of the clubs believed that they could afford not to qualify for the Champions League; the ESL guaranteed at least this to them. Not everyone at the big teams was convinced, and up until the last minute Manchester City and Chelsea had their doubts, but in the end a collective fear of missing out gripped club executives.

UEFA's Slovenian president Aleksander Ceferin reacted furiously. His close personal and political relationship with Andrea Agnelli, president of Juventus, gave it a particularly sharp emotional edge: Agnelli had been assuring Ceferin right up until the last moment that the breakaway would not happen, and that the big clubs were happy to accept the planned expansion of the Champions League format that they had been negotiating together. Then he stopped answering his calls. Ceferin countered by working the phones, and he mobilised the vast majority of the continent's football associations, national leagues and player unions. In Spain and Italy there was muted approval from some of the press and from fans of the big clubs, who like their boards had grown tired of the national leagues they financially dominated, but the opposition quickly monopolised the debate. Javier Tebas (President of La Liga), the REFF (Royal Spanish Football Federation) and the Spanish government condemned the Super League, while thousands of Cádiz fans protested by laying siege to the Real Madrid squad staying in a hotel in the city.[5] In Italy, Prime Minister Mario Draghi offered his support to UEFA and the Italian Football Federation. At a meeting of the presidents of Serie A, Juventus was threatened with expulsion, and the president of Torino described Agnelli and his allies as 'Judases'. In France, Europe Minister Clément Beaune said that the country would use its upcoming presidency of the European Council to challenge the Super League, while President Macron would go on to make his opposition public.[6] Always closely attuned to the winds from the Élysée Palace, Paris Saint-Germain and their Qatari owners, who had been repeatedly approached by the nascent Super League, decided to side with UEFA. In Germany the biggest clubs – Bayern Munich and Borussia Dortmund, mainly fan-owned – refused to even contemplate participation.

All of this might have been enough to scupper the Super League, but England exploded and put the result beyond doubt. The actor Stephen Fry summed up the reaction in a single tweet: '6 clubs achieved something that no politician or public figure has managed in these times of faction, fission and feuding. They have brought together the whole divided nation ... everyone united in disgust and revulsion at such greed and stupidity.'[7] The newspapers, across the political spectrum, from the *Mirror* to the *Mail*, from the *Guardian* to the *Telegraph*, were all incensed and entirely critical of the project. The same was true of dozens of politicians, from Tories like David Burrowes and Huw Merriman to Labour's deputy leader Angela Rayner, who all took to social media to denounce the cartel. Less angry, but reflective of an almost universal mood, Prince William, honorary president of the FA, tweeted in a personal capacity: 'Now, more than ever, we must protect the entire football community ... I share the concerns of fans about the proposed Super League and the damage it risks causing to the game we love.' Well-known pundits, normally loyal to their clubs, were scathing. Ian Wright kept it short: 'Absolutely shameful @Arsenal.' Jamie Carragher invoked the past and wrote, 'What an embarrassment we've become @LFC, think of all the people who have come before us at this club who would be equally embarrassed as well.' Supporters' groups didn't mince their words: 'The death of Arsenal as a sporting institution'; '@Man City hang your heads in shame'; and from the Chelsea Supporters' Trust, who had forgiven everything else Abramovich had ever done: 'This is unforgivable.'

As with British society as a whole, football had been able to tolerate gigantic levels of structural inequality by maintaining the touching belief that any club could, in theory, make it to the top. In closing off even this fantasy route out of poverty, the Super League had miscalculated that there were no limits to that tolerance. The day after the league had been launched, 700 Leeds fans protested outside Elland Road before their game against Liverpool and were allowed to put up a huge banner in the stands saying, 'Earn it on the pitch, football is for the fans.'[8] Before kick-off, a plane carrying a banner with #SayNoToEuropeanSuperLeague was flown over the stadium. Manchester United fans demonstrated at the club's Carrington training ground, while Chelsea fans protested in such numbers before their game with Brighton that both team buses were held up on their way to Stamford Bridge. One home-made banner read, 'We want our cold nights in Stoke!' The following day, 8,000 Arsenal fans demonstrated at the Emirates and called for owner Stan Kroenke to go. Prior to Manchester United's game with Liverpool, 2,000 fans actually stormed the pitch at Old Trafford, forcing the game to be postponed.[9]

Players at Chelsea and Manchester United collectively protested to the management that they had not been consulted over the decision, or even informed in advance. Many were unusually forthright and public with their criticism. Liverpool's James Milner was as unfussy and straightforward as ever: 'I don't like it and I hope it doesn't happen.'[10] The whole Liverpool squad issued a collective challenge to the plan and Jordan Henderson, their captain, prepared to call and host a meeting among all the Premier League's captains to oppose the move. Pep Guardiola, who has kept his counsel on every other one of the very many controversial decisions made by Manchester City's owners, spoke against the league: 'It's not sport if you cannot lose.' Public opinion, just for once, was unambiguous. Among football fans as a whole, 79 per cent disapproved of the super league and just 14 per cent approved. Among fans of lower-league clubs it was even more emphatic, opinion dividing 87 to 9, while even among supporters of the departing clubs, 76 per cent were against the league and just 20 per cent for it.[11] Downing Street, in virtual gangster mode, let it be known that nothing was off the table, and that clubs that left for the Super League might find it 'difficult' in future to get all the visas they would like for players, or to be so generously subsidised by the police, who paid for most of the security costs incurred around their stadiums on match days. In parliament, Culture Secretary Oliver Dowden suggested that the new closed league might be subject to a monopolies and competition investigation. Prime Minister Boris Johnson, having agreed to meet fan representatives and league officials, raised the rhetorical temperature by declaiming, 'We should drop a legislative bomb to stop it – and we should do it now.' UEFA and Europe's national leagues were considering doing so themselves, threatening to exclude the twelve clubs from their competitions.

As quickly as it appeared, the Super League vanished. In half a day, all six of the English clubs, one by one, withdrew their membership. Chelsea were the first to reconsider, then Manchester City. Spurs and Arsenal resigned simultaneously, with the project's biggest supporters Manchester United and Liverpool bringing up the rear. The Premier League, as a whole, treated the secessionists with kid gloves. Aston Villa midfielder John McGinn had earlier suggested that clubs should be punished by enforcing the use of the generic names created by the football video game *Pro Evolution*, Man Blue and Merseyside Red, for example.[12] That might have been more fitting, and humiliating, than the very small serving of humble pie that the

Premier League's official statement set out in front of them: 'The six clubs involved in proposals to form a European Super League have acknowledged once again that their actions were a mistake, and have reconfirmed their commitment to the Premier League and the future of the English game.'[13] In addition, it was agreed that the six would make a £22 million 'goodwill' payment to football's good causes and accept a new poison-pill clause into the Premier League's statutes: that should they be tempted to join another competition, without the league's agreement, they would be fined £25 million each and have 30 points deducted. Senior executives from the six clubs were relieved of some of their roles within the Premier League, losing control of key committees, but no one was in any doubt that the old balance of power would reassert itself. UEFA were equally light touch in their approach: having accepted a format for the Champions League which gave the big European clubs more games and more of the TV money, the punishments were like withholding pocket money – a €15 million fine among them all, and 5 per cent of their UEFA competition revenues to be docked for one season.

The Premier League and UEFA were, perhaps, ready to let the whole thing pass, but much of the English football press had been radicalised by the moment. Sam Wallace, chief football writer for the *Daily Telegraph*, for example, sounded closer to a columnist at the *Morning Star*: 'This had been a furious three-day reckoning and the once secret plans of this wealthy elite of venture capitalists and fossil fuel billionaires, of career football politicians like the old man in charge at the Bernabeu, were over. The limits of their power had been exposed. The people had spoken.' Martin Samuel at the *Mail* was unequivocal in calling for serious legislative change and regulatory intervention to prevent a repeat performance.[14] Gary Neville gathered a cross-section of ex-players and pundits, representatives of fan organisations, and fan TV and YouTube channels, around an open letter calling for the creation of an independent regulator in English football. More than 100,000 people signed a parliamentary petition in support of this. Andy Burnham and Steve Rotheram, Labour mayors of Manchester and Liverpool respectively, released proposals for reform that also called for a shift in club ownership to the German model, giving supporters' trusts a majority of shares.[15] The Conservative government, its populist instincts still intact, read the room and decided to make good on their manifesto promise to commission a review into football's governance. The review was charged with examining the regulation of club ownership, the ways in which fans' interests could be entrenched in football's governance, and whether all of this should be done by an independent regulator rather than the FA and the leagues. Then, as with so many other issues that had momentarily gripped the Johnson government, it disappeared for months. This executive's always limited capacity for focus had been completely broken by the looming end of Covid regulations and an endless series of accusations and investigations into its own probity, a set of affairs that made the case for independent regulation more strongly than even the European Super League.

13.

'Let's Go Fucking Mental!'

Post-Covid Mania at Euro 2020

Euro 2020 was intended to be a celebration of pan-European identity, staged by UEFA in twelve cities across the continent, from St Petersburg to Seville. Covid meant that it was delayed by a year, the number of host cities was reduced, and for the opening games it was played in front of much smaller crowds. Paradoxically, for such a festival of European amity, the final rounds of the tournament would all be held in England, where the ramifications of Brexit were still being played out on and off the field. England, Scotland and Wales had all qualified for the tournament, and Prime Minister Boris Johnson, speaking in the House of Commons, announced his support in advance, wishing 'all the very best to Scotland and England and all the home nations that may be playing'. To which the FAW replied on Twitter, 'And Cymru?!'

Johnson, in keeping with the rest of his time in office, never did get around to acknowledging Wales, but Wales didn't really need it. Covid travel restrictions meant that there was no great cavalcade of Welsh fans following the team to Azerbaijan, where they played their opening games, but Wales itself was awash with flags. Charles Ashburner, the owner of specialist shop Mr Flag in Swansea, reported that he had noticed a change

196

in what fans were looking for. In 2016, before the Euros in France, he had sold countless generic Welsh flags, but four years later, 'There have been many more who want the word "independence" on their flags, or slogans in Welsh rather than English.'[1]

They had, no doubt, seen the flags and banners that had been appearing at Wales games for the previous two years, many of them organised by Welsh Football Fans for Independence. The group first appeared on social media in 2018 and became a small physical presence at games, beginning with a match in Cardiff against Denmark. Over the next two years their numbers appeared to swell to at least four figures, gathering in Womanby Street in the city centre, plastering the street furniture with stickers and marching to the stadium with banners. The group was also a presence in the wider pro-independence coalitions in Welsh civil society like AUOB Cymru (All Under One Banner Wales) and YesCymru. Founder Andrew Benjamin saw football as a gateway drug: 'The idea of Welsh independence is becoming a big thing; you can feel it, and I just wanted to do my part ... We already support an independent football nation. It's just a case of taking the next step politically. Opponents of Welsh independence like to portray Wales as a country of divisions around language, geography, culture – these so called divisions just don't exist following Wales.'[2]

Pandemic restrictions put paid to these kinds of marches and gatherings through 2020 and the spring of 2021, but the polls kept moving, registering at their peak 40 per cent support for Welsh independence in the EU and 31 per cent support for a straight yes in a referendum tomorrow. Alongside these visions of a new kind of Wales, the shift in sentiment was also driven by the pandemic experience of a Welsh government operating very differently from its counterpart in Westminster; the empathy and caution of Mark Drakeford, the First Minister of Wales, contrasted with the seeming indifference and recklessness of Boris Johnson.

Another factor, surely, was the ideological and narrative paucity of the version of Britishness being offered to the Welsh and everyone else. A win against Turkey and a draw with Switzerland were enough to take Wales to the round of sixteen, where they were due to meet Denmark. The day before that match, 25 June, had been designated One Britain, One Nation Day by the UK government, who had encouraged the nation's schools to get their kids to sing along to a specially composed and wincingly awful song also called 'One Britain, One Nation'. The Welsh government countered on social media by suggesting that schools should stop and sing the Welsh national anthem in anticipation of the match. In the end, Wales were soundly beaten by Denmark 4–0; hardly a declaration of independence, but when you are locked into a state whose chief executive can't even remember your presence, or be bothered to call you by your name, it was another small victory.[3]

One wonders if there were many takers for 'One Britain, One Nation' in Scotland that summer, as finally the country had qualified for an international tournament. Some voices on the right, like Alex Massie in *The Times*, argued that this was of no political significance: 'Scots have grown-up. National self-esteem is no longer wrapped up in the fortunes of the national football team.'[4] Others on the left, like Gerry Hassan in *Scottish Review*, thought quite the contrary: 'There are parts of Scottish society that are untouched by the national football team's return to a major tournament. It just does not feel that way. The all-consuming excitement depicts a country that has regained some pride.'[5]

If the atmosphere at Hampden Park, where Scotland played their hearts out and the Scottish crowd were bursting with end-of-Covid energies, was anything to go by then Hassan was probably closer to the mark. Even so, Scotland were beaten by the Croats and the Czechs, ensuring they would not qualify for the knock-out phases, but the team and fans reserved their best for the trip to Wembley and their game against England. With no fan zone to go to in London, and the torrential rain that fell all day making Hyde Park unusable, the Tartan Army assembled in Soho singing, 'No Scotland, No Party'. The last of the nation's social-distancing rules were being relaxed, but they were entirely abandoned here as a rain- and alcohol-soaked reverie began. Politics, for now, took second place to a more general national celebration. As one participant in the Scottish takeover of Leicester Square put it, 'You can be a staunch Tory or an SNP. It's not an issue in the Scotland support.'[6] At Wembley, as ever, the crowd booed 'God Save the Queen', while the team ground out a hard-fought goalless draw with their hosts, and both factions departed peaceably.

In the run-up to the final between England and Italy, a different kind of politics emerged: 'Anyone but England'. Some voices on the unionist end of Scottish politics bemoaned it, arguing, 'From the outside looking in Scots taking the position of "Anyone but England" is embarrassing, it displays a childish ignorance and petulance; a mean spirited closed mind.'[7] There was some evidence of a change of attitude. One fan argued, 'The character of Southgate and his team are part of why anti-English attitudes are softening ... progressive Scots are quietly impressed by their stand on taking the knee and the team's apparent independence from the worst parts of the UK media.'[8] However, the English-centric obsession continued to grate. One member of the Association of Tartan Army Clubs thought 'the English team are a pleasure to watch, but with the sound down ... the media saturation has spoiled it for everyone else.'[9] The polls certainly suggested that ABE was alive. The *Scottish Sun*'s survey found that more than two-thirds of Scots would be supporting England's opponents through the tournament, and that fewer than one in ten would support their neighbours.[10] Once England had made it to the final against Italy, Italian flags started appearing all over Scotland. Pure Radio Scotland rebranded itself 'Pure Radio Italy' for the weekend. Shoppers in Glasgow complained that Tesco was failing to 'help boost national pride' after their local branch played the England fan anthem 'Vindaloo'. The pro-independence *National* newspaper ran a front page depicting Italy's manager, Roberto Mancini, as William Wallace. It went on to describe Italy as Scotland's 'final hope', while the *Daily Record* warned of the 'nauseating possibility' that England could win.[11]

The Scots were not, perhaps, alone in harbouring such thoughts. Certainly, there was a significant minority of both England fans and right-wing politicians who found this England team problematic. England's preparations began at the Riverside Stadium in Middlesbrough, where a small crowd booed them as they took the knee, before beating Austria 1–0 in a friendly. Four days later, a slightly larger crowd did the same before the game with Romania. The right wing of the Conservative Party was delighted and emboldened. Tory backbencher Lee Anderson mounted his own one-man boycott of the side: 'For the first time in my life I will not be watching my beloved England team while they are supporting a political movement whose core principles aim to undermine our very way of life.'[12] Marco Longhi MP raged on Facebook, 'Fans just want to watch football without having the agenda of a Marxist supporting organisation rammed down their throats by overpaid prima donnas competing for who can virtue signal the most.'[13] One online response to this kind of rhetoric was memes of an England team that were actually Marxists, with Gareth Southgate's match notes revealed to be quotes from *The Communist Manifesto* and the *Economic and Philosophic Manuscripts*.

After the opening game of Euro 2020, Home Secretary Priti Patel, when asked by GB News as to whether the booers should stop, gave them the tacit go-ahead: 'That's a choice for them, quite frankly.' Boris Johnson let it be known through his spokesperson that he was even more supportive of their right to boo: 'The Prime Minister fully respects the right of those who choose to peacefully protest and make their feelings known.' Lee Anderson kept up his boycott and the booers never quite went away, but they were drowned out by the vast majority of the crowd who at subsequent games applauded and cheered the knee. The players were unequivocal about carrying on and Gareth Southgate published 'Dear England' on the Players' Tribune media platform.[14]

In retrospect the letter was, perhaps, the most widely read and important statement on English national identity since George Orwell's 'The Lion and the Unicorn'. Thoughtful, polite and authentic, the essay offered a patriotism rooted in Southgate's memories of his grandfather, who had served in the Marines during the Second World War. It was a version of England that was respectful of monarchy, the armed forces and its rituals, but tolerant of difference despite its own conservatism, and above all open and inclusive. It located the national character in the Crown and the armed forces, but in the arts and sciences too, and in an unexpected nod to popular radicalism, in the spirit of the fans that had challenged the European Super League. In his own words Southgate offered an exegesis on Eric Hobsbawm's notion that 'the imagined community of millions seems more real as a team of eleven named people', as powerful as any sociological seminar. He understood that watching England made you 'part of an experience that lasts in the collective consciousness … You remember where you were watching England games. And who you were watching with. And who you were at the time.'

He also thought that with such power comes responsibilities. Southgate defended his players' right to make a statement about racism in the game and in society. Indeed, he argued that it was his and their 'duty to continue to interact with the public on matters such as equality, inclusivity and racial injustice, while using the power of their voices to help put debates on the table, raise awareness and educate'. As for the racists, the trolls and their enablers, 'unfortunately, for those people that engage in that kind of behaviour, I have some bad news. You're on the losing side. It's clear to me that we are heading for a much more tolerant and understanding society.'

Johnson, cunning enough to know when he was beaten, would walk back his statement and rearrange reality, claiming at Prime Minister's Questions: 'Nobody defends booing of the England side.' Indeed, as England progressed through the tournament, he began to adopt the trappings of the superfan. Downing Street was dressed in St George flags and his Twitter timeline became a riot of posed 'Watching the football on TV' pictures. The *Spectator* fawned over these displays, contrasting images of Keir Starmer watching games down the pub – 'in a conventional white work shirt, with the sleeves rolled up to the elbow. Keith from accounts' – with a shot of Johnson with outstretched arms, mirroring a celebrating Harry Kane on a big screen in front of him which apparently said, 'We are both captains of the national team.'[15] In the looking-glass world of British political conversation this was to be expected, for it was Starmer who had the real football credentials, having attended Euro 96 and long held an Arsenal season ticket, while Johnson had never shown the slightest interest in the game. In the end, though, nothing illustrated the insincere and opportunistic nature of the man better than his excruciating appearance at the England–Denmark semi-final game in a very undersized England top, squeezed uncomfortably over his office shirt and tie.

England's run through the knock-out stages was exhilarating, beating Germany 2–0 at Wembley and demolishing Ukraine 4–0 in Rome, before facing Denmark in a semi-final back at Wembley. As the countdown to the end of Covid restrictions ticked down, the nation's commitment to social distancing was evaporating, and the fantastical thought that England would make their first tournament final since 1966 became tangible. England won their semi-final against Denmark 2–1 with an extra-time penalty from Harry Kane, scored on the rebound, and both the Wembley crowd and the internet exploded. Adele's post on Instagram of her celebrating in her living room – 'ITS BLOODY COMING HOME!' – which received more than one and a half million likes, can stand as proxy for the deluge. Gary Neville, at the game, was stunned by both the result and Southgate's measured demeanour: 'The standard of leaders in this country in the last couple of years has been poor. Looking at that man there, that's everything a leader should be: respectful, humble, tells the truth, genuine.'[16]

There was, however, still another side of England in play and warning signs of what was to come. Before the game, fans booed the Danish national anthem, and someone shone a green laser pen in the eyes of Danish keeper Kasper Schmeichel as he prepared to face Kane's winning penalty. Imaan Madsen, a Dane living in England, told the *Observer* that in the aftermath of the match England fans had screamed 'Fuck Denmark' at her, her husband and their nine-year-old son, who had the temerity to show up in a Danish kit and face paint. Jeanette Jorgensen had her hair pulled and a Danish flag snatched out of her hands. Inside the stadium, another Danish supporter reported England fans screaming in her ear how 'shit Denmark was, how shit I was, and that I was a whore'.[17] There was trouble in other parts of London too. An ecstatic, drunken crowd trapped buses in the road near Leicester Square, climbed onto their roofs and let off flares and fireworks, before riot police intervened. In Dulwich, England fans spotted Danish supporters on a bus, which they surrounded, shook and eventually invaded.

On the day of the final, two versions of England turned up. A broadcast TV audience of over 31 million was joined by more than 10 million on streaming services, not to mention those in innumerable public spaces and pubs, all teetering on the edge of the last of the nation's Covid restrictions. These numbers were greater than the audience for Diana's funeral, Boris Johnson's lockdown address to the nation, and even, the 1966 World Cup final. The players took the knee and were applauded. To collective rapture, Luke Shaw put England 1–0 up after just two minutes, a lead they held until Italy's poise and possession brought the inevitable equaliser in the second half. It was penalties again. England's Bukayo Saka, Marcus Rashford and

Jadon Sancho all missed theirs, and the Italians were crowned champions.

Everyone knew that the three Black players who had missed the penalty kicks would be the subject of online racist abuse, and they were duly trolled and racially insulted, thousands of times over. What, perhaps, was less anticipated was the affection they would also receive from the rest of the English nation. Marcus Rashford's mural in Manchester was defaced, only for more than ten thousand people to turn it into a great shrine of love to him: a thousand multi-coloured Post-it notes of support and a tableau of flowers and shirts. Notably, on their return to domestic football, none of the players were abused by the crowd, a kindness afforded to neither Southgate after Euro 96 nor David Beckham on his return from the 1998 World Cup. The Home Secretary and Prime Minister, dog-whistlers-in-chief, condemned the racists, but Aston Villa and England centre-back Tyrone Mings snuffed that one out, tweeting: 'You don't get to stoke the fire at the beginning of the tournament by labelling our anti-racism message as "Gesture Politics" & then pretend to be disgusted when the very thing we're campaigning against happens.'[18] A small victory, perhaps, for a progressive version of England? However, as the Casey Report would reveal in excruciating detail, the real story of the day concerned the other England.

Commissioned by the FA in the aftermath of the unprecedented social disorder that engulfed the final, Baroness Casey's review of the day's events is among the most illuminating documents in the history of English football and its fan culture. The report began bluntly:

The events of Sunday 11 July 2021 (Euro Sunday) at Wembley Stadium were a 'near miss'. I am clear that we were close to fatalities and/or life-changing injuries for some, potentially many, in attendance. That this should happen anywhere in 21st century Britain is a source of concern. That it should happen at our national stadium, and on the day of our biggest game of football for 55 years is a source of national shame.[19]

Wembley Stadium was the epicentre of these events, but an indication of the level of suppressed mania in the football nation could also be found elsewhere in London that day. A crowd of up to 10,000 people, overwhelmingly young men, filled Leicester Square for much of the day, where one fan, to huge applause, lit a massive red flare clasped between his buttocks. Later, the front windows of Burger King were smashed, people invaded the National Gallery, and police proved powerless to prevent hundreds running across the tops of vehicles, not to mention a carjacking on Whitehall.

At Wembley itself, people began gathering early and drinking hard. In fact, many of the early arrivals appeared to be already drunk, arriving with crates of beer and cool boxes of homemade cocktails. What they did not bring with them were tickets. Cocaine and a range of stimulants were being widely and openly consumed on Olympic Way, the pedestrian strip that runs from Wembley tube station to the Olympic Steps in front of the stadium proper. Queues for the small number of bars and restaurants around the ground were huge, as were those at the three supermarkets selling alcohol; many attendees resorted to calling in moped deliveries of booze via Deliveroo. One experienced London Underground employee reported, 'I've been doing this for over a decade and have worked on various other celebratory events, including New Year's Eve. I have never seen drunkenness like this so early on in the day.'

They might have thought otherwise had they been in Porto in 2019 when England played Portugal in a UEFA Nation's League match, where they would have witnessed England fans drinking hard from early morning in the city centre, and clashing with police who baton-charged them through the evening.[20] Indeed, they would have recognised that what was in front of them was the England away support writ large, and on home leave, treating England with the same collective disregard usually reserved for unwitting foreign hosts.

There was, at this point, no police presence on Olympic Way. The first deployment was not planned until later in the afternoon, just one of the many mistakes made by the authorities. There was, it transpired, no real sense among any of them – from the police to the local council, and from Wembley Stadium to the FA – that the day would be anything other than a major footballing event. However, the feel on the streets after the Denmark game suggested that this would be no ordinary occasion. In the first place, the game came on the crest of a wave of excitement around the end of Covid restrictions after eighteen months of control. At the same time, much of the press framed the day as a once-in-a-lifetime opportunity to see England in a final at home, 'as rare as the appearance of Halley's Comet'. The *Telegraph* suggested that 'the delirium dial should be cranked as far as it will go, leap into the madness of the moment conscious that the chance might never come again'. Add to this the well-publicised fact that with the attendance capped at 67,000 there would be a lot of empty seats inside Wembley, and it was inevitable that thousands of ticketless fans, without any other fan zones to go to, would make their way to North London to soak up the atmosphere and, on a day that might never come again, chance their arm at the turnstiles.

At around noon a single-decker bus became jammed in the crowd on one of the streets that crossed Olympic Way and was soon engulfed by fans dancing on its roof and setting off flares. By one o'clock dozens of men were climbing on traffic lights, hanging from lamp posts and launching fusillades of pyrotechnics. One council official at the scene recalled, 'It was like a medieval football match. Stuff was getting chucked in the air – it was dangerous. People were climbing the trees and climbing traffic lights. Things had buckled.'[21] Worse, ticketed fans and families were beginning to make their way through the mayhem.

One recalled, 'I witnessed bottles and cans being thrown at people, children cowering behind parents to hide, trees being ripped up and thrown, climbing on roofs and throwing things into the crowds.'[22] Wheelchair users were forced to roll their way over a thick carpet of broken glass and rubbish. The Co-op supermarket, which ran out of alcohol, had its windows smashed, while one pub landlord was forced to lock his customers inside, in a desperate effort to prevent a large and angry crowd from storming the premises.

At half past four, as planned, the outer security perimeter around the stadium, where fans were to show their Covid passes and their tickets for the first time, were opened. Soon after, a large group of fans charged the fencing at the Spanish Steps on the west side of Wembley, creating the first breach in the outer perimeter and allowing ticketless fans to swarm onto the main concourse that surrounds the stadium and gain access to the turnstiles and other entrances. Over the next few hours more and more breaches in the security perimeter would be made: 'Large groups of fans were observed working together to attack specific points and cause breaches. This would then draw in response teams, stewards and police, allowing these fans to charge an area far further away.'[23]

'Jibbing' – getting into the stadium without a ticket – does occur regularly in English club football, but hitherto it had been neither widespread nor organised at national team games. Despite a small but significant number of incidents at the Denmark semi-final, the authorities had no real idea of what was to come. The Casey Report recorded that many observers on the day had overheard fans exploring how they might evade security and making plans to do so en masse. Emboldened by cocaine mania and the imminence of kick-off, that is precisely what they did. The more of their peers that did so successfully, the more the crowd attempted to replicate their success. The authorities accepted the inevitable and abandoned Covid checks on the perimeter, redeploying staff to try to cope with the chaos now developing at the turnstiles, for within minutes of the initial breach, the first incidents of tailgating had occurred. Ticketless fans used subterfuge, offers of cash to ticketed fans, and bribes to stewards in their attempt to enter the stadium close behind ticketed fans before the turnstile gates closed. When this failed there were many incidents of violence and aggression. While stewards and police desperately attempted to staunch the flow at the turnstiles, roaming groups of men attempted to enter the stadium via its disabled entrances and the emergency gates, not normally opened until just before the end of the game to allow egress. As the father of one wheelchair user said, 'The problem was that each and every time the stewards opened the disabled gates to let [my son] or any wheelchair user in, they were met with a rush of non-paying people charging the gate barging past and pushing disabled people and stewards out the way. I myself had to physically guard [my son] to get in through the gate.'[24] Where force wouldn't work, others tried deceit. Another parent recalled of one jibber: 'He's then taken [son's] wheelchair and pushed it towards the door … Just as we got to the door we twigged what was going on and it turned out he's just an England fan in a high-viz jacket that was literally hijacking a wheelchair to get into the stadium.'[25]

Over the two hours before kick-off there were at least seventeen major breaches of the stadium's gates. Many of them occurred when staff opened pass gates for wheelchair users from the inside to eject a tailgater and were ambushed by a group on the concourse, who typically held the external door open, allowing others to rush through. Three mass breaches occurred when ticketless fans used brute force, along with crowbars and scaffolding, to open the pass gates. The largest breaches took place through emergency fire doors, and between 6.50 and 7.10 p.m. approximately 690 people broke through. One witness told the Casey inquiry, 'There was a wave of bodies just flung to the floor, including a young lad in a wheelchair – it was terrifying, disgraceful.'[26] It might have been even worse had police not deployed the bulk of their riot-control units at the top of the Olympic Steps, where they faced an enormous crowd for much of the next four hours in an aggressive standoff that was punctuated by huge and maniacal charges when the national anthems played just before 8 p.m., and later while the penalty shoot-out was taking place.

Inside Wembley most of the mob had headed straight into the lower level of the stadium, where there were almost no empty seats, and proceeded to occupy the aisles, other people's seats, and much of the area reserved for wheelchair users. By this time the decision had long since been taken that they could not be removed from the stadium during the game, and so the ugly mayhem of the Olympic Way was now firmly in the stands. The mood was manic, aggressive and racist. One attendee recalled, 'One fan tried to hit me personally because I was saying not to boo the Italian national anthem. I witnessed a fight by the bar area and that was set off just because somebody bumped into someone else.' Another wrote, 'A large group of drunken, drugged men suddenly filled the area around us and spent the entire game shrieking racist chants, swear words etc behind my 12yr son, when I asked them to tone it down due to my son being there they threatened violence.'[27]

The police estimated that 6,000 people remained outside the stadium at kick-off and stayed there for the duration of the game, an angry, brooding and menacing presence. As extra time turned to penalties, senior staff were contemplating what would happen if England were to win, and whether it would trigger a vast final surge from those still outside. One senior member of the Wembley control room staff recalled, 'I wanted Italy to win under penalties, I was begging for the scenario that unfolded because there was pressure building and building and building.' Another remembered thinking, 'If they win, that charge is uncontrollable.' England lost, and then the rain, mercifully, began to fall. The crowd outside remained aggressive, demolishing a temporary toilet block on Olympic Way, which meant, for the now departing fans, that 'the smell in the air was extremely strong and horrid, best described as a mix of alcohol and urine'.[28] Given the Covid regulations still in place, there weren't many travelling Italian fans, but the mob still found a few to abuse. A British Transport Police officer described a situation that was repeated many times over: 'On the train, we had staff intervene to protect Italian fans from being abused. One family of three generations, grandparent and grandchild were shouted at by England fans.'[29]

On a normal match day, Brent Council would have had to deal with around three tonnes of litter. On this occasion they had to deal with thirty-three tonnes, not to mention all the drug debris, faeces and broken bottles. What would normally take a day took five days to clear up, as good an analogue for life in Britain after Covid as one could hope for.

Part III

Injury Time

Football in a State of Emergency, 2022–24

14.

Poetry in Motion

Football, the Arts and the Polycrisis

In 2023 *OOF* magazine, in association with the artist Jeremy Deller, put on 'The World of Gazza!!', an exhibition featuring art, memorabilia and archive materials that presented a complex, multi-layered version of Paul Gascoigne. Douglas Gordon's neon piece *Tears Are Not Enough* referenced his lachrymose performance at the 1990 World Cup, while Rosie McGinn's writhing sculpture of Gascoigne spoke to the torments and dislocations of sudden fame, and the precarious states of mental health it can produce.[1] Artistic merit aside, what made it such an extraordinary act was that in 1994 Deller had created a series of posters for imaginary art exhibitions on subjects not normally considered suitable for the gallery or the museum. One of them was 'The World of Gazza!!'. Now, just under thirty years later, football and art, once almost entirely separate realms in British culture, had been conjoined.

For much of the twentieth century there had only been limited encounters between art and English football. A few fabulous posters for the FA Cup final were commissioned by Frank Pick at London Transport in the interwar years. There was a burst of activity for the Football Association's 1953 'Art and Football' exhibition that featured L.S. Lowry's *Going to the Match*, alongside work from leading impressionists, abstract painters and engravers. Then there was almost nothing for the next four decades. Like everything else in the game, something began to change in the early 1990s, and a new wave of football-related art emerged alongside the launch of the Premier League and the wider cultural and economic transformation of English football. Since 1992, the year of the league's debut, at least six winners of the Turner Prize, Britain's most prestigious award for visual art, have made a connection to the game. Mark Wallinger preceded them all in 1988 with *They Think It's All Over … It Is Now*, a Subbuteo homage to the 1966 World Cup final set atop a museum-style marble plinth, slyly reflecting on football's place in the nation's historical narrative and sense of identity. Damien Hirst, always operating on the borderline of art and his own celebrity, was part of the group Fat Les who recorded the football anthem 'Vindaloo' for the 1998 World Cup and appeared in its video. More recently, he has made a dull and formulaic spot painting featuring Lionel Messi. In 1996 Grayson Perry, repelled by football's often uncouth and violent masculinities, made a pot called *Football Stands for Everything I Hate*. In a shift of mood that reflected much of the nation, he tweeted a picture of it in 2018 during the World Cup and wrote, 'Me and soccer had history. Gareth Southgate and his team are helping me find closure.'[2] Chris Ofili made tapestries and drawings featuring Italian striker Mario Balotelli. Douglas Gordon – with Philippe Parreno – made *Zidane* in 2005, a seventeen-camera microscopic examination of the player filmed during a single Real Madrid match, and made it impossible to look at a football match in the same way again. Nostalgia, history, memory and memorabilia – all central components of mainstream football culture – have been the concerns of Jeremy Deller and Mark Leckey. Deller's breakthrough exhibition, 'Open Bedroom' – staged in his actual bedroom in his parents' house – featured a set of calling cards modelled on those used by the football firms of the 1980s, to be left for their victims after a fight. Mark

Leckey's 1999 film *Fiorucci Made Me Hardcore* featured football casuals and their style as part of a found-footage collage that celebrated the protean working-class youth movements of the 1970s and early 1980s that would eventually give ecstatic birth to rave culture.

Plenty of other artists have followed similar paths. Sarah Lucas's 2002 *Geezer* was a multi-media portrait of the Arsenal striker Charlie George, who had grown up on the same estate as her. Banksy, in a previous life, played for the Easton Cowboys FC in Bristol, and went on a tour of Zapatista-controlled Chiapas in Mexico in 2001, where he painted a number of football-themed murals. Caroline Coon, perhaps the first to do so, painted dazzling female football players. The noted portraitist Tai-Shan Schierenberg said that he had no connection to football until he was made artist in residence at West Bromwich Albion in 2017 as part of a TV documentary. He painted, among others, manager Tony Pulis and striker Darren Moore, and finished the season an Albion addict. David Shrigley, who long ago lost his heart to Partick Thistle, created 'Kingsley', an angry, crumpled star who serves as the club mascot, without doubt the best in world football.

'World of Gazza!!' was just one of many exhibitions that *OOF* has staged in the gallery space next to Tottenham Hotspur's stadium, featuring a new generation of artists taking football as their theme, and bringing more female and queer perspectives to the genre. Lydia Blakeley, for example, celebrated the owner of Norwich City, Delia Smith, giving her legendary half-time talk to the crowd, imploring the team to come back out and win, crying, 'Let's be 'avin you!' Jakob Rowlinson has been making tapestries and hand-embroidered club crests that blend football iconography with quasi-religious imagery and queer references.

What explains this surge of creativity? Neither the FA, nor the leagues, nor many clubs have actually commissioned works. Certainly, there has been an explosion of club and player murals on urban English walls, some spontaneous, many paid for by sponsors, but it is hard to see the football authorities as a direct catalyst for, or patron of, artistic innovation. Rather, as football, at all levels, has become the most popular form of storytelling and allegory in modern Britain, so artists of all kinds have taken note. The game's arrival in the world of high art was just the last frontier in its expanding reach, as a cursory glance at the worlds of poetry, music and theatre demonstrates.

Rhythm, rhyme and meter are no strangers to the world of football. The game's innumerable chants and songs make it natural territory for the poetic imagination, so that even T.S. Eliot, hardly a sporting man, could consider the FA Cup final an essential element of the national culture, while both Seamus Heaney and Ted Hughes wrote small but beautiful recollections of childhood games. In the mid-1980s Tony Harrison's epic poem *V* described the graffiti sprayed on gravestones by Leeds United supporters, and took the rage of football fans as a symbolic starting point for exploring the anger and conflicts of the Britain that was just emerging from the bitter end of the miners' strike: 'More expansively, there's LEEDS v. the opponent of last week, this week, or next/And a repertoire of blunt four-letter curses on the team or race that makes the sprayer vexed.' In a similar vein Don Paterson's 1993 collection *Nil Nil* used the dismal fate of a small Scottish club to tell the story of a battered post-industrial town in the west of Scotland. The BBC, perhaps alert to these trends, if not quite the tone of Harrison and Paterson's verse, broadcast a montage of the 1998 World Cup accompanied by Des Lynam reciting the words of Kipling's 'If'.

More recently, poets have not just been writing about football clubs, they have been working for them, as dozens have been appointed poets in residence, from Ian McMillan at Barnsley to Jamie Thrasivoulou at Derby County. Scottish football has been a particularly welcoming space for poets, with clubs like Selkirk, Kilmarnock and St Mirren all enthusiastic supporters of the form, while the Scottish FA has its own dedicated poetry library and programme. In fact, only Brazil could produce an anthology of national football poetry close to the size and literary quality of Alistair Findlay's stunning collection of Scottish football verse. Simon Armitage, reflecting on England keeper Robert Green's performance at the 2010 World Cup, went as far as to suggest poets were, metaphorically at any rate, footballers themselves: 'I've always thought of poets as the goalkeepers of the literary world – the last line of defence.' Poet Laureate Carol Ann Duffy wrote a lament for David Beckham's ruptured Achilles tendon to coincide with the 2010 World Cup finals. Since stepping down from the post, she has continued to find inspiration in the game, spotlighting Pat Dunn, the country's first ever female referee, in a poem that celebrated the Lionesses after their victory at Euro 2022: 'Red card for misogyny/Free kick for progress/We're all onside.'[3]

Prose and fiction have, by contrast to poetry, been almost conspicuous by their absence. The wave of fan autobiographies that followed Nick Hornby's *Fever Pitch* has dwindled, and none have ever matched its acuity or comedy. Similarly, the defining football and travel texts of the early 1990s – Bill Bruford's *Among the Thugs*, Pete Davies's *All Played Out* and Simon Kuper's *Football Against the Enemy* – have had many emulators, but few equals. The great wave of 'hooligan memoirs' published in the 1990s and 2000s has provided a rich stream of evidence for social historians, but little that stands the test of literary time. As that generation has aged, and even passed on, the genre has virtually disappeared. Novelists, too, have been remarkably shy. Irvine Welsh has certainly woven references to Hibs into every one of his Edinburgh stories, but he has only made the game a setting for action in *Dead Men's Trousers*. Published in 2018, it reincarnated the characters from his 1993 novel *Trainspotting*, and by his own admission he was only able to imagine them coming together in a meaningful way at a football match – specifically Hibernian's miraculous Scottish Cup win over Rangers in 2016. That said, acknowledging football as the common denominator of ageing and damaged masculinities is hardly news, and the place of the game is lost in his now trademark miasma of sex and drugs and violence. In fact, the only recent additions of any weight to the thin skein of twentieth-century football novels – like *The Unfortunates*, B.S. Johnson's experimental book in a box, or the surreal whimsy of J.L. Carr's *How Steeple Sinderby Wanderers Won the F.A. Cup* – have been David Peace's coruscating football trilogy – *The Damned United*, *Red or Dead* and *Munichs* – and Anthony Cartwright's *Iron Towns*, set in Middlesbrough, which finally broke out from the self-referential and claustrophobic world of football to explore its presence and meanings in wider British society.

Music has, perhaps, been even more intimately entwined with football than poetry: obviously enough by the singing of crowds, but also by the use of recorded music in the stadiums and the release of official songs by clubs and national teams. There was even a short wave of football players turning wannabe pop stars, like Chris and Glenn – aka Chris Waddle and Glenn Hoddle – who took 'Diamond Lights' to number two in the charts in 1987, and Paul Gascoigne, who covered Lindisfarne's 'Fog on the Tyne' in 1990. In the last decade the relationship between music and football has changed. Popular music continues to furnish the basis of many chants, and their distribution through YouTube and social media has proved as efficient, if not more so, than terrace networks. In 2018 one Liverpool fan's online reworking of the Archies' 'Sugar, Sugar' in praise of their front line and smart transfer dealings – 'We've got Salah/Mane, Mane and Bobby Fermino but we sold Coutinho' – not only went viral, but was widely sung at the club's games. That said, the taste for official songs has diminished. England, for example, only had a new song for the men's World Cup in 2010 (Dizzee Rascal's 'Shout for England') and Euro 2020 (Krept & Konan's 'Olé (We Are England)'), but both disappeared without a trace.

In fact, the crowd has reverted to the 1996 hit 'Three Lions' and, in an ever deeper nostalgic mode, embraced Neil Diamond's 1969 wedding disco classic 'Sweet Caroline'. In a similar embrace of the past, Coventry City paid homage to the Specials and the 2 Tone Records label that emerged there in the late 1970s with a 2019 third kit featuring the label's characteristic chequerboard pattern. Manchester City did much the same, putting the yellow-and-black stripes that once adorned the walls of the Haçienda nightclub on the shoulders of an away kit. Footballers, wisely perhaps, have foresworn the charts, though Yannick Bolasie and Bradley Wright-Phillips faced off in a grime sound-clash hosted by Lord of the Mics in 2014, while Cole Palmer's rendition of the reggae dancehall tune 'Clarks' went viral in 2024.[4]

For the most part, though, the traffic is in the other direction, as musicians have flocked to football. In their long and now rescinded retirement, the Gallagher brothers' main claim to fame appeared to be their fidelity to Manchester City. Fatboy Slim (Brighton) and Goldie Lookin Chain (Newport County) were the turn-of-the-century pioneers in sponsoring club shirts, but they have been joined by a whole raft of new arrivals. Ed Sheeran put his tour and album logos on Ipswich Town's strip, and for those without his deep pockets, lower-league sides have offered a less expensive option – one taken up by the Libertines at Margate, Enter Shikari at St Albans, and Jake Bugg at Notts County.

Inside the stadium, now equipped with deafening PA systems, music is an unavoidable element of the match-day experience, now so loud that one does not know if it is there to beat the crowds' cheers into submission or to mask their absence. Either way, it is a small mercy that the ubiquitous use of AC/DC's 'Hells Bells' has moved on, but in the Premier League, at any rate, the walk-on songs are a motley selection. Looking at the playlist for the 2023–24 season we find that a few clubs stood by tradition, playing modern recordings of old songs, notably

Brighton's Edwardian ditty 'Sussex by the Sea' and West Ham's music hall singalong 'I'm Forever Blowing Bubbles'. Some opted for 1960s pop classics, like Manchester City's doo-wop version of 'Blue Moon' and Liverpool's longstanding choice of 'You'll Never Walk Alone', originally released by Gerry and the Pacemakers in 1963. Not quite a popular hit like these, but of their era, Everton have stayed faithful to the theme tune of the BBC's 1960s Merseyside police drama *Z-Cars*. More conventionally, Brentford played 'Hey Jude', while Crystal Palace walked out to the Dave Clark Five's 'Glad All Over'; 1970s easy listening was the choice at Wolves – 'Hi Ho Silver Lining' – and Nottingham Forest – 'Mull of Kintyre' – while Spurs and Newcastle opted for orchestral film music. The 1980s got a look in at Manchester United, who played the Stone Roses hit 'This Is the One'. By contrast, contemporary tunes, like Louis Dunford's 'The Angel', which was played at Arsenal, were rare. A preference for unthreatening nostalgia aimed at an ageing audience is not surprising, but what perhaps is most remarkable about this playlist is that with the exception of Chelsea and the Harry J Allstars tune 'Liquidator', they are all performed by white artists. To find football's connection with Black urban Britain, which continues to supply a disproportionate number of its players, one must get outside the stadium, where a new wave of hip hop, grime and drill artists have made the game a regular theme of their lyrics.

Look closely enough and, in fact, Britain's Black musical cultures have always had an eye on football.[5] From the Windrush generation, we have King Timothy's 'Football Calypso', which ran through the clubs of the then First Division and incorporated recorded match atmosphere into the song. Lord Kitchener and the Fitzroy Coleman Band's 1956 tune 'Manchester Football Double' celebrated United winning the league and City winning the cup. Reggae artists, both Jamaican and British, found the game irresistible and a space for political commentary, too. Dennis Alcapone's 1982 'World Cup Football' celebrated the international game before demanding that Ron Greenwood, England's manager, put black players – specifically Cyrille Regis and Garth Crooks – on the pitch. In 1985 Asher Senator's 'The Big Match' upped the stakes and called for all eleven slots to be given to the new generation of Black footballers, name checking, among others, John Barnes, John Chiedozie, Paul Davis, Ricky Hill and Alex Williams. For the current generation of musicians and performers the intersection of football and music stems, at least in part, from the fact that many young musicians have themselves been aspirant footballers before opting for music, like MC Zakhar, who attended Brentford's academy, Tiggs Da Author, on the books of Gravesend and Northfleet, and Kano, who played youth football at West Ham and Chelsea. Players or not, these artists and producers have all grown up in a milieu where football and music were not only sources of self-expression, but offered a narrow path of social mobility where there were few other options and were central elements of everyday life and conversation. This close interaction between the two has made for a rich lyrical palette. CASisDEAD, on his tune 'All Hallows', playfully mixed football and politics: 'Yeah we fucking party/Middle fingers up like fuck the Tory Party/They're about as far right wing as Nani/So we start riots like we just lost the derby.' Stormzy, a Manchester United fan, in 'Know Me From' made the luckless David Moyes and his short-lived reign at the club an exemplar of disaster and disruption: 'I come to your team and I fuck shit up/I'm David Moyes', while Skepta thought Thierry Henry's departure from Arsenal to Barcelona the epitome of betrayal: 'My Man are United like Giggs, I will never leave my young gunners like Thierry.' It is a matter of considerable regret that, while Stormzy may have played Glastonbury, English football has yet to showcase the musical genres and the performers who are its closest and most dextrous observers.

Football, performed in front of a live audience, often under lights, offers an obvious analogy to the theatre, but playwrights were slow to explore this connection. Harold Brighouse, author of *Hobson's Choice*, wrote *The Game* and saw it performed in Liverpool in 1914, but this surprisingly contemporary tale of corruption and match fixing didn't receive a revival until 2012. By then, Peter Terson's 1967 play *Zigger Zagger* had become a staple of youth theatres, and Arthur Smith's 1991 domestic comedy *An Evening with Gary Lineker* had become the best-known football-themed drama. The former told the story of Harry, a teenager caught between the adrenaline rush of football disorder and the economic pressures to conform, settle down and take up an apprenticeship; the latter was a domestic tragicomedy in which a football-obsessed man plots how to watch the 1990 World Cup in preference to spending holiday time with his long-suffering partner. In the early 2000s they were joined by Andrew Lloyd Webber's saccharine musical *The Beautiful Game*, set in Northern Ireland on the eve of the Troubles, and Roy Williams's altogether more serious *Sing Yer Heart Out for the Lads*, a study of racism and masculine aggression among a pub team watching an England–Germany match, which opened at the National Theatre.

Over the last decade this small body of plays has been significantly enlarged. Questions of sexuality, untouched by past works, have been examined. *Jumpers for Goalposts* was a comedy that pitted two LGBT teams, Barely Athletic and Tranny United, against each other, while John Donnelly's *The Pass* was a brilliant duet in which a star striker, eventually married with kids, struggles with the sexuality that he has hidden from friends and colleagues all his life. *The Christmas Truce*, a big-money production for the Royal Shakespeare Company, did its best to make the fabled First World War Christmas game – played between British and German soldiers on no man's land in 1914 – into compelling theatre, but struggled to effectively counterpoint this moment of humanity with the scale and senselessness of the slaughter within which it occurred. Much more satisfying and harder edged, *Red Lion* and *Red Pitch*, opening in 2015 and 2024 respectively, set new standards for the genre. The former, written by Patrick Marber and staged at the National Theatre, was a compelling, claustrophobic three-hander set in the changing room of an impecunious small-town non-league club. Here, the romantic and loyal kit man and the ambitious and cynical manager struggle over the soul of the team's young striker; the former hoping to nurture him within the club and to transform its fortunes, the latter eager to sell him on and take a cut of the fee. *Red Pitch*, by Tyrell Williams, was an electrifying experience in which three Black sixteen-year-old boys from a London estate played out their football dreams and their real-life setbacks on one of the caged pitches, now synonymous with the city's football culture. Both would go on to have successful West End runs. However, their performance can't compare with that of James Graham's *Dear England*, in 2023, without doubt the most successful English football drama ever.

Taking its title from the open letter written by Gareth Southgate on the eve of the European Championship in 2021, *Dear England* starred Joseph Fiennes, who gave a remarkable performance as Southgate. Neither impersonation nor facsimile, he brilliantly captured Southgate's physical and verbal tics, his inner strengths and his enduring frailties. It told Southgate's own England story: how he coped with the disappointments and harsh scrutiny that followed from missing a penalty in the semi-finals of Euro 96, and how this was ultimately a source of learning and strength that he would deploy as England manager. Staged with aplomb, deeply human, often funny, no football play received the accolades or the audiences that *Dear England* acquired, and surely no other drama has managed to turn the habitués of the National Theatre into a raging football crowd. On the other hand, it was, for the most part, a study in leadership, individual psychology and emotional intelligence. The opportunity to link Southgate and his football story to deeper and wider social currents of racism and nationalism, though presented, was rarely taken. It was not alone in this. Brilliant as *Dear England* and the rest of the new football plays were, instructive as the new poetry and music of football have been, intriguing as the art world's take on the game has become, nothing has really risen to the challenge of narrating and exploring football's relationship with contemporary history. Nothing, that is, except football itself.

With the lifting of the last Covid restrictions on football crowds in the summer of 2021, the new season was seen as a return to normality. As one Watford fan, attending his first live game for two years, put it: 'A sell-out crowd, a great atmosphere and beautiful football to end it! Life may not be completely normal, but being back watching football live again is definitely bringing it back!'[6] For fans, at any rate, there were no masks, no checks, no digital passes, just the football, just like it used to be. However, the next two years were to prove to be anything but normal, and nothing would be just like it used to be.

In the first place, the return of crowds to the game brought with it the strange accumulated psychic baggage of an eighteen-month pandemic, which manifested itself in the biggest outbreak of disorder and anti-social behaviour in football for decades, from raging coaches to fist fights and pitch invasions. Then, in early 2022, Russia's invasion of Ukraine triggered the departure of Russian money from English football, above all Roman Abramovich's enforced sale of Chelsea, a moment that exposed the degree to which many national assets had been sold off to oligarchs, chancers and foreign private equity. It also triggered a sharp rise in the cost of energy and food. Football could live with Chelsea's short-lived demise, but the cost of living crisis that the war ignited would prove much tougher to weather. In this context the victory of England's women at Euro 2022 was all the more joyous: a few weeks of glorious sunshine and hope, an alternative version of the football nation and England's first major trophy since 1966. This, in turn, transformed the status of the women's game and began a process that will seriously change the gender balance and culture of the wider game. English football will never look the same again.

The 2022–23 football season that followed was always going to be unusual, with the FIFA World Cup to be played not after the season had ended, in July, but, due to host nation Qatar's extreme heat, mid-season, from late November to mid-December. Given the possible loss of momentum occasioned by the break and the likelihood of exhaustion thanks to the extended football calendar that year, one might have expected upsets, but no one predicted that in the course of a season the UK would go through three prime ministers, an unprecedented cost of living crisis, the death of the Queen and then the hottest year on record on Earth.

Football tracked each of those moments. For five weeks the Qatar World Cup replaced the Premier League as the world's premier spectacle, while Middle Eastern influence in the game grew. Manchester City's long-running battle with the Premier League over its financing highlighted the abject nature of corporate regulation in Britain, which has been captured by the powerful interests that it was meant to control; a state of affairs that is responsible for not merely City's evasion of football's financial rules, but the scandal of Britain's negligent water companies pumping sewage into rivers and the tragedy of Grenfell Tower. The cost of living crisis was sharpest in grassroots and youth football, where clubs were folding and parents struggled to pay their kids' subs. The rituals and counter-rituals of royal mourning in football was in keeping with the wider divide in the country between royalists and republicans. And finally, football's encounter with the climate crisis – the extreme weather and storms of these seasons and environmental campaigning inside stadiums – illuminated both the nation's vulnerability to the emergency and its desperately sluggish response to it. Never had football's capacity to tell the story of the nation been so powerful and the result so vivid and multi-stranded, so much stranger and more real than fiction. To paraphrase Oscar Wilde, we have reached the point where football imitates art far more than art imitates football.

15.

The Fall of the Roman Empire

Ukraine, Russia and the New Geography of Football Club Ownership

Back in 2014, any qualms that English football might have had about its relationship with Russian money after the annexation of Crimea in March of that year were soon dissipated. For the Russian emigré oligarchs in Belgravia and their English facto-tums – from the Conservative Party to the money launderers in the City – it was back to business as usual. Aeroflot became top-tier sponsors of Manchester United. Maxim Demin, a low-profile Russian petrochemical trader, quietly bankrolled Bournemouth's ascent to the Premier League. Alisher Usmanov, an Uzbek oligarch with close links to the Kremlin, abandoned his long-term ambition to own Arsenal and invested in Everton instead, through big sponsorships from his companies USM, Yota and MegaFon. Roman Abramovich remained firmly in place at Chelsea, where a banner reading 'The Roman Empire' permanently hung from the top deck of the Matthew Harding stand. Chelsea fans sang Abramovich's praises as the team, coached by the demonic Italian Antonio Conte, won their fifth Premier League title in 2017.

This kind of presence in British life began to look a little different when, in early 2018, Sergei Skripal, the former Russian intelligence officer and double agent, was poisoned in Salisbury by officers of the Russian FSB. Two months later Abramovich's visa ran out and was not renewed, while the Home Office began to have second thoughts about many of the 700 top-tier 'entrepreneurial' visas taken up by Russians since 2015 – a steal for just a loosely interpreted £50,000 investment in the UK. Abramovich cancelled his plans to rebuild Stamford Bridge but kept paying the bills. In 2021 he received his final dividend when Chelsea won the Champions League, and Abramovich, who had been absent from Stamford Bridge for three years, went on to the pitch in Porto to celebrate.

Russia's invasion of Ukraine in February 2022 stopped all that. The British government sanctioned Abramovich and a dozen other Russian oligarchs, freezing their UK assets. Demin would go on to sell Bournemouth and disappear, Manchester United terminated their Aeroflot contract and all of Everton's Russian sponsorships were cancelled. Within a week, Abramovich agreed to hand over the running of the club to the Chelsea Charitable Foundation, wrote off more than £1.5 billion in the form of loans and stock purchases he had subbed the club since he bought it in 2003, and announced that he would sell it immediately, with any profit from the sale being passed to a newly created trust to support victims of the war in Ukraine. The club itself, while still owned by Abramovich, was required to operate under strict sanctions that prevented it from selling any further tickets or merchandising, or receiving any further sponsorship or transfer income, and was permitted only to spend the bare minimum on club expenses. Chelsea fans mourned Abramovich's passing and chanted his name at a dozen games, most pointedly during a show of support for Ukraine at Burnley.[1]

The departure of Abramovich, Usmanov and Demin did not herald the end of foreign ownership in English football. If anything, it had become even more entrenched over the previous decade. As of the 2023–24 season just three clubs in the Premier League were owned outright by British citizens –

Matthew Benham at Brentford, Tony Bloom at Brighton and Joe Lewis at Spurs – though Joe Lewis's tax-exile status ensured he wasn't around too much. All three made their money from gambling, Benham and Bloom on sports, Lewis on currencies. West Ham United continued to be owned by ex-pornographer David Sullivan, but he had sold a quarter of the club to Daniel Křetínský, a Czech billionaire; while Steve Parish held on to a small share of Crystal Palace, otherwise sold to Americans. The other fifteen clubs' ownership consisted of: two Middle Eastern state-backed projects, Manchester City and Newcastle United; a member of the Saudi royal family at Sheffield United; eight by American billionaires and their investment vehicles (Arsenal, Aston Villa, Bournemouth, Burnley, Chelsea, Fulham, Liverpool and Manchester United, though Villa was part owned by Nassef Sawiris, the richest man in Egypt); Evangelos Marinakis, a Greek shipping oligarch at Nottingham Forest: an Iranian billionaire at Everton (now sold up to another American fund); Chinese billionaires at Wolverhampton Wanderers; and, amazingly, Luton Town was owned by its supporters' trust.[2] Thus, the Premier League, composed of institutions nearly all created in late-nineteenth-century working-class Britain, was more than three-quarters owned by the global super-rich. An extraordinary turn of events, it would seem – until one looks at the ownership of the rest of Britain's Victorian infrastructure.

The privatisations of the 1980s and 1990s had created a railway network in which, by 2017, 70 per cent of the rail companies were foreign owned, almost all by foreign states. The water industry, outside of Scotland, was 72 per cent foreign owned, with major shareholders including Chinese state entities, the Qatar Investment Authority, the Abu Dhabi Investment Authority, the US company BlackRock, the Hong Kong tycoon Li Ka-shing, and the Malaysian magnate Francis Yeoh.[3] The parallels with football became even closer in the 2010s and 2020s, as, with the biggest and most obvious targets all taken, foreign investors began to pursue the slumbering giants and smaller clubs of the lower leagues, while the Conservative governments of the era flogged off the last of the public realm, selling Royal Mail and many of the nation's ports and airports to foreign companies. By 2023–24, an incredible seventeen of twenty-two clubs in the Championship had majority foreign owners, as did more than a third of both League One and League Two clubs. Even the National League, tier five of the English pyramid, was not immune, with Ebbsfleet United and Dagenham and Redbridge in foreign hands. By the same token, outright social ownership below the Premier League had shrunk to just three clubs – Newport County, AFC Wimbledon and Exeter City – after supporters' trusts at Swansea City, Wycombe Wanderers and Portsmouth sold up to new billionaire investors.

Who, then, are this new generation of patrons, domestic and foreign? What possesses them to invest their capital in a sector in which almost every business loses money every year? A number of British clubs have enjoyed the largesse of lottery winners. Poor John McGuinness lost all of the £10 million he won propping up Livingstone, while in 2009 the more cautious Les Scadding put £1.25 million of his winnings into Newport County and got them promoted back to the Football League. Paul and Thea Bristol put £3 million into Torquay United and rescued them from debt, if not from lower-league football, while Colin Weir, who won £161 million, bought Partick Thistle a new training ground and academy. In the absence of this kind of winning ticket, the next best thing has been the 'local boys made good', preferably with fortunes in the low hundreds of millions; Steve Gibson, the patriarch of Middlesbrough, and Tony Stewart, the long-suffering owner of Rotherham United, are exemplars of this kind of patronage. Local girls, it should be noted, have been thinner on the ground, with just a few female owners like Delia Smith at Norwich and Carol Shanahan, who used the money she made in fintech to rescue Port Vale from bankruptcy. Lower down the leagues the fortunes are smaller, but the losses still pile up. Among those local heroes ready to drop a few million pounds a year have been: Ronald Wycherley, whose vending-machine monies sustained Shrewsbury Town for more than two decades; Andy Holt, the moulded plastics king who has sustained Accrington Stanley; Paul Barry, who made a lot of money in the US travel industry and spent it on Cambridge United; and IT and insurance folk like Robbie Cowling at Colchester, Charles Grant at Crewe, Jason Stockwood at Grimsby Town and Ben Robinson at Burton Albion. Less money but more glamour was provided by Manchester United's 'Class of 92' who, with Singaporean financier Peter Lim, bought Salford United in 2014.

Adopted son's money is also accepted. Dale Vince spent much of the 1980s with no fixed abode as he moved around the country as part of the network of new age travellers and free festivals. He stopped in Stroud long enough to build his first windmill, create his renewable energy company Ecotricity and buy the nearby Forest Green Rovers. Pete Winkelman grew up supporting Wolverhampton Wanderers but moved to Milton Keynes in 1993 as he transitioned from music executive to property developer. Rightly recognising that what would become a city of near a quarter of a million people had no league football club, he ruthlessly engineered Wimbledon's move to the city in 2003 and onto land he had bought. He then built a stadium with a lot of money from IKEA and Asda, who set up next door, renamed the side MK Dons and spent over twenty years as chairman of perhaps the most unloved club in the league, watched by a decent League One crowd of 7,500 in a windy, cavernous stadium built for 30,000, before finally selling up in 2024 to a consortium of Kuwaiti businessmen.

These owners are all wealthy men and women, their personal fortunes in the tens, even low hundreds of millions, but they have been joined by a new generation who have entered the lower ranks of the super-rich. Local billionaires in the lower leagues include Bristol City's Steve Lansdown, the late Trevor Hemmings at Preston, and the Coates family, owners of Bet365, at Stoke City – all have spent heavily, but not enough to take their clubs to the top or keep them there. Recently, they have been joined by Simon Sadler, who made his money in finance and in 2019 removed Blackpool from the clutches of the Oyston family, who, in a highly competitive field, were surely the most odious and unpleasant owners in English football. In 2021 David Clowes, scion of the huge property development firm, took over Derby County after Mel Morris had blown the best part of the £200 million he made from *Candy Crush Saga* and taken the club into administration. A similar act of salvage was performed by Mike Danson, a data company billionaire, who bought out Wigan's hapless Chinese owners and their considerable debts.

Amid all this wholesome patrician largesse, it is a relief that English football still has room for some old-fashioned wideboys. Andy Pilley bought Fleetwood Town in 2003 and bankrolled them through seven promotions, from the tenth level of English football to League One.[4] In many ways he was a model owner, developing the stadium and the training ground, and generously supporting a range of local charities in one of the poorest towns in the country. Sure, he had in the late 1980s done four months in prison for stealing disability benefit cheques and cashing them, but nobody's perfect. By the 2000s he had learnt the basics of corporate malfeasance working for Enron, and then set up his own energy company, BES Utilities. While the company made a lot of money for Pilley and for Fleetwood, it was also systematically defrauding many of its customers, locking them in to unnecessarily expensive contracts. Pilley denied everything, and then in 2023 was found guilty of fraud and sentenced to thirteen years.

Jason Whittingham and Colin Goldring's time is perhaps yet to come.[5] This unlikely duo – Whittingham an older and secretive financier among the London super-rich, Goldring a trainee solicitor with a taste for cutting corners – teamed up in 2018 and bought Morecambe FC. Somehow nobody at Morecambe or the EFL managed to notice that Goldring had been censured by the Solicitors Disciplinary Tribunal and banned from working as a solicitor, for his part in some very sharp practice involving £9 million, a Saudi cabinet minister and expensive cars. They even managed to look the other way when the pair bought into the rugby union club Worcester Warriors and swiftly drove them into administration and liquidation. The Department of Culture, Media and Sport (DCMS) select committee investigation into this debacle thought that the 'unscrupulous owners mismanaged club finances while attempting to strip the club of its assets'.[6] The pair were, at least, forced to step down from the Morecambe board before they could play the same game with that club. They have not, however, relinquished ownership; and though the fans, the board and the league have been begging them to do so, it could be worse, considering their much-publicised plan to sell Morecambe to 21-year-old Sarbjot Johal, who was apparently a 'soft drinks' entrepreneur, but whose digital trail mainly led to implausible cryptocurrency schemes, before he disappeared from view.

These kinds of local owners are not an endangered species, but over the last decade or so many of them have been replaced by foreign owners. In the lower leagues they fall into four broad categories. Some are straightforward and very rich romantics who have fallen in love with the game and whichever small town they have alighted upon. More cynical Europeans, often with some experience in football, are a second and eclectic group of owners. Others, primarily Americans, are private equity investors who maintain the touching illusion that their advanced financial engineering and management skills will allow them to transcend the impossible economics of English football where everyone else has failed. Finally, there is the serious money, predominantly from Asia, from men who have lots of agendas, none of which involve breaking even.

Darragh MacAnthony, an Irish property developer specialising in expensive holiday homes, became at the age of thirty the then-youngest chair of a Football League club when he bought Peterborough United in 2006. MacAnthony quickly graduated from dilettante to obsessive, so much so that he has bought the club twice. Having sold around half of his shares to Canadian businessmen in 2021, he was forced to buy them back when their plans for funding a new stadium disintegrated. Millwall might still be singing 'No one likes us,' but it is simply not true. John Berylson, a Jewish-American East Coast banker purchased the club in 2007 and lavished his love, time, attention and more than £100 million of his money on it, until his untimely death in a road accident in 2023. Australian businessman Clem Morfuni got bitten by the same bug. He spent twenty years building a multinational plumbing business in Sydney, opened a branch in England and made the mistake of watching a lot of football. In 2021, after a vicious legal battle with the former majority owner of Swindon Town, he took control of the club. In a magical first season he put on an adrenaline-fuelled Antipodean orgy of 'can do' optimism: pulling pints for the fans, personally driving around Swindon in a mobile billboard truck promoting season-ticket sales, and playing six-a-side football with supporters. Welcome as this was, no one could claim that due diligence was his strong suit. Having, on purchase, paid off around £6 million of the club's debts, he discovered, much to his surprise, that there was another £2.9 million on the books and payment was suddenly due. A sale of some of his shares covered that, but the bills kept rolling in and by 2024 he was £8 million down and the club just a few places off the relegation zone in League Two.

Portsmouth's history of foreign ownership had not been an entirely happy one. Under Serbian-American billionaire Milan Mandarić, the club made it to the Premier League and won the FA Cup in 2008, but Mandarić sold up and a succession of calamitously bad owners followed. In 2010 the club passed from the Russian-Israeli Gaydamak family, who made their money in arms dealing, to Sulaiman Al-Fahim, a UAE real-estate developer who also hosted the country's version of *Dragons' Den*. It took him six weeks to realise that the sums would never work, and he sold Portsmouth on to Saudi businessman Ali al-Faraj, who in turn could only keep the club going by taking out a large loan from Hong Kong businessman Balram Chainrai. Farah defaulted on the loan and the club passed to Chainrai, who put it into administration. He would later take it out of administration and sell it to Vladimir Antonov, a Russian con artist then busy asset-stripping Lithuania's largest bank, Bankas Snoras. When this company failed in 2011, Antonov departed and the club went back into administration, finally rescued by the Pompey Supporters Trust. The trust was able to stabilise the club, but any return to the heights Portsmouth had reached was inconceivable. When Michael Eisner, chief executive of Disney for over two decades, came calling in 2017 they voted by a huge majority to sell their stake. Since then the Eisners have spent tens of millions of pounds, been model owners and helped Portsmouth back to the Championship; but what is interesting about them is not their capacity to absorb these kinds of losses, or even their model of management, but how they exemplify what combination of needs and desires English football sates in the super-rich.

In a revealing interview Eisner explained that this was, in the end, all about family matters: 'We came up with "the family that plays together, stays together", a play on the old line about families praying together. So, that worked for Disney and it's what Disney is. Well, having three children, nine grandchildren and tons of cousins, I thought having something where the family could play together would help keep the family together.'[7] Family dynamics, the creation of an heirloom and the sinews of a dynasty aside, what is it that attracts America's new super-rich to the lower levels of English football? In part it appears to offer a sense of authenticity, localism and human connection that American sports are not delivering. In 2023 Brad Galinson, a multi-millionaire property developer from Florida, bought

Gillingham from its long-standing and irascible owner Paul Scally, who had made his money in photocopiers and kept most of it in tax exile in Dubai. Galinson had been looking for a sporting project but could not find one in America. In part this was a function of costs, as major league US franchises had become too expensive for a mere billionaire to purchase. More than that, they were, in their hyper-commercialised and advert-fragmented form, losing their appeal. Galinson eulogised to the local press, 'What you don't realise is that English football is so much more than, and so different to, U.S. sports. I'd never seen something like that and I'm bored watching NFL now with the time-outs and huddles.'[8] Kevin Nagle, who made billions when he sold his healthcare company, was looking for a club and 'in about ten days I went from barely knowing Huddersfield existed, and I don't mean that pejoratively, to buying it. It's not just the club that impressed me, though, it's the community. It reminds me of where I grew up and I really relate to it.'[9] Peter Freund, a New York investor, transferred his affections from baseball to football after seeing Dagenham and Redbridge win promotion to League Two, and having bought the club in 2018 said 'there is no experience like it in the world – sharing a pint after the match with your supporters – we can either drown our sorrows or celebrate, but either way we are drinking after the match. It is the most authentic sporting experience in the world.'[10] Berke Bakay, a minor investor at Ipswich Town, saw them get promoted from League One to the Championship and gushed, 'When I got back home I told my family that this is the most meaningful event I have ever been part of during my entire life. I put it up there with the day that I got married and the birth of my four children. To see in the eyes of thousands of Ipswich Town supporters the sparkle and to see them so happy meant the world to me.'[11]

It was precisely this kind of schmaltz that had been making Hollywood take note of English football. However, attempting to bend football narratives to the traditional arcs of a ninety-minute movie proved almost impossible to engineer. Then, in 2020, with the arrival of Apple TV's surprise football sitcom hit *Ted Lasso*, the industry began to find a football format that it could work with. But why trouble oneself with a writers' room when the game itself was a multi-stranded soap opera of its own? It was this realisation that led first Rob McElhenney, the lead in sitcom staple *It's Always Sunny in Philadelphia*, and Ryan Reynolds, star of the *Deadpool* Marvel movies, to buy Wrexham from its supporters' trust for £2 million. The story, since documented in their global hit show *Welcome to Wrexham*, has almost everything they could have asked for: the third-oldest professional football club in the world is out of the Football League and, like the town, down on its luck; a still loyal and large local fan base is hungering for better times; and two out-of-town bros ride to the rescue, making it up as they go along. Three wild seasons followed: just missing promotion back to the League in 2022; then returning to the League in 2023 in an epic battle with Notts County at the top of the table; and a miraculous second promotion in 2024 taking them to League One, with the promised land of the Championship and the Premier League in their sights. It helped, of course, that the owners had lost another $9 million to get them there, but at the same time the extraordinary power of their own celebrity and the global audience they were attracting online saw income soar. Shirt sales exploded, Wrexham toured the United States playing to full houses against Chelsea and Manchester United, and where before they were sponsored by Ifor Williams Trailers, they now sported the logos of United Airlines, TikTok and Expedia.

New European owners of English football clubs have not been able to rely on a global television hit to boost their brand, but there has been no shortage of great storylines. Bradford City's is perhaps the clearest tale of a football club as financial albatross. In 2016 the club was bought by German duo Stefan Rupp and Edin Rahic. Rupp was a very wealthy semi-retired and bored businessman who had made his fortune manufacturing helicopter seats. Before he came to take a look at Bradford in 2015, he had never been to a football match. Rahic was an ex-professional with some scouting experience in the Bundesliga and a short time on the board of Stuttgart Kickers, but he had never actually run a football club. The two did share a bank manager, and through this connection they made a deal where Rupp would put up the money and Rahic would run the show. Defeat in a play-off for promotion to the Premier League in 2017 was the high point for the pair, but it has been all downhill ever since. Rahic ran up a giant transfer bill, kept very poor financial records, spoke rarely, alienated staff and supporters, and was drummed out of the club in 2018. Since then, Rupp, a largely absentee chair, has barely been to a game, has written a few desultory open letters, made heartfelt apologies to the now exasperated and angry fans, and landed the club in the fourth tier – where they have been becalmed and where no one wants to offer him the kind of money for Bradford that he stumped up in the first place.

Watford's story has been an Italian holiday affair gone sour. Owner Gino Pozzo came from an Italian business family whose successful toolmaking company enabled them to buy Udinese, which launched Gino into the world of football management and scouting. In the 1990s he built an innovative global scouting network that helped transform the Udine-based club's fortunes. In 2012 the family bought Watford, installed Gino as the chairman and attempted to apply similar methods. For a time it worked, as Watford moved in and out of the Premier League and made it to the 2019 FA Cup final, though a 6–0 humiliation by Manchester City took some of the gloss off the occasion. Relegation to the Championship swiftly followed. In the meantime, the rest of the football world appeared to have caught up with Pozzo's methods, and his recruitment policy became increasingly ineffective, though not for Pozzo's close friend, the French agent Mogi Bayat, who personally earned more than £40 million for the transfers he arranged for the club, when he wasn't fending off investigation and accusations of fraud and money-laundering in France and Belgium. Hiring and firing seventeen mangers in as many years didn't work too well either. By 2023 a fan base that had once sung, to the tune of 'Mrs. Robinson', 'Here's to you Pozzo Family/Watford loves you more than you would know/wohohoh' was putting up 'Pozzo Out' flags. Communications with supporters were so infrequent that the EFL threatened to sanction Pozzo unless an open meeting was held with the fans, a legal requirement of League membership. In the absence of communication, the fans turned to satire and in 2022 voted to give the player of the season award to Hassane Kamara, an Ivorian left-back who arrived in January, scored one goal and made no assists but played wholeheartedly and occasionally acknowledged their existence.

Sunderland, whose demise under American billionaire owner Ellis Short had been so brilliantly captured by the *Sunderland 'Til I Die* series, provided further fabulous content under the next set of owners, a consortium led by British businessman Stewart Donald. Inevitably, bad turned to worse as Sunderland remained borderline insolvent and stuck in League One. Donald confided, 'I know fans want me out and I'm desperately trying to get out.'[12] Misery can make for great television, but there has to be an upswing, too, and series three delivered on that with the arrival of 23-year-old French billionaire Kyril Louis-Dreyfus, fresh from an incomplete degree in sports management and equipped with a $2 billion trust find inherited from his father Robert, who had run Adidas and owned Olympique Marseille in their heyday. So far, the youngest chairman in the league with the youngest squad has won promotion back to the Championship and lost the kind of money necessary to get them back into the Premier League in 2025. Netflix have surely commissioned series four.

There will surely be a movie, when the time comes, about the garrulous Turkish media magnate Acun Ilıcalı, who bought Hull City in 2022. In fact, he will probably make it himself and star in it. Ilıcalı, a dedicated Fenerbahçe fan, had started out in sports broadcasting, moved into game shows and light entertainment, and created one of Turkey's most successful media channels and streaming service on which he hosted the Turkish versions of *Deal or No Deal* and *The Voice*. Not one to hide his emotions, he told the fans on arrival, 'Destiny has brought me here from the other side of Europe ... I believe in destiny and I believe we are going to have many good things together. I am in heaven now.' At home Ilıcalı had stayed close to President Erdoğan, playing on his team in a televised seven-a-side match. In England it seemed he had plans for his own soft-power initiative, writing, 'I want to fly the flag of our country in England with the success of Hull City.' He planned for a Turkish outpost on the Humber: 'I hope that Hull City will consist of Turkish people, from their coaches to certain players in the future. My goal is to create a team that makes a sound in the world.'[13] That was certainly the consequence if not the intention of Alan Hardy's brief tenure at Notts County. Hardy, or 'Big Al' as he excruciatingly preferred to be known, bought Notts County in 2017 and communicated more than was good for anyone. In just two years he alienated most of the club's staff, fans and the local press, and having spent tens of millions of pounds led them out of the Football League in 2019 in what he described as the worst six months of his life. Bad as this was, perhaps the real low point came when, in an angry online conversation with a disgruntled fan, Hardy attempted to repost two of their contradictory tweets but ended up posting one from the fan and a picture of his own penis.[14] At County's next home game, Lincoln fans acknowledged this by holding up dozens of inflatable genitals in the away end. He sold up to the more reticent Danish Reedtz brothers, who had made money in the game with the analytics company Football Radar. Under their rather less confrontational regime, Notts County made it back to the Football League in 2023.

In addition to all these new individual and family owners, the last decade has seen many private equity funds and investment vehicles take stakes in English football. They are, in truth, just a tiny part of a much bigger wave of American private equity purchases of UK companies, from care homes to vets, from food processing to hotel chains.[15] The script is nearly always the same: the usual genuflections to city, fans, tradition and stewardship, followed by a lot of PowerPoint talk about data-driven recruitment, new analytics departments, multi-club synergies, innovative scouting and succession planning, all taking the club to the sunlit, cash-rich uplands of the Premier League. They were, however, preceded by a domestic textbook example of why this might prove problematic. In 2007 the Mayfair-based hedge fund and investment company SISU bought Coventry City, recently relegated from the Premier League. In just over a decade they managed to reduce the average attendance from nearly 20,000 to 6,000, got the team relegated twice, endlessly fought with the owners of the stadium that they rented – as a consequence of which they moved them for a season to Northamptonshire, and sacrilegiously to Birmingham for two more – and all that for nearly a hundred million down the drain before selling out at a loss. No one has quite managed the combination of incompetence and self-regard that SISU achieved, but more recent American private equity takeovers have generally performed poorly. Swansea City were sold for £110 million to a fund run by Americans Steve Kaplan and Jason Levien, the former already in private equity, the latter a sports lawyer and NBA executive. After a decade of poor performances and relegation from the Premier League, they, like many other owners, have realised that the club would be marooned in the lower end of the Championship unless they were prepared to gamble even more money on getting back to the Premier League. If they didn't, they would never recoup the enormous and overvalued outlay they made on the club. In late 2024 the two appeared to accept the inevitable and sold up. US hedge fund owner Tom Wagner and his private equity vehicle Knighthead are about to discover the same dilemma, having bought Birmingham City in 2022 and promptly overseen their relegation to League One. Meantime, they are relying on their plans for a new stadium, indeed an entire £3 billion sports quarter in Birmingham, and the irregular presence of celebrity minor shareholder and NFL legend Tom Brady.

At least it was a strategy, which is something that Barnsley's owners have found harder to assemble. The club was purchased in 2018 by a consortium led by Pacific Media Group, under American banker Paul Conway and Chinese hotelier Chien Lee, who had been running their own hedge fund. Barnsley were just one of seven European clubs that the group had bought into, and all of them have fared poorly under their management. Indeed, at the end of the 2021–22 season four of them, including Barnsley, were relegated, and financial problems and fan protest have been mounting at them all. Ipswich Town have proved the exception to the rule. After nearly two decades of lower-level mediocrity under English businessman Marcus Evans, the club was sold to American investment vehicles Bright Path and ORG, and miraculously they achieved back-to-back promotions to the Premier League. Suffolk celebrated alongside, one imagines, Native American sports funds and Arizona's retired police and prison officers, the main clients of the two corporate groups that now owned the club.

The first foray by an Asian oligarch into English football was Thaksin Shinawatra's brief reign at Manchester City. The then prime minster of Thailand was deposed by a military coup when outside of the country, and he bought City as a way of sending messages from exile back to Thailand, where he still hoped to revive his political career. Shinawatra sold up to the UAE in 2008, but he was followed by new Asian owners at Birmingham, Blackburn, Cardiff, Leicester and QPR. Leicester aside, none of these have proved entirely happy encounters, but three more recent episodes of Asian ownership have proved particularly disastrous.[16] In 2015 Thai billionaire Dejphon Chansiri, son of the country's leading tuna-canning company, bought Sheffield

Wednesday and has so far dropped more than £150 million on
the club. Maybe things would have been different if they had
won their play-off in 2016 and made it to the Premier League,
but they didn't, and despite all the money things went badly.
Desperate to reduce the club's now considerable debt and
comply with the Football League's financial rules, Chansiri
bought Hillsborough Stadium from the club, a move designed
to inject another £69 million. The EFL ruled that this was inad-
missible, and a six-point deduction and relegation to League
One followed. Chansiri had a second life when, in 2023, after a
truly extraordinary comeback in the following season's play-off
semi-finals against Peterborough (overturning a four-goal def-
icit), Wednesday went on to beat Barnsley at Wembley and get
themselves back in the Championship. Chansiri then fired the
coach who had achieved this, Darren Moore, while his replacement, Xisco Munoz, delivered just two points from their next
ten games. For good measure, he then put up ticket prices and
goaded the fans with the prospect that he might leave them and
the club's debts behind. When, later in the season, HMRC came
calling for a £2 million unpaid tax bill, Chansiri asked the
supporters to rustle up the money themselves. Wednesday stayed
up, just, but fan protests grew all season.

In 2016 the Central Committee of the Chinese Communist
Party published its plans to turn China into a world-class soccer
nation. Fifty thousand dedicated football schools were to be
established, the football association and league were to be
reformed, and official government policy was to achieve
President Xi Jinping's 'three wishes' – that China should qualify
for, host and win the men's World Cup by 2050. Ever eager to
manage upwards, China's new billionaires took this as a signal
that massive investments in football would reap political
rewards. Some chose to spend their money on the Chinese Super
League, while others rushed to invest in foreign football teams
in Spain, France, Italy and England – like billionaire Tony Xia,
who owned Aston Villa between 2016 and 2020, and conglom-

erate Fosun International, who bought Wolverhampton Wanderers. In 2016 West Bromwich Albion, then in the Premier League, were purchased by Chinese businessman Guochuan Lai for over £175 million. The following season he hired and sacked three coaches, the chairman, the CEO and the technical director, but Albion still got themselves relegated. They did manage another promotion to the Premier League in 2019 but were back in the Championship for 2021 and the club's finances declined. By 2023 it became common knowledge that Lai, who had only visited the club once in the seven years he had owned it, had taken out a series of loans secured against club assets and at eye-watering interest rates. He also appeared to be funnelling the money home to his troubled post-Covid businesses. Fan discontent, organised by Action for Albion, saw thousands march on the stadium, demonstrations held at the directors' entrance to the Hawthorns, and 'Shine a Light' protests using cell phones on the twelve-minute mark (a reference to one of the loans) at home games. However, given the club's precarious balance sheet, no alternative to Lai has yet appeared.

A not dissimilar tale unfolded at Reading in 2017, when it was snapped up by billionaire Chinese businessman Dai Yongge, who had made his fortune, slightly improbably, converting the People's Liberation Army's surplus air raid shelters into shopping malls. The club then came within a whisker of promotion to the Premier League, losing a play-off final to Huddersfield on penalties, and this must have whetted Yongge's appetite. Money began to flow, a new training complex was built, players came in wholesale, and by 2021 the club had a wage bill that was twice the size of its annual revenue and the biggest debt of any club outside the Premier League. The EFL deducted six points from the club in 2021 and relegation to League One followed. In the subsequent three years another twelve points were docked for a variety of late payments and financial misdemeanours. Meantime, two other Belgian clubs owned by Yongge went into liquidation, his main company China Dili was suspended from the Hong Kong stock exchange and its bank account frozen after repeated failures to pay back loans and creditors. Things were so financially tight in the winter of 2023–24 that staff at the training ground were wearing coats indoors, as the heating was turned off. The first team trained late in the day to reduce the costs of undersoil heating. Suppliers who had not been paid withdrew, leaving the medical team responsible for organising players' food; fan group 'Sell Before We Dai' were now organising protests on the eighteenth minute of every game, a reference to the eighteen points that, cumulatively, the EFL had docked from Reading for financial misdemeanours. The League issued regular requests to Dai that he pay some bills, or better that he sell the club, but had no powers to do more until in 2025 a new owner, the American lawyer Rob Couhig, met Dai's price.

Now, more than two decades since Roman Abramovich bought Chelsea and triggered the great sell-off of England's football clubs, the majority are in the hands of foreign owners. The old school of English owners remain driven by a mixture of hucksterism, homesickness, nostalgia and a sense of local duty. Some new arrivals have bought in on a whim, football as an adventure for the terminally rich and bored. Others have sought out the chance to play Lord of the Manor meets *Football Manager* and turn their ice-cold capital into love and respect. The investment funds are driven by finance and tech fantasies of easy profits, nation states by the possibilities of global political messaging and oligarchs by the accumulation of domestic political kudos. None of them, whatever their motivations, have actually been making any money, and some of them have lost a lot, though a few have managed to sell on their financial albatross to the next sucker. Those that remain have found that not only is English football an impossible place to make money, but that retaining the affections of its fans is almost as difficult. Yet such is the draw of English football, its perceived political and cultural heft, that there is no shortage of rich and powerful people ready to disregard these truths.

16.

The Return of the Repressed

Football Crowds, Pitch Invasions and the New Disorder

With the lifting of all Covid restrictions in July 2021, the 2021–22 season saw the emphatic return of crowds to football. Home advantage – radically diminished, even extinguished, in their absence – instantly reappeared, but the mood among players and managers had changed. Coaches, whose touchline behaviour had been getting increasingly unconstrained and angry before the pandemic, returned in a state of fury and paranoia. Sometimes they would turn on each other, as when in August 2022 Chelsea's Thomas Tuchel and Tottenham's Antonio Conte took a handshake to the brink of all-in wrestling. For the most part the officials were the targets of their ire. In the autumn of 2022 Liverpool manager Jürgen Klopp was sent off for his maniacally angry tirade in the face of the assistant referee Gary Beswick; Manchester United's Bruno Fernandes escaped censure despite shoving an assistant referee on the touch line; Fulham's Aleksandar Mitrović pushed referee Chris Kavanagh and was sent off, as was his coach Marco Silva. In an effort to curtail this kind of behaviour, referees were instructed to crack down on dissent. In the first six months of the 2023–24 season the number of bookings doubled, and in the Premier League they trebled. By February 2024, 155 yellow cards had been brandished compared with just 86 for the whole of the previous season.[1] Brighton's captain Lewis Dunk was the first player to receive a straight red card for dissent since 2012, after he called referee Anthony Taylor a 'fucking bellend'. It appeared to be having some effect, as the number of charges reaching the FA itself for technical-area misconduct, mass confrontations and surrounding referees declined, while fines levied on clubs rose: more than a million pounds' worth for Premier League clubs that year.

Many fans were, it seems, in an equally volatile state of mind, and not just in England. Scandinavia and the Netherlands also returned to football amid a flurry of dangerous pyrotechnics, aggressive confrontations and widespread missile-throwing at players and officials on the pitch. In the decade before the pandemic, the number of football-related arrests had dropped every year, declining by almost two-thirds in total over ten years. In the season after the pandemic, the number of arrests in England rose by 58 per cent. More than half of all matches saw some kind of incident: use of pyrotechnics was at an all-time high, on over 440 occasions objects were thrown from the crowd and the number of pitch invasions more than doubled.[2] One football security expert, quoting the Clash song 'Bankrobber', describe the situation: 'Imagine if all the boys in jail could get out now together.'[3] Incidents were occurring at every level of the English game. Rotherham fans were among the most active, with coins thrown at the assistant referee in a game against Crewe, a pitch invasion in a game against Fleetwood, and one supporter who ran onto the pitch at Accrington Stanley and assaulted the home side's Harry Pell, just as he was about to take an 89th-minute penalty, which inevitably he then missed. Bolton fans at Morecambe, in just one game, managed to get arrested for pitch encroachment, disorder, racial slurs and an assault on a police officer. The Premier League was by no means immune to this kind of behaviour: water bottles were thrown at and struck Aston Villa's Matty Cash and Lucas Digne as they celebrated a goal against

Everton, while two Arsenal supporters got on to the pitch during the Carabao Cup semi-final, making a beeline for the Liverpool players celebrating their winning goal.

Scottish football fans' proclivity for pitch invasions and pyro-technics had been rising in the years before Covid. It was almost like old times at the 2016 Scottish Cup final, where victorious Hibernian fans invaded the pitch at Hampden Park in their thousands, assaulting Rangers players and the few foolhardy Rangers fans who'd joined them. After the pandemic these ener-gies were released all over again. In fact, a stoppage was required two minutes into the Scottish Premiership's first game between Livingston and Rangers, as the number of smoke bombs set off made it almost impossible for players and officials to see the ball. The Edinburgh derby proved particularly volatile, with the game at Hibernian's Easter Road witnessing coins thrown at Hearts players, match-stopping levels of pyro when the visitors took the lead and a mass pitch invasion when the home side got a late equaliser. Pyrotechnics had become so commonplace that at the end of the 2023–24 season, Dundee United's procession to the Championship title, Scotland's second tier, saw four consecutive matches stopped by pitch invasions conducted beneath great clouds of orange smoke.

Pitch invasions could, on occasion, be simply comical. When Norwich City were losing 1–0 away to Crystal Palace in December 2021, having gone more than five matches without scoring a goal, another mis-hit cross was met by a fan who had jumped the advertising boards and saved the ball from going out. Norwich fans chanted, 'Sign him up,' to which the Palace fans responded, 'He's too good for you.' At 2–0 down and in the final minutes of a League Cup defeat to Liverpool, one Arsenal fan made a beeline for the team's goalkeeper, Aaron Ramsdale, who theatrically kept the ball away from him and refused to shake his hand before the stewards brought the invader down. Some fans were looking for more than a handshake, though – like the Leicester supporter who, with his side three goals down, rushed the field, sprinted towards the Nottingham Forest players and assaulted Brennan Johnson, Keinan Davis and Djed Spence.

Fans were also fighting each other. Tottenham's visit to West Ham in late 2021 produced a huge brawl among hundreds of fans in the lower concourses of the Olympic Stadium. Middlesbrough's game against Derby in early 2022 saw violent encounters before, during and after the match, inside and outside the stadium, including attacks on emergency workers, resulting in eighteen arrests. The final weeks of the season saw the level of delirium and disorder rise once again, with Bristol Rovers providing the comedy. Rovers went into their final game of the season needing to win by at least seven goals against Scunthorpe to guarantee promotion to League One. The visitors, who had recently gone into administration, did their best to help, fielding a youth team including a seventeen-year-old goalkeeper who was making his league debut. Even so, it was a tall order for Rovers. And yet, in the eighty-fifth minute, miraculously, they made it 7–0, triggering a pitch invasion from every corner of the Memorial Stadium. Proceedings ground to a halt for more than half an hour as the officials, Rovers manager Joey Barton and owner Wael al-Qadi, implored the delirious crowd to get off the pitch lest the whole game be rendered null and void and Rovers' promotion cancelled. The crowd eventually complied and then, on the final whistle, invaded the pitch all over again.

Things had a distinctly nastier edge in the semi-finals of the promotion play-offs that season. At League Two's Northampton Town the home fans invaded the pitch, threw flares and shoved Mansfield Town's Jordan Bowery during injury time. In League One, Port Vale fans invaded the pitch at Swindon and punched and kicked players as the home side beat them on penalties. Nottingham Forest winning their semi-final in the Championship against Sheffield United triggered a huge celebratory invasion, only for one Forest fan to make a run at United's Billy Sharp, whom he headbutted hard enough that Sharp required stitches. On the final day of the Premier League season Everton escaped relegation by a whisker, unleashing a delirious pitch invasion during which Crystal Palace manager Patrick Vieira was assaulted by a fan and then caught on camera kicking him back.

The Premier League, the EFL and the FA all issued pleas to fans to control themselves and promised more and greater legal punishments and bans, but rather less was said about what might be driving all of this. There was some suggestion that the loss of experienced stewarding staff – many of whom had moved into minimum-wage work in logistics and retail in the absence of football – and the departure of police liaison officers over the pandemic had made clubs more vulnerable to social disorder. Stewards were recruited in ever-greater numbers, though they were increasingly young and inexperienced, and police numbers at games actually rose through the season, but to no avail. Clearly, the strange mixture of mania and hedonism with which many emerged from the lockdowns was a factor in the new misbehaviour. The evidence from schools, which reported a massive increase in post-pandemic disorderly behaviour and began to sharply increase the rate at which pupils were excluded, suggested as much.[4] It was, perhaps, made worse by the fact that breaking the rules through the pandemic had been the norm for the Prime Minister and those close to him, and so far they had got away with it.

However, while these contingent factors explain some of the new disorder, they were put to work in a football culture that still harboured a significant number of supporters with a taste for trouble.[5] The old mass charges at away ends, collective vandalism on trains and mass thefts from off-licences may have passed, and most of the old organised firms were effectively retired, but the search for transgressive adrenaline and excitement at football was still on. Regular away fans were perhaps the clearest example of this, but there were plenty of takers at home games and a large fringe beyond the core who could and would be swept up into the volatile situations they created. Here, the pleasures of match-going were rooted in a wider culture of shared travel and the intense camaraderie created by all-day drinking and drug taking. All through the 2010s most games would see large groups of fans occupying public space in the vicinity of stadiums and, where they could, local pubs and bars; both opportunities for the aggressive assertion of identity and power through singing, chanting and, when they could find the opposition, taunts, insults and threats. Violence, though it was very rarely pre-planned, could still be found in the side streets and car parks around football. Within this milieu a small subculture of jibbers emerged, who, if they could evade the police and stewards checking for tickets, would try to get into games for free, jumping over the turnstiles, getting through behind legitimate ticket holders and overwhelming stewards. Confrontations with other fans, and especially the police, remained the stuff of local legend, enhanced the social capital of the 'top boys', and provided the story of the week for those that returned to dull jobs and shrunken horizons. Perhaps, most importantly, these actions served to underwrite a sense that they were still the most authentic of fans, the real representatives of their town or neighbourhoods, bound by an unbroken thread of dedicated hedonism and local pride to the 'golden age' of football disorder.

The combination of pandemic mania with this kind of milieu was certainly an important element in explaining the wave of disorder, but it was supercharged by the increasingly prevalent use of cocaine in English football. Eyewitness reports from the Euro 2020 final at Wembley noted people visibly taking a snort in the stands and drug debris in the bathrooms. Speaking about the problem across football, one anonymous investigator told the *Observer*, 'There's no doubt that even at smaller clubs the toilets look like a launderette by the end of the game, there's powder all over the place.'[6] The *Athletic*, speaking to a specialist police officer, heard that in football pubs the presence of the drug was so overwhelming that their sniffer dogs didn't 'know where to start'.[7] A 2022 survey of match-going fans found that more than 30 per cent had seen cocaine being consumed at the game, with rates of reported use among football fans, at 6 per cent, about double the national average.[8] In this, football was just a more exaggerated version of the nation's large and rising use of the drug. Since the turn of the century cocaine in the UK has been imported in greater quantities, become much more easily available, purer and more reliable in quality, and relatively cheaper. Hardly surprising, then, that usage has risen, and not just among its traditional constituency of City wideboys, rock stars and advertising executives, but as the weekend drug of choice for both working- and middle-class youth – and the middle-aged too. Cocaine levels in the country's sewage systems showed not only more of the drug being taken, but with such a great surge in concentrations at the weekend that its recreational use had become pervasive.

One of the impacts of the drug at football was to make the already garrulous unstoppable. I have, for example, watched Manchester City games in dedicated pubs and been literally pinned to my seat by the torrent of words emerging from my companions as they flitted, in seconds, from their love for Pablo Zabaleta to the corruption of the Premier League and the organised bias of the media against the club. At Bristol Rovers I have sat behind a supporter who, from the kick-off to the final whistle, stood and actively coached the team in an unbroken maniacal dialogue with the players who could not hear him, and his long-suffering assistants who could not get away. For the most part, though, the drug has served to make the loud and aggressive louder and more aggressive, to bind individuals into a collective mania that easily turns to fury, and to convince many that they are smart and fast enough to invade the pitch or take on the police and get away with it. Rarely has a narcotic promised so much and, the comedown aside, delivered so little.

Difficult as all these circumstances were, it is still a little surprising that the police were caught seemingly so unaware and, for a time, appeared so ill-equipped to tackle them. It is not as if a lot of money was not being spent on policing football, or that the police did not have access to remarkable levels of technological surveillance and coercive power.[9] Estimates put the annual bill for policing English football at between £40 million and £50 million, of which the football clubs themselves pay less than 20 per cent, accounting only for police deployed on their property. All of the resources required to police city centres, pubs, railway stations and routes to and from the game are borne by the taxpayer, a not inconsiderable subsidy. For those games categorised by the police as high-risk events this can involve up to 500 officers. This will include: spotters, or as they are now more prosaically called, dedicated football officers (DFO), whose responsibility is to directly monitor and interact with supporters; police support units (PSU) – the official euphemism for three vans' worth of trained and equipped riot police; specialist dog units; and, for good measure, mounted police. Not only does this cost a lot of money, but it has huge implications for the police force more widely, with large numbers of officers having to cancel leave or be withdrawn from other duties. On these occasions much of the police strategy rests upon the active segregation of home and away fans, the allocation and policing of separate pubs for pre-match drinking – or even their closure – and the creation of secure corridors for away fans from their transport to the game, which often turns into something closer to kettling and forced marches.

By contrast, much of the best work done by the police eschews the riot shield and baton in favour of dialogue and engagement with supporters. DFOs accumulate a great deal of knowledge about their supporters, become known faces with much of the crowd, and have thick skins and a knack for football banter that allows them to develop relationships of trust. They also have a gut instinct for what might or might not be about to go off. As one DFO put it: 'Because you tend to work most of the games, you get that feeling … You know if it's boiling or if it's a bit subdued.' If it does start boiling they are often able to defuse situations and draw lines of acceptable behaviour that, for the most part, supporters will accept, because they know the PSUs are a much less negotiable prospect.'[10] Another DFO reported, 'I say there's a line, our line's probably a bit further back than some other officers but they [the fans] appreciate that as well.'[11] In the aftermath of the pandemic, DFOs effectively had to start all over again, reestablishing their intelligence networks and their credentials with fans.

While these tactics contributed to the long-term fall in football arrests and incidents of serious disorder before the pandemic, a number of significant problems remained unaddressed. In many cases the police have been assigning risk levels to matches and fans on the basis of historical reputation rather than contemporary information, reinforcing a predilection among commanders for very highly resourced operations. In particular, the idea that things might go wrong and that one had made a lax assessment of an event or refused offers of additional resources weighed heavily on officers in charge of planning operations. That said, there are reports that even when reliable intelligence came to light suggesting that rumours of organised trouble were in fact just that, senior officers never lowered their risk assessments. In some police forces this kind of overkill was made worse by units being set targets for issuing football banning orders. Repeated observations of this kind of operation revealed that PSUs, who made up the bulk of officers present at high-risk matches, consistently failed to engage with fans, failed to de-escalate tense situations among opposing supporters and made threatening interventions that made conflicts worse. Heavy-handed use of preventative measures was so egregious that a number of police forces were taken to court for transgressing fans' human rights of assembly. In 2015, for example, fifty Bristol City fans drinking outside a pub before their away game with Birmingham were surrounded by West Mercia police officers.[12] They were then threatened with police dogs, publicly accused of being hooligans by an inspector using a megaphone and detained for over ninety minutes, before being put on a train home while the game was being played. Similarly, in 2016 a minibus full of Wrexham fans, none with any reputation for trouble, heading for their game against Grimsby Town, were forced to pull over by the local police, held for half for an hour and forced to turn around and go back to Wales.[13]

Both of these cases, as well as dozens of other examples of draconian police behaviour over the last decade, have been documented by the Football Supporters' Association (FSA) and legal challenges mounted. It is disappointing then, if unremarkable, that the main response to the disorder of the 2022–23 season was not any serious review of policing strategies, but the creation of more minor offences at football and the demonisation of football fans. Chief Constable Mark Roberts, the lead officer of the UK Football Policing Unit and among the most bellicose on the matter, when challenged by the FSA, responded, 'I would like to see the FSA giving a voice to those supporters [who feel intimidated to go to away games] as well as being apologists for hooligans.'[14] In the years since, the levels of disorder and arrests have dropped, if not quite yet back to what they were pre-pandemic; but as with the aggressive policing of demonstrations and political dissent, there has been no attempt to dial down the rhetoric or the police's armoury.

If the years since Covid have highlighted the potential of football crowds for disorder, they have also demonstrated precisely the opposite: the capacity of football supporters for organised political and social action. Indeed, this period represents the culmination of more than three decades of organising and campaigning that have seen football supporters' organisations achieve more impact on the governance of football than ever before. Previously, most of football's protests and campaigns had been conducted at club level. In the 1980s fans at Brighton and Hove Albion and Bristol Rovers had mounted long-running campaigns to acquire a new stadium, after both had seen their old homes flogged off for retail development without alternative plans being made. Reading and Oxford United supporters had combined to prevent Robert Maxwell – the then media tycoon – from carrying out his plan to merge the two as the Thames Valley Royals. More recently, supporters' trusts demonstrated high levels of mobilisation when it came to rescuing clubs – like Exeter City and Portsmouth – from bankruptcy and liquidation. Attempts by owners to change the name or the colours of clubs were met by furious campaigns, like those at Cardiff City when Malaysian billionaire Vincent Tan proposed they play in red rather than blue, or at Hull City where owner Assem Allam had decided that 'City was a shit name' and hoped to rebrand them as the Hull Tigers. For the most part, though, club-level protests centred on performance, or rather the gap between expectations and performance. Disappointment with Arsenal's long spell in the doldrums since the heights of the early 2000s would, in 2017, eventually erupt in the long-running 'Wenger Out' campaign that saw a considerable minority of the fan base turn against their manager, a course that would make the Emirates a toxic and unhappy place until his retirement in 2019. Similar disquiet could be found at West Ham over coaches and owners. In 2018 a game marking the twenty-fifth anniversary of Bobby Moore's death turned very sour when visitors Burnley took a 1–0 lead in the second half and hundreds of fans gathered to protest in front of the directors' box, while others invaded the pitch. A mass rally in 2020, on the occasion of David Gold and David Sullivan's ten-year reign at the club, was just one of many protests inside and outside the stadium over the last five years, not least a season of banners and booing directed at coach David Moyes in 2023–24, despite his having led the club to victory in the previous season's European Conference League. Crystal Palace fans were more cryptic, if no less angry, hanging banners at the club's training ground during Covid that read, 'Palace pandemic of apathy. Change this mentality. Restore the pride ambition and vision,' while in 2024 Roy Hodgson's departure as manager was prefaced by a huge banner in the Holmesdale End that read, 'Wasted potential on and off the pitch, weak decisions taking us backward.'

Fans have been calling for their boards to be sacked since time immemorial, but in a few notable and more recent cases, club owners proved to be so toxic, irrespective of the team's fate, that significant and long-term movements emerged to challenge their incumbency. Manchester United's fan base successfully opposed the proposed BSkyB takeover of the club in 1999, and though unable to halt the arrival of the Glazers, they contested their ownership in more than a decade of campaigns, most notably the green-and-gold movement that adopted the colours of the club's nineteenth-century predecessor Newton Heath. The obviously predatory intentions and disingenuous promises of Liverpool's American robber barons Tom Hicks and George Gillett gave birth to Spirit of Shankly, whose protests, petitions and walkouts helped force the two out. Once the honeymoon was over, at best a few months, Newcastle United fans spent a decade rejecting Mike Ashley. But perhaps the most powerful protest movement was at Blackpool, against the Oyston family, specifically Owen Oyston and his son Karl. The team's one season in the Premier League was used to enrich the owners, as were subsequent parachute payments, while the club dropped into the fourth level.[15] Fans were taunted and slandered on social media and threatened with vicious legal actions. Consequently, the campaign to remove them mobilised a bigger percentage of supporters than any other, mixing marches to the stadium, boycotts of all catering and commercial operations, protest at the Oystons' homes, running an Oyston Out parliamentary candidate, and, most impressive of all, a pitch invasion and occupation during an end-of-season game with Huddersfield Town that saw the fixture abandoned. The Oystons put the club up for sale but hung on until 2019 – when the club, now bankrupted, was finally put into receivership and the family swept from the board.

In contrast to club-level protest, supporters have been almost invisible within the wider governance of the game. It was not until 2007 that the FA Council, notionally the space in which the game's broad swathe of stakeholders were represented, actually had a representative of fans. Even today they have only three out of more than a hundred seats on the council, while places are still allocated to Oxbridge, the armed forces and the rest of England's universities. As late as the 1980s they had virtually no representation and voice within the mainstream football media, and it was this that prompted the first efforts to organise supporters nationally in the wake of the Heysel disaster in 1985. It became clear that no one in the FA, the press or among the coterie of ex-professionals giving their opinion on television had any detailed knowledge of the mechanics of crowd control, or were able to approach the subject with supporters' interests in mind. The Football Supporters' Association was born of this problem. Beginning in Liverpool, but eventually establishing regional branches across the country and gathering more than 2,000 members, the FSA would create a loose activist network which over the next five years combined the voices of the burgeoning fanzine movement with the new independent supporters' associations being formed around some clubs. It was enough to give the FSA a place in the conversation after Hillsborough and during the debates about the reform of stadium safety that culminated in the Taylor Report in 1990, albeit a place with very little weight.

Since then, the FSA (the FSF – Football Supporters' Federation – between 2002 and 2019) has established itself more effectively in football politics, with full-time staff and an increasingly sophisticated policy and press operation. It has absorbed Supporters Direct, which the Blair government created to develop fan ownership, connected itself to similar groups across Europe, and struck deeper roots among supporter organisations at all levels of the game. It has also found an increasingly large and sympathetic constituency at Westminster in the All-Party

Parliamentary Group on Football. There have been some not-able successes. In 2007 the then FSF was a key part of the coali-tion that defeated the Premier League's proposal for a thirty-ninth game, in which a real league fixture would be played in a lucra-tive overseas market. More recently, it was instrumental in getting the Premier League to cap the cost of tickets for away fans at £30. Not quite the aim of the 'twenty's plenty' slogan that it had been running since 2013, but remarkable nonetheless – perhaps, above all, for the campaign's success in making all the stakeholders publicly acknowledge the vital role that away fans play in generating the atmosphere in stadiums that the broadcasters and global audiences find so alluring. Other campaigns have, so far, proved less successful, and certainly ticket prices for home fans have continued to rise at a speed far ahead of the rate of inflation. Campaigns to try to halt the endless proliferation of kick-off times to suit the global televi-sion audience, and thereby to improve the situation for travelling fans unable to get to and from these games in a day, have made little progress. Similarly, attempts to persuade politicians and the police that there should be some relaxation in the alcohol pol-icies of the leagues have met implacable opposition, while the complaint that fans would much prefer the old arrangements to the FA's insistence on playing FA Cup semi-finals at Wembley has fallen on deaf ears. However, on two issues the FSA and the wider supporters' movement have registered significant gains: safe standing and the wider governance of the game.[16]

The recommendation of the Taylor Report on the Hillsborough disaster that the grounds of the top two divisions in English football should become all-seater stadiums had more impact than any other of its many proposals. Implemented over the next five years, clubs hiked ticket prices and made generous use of lottery money diverted to them to pay for the transformation. While the removal of the crumbling terraces and what remained of the fences and barriers erected in the 1980s made watching football unquestionably safer, it also disturbed the ecology of football crowds. Where once the most boisterous and voluble could gather together, numbered seats made this impossible. Even if a critical mass of singing fans was, by chance, established, no choir chooses to sit when it performs. An older, more affluent crowd might account for some of the diminution of atmosphere and noise that has occurred, but the new seating arrangements were even more culpable. Many fans have found it impossible to stay in their seats and, at away ends especially, persistent standing, as the authorities bumptiously describe it, has become widespread. Various attempts by clubs to stop this over the last quarter of a century have led to short bouts of banning orders, and a lot of discontent and anger among fans who feel they have been aggressively over-policed, but a considerable minority continued to stand. The FSA campaigned on this issue in the early 1990s, calling on fans to 'stand up for your right to stand up', but opposition from the police, the government and, not surprisingly, the Hillsborough Family Support Group easily trumped them. Efforts in the late 1990s to get Labour's Football Taskforce to consider the issue were ruled out, and Chris Smith, then Secretary of State for DCMS, condensed the received wisdom in a speech to Parliament: 'Whilst I understand the desire of some football supporters to stand at matches and had considered the case for a return to terraces ... the review concluded that all-seater stadia are demonstrably safer than standing terraces ... At all costs, we must ensure that Hillsborough cannot happen again.'[17]

In Germany, however, a different view prevailed: in the early 2000s designs for what was called rail seating were developed and deployed in many Bundesliga stadiums. Rows of individual seats were set behind waist-high rails, making terrace crushes virtually impossible. The FSA brought the idea to England but chose to talk about 'safe standing' rather than terracing, and to emphasise, alongside safety, the importance of consumer choice for fans, who were by now primarily treated as customers by the clubs. Smart use of surveys – all showing big majorities among match-going fans for the introduction of safe standing – and a road show that took the new technology to dozens of grounds in England – began to change the landscape. As one participant put it: 'To focus the campaign on something that was not a terrace and took the status quo – seated stadiums in which fans are standing anyway – and made it safer ... was a logical proposition that even the most sceptical politician could get on board with.'[18] Scottish football, which had never been subject to the same strictures as its English counterpart, revoked a voluntary ban on standing areas in the Scottish Premier League in 2011, and Celtic, who had suffered more than most from persistent standing, introduced the new seats in 2016. In England the DCMS review of the matter in 2018 gave its blessing for safe standing to be trialled, and over the next six years dozens of clubs would take up the offer. Whether these new zones will be able to recreate some of the drama, if not the turmoil, of the old standing spaces remains to be seen.

The cumbersomely named Fan-Led Review of Football Governance had been established by the Conservative government in the wake of the launch and then collapse of the European Super League in April 2021. In addition to the issue of whether clubs should be allowed to tear up a century and more of English football culture, the review was also tasked with the great back catalogue of economic problems facing the game and the discontent of supporters over owners' unregulated power. The review's chair, Tracey Crouch, was certainly a Tottenham Hotspur supporter, but her key credential was that she was a Tory MP who previously had served as minister of sport. Similarly, Danny Finkelstein, billed as an independent member and keen Chelsea fan, was a Tory peer. Alongside them, the other members of the review were senior club and league officials, finance experts, Roy Hodgson for the managerial voice, and Clarke Carlisle, chair of the Professional Footballers' Association. In fact, the only unambiguous representative of fans was Kevin Miles, chief executive of the FSA.

Nonetheless, the agenda that was set for them, and the prevailing ideological winds within which it was tackled, had been significantly shaped by the work of the supporters' movement. When the review issued its report in November 2021, its proposals, if not revolutionary, would, if implemented, constitute the most serious reform of the governance of the game since the establishment of the Football League in the nineteenth century.[19] At its core was the insistence on the creation of an independent football regulator with significant auditing and licensing powers over clubs and leagues. It proposed giving the Independent Football Regulator (IFR) the power to impose a financial settlement on English football that would make it more economically sustainable and egalitarian, including the introduction of a 10 per cent transfer levy that would fund grassroots football. With a nod to the fan-led struggles with owners, it also proposed a much more serious owners and directors test and the creation of fan-led shadow boards at clubs whose 'golden share' in the club would give them veto power over plans to move stadium, change club colours, names or crest, and to leave or enter competitions. There were also calls for greater support for the women's game, stricter equality and diversity requirements for clubs, and the protection of player welfare at academies and beyond, all well received. By contrast, the issues of regulation and finance – the distribution of power and money in the game – proved highly contentious.

The Premier League clubs, and their owners and executives, responded with the kind of rhetoric and specious arguments that the rich usually reserve to oppose wealth taxes and all forms of public regulation. Angus Kinnear, chief executive at Leeds United, reached for the most implausible of historical analogies, suggesting that the review would create a situation like 'Maoist China. Redistribution of wealth will simply favour the lowest common denominator.'[20] Christian Purslow, his equivalent at Aston Villa, a club that had persistently lost large amounts of money for two decades, thought that the proposals amounted to 'killing the golden goose if we over-regulate a highly successful financial and commercial operation'.[21] Steve Parish, chair of Crystal Palace, attacked the proposed transfer levy: 'We are in a global market for talent and a further ten per cent levy would make English clubs extremely uncompetitive.'[22] Except, of course, that the EPL's total, and indeed average, club income was much more than 10 per cent larger than that of any other league. The Premier League itself was a little more cautious in its commentary and accepted that an independent regulator was coming, but fought for its powers to be as limited as possible. When Richard Masters, chief executive of the league, was questioned by the DCMS select committee as to whether he would 'welcome' the regulator into the game, the best he could muster was: 'I don't like yes or no answers because there's always a nuance in between.' At the same committee Tracey Crouch thought, when asked, that the Premier League had spent most of their time trying to get things 'kicked into the long grass'.[23] The government, moving at a glacial pace, made an official response to the review in April 2022 and accepted all of its recommendations. It finally issued a white paper in February 2023 and put a bill forward in the King's Speech that autumn. While many details remained unresolved, the broad thrust of the review had remained intact, testament to the now much more sophisticated lobbying power of the FSA.[24] The bill was lost when, in 2024, Prime Minister Sunak called a snap election, but the momentum established by the FSA ensured that it would be back under a sympathetic Labour administration.

The coda to the 2021–22 season was the Champions League final held in May 2022 between Liverpool and Real Madrid at the Stade de France in the Paris suburb of Saint-Denis. It highlighted both the new power of fan organisations and the still dismal state of how fans were policed, albeit on this occasion by UEFA, the French government and their security forces. While Madrid fans were afforded the luxury of a fan park a few minutes' walk from the stadium, Liverpool's was located ten kilometres and a full train ride away. Rail strikes on Line B, the normal route from central Paris to the stadium, meant that the majority of fans had to take Line D and approach the stadium through narrow and congested passages too small to manage the flow of people. Under-stewarded and under-policed, the Liverpool fans were then forced into cramped spaces, where the turnstiles had ceased to work or were closed. The police took this as an opportunity to tear-gas and pepper-spray them. Kick-off was delayed for almost forty minutes, and in the aftermath of the game there were hundreds of assaults outside the stadium as local gangs fought the police and preyed on departing supporters. In a horrific replay of the Hillsborough disaster, the French police and politicians attempted to blame Liverpool fans' tardiness and their purchase of fake tickets for the disaster. However, unlike Hillsborough, neither government nor the police could monopolise the response to the game, or corral friendly newspapers into accepting their narrative. In fact, it was Liverpool's many fan-run media channels, not least the Anfield Wrap, that offered a supporter's-eye view, which proved to be entirely accurate.[25] A year later, UEFA's report on the final would absolve Liverpool supporters of all blame, accepting that UEFA itself, alongside the French authorities, had been responsible for the chaos. It was a reminder that of all the dangers and threats presented by a fractured and febrile society, football fans, however they behave, are as nothing to an armed and un-accountable state.

17.

Alternative England

Euro 2021 and the Rise and Rise of Women's Football

The joke going round on Twitter read: 'Men: It's coming home … Men: It's coming home … Men: It's coming home … Women: Oh fuck it, I'll do it myself.' After more than half a century of waiting, England had won a major football tournament and it was the women who had done it. The final of the Women's European Championship, played at Wembley against Germany in July 2022, was a remarkable moment, one that offered an almost entirely different version of the English nation from the one on show the previous year, when the men lost their Euro final to Italy. It was, of course, partly a matter of demographics, with a crowd that was majority female, with more young women and girls than any men's game would ever attract. But not just that: cocaine was not visibly being consumed and the queues for the water fountains were many times longer than those for beer, while on Olympic Way there were no flares up anyone's arse. There was also no evidence of what Jonathan Liew so perceptively noted at an England game in Germany: 'grown men in polyester shirts urinating into foliage'.[1] Perhaps most unusual of all, though, this was an England game against Germany that passed without a single visual or aural reference to the Second World War or any kind of militarism. It was not that the crowd were not partisan, capable even of booing the referee for what was perceived to be overly gentle treatment of the Germans, but it was a crowd without spite or rancour. The game itself was a perfect drama, both teams scoring in normal time, followed by an excruciatingly close period of extra time in which it seemed that either side could win. Chloe Kelly's winning goal and exuberant celebration, running the length of the field while whirling her shirt above her head, made for delirium. The following day tens of thousands filled Trafalgar Square to hail their champions. Women's football, for the first time ever (in England, at any rate), was at the very centre of the national story and national consciousness.

It was a moment more than fifty years in the making, half a century since the FA first rescinded its ban on the game and thirty years since it grudgingly took on the task of overseeing and developing women's football. Progress had been desperately slow for much of that time, but in the decade or so running up to the Euros serious shifts had begun to occur. First, in 2011, the FA established the Women's Super League, bringing the game within the wider football pyramid and establishing the first elite, semi-professional competition. In an effort to distinguish itself from the men's game and build a new audience, it was initially held as a summer league and festooned with face painting and mascots. Second, the women's England teams had been a marginal concern of the FA for decades, but were now incorporated into the new national team coaching and support structures at St George's Park; the team made the quarter-finals of the World Cup in 2015 and the Euros in 2017, and then the semi-finals of the 2019 World Cup, all extensively broadcast on the BBC. Most important of all, however, was that many more girls and women were playing football. In 1993, when the FA first took responsibility for the development of the women's game, there were just 10,400 registered players and a few hundred clubs. By 2017 there were more than 5,000 teams, and by 2024 more than 12,000. In 2018 the FA estimated that 1.7

million women over the age of five were regularly playing, and that had grown to 2.6 million by 2024.[2] A report from Sport England the same year found that, in the week of the survey, 777,000 girls under sixteen had played football in a formal setting while another 200,000 had joined a kickabout in a park or a small-sided game with friends.[3]

It helped that the grassroots game had become significantly more inclusive, with single-gender teams only becoming compulsory among teenagers and mixed teams recently permitted all the way up to under-18s; but I suspect that there was something more than just new formats and institutional strategies at work, something closer to the joyous experimentation, liberation and ludic mania that accompanied the first eruption of the women's game during and immediately after the First World War. Then, as now, the merest access to the game ignited a football fever, just as it had among working-class men and boys in the 1870s and 1880s, because people just love to play football. As Suzy Wrack put it: 'How could you not be sucked in? How could you not be drawn towards a sport that united everyone around you? I would spend hours with my football in the playground ... weaving it around climbing frames and swings, crazy-golf-style obstacles on our tough pitch.'[4] In this light, the FA's 1921–72 ban on women playing on the pitches of any FA affiliated clubs, and indeed prohibition of them from playing against those clubs anywhere, appears an act of almost unique patriarchal meanness: a half century that entrenched an almost impenetrable masculine culture in the game. Of course, there were already plenty of established zones of exclusive male privilege in the country, but since 1921 it is hard to think of another form of newly imposed gender segregation in British society. Having exiled the women's game to the margins of boggy municipal parklands, football effectively excluded women from the men's game. Old photographs of stands in football grounds suggest that women made up below 10 per cent of the crowd, and in many cases even less. Many of the big standing terraces would, like the press box, have been entirely male. The number of women owners or directors prior to the 1990s can be counted on one hand. Even then, they would have been excluded from the boardroom and shuffled off to a separate dining room for wives. As late as 1997, Rachel Anderson, the first female football agent in Britain, was excluded from the PFA's annual dinner. The FA rescinded the ban in 1972, but it took until 1993 for the FA to actually assume responsibility and integrate the women's game into its central strategy and management, a rate of reform that put it on a par with the other great hold-outs of male privilege: boys' public schools, which decisively shifted to coeducational formats in the 1990s, the British armed forces, which integrated women's units into the core of the army in 1992, and the Church of England, which first ordained women priests in 1994.

This new grassroots culture of women's football has in turn generated the fans, players, coaches and administrators who have developed the women's game since 1993; but alone, in the face of such entrenched exclusion, they would have been unable to turn their work into the mass sporting and cultural phenomenon it has become. For that to happen, the sporting media needed to change the way it reported on the game and the money had to be found to allow the game to professionalise. Having been almost entirely absent from the sport pages of the main newspapers, women's sport in general – and women's football in particular – was given a decisive boost by the coverage accorded to the London 2012 Olympics. With more than a third of the country's medals won by women, female athletes not only received their due coverage, but were hailed as national heroes. The Great Britain women's football team (really England in disguise) sold out its games and made the quarter-finals, and Wembley was full for the final between the USA and Japan. That said, six years later, Women in Sport were reporting that coverage of female sport made up between just 3 and 12 per cent of newspaper and broadcast output.[5] However, for major events this could change. The BBC's coverage of the 2015 and 2019

Women's World Cups, both of which were shown in their entirety on the network, saw England games given prime-time billing on BBC One and accorded the wraparound promotions, features and news stories usually reserved for the men. On both occasions the England team made the semi-finals, a run of form that at the time exceeded anything managed by the men's team since 1966, and the traditional football public began to take note.

A fascinating survey of men's responses to these tournaments revealed three distinct sets of attitudes, which characterise much of the way in which male football culture is attempting, or not, to come to terms with change.[6] Around a third of male football fans surveyed were already supporters of women's football or had been converted by the coverage. One respondent said, 'I used to see it as a bit of a joke, but having watched the World Cup, I now feel the opposite.' Another small constituency had abandoned outright hostility to the women's game, but remained, sotto voce, unconvinced by its real value: 'I may appear to be sounding sexist but I'm not ... I have become more politically correct in my view of women's sport, I tell them I respect their ability. However, deep down I still view women as the weaker sex and the standard of their sport when compared to the men's reflects this view.' Close to a majority, though, remained old-fashioned misogynists. Most continued to see men's football as the authentic standard against which the speed, technique and fan culture of the women's game could never compare. A significant minority considered the women's game just a media invention and a censorious 'politically correct' campaign. Others did not need conspiracy theory or culture wars to underwrite their distaste; a deep-rooted biological essentialism appeared widespread: 'Women are just not made for football and women should just not take part in a man's sport.'

Given this constituency, Conservative populists and culture-war provocateurs have found women's football an irresistible space for sniping. The *Spectator*, as one might expect, has been generous in the space afforded to them. Philip Patrick, for example, found the coverage of the 2019 World Cup a good stick to beat the BBC with: 'What is disturbing is that it isn't always women's football itself that seems to get BBC executives so energised, but the gender politics at play.'[7] He was not entirely wrong, for on the television and in the press, journalists highlighted the still huge inequalities between men's and women's football, but for Patrick it was more a question of whether the national broadcaster should dare to dwell on such matters: 'Does the BBC know its place anymore?' In 2023 Toby Young asked, 'Am I allowed to make fun of women's football?' But no one imagined he wouldn't be doing so. Even then it was fun with a sour taste, more interested in lampooning Megan Rapinoe and Sadiq Khan than anything else. It was also rather thin-skinned. Young seemed to view the normalisation of women's football, and its new space in the culture, as the result of compulsion: 'You've given all of us who dislike being told what sport we should enjoy a good laugh.'[8]

The *Spectator* and its friends may have been struggling to enjoy women's football, but alongside the successes of the national team, the English professional game has seen remarkable growth. In the late 2010s the leading clubs finally began to take women's football seriously, though there remained some significant laggards like Manchester United, who did not create a women's team until 2018. Most, though, had already embraced the women's game. Manchester City, for example, made the move to integrate all their social-media feeds rather than having separate digital identities for their men's and women's teams. In 2018 this work was consolidated by the relaunch of the now professional Women's Super League and a second-tier Championship. In just five seasons it became the richest and most watched women's league in Europe, particularly once clubs began to make their main stadiums, on occasion, available for women's games. In 2019 the first women's Manchester derby at the Etihad drew more than 31,000 spectators, while the

North London derby at Tottenham's stadium drew 38,000. After the pandemic Arsenal began to play regularly at the Emirates and successively smashed this record, peaking in 2024 when more than 60,000 people saw them beat Manchester United. The same year, the Women's FA Cup final between Manchester United and Tottenham brought 76,000 fans to Wembley.

If the size of these crowds was something close to the men's game, are the crowd itself and its cultures any different? They are, of course, much more feminine, probably around an even split, but with a much bigger presence of young women and girls than in the men's game. There are, visibly, more family groups, of all kinds, in the crowd, and there is certainly a bigger and more visible queer presence. Gay and lesbian couples showing open affection are the norm rather than an exception. Will Unwin, in the *Guardian*, observed with some surprise that 'everyone wanted to enjoy themselves, a concept I fear is sometimes lost on supporters in the men's game'.[9] The crowd is more mixed in every way, and above all home and away fans are not segregated. Consequently, for all the flag-waving, singing and amity, the atmosphere can sometimes be a little flat; but that is also true of a lot of men's football and is, perhaps, the price for dispensing with its permanent sense of edge and rancour. It is a trade-off being explored over the question of cursing, the norm at the men's game, but hitherto considered inappropriate for a family occasion. To the dismay of some, Arsenal fans adapted a song about Martin Odegaard for Kyra Cooney-Cross, 'When she's on the ball, she's fucking magical,' while her teammate Lotte Wubben-Moy asked the Arsenal fans to tone it down when they greeted a wayward shot with, 'What the fucking hell was that?' Although playing at a club's main stadium has brought huge crowds, the smaller stadiums in which the WSL has played most of its games have brought a simplicity and intimacy that many value. Refugees from the men's leagues in particular have found a romantic reconnection with the game after shifting to women's football. One Newcastle supporter thought, 'It felt more real and grassroots than the empty men's Premier League experience.'[10] In this context fans appear to have a closer physical and emotional connection with the players, who have worked hard on social media to establish these relationships and given a lot more time and attention to fans, handing over their kit and signing autographs, than their male peers.

While the women's game has grown, it operates inside a footballing universe that has taken men, especially as players, as the unspoken default. Consider just the hidden gendering of kits.[11] Socks, notionally unisex, are sized on the basis of average masculine dimensions. Women who chose a sock that fitted their feet found that it barely covered their calf. If they chose a sock that reached their knees they would have sock feet so large that wearing a boot was uncomfortable. Football was not alone in this. In a 2024 BBC survey of elite sportswomen in Britain, a majority reported that they were using equipment that was not suitable for women and a quarter felt that in doing so they risked injury. Boots have no pretence to be unisex. Eni Aluko, even as an England player, said, 'I buy a size four version of men's boots, they're not designed for a woman's foot.'[12] In a 2023 survey of 350 women professionals conducted by the European Club Association, 82 per cent said their boots were uncomfortable and affected their performance, and a fifth of them had to customise their boots to make them usable.[13] An exasperated Parliamentary Women and Equalities Committee noted in 2024: 'It is symptomatic of gender inequality and sexism in the sports sector that the first football boot in the world designed around female feet came to the market less than four years ago.'[14] Even then, those specialised female boots were retailing at £200 a pair, way beyond the means of many women players. Shirts have always been sized and shaped for men, and it was only in the late 2010s that the sportswear companies first sold specialised women's kit. While slightly more appropriately sized, there has been little effort in the new designs to accommodate women's distinct physique, and there is a tendency to 'shrink it and pink it', reproducing masculine shapes with feminised decoration. Often that has meant sexualisation, with a preference for special editions with plunging necks and cuts that expose the midriff, both of them inappropriate for actually playing the game. Not that playing the game is a guarantee that the sportswear companies will take women's kit any more seriously. Prior to the 2023 Women's World Cup, England's goalkeeper Mary Earps discovered that Nike were not making or selling goalkeeping shirts bearing her name. An online petition, signed by more than 150,000 people, forced the company to change course, and for good measure the public voted her BBC Sports Personality of the Year.

The issue of shorts takes us from the gendering of garments to the gender biases of medicine, for neither manufacturers nor sports scientists have been paying any attention to the fact that women players have periods. Given the still-prevalent taboos and shame around bleeding, women players have been forced to take evasive action. One option is to take the contraceptive pill, another is to customise their kit. One player recalled, 'When I was fourteen, fifteen, I used to wear two pairs of cycling shorts, just because of the absolute paranoia.'[15] The issue has been particularly pressing for women playing in white, so much so that the England women's team pressed the FA to switch from an all-white kit to dark blue shorts, a move greeted with a sigh of relief across the women's game. Stephanie Hilborne, CEO of Women in Sport, said, 'It sends out a signal that society cares about how women and girls are feeling, not just how they are looking.'[16] Menstruation can also have a significant impact on an athlete's physical health and performance levels through tiredness, cramping and chronic pain, though there is evidence that performance can be boosted by rising hormonal levels at other stages of the menstrual cycle. Either way, almost no serious research has been conducted in this area, nor has it become a core part of the coaching and sports medicine curricula.

The same is true of the long-term impact of breast damage and the value of different kinds of breast protection.[17] One injury, though, has been too prevalent to ignore. Studies report that women players are suffering damage to their anterior cruciate ligament at two to eight times the rate of their male peers. Theories abound, but detailed studies are absent. Some have argued that girls, generally recruited later than boys into regular training and academies, are missing out on the early strength work that would protect their knees later in their career. This is made worse by the fact that girls reach their maximum velocity of height growth – precisely when this kind of training is most needed – earlier than boys. Others have argued that the different ratio of front and back leg strength in men and women accounts for the prevalence of the injury, but no one has really looked into it. The Parliamentary Equalities Committee was scathing: 'We have no doubt that a health issue of similar magnitude affecting elite male footballers would have received a faster, more thorough, and better coordinated response.'[18]

If the number and quality of toilets in most British football stadiums are anything to go by, then men remain the default football supporter. Despite this, the female component of the crowd has been growing. After the first decade of the Premier League and the introduction of all-seater stadiums, women made up 15 per cent of the crowd, growing to 19 per cent in 2015. By 2024 they made up over a quarter of the crowd and more than 30 per cent of the TV audience.[19] It has not always been a comfortable experience. In 2021 the FSA's 'Women at the Match' survey found that a fifth of women had experienced unwanted physical attention during a match, double the proportion from its 2014 survey.[20] On a positive, if limited, note, the report also found that nearly a quarter of women were willing to laugh off sexism in the stadium in 2014, but that only half that number would do so in 2021. Willing or not to laugh at sexism, they were still going to experience it. Three years later, in 2024, a Kick It Out survey found that one in four women had felt unsafe at football grounds, and 52 per cent had experienced sexist behaviour or language on match days. More than half of respondents had been told that they should be somewhere else – inevitably the kitchen – with almost as many subject to 'lewd requests' – code, one presumes, for 'get your tits out for the lads' – and over a quarter had experienced sexually aggressive comments. Eighty-five per cent of the women who experienced abuse never reported it, as they did not believe they would be taken seriously. Women's experiences of online fandom were not dissimilar: 'Sometimes you'll put up a comment and someone you don't even know will reply saying … "what do you know" or "should have guessed you're female making this comment".' In 2022, Bristol Rovers fans Caz May and Lucy Ford launched the campaign Her Game Too, after they'd had enough of receiving sexist abuse on Twitter. Their launch video featured twelve women fans in their club shirts holding up signs with comments that they had received from men at football matches: the usual depressing litany of 'It's a man's game,' 'Get back to the kitchen' and 'Fancy a shag?' It received almost a million views and sparked a massive outpouring of support on social media, as well as practical action. More than two dozen league clubs partnered with the campaign, Torquay United gave out a thousand free match tickets to local women and girls, while Forest Green had Her Game Too logos emblazoned on their women's kits and pitch-side LED boards. Just as the MeToo campaign brought everyday sexism and sexual assault out of the shadows, Her Game Too has been doing so in football, but it has a lot of shadow to navigate.

If women fans were deemed by many men to be unwelcome interlopers, perhaps even greater disdain and fear was evoked by women as officials, commentators and pundits. The Keys and Gray affair in 2011, when the Sky Sports presenters were caught off camera raining sexist abuse down on assistant referee Sian Massey, had seen the pair fired and a line drawn between what constituted banter and misogyny, but female officials have remained very rare in the men's game. It was only in December 2023 that Rebecca Welch took charge of a Premier League game, the first woman to do so. However, if female officials were grudgingly accepted, there remained, among some men, a deep antipathy toward women as match commentators and, above all, their presence in the inner sanctum of punditry. Jacqui Oatley had broken the glass ceiling in 2007 as the first woman to commentate on *Match of the Day*, and received plenty of criticism – not for her unimpeachable football knowledge and mastery of its syntax and cliches, but for the tone of her voice. Five years later, Des Lynam, once the doyen of BBC football coverage, thought 'the female voice is not so attractive for actual commentating and in some cases became grating'.[21] Since then, as more women have commentated on games, including Vicki Sparks's debut in 2018 as the first woman to talk us through an England men's game at the World Cup, the old guard has conceded the field, but the new red line has become punditry and analysis. Lynam in 2023 told *Radio Times*, 'I've got no gripe with female presenters, but when you're a pundit and you're offering opinions about the game, you have to have played it at the level you are talking about – i.e. the men's game.' Kevin Keegan, on a speaking tour in Bristol, shared this with his audience: 'I'm not as keen, I've got to be honest, and it may not be a view shared. I don't like to listen to ladies talking about the England men's team at the match because I don't think it's the same experience. I have a problem with that.' Women in Football tartly responded on Twitter: 'There is more than one reason why Keegan is seen as an icon of the 1970s.'[22] Another reason was, despite his grating sexism, he retained a certain politeness and control.

Neither were possessed by Joey Barton, who as part of a new, angrier and ruder generation of men, tweeted in 2024: 'I tried to play nice, you didn't listen.' Having recently been sacked by Bristol Rovers and then launched his own podcast, Barton was out for clicks. In a series of vicious posts he described ITV pundits Eni Aluko and Lucy Ward as 'the Fred and Rose West of football' and argued that women 'shouldn't be talking with any kind of authority' on men's football, before comparing having women on co-commentary or punditry duty as 'like me talking about knitting or netball'. As ever getting his retaliation in first, he lambasted his opponents as 'eunuchs'. Barton took a lot of flak, but as the playbook demands, he doubled down, tweeting a video of his sons having a kickabout accompanied by the words: 'When they stop playing and are middle aged, there will be no jobs for them in the football industry because they are white, middle aged and male ... We have to take this fight up for future generations. This is not about us. The British, White, Middle Aged men [sic] is under attack.'[23] Emma Hayes, Chelsea's coach, wearily replied to this latest assertion of wounded masculine power in the game: 'The realities are male privilege has always been at the centre of football in this country. I feel that sport is the last place in society where that male privilege exists.'[24]

Men might be, in Barton's fevered imagination, under attack in the football industry, but at home they are, unambiguously, the aggressors. Over the last two decades a gruesome body of research has revealed a close correlation between football and the incidence of domestic violence after Old Firm games in Glasgow and on the days when England played at the 2006 and 2010 World Cup, especially on days that they were beaten.[25] A 2014 study confirmed this, finding that an English win or draw saw a 26 per cent increase in incidents, a defeat a 38 per cent increase.[26] In 2021 research drawing on more than half a million incidents of domestic violence recorded by Greater Manchester Police between 2012 and 2019 attempted to correlate their frequency with the type, location and outcome of football games in the city.[27] They found that the overwhelming reason for an increase in domestic violence was not the football itself, but the impact of alcohol consumption. The research showed that domestic violence actually fell during games, increased during the four hours after the game, and peaked ten hours after the final whistle at the end of a very long day of drinking. Football is not the only occasion on which Britain dangerously abuses alcohol – Christmas and New Year are also associated with spikes in domestic violence – but it is the most frequent and unhinged. It remains the case that the day of England's quarter-final game against Sweden during the 2018 World Cup holds the record for the number of alcohol-poisoning cases dealt with by the NHS. However, there does seem to be evidence that the culture of football support is part of the problem. One survivor of football-related abuse argued, 'Football doesn't cause domestic abuse. Nor does alcohol, but if you have someone who is controlling and abusive by nature and you maybe add some alcohol to that … I lost count of the times I was assaulted after my ex-husband's team lost.'[28] A study drawing on the records of the West Midlands Police found that on the day of England men's games in major championships, incidents of domestic violence increased by 47 per cent and by 18 per cent the following day, while on the days England's rugby team played, also an occasion for alcohol abuse, there was no difference at all.[29] A second survivor found that the outcome of games mattered too, with a win more likely to result in sexual abuse, whereas a defeat would mean violence; a third thought that football generated a toxic mix of entitlement and the normalisation of force: 'You put a man in a football environment and he feels allowed or entitled to behave perhaps in a way that he would not do in any other scenario … it's OK that we're talking about violence, it's become normalised, that's what you do, so that's what they do.'[30]

Another form of normalisation has been the way in which football clubs have dealt – or not – with players accused and convicted of domestic and sexual assaults. While not unheard of in the past, and certainly under-reported, there have been dozens of cases over the last ten years. In 2024 the *Athletic* reported: 'At one stage last year, six of the 20 Premier League clubs employed footballers who were being investigated by the police for offences against women or, in a case that has now been dropped, unlawful sexual activity with a girl under the age of 16.'[31] Some clubs have been reticent to suspend players that have been charged and face trial. Others have appeared to have treated these issues as merely a PR problem, like Mason Greenwood's departure from Manchester United after charges against him were dropped. In some cases, fan protests have dissuaded others from signing convicted players. David Goodwillie, who maintains his innocence, was thrice convicted of assault, and in 2016 found in a civil case to have raped a woman with a teammate. He was accepted by Clyde, but on signing for Raith Rovers faced a fan backlash so fierce that the club released him. That said, many fans appear indifferent, and a peculiarly cruel segment of the crowd at Sheffield United chanted for Ched Evans even before he was cleared of charges of rape: 'He'll shag who he wants to.' That, one suspects, was the policy of Mohamed Al-Fayed, owner of Harrods, and Fulham between 1996 and 2013, who now, safely departed, has been accused by hundreds of women, from both institutions, of sexual assault and rape. The leaked emails of Richard Scudamore, then chief executive of the Premier League, in which he joked about 'female irrationality' that follows women having children and 'big titted broads', suggest that the misogyny and disrespect that thrives in dressing rooms and on the terraces is alive and well in the boardrooms of the game.[32]

It is one measure, then, of a changing balance of power in English football that Greg Clarke's successor as the chair of the FA in 2021 was Debbie Hewitt, the first woman to hold the post in more than 150 years. Yet, as Simon Kuper has argued, 'Football's best known female leader is probably still Hannah Waddingham who plays the fictional owner of AFC Richmond in the television series *Ted Lasso*.'[33] Hardly surprising when one looks at the gender imbalances of football's workforce. In 2018 women made up 27 per cent of the total, but just 14 per cent of those in the top pay quartile.[34] As one got closer to the centre of power the numbers dropped further, with women comprising just 8 per cent of board members at clubs and 6 per cent of CEOs. The female presence in FTSE boardrooms, by contrast, is now almost 40 per cent. An improvement on the situation of thirty years earlier, perhaps, when there was just one female board member across all ninety-two league clubs, but even these advances disguised the peripheral location of women in senior positions in football, with over half concentrated in four areas – commercial, club secretaries, ticketing and finance – none of which entailed close or regular contact with the male playing staff. In recent years women have broken into some of the new areas of employment at football clubs, like disability liaison, safeguarding and DEI (diversity, equality and inclusion), but the team remains off limits, an all-male sanctum of players, coaches, directors of football, physios and doctors. There are just a handful of full-time female scouts, and the one female doctor in the Premier League – Eva Carneiro at Chelsea – was driven out of the club after her scolding by José Mourinho for actually doing her job and, as the referee requested, going onto the pitch to treat an injured player. Hannah Dingley's two-week tenure as caretaker manager at Forest Green Rovers in 2023 remains the only female appointment in men's professional football in over 130 years.

In a working environment that remains both exclusionary and hierarchical, and in which banter is the currency of power, sexist comments continue to abound. In fact, as women eke out a little more space and authority in these organisations, it is more starkly obvious than ever. A 2023 survey conducted by Women in Football found that 89 per cent of its members, who all work in the game, reported experiencing some form of sexism, sexual harassment or derogatory comments at work, up from 66 per cent in 2020. Sixty per cent of those that reported sexist incidents saw no action taken by their employers, and 16 per cent were simply not listened to at all; the figures were even worse for women of colour.[35]

One wonders whether this might, in part, be the fate of the Carney Report. Commissioned by the government in 2022 to chart the future of women's football, and chaired by ex-England player and journalist Karen Carney, the report was published in 2023. It called for full professionalisation of the top tiers, more diversity and better grassroots facilities in the women's game, and equal access to football in school sport. While the report was greeted with much noting and nodding, it has been outflanked. The decisive move in the shaping of women's elite football was made by the Football Association. In 2023 it handed over the ownership of the Women's Super League to a newly constituted private company. The new league has been quietly celebrating, pointing rightly to the record revenues it is receiving, a £30 million sponsorship deal with Barclays and growing crowds, making it the best attended and richest women's league in Europe. The parallel with the men's Premier League does not stop there. Growing income has been matched by growing inequality. More than half of the league's £71 million annual turnover is accounted for by just four clubs, all with a familiar ring: Arsenal, Chelsea, Manchester City and Manchester United. At the same time, clubs have inadvisably high wage-to-income ratios, closer to the financial mayhem of the Championship. Needless to say, none of these clubs were actually profitable. Indeed, in keeping with the men's game, all the WSL teams are now beginning to accumulate similar debts. In the absence of systems of equalisation and collective restraint on wages, the increasing popularity and cultural weight of women's football are unlikely to turn this around, for it seems on course to enter the same unsustainable spiral of aspiration, spending and losses that the men's game has perfected.[36]

The Women's World Cup in Australia and New Zealand in 2023 should have been a celebratory moment, one that gave women players global exposure and England, going as European champions, a real chance of winning. England made it to the final, but the prospect of winning was insufficient for Prime Minster Rishi Sunak to attend. His and Prince William's concerns over their carbon footprint were praiseworthy, but one imagines that they would have lasted for about two seconds had the men been in an equivalent position. Despite the time differences, more than 14 million other people watched Spain beat England 1–0, but none of the players of either team would claim the headlines or define the moment. One man, wearing an anti-Putin T-shirt, had already sought to steal the limelight with a first-half pitch invasion; but it fell to Luis Rubiales, president of the Spanish Football Federation, to finish the job. Already under suspicion for his patronising attitude to the women's team and his support of coach Jorge Vilda, subject to a boycott by many previous members of the squad, Rubiales had expressed his support towards the end of the game by grabbing his crotch and pointing to the players. When Jenni Hermoso came onto the dais to receive her medal, Rubiales, uninvited and unwanted, kissed her on the lips. He would go on to deny the accusation of sexual assault, pressure her to change her story and eventually be forced to resign. A satisfactory outcome, perhaps, but one bought at the price that the calibre of football at the tournament and the fervour of the crowds were obscured by the antics of another toxic man at the top of a football federation.

18.

Playing for a Pittance

Grassroots Football and the Cost of Living Crisis

In the summer of 2022 the impact of Russia's invasion of Ukraine and the disruption of global hydrocarbon markets began to bite. UK inflation climbed above 10 per cent and household energy bills were forecast to quadruple, while real-wage increases lagged behind. The cost of living crisis had arrived and would intensify through the autumn and winter. The short-lived premiership of Liz Truss and her disastrous 'Dash for Growth' saw the end of low interest rates, while the cost of mortgages and rents climbed. Not everyone, though, was feeling the pinch. Not the UK's 170-plus billionaires, whose collective wealth in the two years since the start of the pandemic had grown by £150 billion. Not the Premier League, which, with the crowds returning and its TV income increasing, including a record round of newly signed foreign media deals, posted its highest revenues ever, spent a record £1.5 billion on transfers over the summer, and racked up another round of losses and debts. Despite this, it remained the case that, as of 2022, only twelve out of twenty Premier League clubs were paying the real living wage to security and ground staff – a mere £11.95 an hour in London and £10.90 in the rest of the country – and were also committed to ensuring that all of their subcontractors did the same. Beyond the Premier League just a handful (Hearts, Luton Town, Grimsby Town, FC United of Manchester and Dulwich Hamlet) signed up to the Living Wage Foundation.[1] Ticket price policy was also mixed, with some clubs freezing prices and making a greater number of cheaper tickets available, while many more passed on their costs to their supporters. By 2024 they were in the majority, as every Premier League club bar Crystal Palace raised its ticket prices and trimmed its discounts. Spurs, for example, decided this was the moment to revoke the 20 per cent discount made available to the over-65s, while Wolves put up the price of some youth season tickets by more than 150 per cent and West Ham confined concessions to the most distant seats in the stadium.

Fans, meanwhile, were mobilising to counter hunger and cold in their communities. The impact of austerity, the harshness of the benefits system and the decline of real wages for the majority had seen a steady and appalling rise in the number of people using food banks over the 2010s. Football had first responded in Liverpool, where in 2015 Dave Kelly, an Everton supporter, and Ian Byrne, a Liverpool supporter, founded Fans Supporting Foodbanks by taking a wheelie bin to Goodison Park and Anfield on match days and asking for donations.[2] They drummed up so much support and collected so much food that by 2017 they were supplying a quarter of north Liverpool's food banks. By 2022 they had inspired dozens of similar operations at other football clubs, and they were also operating six mobile pantries across the city, feeding 120,000 people. Through the winter of 2022–23 clubs also began to use their own facilities to run pantries and food banks, and opened their cafeterias to offer free warm meals and warm spaces.[3]

Between these two extremes – the soaring wealth of the super-rich and the grinding poverty of the poorest – grassroots football, much like the rest of the nation, was squeezed by the financial aftermath of Covid, economic recession and soaring energy bills. Over the 2020–21 season, paralleling the record number of bankruptcies of small businesses in the wider economy, 2,600 grassroots clubs folded. More than 8,000 were expected to follow suit the following season as the cost of football's basic inputs – energy, transport, grass – spiralled upwards.[4] John Bailey, chair of eighth-tier Didcot Town, said, 'I've been doing this for 30 years – it's never been as bad. The cost of living crisis poses the biggest threat to non-league football since World War Two.'[5] Some clubs, including Didcot, moved to early kick-offs to save on the cost of floodlights, but then lost out on their bar takings. Some reseeded just parts of their pitches. In Scotland a survey of parents reported that almost a quarter had not been able to afford the subs for their kids' football practice since the pandemic; a third predicted that they would not be able to afford them in the coming year; and one fifth were only able to send their children to football if they had made sacrifices elsewhere.[6]

As with so much of Britain's threadbare social services, it has been these kinds of sacrifices and the millions of hours of free labour and free transport given by coaches, officials and families that have kept grassroots football going. Indeed, football has seen a significant rise in levels of participation over a decade in which both overall levels of physical activity and rates of participation in organised sport first stagnated and then declined. In 2012 the Football Association reported that 7 million adults were regularly playing football in England. By 2015 the number had risen to 8.2 million, a quarter of whom were women, as well as 3.4 million kids, and by 2019 there were 9 million adult footballers and 4.5 million children playing, 13.5 million in total.[7] Admittedly, the statistical bar for playing is low: once a month for adults, once a week for children, and any form of football – from a kickabout in the park with your kids to half an hour's five-a-side on a commercial 3G pitch – is counted. Even so, the fact that around a quarter of the population of England and more than a sixth of Scotland are playing in any way is remarkable. At the same time there is a pervasive sense, confirmed by what little reliable data there is, that grassroots football is in decline, its clubs struggling to make ends meet, its leagues shrinking and its facilities impoverished. The declinists, however, are not talking about the small-sided or recreational football (which accounts for much of the overall growth in numbers), but the two versions of the game that dominated the grassroots scene in the twentieth century: street football and league-based, competitive eleven-a-side.

Perhaps the most important change in grassroots football is one that no official statistics ever capture: the decline, indeed almost total disappearance, of street football. A survey of the biographies of footballers whose professional careers ran from the 1930s to the 1990s reveals the ubiquity of informal urban football in mid-century Britain. Dixie Dean practised heading against the wall of the Birkenhead Methodist Wesleyan Hall, while Nat Lofthouse used a stable block. Steve Perryman learnt the game in a West London cul-de-sac, Ian Callaghan on the concrete squares of Toxteth, George Best on the narrow paths of the Cregagh Estate in Belfast. Their modern equivalents have, overwhelmingly, got their training in more formal settings, socially and geographically sequestered in the new academies. Wayne Rooney, described by David Moyes, his manager at Everton, as 'the last street footballer', was a rarity, playing all through his youth on the streets of Croxteth in north Liverpool and even returning to his old haunts to play after breaking into the Everton first team.[8] Contemporary sightings are rare. As Neil Lennon, then coach of Celtic, remarked, 'Football doesn't seem to be the priority any more. Football was never won on an iPad – it was out in the parks and streets. I walk around the west end of Glasgow and very rarely see kids out playing football.'[9]

Increasingly, one seldom sees kids playing out at all, and while the lure of the digital screen is part of the story, it is also a consequence of significant changes in the character of the urban environment and our culture of parenting. While increasing levels of parental paranoia and inflated fears of stranger danger have made many reluctant to allow their kids out, there is a real and practical danger facing street footballers. The streets that once provided play space now primarily provide parking spaces for the 41 million vehicles on the UK's roads, more than double the number of even the 1990s.[10] Simultaneously, access to green space has diminished in many urban areas, while post-millennial housing developments include less and less area for play. Save the Children found that only just over a quarter of children regularly play outside their homes, compared with 71 per cent of their parents' generation.[11] Most shockingly of all, we have reached the point where three-quarters of UK children spend less time outdoors than prison inmates.[12] Impossible to truly calibrate, there is a widespread sense that the loss of street football has not only diminished the skill sets of young players – instinctive understanding of how to operate in tight spaces, the determination to stay on your feet in the tackle for fear of the tarmac – but there has also been a loss of self-organisation, learning and imagination. Dave Parnby, director of youth football at Middlesbrough, contrasted the stifling style of modern coaching with the freedom accorded to earlier generations who 'weren't interrupted by adults saying "do this, do that" ... They just created their own games from their own imaginations with very little intervention from adults. We're now in an era of sports science, coaching, psychology ... It's coached, boxed, scientific. That freedom of expression, freedom of play, has gone.'[13] The last enclave of this culture survives in the small caged pitches that dot the major social housing estates of the post-war era.[14] Free to use, available around the clock, they have been the training grounds of a new generation of talent. South London estates, in particular, have sustained an extraordinary scene, nurturing players of the calibre of Eberechi Eze, Joe Gomez, Jadon Sancho and Wilfried Zaha. Where once the intricate skills and small-space tricks that cage football nurtured were considered showboating by mainstream coaching, and its many black players racially stereotyped as ill-disciplined, they are now celebrated and actively sought out by a new generation of coaches.

If street football is close to extinction, then the traditional eleven-a-side game is heading for the endangered list. In 2015, Sport England found that the level of weekly participation in the eleven-a-side game had dropped by almost a quarter, from 5.2 per cent of the adult population to 4.2 per cent. Although the total number of people playing football has risen, the number of teams playing eleven-a-side has been falling, from 131,000 in 2012 to 119,000 in 2015, and just 102,000 in 2019.[15] At the county level, district leagues have been shrinking or disappearing altogether. At the turn of the century the Southampton Saturday Football League had 182 teams in thirteen divisions, but by 2015 it had just 43 teams in six divisions. The North Lancashire and District Football League, over a century old, still had more than 50 teams and five divisions in 2012, but by 2024 was forced to close down entirely.

The biggest decline in eleven-a-side football has come in Sunday leagues. In the early twentieth century, the Football Association and its lower amateur leagues, in deference to the lingering puritanism that surrounded Sunday leisure pursuits, only played games on Saturdays. However, for many working-class men, often working on a Saturday morning, Sunday was a much better option – to the dismay of the FA. Beginning in the late 1920s in north London, the interwar period saw the creation of hundreds of clubs in dozens of Sunday leagues in the bigger cities. After the Second World War, the leagues boomed and the Football Association, albeit through gritted teeth, finally acknowledged their existence and in the early 1960s brought their operation under the loose control of the county FAs. Hackney Marshes in East London – long a metonym for the Sunday League game – is a good barometer of its health. Laid out in 1948 using rubble from the Blitz for sub-surface ballast, Hackney Marshes at its peak in the late 1960s could boast 120 full-size pitches. By 1990 it had shrunk to little over a hundred, and today there are just eighty-eight, of which only sixty are full-sized adult pitches.[16] This halving of facilities is reflected more widely in the declining numbers of teams and leagues across the country. The Nuneaton & District Sunday League, for example, had six divisions in the 1980s, now it has just three. Scarborough's Sunday league went from four divisions in 1991 to just one in 2021. Ellesmere Port went from four divisions in the 1970s to none at all. As with the rest of grassroots football, increasing time pressures, weekend working and a greater range of leisure options available to players have eaten into the game's popularity. The increasingly peripatetic population has diminished the social networks that sustained teams, while some observers have suggested that many players have migrated to small-team and midweek formats, which require less time, travel and commitment. Others have suggested that the enduring roughhouse edge to Sunday league, scything tackles and performative aggression, are fuelling the exodus too. Sunday leagues have also been hit by the decline of three of its traditional recruiting grounds – working men's clubs, medium-sized manufacturing firms big enough to support a team, and popular pubs. Their replacements – fast-food chains, warehouses and themed bars – have proved, it seems, less successful in either paying a living wage or supporting football teams.

Even where a team can be assembled, finding a playable pitch is, increasingly, a challenge. The vast majority of the nation's football pitches, more than 80 per cent, are owned and administered by local authorities. Since 2010 they have borne the brunt of the Conservative's policy of austerity, their central government funding cut by more than 40 per cent. Unable to raise council tax to fill the gap, and facing the spiralling and statutory costs of social care, homelessness and child protection, local government's discretionary budgets for sport, leisure and youth services have been eviscerated, and capital assets have been sold off. Between 2010 and 2018, 710 local authority football pitches were lost to the game, 164 in the North West and 129 in Scotland alone. Over the same period another 220 school playing fields were decommissioned, mostly sold to property developers.[17] Those that survived the cull have not been well looked after. The chief executive of the Football Association of Wales, Noel Mooney, said shortly after taking up the post, 'The first thing I picked up on was the chronic Third World grassroots facilities we have across the country.' The coach of Maesglas FC in the second division of the Ceredigion Costcutter League, who had been using the same mildewed shipping container for a changing room for twenty years, described his club's facilities as 'despicable and dangerous'.[18] At least there were some facilities. Many pitches offered neither changing rooms nor toilets, and even where they did, specific provision for women and girls was usually absent. In Merseyside full-sized grass pitches have been abandoned and locked up due to a shortage of funds. Cuts to leisure services in Blackburn saw pitches left uncut or unmarked at the height of the football season. In Newcastle a grassroots coach observed that 'there are very few facilities that are available for casual football … most have been closed'.[19]

What explains the higher rates of participation in football, despite the decline of eleven-a-side, is the rise of other versions of the game. Small-sided formats, from five- to seven-a-side, have become the mainstay of all children's organised football, and increasingly of the adult recreational game. The emergence of commercial operations renting out caged artificial pitches and organising small local leagues has proved immensely successful and accounts for the bulk of the increase. Futsal, the now internationally codified indoor version of small-ball, small-sided football, has seen levels of participation increase, albeit from a low base, at around 15 per cent a year, and is the fastest-growing sport within Britain's universities.[20] Walking football, formalised by the Walking Football Association in 2016, is another growth area.[21] Football is unforgiving, demanding a level of running, turning, twisting and contact that an ageing and increasingly inactive population can't cope with. Originally aimed at men over fifty struggling with physical or mental-health issues, walking football has proved enormously popular, adding the under-fifties, women and disabled players to its roster. One foot must remain on the ground at all times. Heading is not permitted, nor balls above head height, and penalties are taken with a one-step run-up; but walking football retains the spatial essence of the game while dropping it down three or four gears. That said, players still manage to hurt themselves, get out of breath and behave badly; sin bins are a standard feature of the game.

In a wider landscape of decline, there have also been zones of growth in the eleven-a-side game. First, within established clubs there are significantly more women's teams, the total doubling from 5,600 in 2017 to over 12,000 in 2023. Second, three types of new club have sprung up: YouTube- and social-media-driven outfits; a wave of refugee and asylum-seeker teams; and a new generation of self-consciously activist clubs. English grassroots football's first serious encounter with the internet came in 2007, with the launch of crowdfunding website MyFootballClub, which planned to use the money raised to buy a lower league team and offer funders the opportunity to play *Football Manager* for real, voting on key club decisions, including team selection.[22] More than 30,000 people signed up, and in 2008 MyFootballClub bought Ebbsfleet Town, then in the fifth tier. With the injection of new funds and energy, Ebbsfleet went on to win the FA Trophy that year, beating Torquay at Wembley. Things, however, went downhill from there. The membership voted not to pick the team, and lost a big minority for whom that was the main selling point. In the absence of much communication with what remained of the membership, enthusiasm waned. The club got relegated and the money dried up, after which the club was sold on. However, by the time the experiment with Ebbsfleet was over, the internet had significantly changed. The arrival and subsequent ubiquity of social media of all kinds offered the next generation of digital clubs an entirely different way of interacting with their fans.

Foremost among this new generation is Hashtag United. It was created in 2016 by Spencer Owen, whose Spencer FC YouTube football channel had acquired more than a million subscribers. Initially, the team, made up of friends and family, played in an imaginary league that took its cue from the gameplay formats of EA Sport's *FIFA*, where a side plays ten games but is the only club playing for points. Video-game narratives were then fused with the DIY aesthetics of YouTube content creation. Coverage of games was reduced to less than fifteen minutes of highlights; players' personal and home lives were given prominence; and the camera had access to an unfiltered and uncensored dressing room. As Hashtag's head of content explained, 'Kids now just want to see the goals, assists and skills rather than a full match and they'll follow individuals more than teams.'[23] For those alienated by the inaccessibility of the professional game and the mannered inauthenticity of its media interactions, this new model was irresistible. By 2018 the club's channel could boast 400,000 subscribers and draw more than 30,000 people to a charity match played at Wembley Stadium – the kind of numbers that bring corporate brands calling. Hashtag were now sponsored by the simulation game *Football Manager*, had their kits made by Adidas and were an option for players of *FIFA 19*. Buoyed by this extraordinary level of success, Owen took Hashtag United out of its digital existence and established the team in real life, aka the Eastern Senior League in Essex, in the tenth level of the English pyramid, and employed a professional coach; six seasons and three promotions later they had climbed up to the seventh level Isthmian League Premier. Along the way a series of mergers with local clubs allowed them to field additional men's teams, Sunday league teams, a women's team, more than forty youth sides and, at this level of football, draw a very decent crowd for the first team. The digital public has been lapping it up and the club's YouTube channel now boasts more subscribers than – the big six aside – any Premier League club.

A similar combination of YouTube and Instagram content, DIY previews, commentary and post-match analysis has been working for Sunday league sides too. SE Dons, kings of the Orpington & Bromley District Sunday League, were created by grime DJ Don Strapzy and his friends in South London, and have added a rap, grime and jungle soundtrack to the genre.[24] Stretford Paddock FC were founded in 2019 by Stephen Howson, supported by and named after his Manchester United fan channel. Baiteze FC, an East London Sunday league side, are the grassroots champions of TikTok, with the kind of following you would find at the top of the Championship and enough class to win the national Sunday league cup in 2022.

Every major wave of migration to modern Britain has produced new football clubs. The arrival of Jews at the turn of the twentieth century saw the creation of so many new clubs that distinct Jewish soccer leagues were established in Manchester and London. The Windrush generation and its children set up new Black and Caribbean clubs in the 1960s and 1970s, like Highfield Rangers in Leicester and Constantine United in Willesden – a club that nurtured future professionals Ricky Hill, Enoch Showunmi and Junior Agogo. Greek Cypriots had their standard bearers too, like New Salamis FC, and a dense enough presence to staff a Cypriot league in North London in the 1970s. A generation later, British Asians have been doing the same, founding Sporting Bengal, London APSA (All People's Sports Association), Punjab United in Gravesend, and Sporting Khalsa Sikhs, the first British Asian club to own its own ground. Now, alongside these established communities and their clubs, a wave of contemporary refugee football teams have emerged. As with previous generations of migrants, football offers a safe space for minorities in an often hostile landscape, nurtures camaraderie and friendships, and offers rare moments of escape from an often traumatic past. As one Yemeni refugee put it: 'Until I started playing again I could not get one moment of peace. You know when you're thinking and thinking and thinking so much that you're just overthinking? That was me every day since I'd left Yemen. I think every person who plays football knows what happens when you step out on the pitch. Everything disappears for a while.'[25] Getting playing, though, has proved hard. Given that refugees are unable to work and obliged to live on starvation-level benefits, access to transport and social clubs let alone football equipment is close to impossible for many. The widespread dispersion of refugees, often to inaccessible hostels and military camps, has made establishing teams difficult. At the same time trauma, depression and isolation have sapped the organisational energies of even the most resilient.

Many refugee clubs have emerged from the wider patchwork alliance of local charities, churches and volunteers that, in the virtual absence of state support, are a refugee's threadbare safety net. Scotland has proved particularly hospitable to refugee football and now boasts a ten-team league, including Dream Team Glasgow – created in response to the trauma of refugees housed at the Park Inn where one of their number, in acute mental distress, stabbed six people before being shot by the police – and Afroscots and Scoutable United FC, who see themselves as stepping stones, with a remit to promote talented players from refugee and minority ethnic backgrounds to semi-pro and pro clubs.[26] Outside of the refugee leagues, the environment can be hostile. Changing Lives FC, for example, play in the Harlow District League in Essex with an all-refugee line-up, and for their troubles saw their team bus deliberately burnt out. Coach and founder David Simmons wearily reported, 'We've had a lot of trolls and abuse. I've had personal abuse and the players we work with get discriminated pretty much every Sunday.'[27]

Many football clubs, to their credit, have given out free match tickets to refugees and put on free football sessions. Out of these encounters, their charitable wings and local refugee-support networks have brought new teams into being. Club Together FC, for example, was created by Middlesbrough's charitable foundation and the Methodist Asylum Project, but some refugees have just taken the initiative themselves. Justice FC, a Middlesbrough Sunday league side, was created by a Cameroonian refugee, John Yarro. Walking through his local park and finding a group of young refugee men selling drugs and fighting, he recalled asking them, '"Would you be happy if I can bring a football and we play?" And they all said, "Yeah, yeah, yeah." That's how the team started.'[28] Malik Al Shahadat, himself a refugee from Syria's civil war, created Phoenix FC out of nothing for his compatriots who had also settled in Liverpool, and the club are now playing in the city's County Premier League. The club has enabled him to achieve almost every migrant's dream: 'Football has enabled me to find something so we can integrate and make a positive impact in Liverpool.'[29]

Even at the height of the workers' sports movement in the interwar era, the links between socialist politics, the labour movement and football had been thin on the ground. If anything, radical politics found more of a home among ramblers, walkers and cyclists than footballers. However, in the 1980s and early 1990s a new generation of anarchists and socialists, alert to the game's political potential, began to gravitate to football, coalescing in Bristol as the Easton Cowboys (later also Cowgirls) and in Leeds as Republica Internationale, where Sunday league football was combined with anti-racist action and international solidarity tours to Palestine and Oaxaca. Bigger clubs, fielding more teams, emerged at FC United, created as a post-Glazer breakaway from Manchester United in 2005, and at Lewes FC, which became fan-owned in 2011 and turned itself into an explicitly community-oriented activist club. Mount Pleasant Park FC, founded in Sheffield in 2013, is an anti-fascist club, welcoming all abilities and genders under the motto 'Love Cantona, Hate racism', that combined Wednesday night matches and Sunday league with games played at pro-migrant demon-strations outside the Home Office's Sheffield headquarters.

More recently, East London has produced two remarkable new clubs, Clapton Community FC and Hackney Wick. The former is a fan-owned team created when ultra groups broke away from the original Clapton FC to set up their own club. With more than a thousand members and the biggest crowds in their league, the club has managed to buy back Clapton FC's abandoned stadium and fund itself with huge sales of an away shirt based on the colours and insignia of the leftist International Brigades that fought in the Spanish Civil War. Hackney Wick was the creation of Bobby Kasanga, who after doing an eight-year stretch for armed robbery and acquiring an Open University degree along the way, decided on his release to create an inclu-sive and successful football club for Hackney: 'I was broke and working night shifts in a bagel factory in Hackney Wick to feed myself and provide for the football team ... I'd literally go door-knocking with a yellow bucket, explaining I had been in prison and asking if people would support our new team. Some would just close the door. Others would leave it open, go upstairs and find some money.'[30] Eight years later, Hackney Wick were fielding twenty teams and signing players on the condition that they did two hours' volunteering a week, collab-orated with local artists and musicians, and secured sponsorship from the Netflix hit series *Top Boy*.

The catalyst for new teams in North Kensington, on the west side of London, has been trauma and tragedy. The former was the source for Minds United, the creation of Tarik Kaidi, still serving as the coach, driver and kit man, who founded the team after emerging from a long bout of psychosis. Like Kaidi, many of Minds United's players have been patients at St Charles' Hospital in Kensington, often with mental-health issues so ser-ious that they have been sectioned. Similar efforts to use foot-ball as a space for addressing mental-health concerns have emerged across the country – VCS (Vulnerable Citizen Support)

United in Leeds and Blantyre United in Lanarkshire among many others – all of them offering a combination of exercise, socialising and empathy.

Tragedy arrived on 14 June 2017, when Grenfell Tower, a twenty-four-storey block in North Kensington, went up in flames, killing seventy-two of its residents, doomed by the use of combustible cladding and the disastrous disregard for their safety shown by the regulators of the construction industry, the London Fire Brigade and their own housing association. Those that survived were left homeless, bereft and woefully under-supported by Kensington and Chelsea Council. Rupert Taylor, a local youth centre worker, fell into conversation with a young survivor of the fire. The young man talked about how he had coped with the loss of both parents just a year earlier. Taylor recalled, 'I asked how he coped at the time. "Football", he simply replied. It gave him the support he needed when he was at his most vulnerable. I responded: "Right, we'll create a foot-ball team then."'[31] Grenfell Athletic started life in the third division of their Sunday league in the 2017–18 season.[32] They held a seventy-two-second silence in honour of the victims of the fire before their first game, which they won 6–3. Since then, they have added more new teams and social programmes. Still going in 2022, five years on from the tragedy, the club staged the Grenfell Memorial Cup, where more than 600 players and 4,000 spectators stood to hear the seventy-two names of those who lost their lives. At the current rate of progress Grenfell Athletic, still without their own pitch, will have raised enough money to build a new home long before the public inquiry into the tragedy is complete or the burnt shell of the tower is demolished.

Grenfell Athletic are an exception, with the scale and notoriety of their story sufficient to attract sponsorship from corporates like Nike and Cadbury and support from prominent footballers. Most grassroots clubs and charities are surviving on money from small local businesses, personal donations and what few scraps are available from the National Lottery. At best, this helps cover their running costs, but capital expenditure is out of the question. In the absence of any local government investment, the development of grassroots facilities has fallen on the rather narrow shoulders of the Football Foundation. Established in 2000, the Foundation has been jointly funded by the FA, the government via Sport England and the Premier League. By 2023, the foundation had spent £931 million on building or improving infrastructure, though £180 million of that went to the stadium-improvement fund for lower-league professional teams, leaving less than £40 million a year for grassroots projects. Since 2022, spending has inched up to around £100 million per year and the Foundation can reasonably point to a lot of good work: new drainage for grass pitches, thousands of refurbished changing rooms, the creation of football hubs with club rooms serving grassroots teams, and more recently the multi-pitch PlayZones built in deprived areas that actively seek to engage poorly served demographics. On the other hand, this is all a drop in the ocean, the Premier League's contribution coming in at around 1 per cent of its annual revenues, less than a third of the annual parachute payments received by a handful of relegated clubs. Little wonder, then, that in 2018 the FA were tempted to sell Wembley Stadium to Shahid Kahn, the American billionaire owner of Fulham, and spend the lot on the renewal of the grassroots game. After much protest, the deal was cancelled, but it is extraordinary that, in the country with the richest football league in history, the governing body should think that selling the nation's most important asset was its best option. Martin Glenn, FA chief executive, insisted: 'Receiving an offer to sell Wembley Stadium is not a "betrayal". It is not selling the "soul of the game".' Yet one suspects that the latter has long-since departed.[33]

19.

When the Fun Stops

Gambling and Cryptocurrency
in British Football

For its first half century, English professional football, its upper reaches staffed by many pious Anglicans and non-conformists, was militantly anti-gambling and furiously resisted the pools companies through the 1920s and 1930s. In retrospect, the pools model appears rather quaint. For a small stake but potentially large returns, punters attempted to predict the weekend's score draws. It was hugely popular, and though occasionally its jackpot winners would descend into mania, it didn't nurture a population of problem gamblers. Illegal bookmakers, from the late nineteenth century, took wagers on football matches, but their main business was the horses and the dogs. Even when high-street bookies were legalised in the 1960s, football betting was a distant second to the turf and retained curious limits – like the requirement for football bets on non-televised games to be trebles rather than single-game wagers.

The advent of the National Lottery in 1994 saw the casual gambling market shift almost entirely away from the pools – which closed down in the early twenty-first century – while more serious punters moved online. It is with this shift, massively accelerated by the arrival of the smartphone and the possibility of real-time, in-game betting, that football gambling has taken off.

Government deregulation, like replacing the old tax on punters' stakes with a levy on bookmakers' profits, helped stimulate the market, but the most important change came in the Gambling Act 2005, which, for the first time, permitted bookmakers to advertise. They didn't need a second chance. By 2010 they were spending £150 million a year on advertising, and by 2017 £1.5 billion. Their annual turnover hit £10 billion in 2018, £1 billion of which was bet on football. Takings fell during the Covid lockdowns when the game ground to a halt, but they bounced right back in 2022, when over £2 billion was wagered on football and from which the bookmakers took away a £400 million profit.

This was proof, surely, that advertising worked, and nowhere was it more publicly visible than in football. In 2002 just one Premier League club had a gambling company shirt sponsor, but between 2017 and 2020, half, or almost half, of the twenty clubs had gambling company logos on their strip; and although that number has fallen to just three by 2023, every single member of the league had a 'responsible gaming partner'. In some cases clubs had more than one, like Spurs, who had Fun88 as their Latin American and Asian partner, Betway in North America, and BetMGM as their training-top sponsor. The entire EFL had been sponsored by Sky Bet since 2013, with, at any one time, at least half a dozen teams in the Championship carrying front-of-shirt betting brands. Most perniciously, until 2020 every club across the Football League also received a share of Sky Bet's takings from losses incurred by their own fans. Of course, it's not just the shirts. It's the huge pitch-side digital boards, the sleeve sponsors, the innumerable adverts in the build-up to the game and at half time, not to mention the alerts, emails and advertising everywhere on club websites and social media. Football players and celebrities were central to the pitch. For almost a decade, Ray Winstone was the face and voice of Bet365, telling us with avuncular menace that it was 'all about the in-game'. Among many others, ex-players Micah Richards and Roy Keane and Sky Sports presenter Jeff Stelling were regulars on Sky Bet commercials, while José Mourinho and Jack Wilshire shilled for Paddy Power.

A study from 2020, which looked at five major football matches, including Premier League fixtures, found that a gambling sponsor was referenced every twenty-one seconds during a typical TV broadcast.[1] A survey of ten games in 2022 found that a logo appeared every sixteen seconds on average, and at one game at West Ham, who were sponsored by Betway, it was every two seconds, totalling more than 3,000 gambling images in a single match.[2] Analysts of television coverage of six matches played over one weekend in September 2023 counted 7,000 gambling messages.[3] Away from direct coverage of a game, a study of Sky Sports News found that there were 600 gambling images or references in just two hours of broadcasting, and anyone who listened to Talksport will have struggled to hear any content devoid of gambling tips and offers. Meanwhile, the next generation of punters was being groomed. Betway was fined £400,000 after it was found advertising on the children's section of the West Ham United website, including a direct link on a page in which kids were invited to colour in a teddy bear. Sticker books and magazines were another way to put gambling messages in front of young eyes. In 2020, 42 per cent of Panini Official Premier League stickers featured a visible gambling logo, while the BBC's *Match of the Day* weekly magazine featured thirty-seven in a March 2019 edition, fifty-two in May 2019 and thirty-eight in January 2020, basically one on every other page.[4]

As profits have been mounting at the gambling companies, the social costs of 'responsible gaming' have also been climbing. Gambling in general, and football gambling specifically, have been linked to financial stress, obviously enough, but also to: a precipitous decline in gamblers' physical and mental health; relationship and family breakdowns; homelessness and ultimately suicides. This is not, however, the view of the gambling industry and its regulators, who are in a state of denial, claiming first that gambling is not addictive, and that in any case the number of problem gamblers – the industry's preferred term for addicts or those at risk of addiction – was just 150,000 people, or 0.3 per cent of the population. The chief executive of the Gambling Commission itself, the government's regulatory body for the industry, has argued that advertising makes no difference to the rate of problem gambling, while the main trade body – the Betting and Gaming Council – does not consider sport sponsorships to be a form of advertising at all. However, the 0.3 per cent figure has been based on a methodologically flawed, small-scale telephone survey, which even the Gambling Commission has recognised as an understatement. Its own work in 2023 suggested the number of problem gamblers might be 1.3 million people, or 2.5 per cent of the population, a figure confirmed by a YouGov survey in 2022 that found not only that 1.4 million people were problem gamblers in the UK, but that another 3.6 million have been indirectly harmed by their gambling behaviours.[5] The combination of stress, shame and financial problems is so bad that people with a gambling disorder are twice as likely to have depressive episodes and attempt suicide than those suffering from other addictions, increasing their mortality rate by 37 per cent. Consequently, in 2021 Public Health England estimated there were over 400 gambling-related suicides each year in England, while in 2023 the estimate from the Office for Health Improvement was close to 500.[6]

The problem gamblers really matter to the industry, because the vast majority of its profit comes from a very small group, the 5 per cent who are either addicted or at risk. It is here that football's relationship with gambling is at its most insidious. As James Grimes, a recovering addict and Tottenham fan, recalled: 'Spurs had a casino on the front of their shirts at that time: Mansion. That was a company I went on to use and it quickly consumed all of my life. Football was a constant in it. Whenever I saw new companies pop up on shirts or the side of the pitch, I would use those sites. It sucked everything away from me. I turned from a happy, normal boy into a hopeless, helpless wreck of a man.'[7] One NHS consultant psychologist working with gambling addiction observed, 'One of the first things I noticed was that groups were filled with young men wearing football shirts. That hasn't stopped.'[8]

Once recruited, the industry really gets to work on them. Vulnerable gamblers are exposed to gambling products that are devised to be compulsive, predatory communications from bookmakers, and a disingenuous system of regulation and intervention. In-play betting on football is bad enough, but companies constantly offer regular football punters free spins and bets on their casino and slot-machine games, which, according to the charity Gambling with Lives, are 'the most dangerous gambling products, some with addiction and at-risk rates as high as 45%, higher than heroin.'[9] Once gambling companies have identified regular and compulsive gamblers, they do not leave them alone. Gambling with Lives also reported that this group were nine times more likely to receive daily incentives to bet than other gamblers. The parents of Ryan Myers, who committed suicide in 2014, found that even two years later his email inbox was jammed with offers from gambling companies to take up a free bet and come back to their site. Despite protocols for monitoring problem gamblers and intervening to staunch their losses, companies rarely deploy them, as in the case of Luke Ashton, who was making more than a hundred bets a day in secret, desperately chasing his enormous losses, but was ignored by the bookmakers until he took his life in 2021.

In the face of this epidemic, the industry and its regulators have put their faith in the notion of 'responsible gaming' and a model of behaviour that places all of the responsibility on vulnerable and potentially addictive individuals to control their addiction. Thus, alongside every advert is the ubiquitous slogan 'When the fun stops, stop!' The injunction has a horrible poignancy. In a survey of gamblers' motivations, the vast majority said they were betting in the hope of making some money; less than a fifth said they did so for pleasure. For the majority of punters the fun never even started.[10]

Having opened the doors for the gambling industry's explosive growth, governments have been fighting a rearguard action to rein it in: tweaks have been made to the legislation to restrict children's access to gambling imagery; maximum bets on slot machines have been introduced; the use of celebrities and footballers in advertising has been curtailed; and companies are paying more blood money to fund adverts that call for responsible gambling and, when that inevitably fails, into addiction-recovery programmes. Yet even these minor reforms have been actively resisted by the gambling industry. The Football Association and a handful of clubs – like Luton Town, for example – have publicly announced that they will not accept gambling money, but for the most part the clubs and the leagues are silent. The Big Step – a charity established by recovering gambling addicts and the families of victims, which campaigns to try to get football to confront its gambling problem – has, since 2017, organised a number of cross-country walks to clubs' stadiums to try to force the issue. Its founder noted that 'fifty of us walked through the rain to the three big north-east clubs, Newcastle, Sunderland and Middlesbrough and no-one ever came out to meet us. This has been the case on every walk we have done.'[11] In 2023 the steady drip of gambling-related suicides, this kind of campaigning work, and the case of Ivan Toney – Brentford's striker who was harshly punished for his compulsive betting on football matches, receiving an eight-month ban in 2023 – raised the pressure on government and industry to reform. The best the Premier League could manage in response was an agreement to end front-of-shirt sponsorship by gambling companies in 2026.

Huge as the UK gambling industry may be, it is minuscule compared with the predominantly illegal global betting market. The UN estimates the annual turnover of the sector at around $1.7 trillion – of which $1 trillion is entirely untraceable and almost certainly part of money-laundering operations.[12] The bookmakers in this market, mainly based in East and South East Asian countries where gambling is illegal, will take a bet on anything, but their punters love the Premier League – so much so that many of these bookmakers run illegal streams of its games on their website to keep their customers hooked. To evade their own national regulators, these companies have established themselves in the Philippines, where they are not permitted to take bets from the locals but are free to take anyone else's money. From there they take advantage of the UK's unparalleled system of legal loopholes for corporations and the rich, by buying a UK gambling licence from shell companies incorporated in the Isle of Man, which offer the additional virtue that the ownership of these operators is almost entirely obscured.[13] In 2023 just one of these 'white label companies', TGP Europe, was managing the websites of seventeen Asian bookmakers. This arrangement allows them to then advertise in the Premier League, sponsor shirts and run a UK gambling website. However, the adverts, often entirely in Chinese script, are not aimed at the UK, while their UK websites are invariably 'in development' and unable to take bets. The real business, of course, is at home, where their Asian websites will most certainly take your bet, in any currency you choose.

In keeping with the industry's hapless record of due diligence, football is now taking money from not only one of the main hubs of the world's criminal money-laundering sector, but one that is associated with human trafficking and appalling working conditions for their staff. Reports include accounts of Chinese and Vietnamese staff forcibly relocated to the Philippines, who have had their passports removed and are subject to physical and sexual abuse. Filipino Senator Rosa Hontiveros wrote, 'Women and girls … are prostituted to serve the sexual appetites of an exploding market of Chinese workers in the Philippines offshore Gaming Operators (POGO) industry.'[14] BK8, the shirt sponsor of both Burnley and Aston Villa in 2024, was closely linked to operations in the notorious criminal gambling enclaves of Cambodia, where human rights abuses of workers were the norm, while Leicester City and Manchester City gambling sponsor 8Xbet was linked by the UN to similar practices where 'prison-like conditions and torture have been well documented and corroborated'.[15]

Football has been equally lax in the due diligence of other purveyors of high-risk bets – NFTs (non-fungible tokens) and cryptocurrency. Its first notable encounter with the latter came in 2017 when Harry Redknapp tweeted: 'Proper excited about Mobile Cryptocurrency! I'm in, get involved @electroneum #Electroneum.' Given Redknapp's track record with new technology – in a tax-evasion trial in 2012, in which he was cleared of the charges, he claimed that he didn't know how to send an email and had never sent a text – the response was sceptical. However, purveyors of crypto and NFTs have since found more compelling recruiting sergeants for their schemes and scams. The wave of market hysteria and hype around NFTs began in the art market, and in the late 2010s some items of digital art sold as NFTs were commanding prices in the tens of millions; a lot of money for what is, in effect, ownership of a ledger item in a blockchain register tied to a JPEG, but without copyright ownership of the image. At this point football's relationship to the market was mainly as a source of gullible purchasers, including Neymar Jr, who spent more than a million dollars on the ugly cartoons of the Bored Ape collection. Useful as this kind of foolhardy celebrity money was, the NFT and crypto operators were much more interested in the mass market: the same kind of punters – predominately young men – ready to lose money in a display of ill-informed financial bravado. And where better to find them than among football supporters?

The absurdly named startup Sportemon Go were first into the market, doing sponsorship deals with Rangers and Hibernian, trying to sell their fans crypto-trading tokens and offering a lot of NFTs of the clubs winning things and celebrating. Just a year later the tokens were valueless, the few NFTs that had been sold likewise, and the company had ceased trading. In the meantime, they had signed up three Premier League players – Andy Robertson, Luke Shaw and Callum Hudson-Odoi – who all promoted their tat on social media, including imagery of themselves, but received more grief from fans than purchases; these NFTs are now not even available on resale sites. Michael Owen first backed a horse-racing-themed set of NFTs called 'deRace', which collapsed in value almost as soon as it was launched, but, undeterred, he then backed a football NFT collection which he claimed 'can't lose value'. The Advertising Standards Agency censured Owen, for what in fact this meant was that while the NFT you bought could only be sold for at least the price you paid for it, all lower bids would be rejected. Consequently, if the price permanently fell – which it did – purchasers would be permanently stuck with, in effect, negative equity. Manchester United's Paul Pogba, signed up by Cryptodragons, was unfathomable rather than misleading. Promoting the purchase of the company's NFTs, he tweeted: 'This is huge. You see I'm going to get some dragon eggs – so as you know what's gonna happen I'm gonna be the father of the dragons and the next run of reservations is coming soon so keep your eyes open.' Pogba later revealed that he had paid $162,000 for a digital dragon egg that made him 'master of dragons', but he has yet to tell us what happened when the egg hatched or how the value of his considerable investment is holding up.[16] One can only hope it did better than John Terry's Ape Kids Club FC, which was flogging gruesome football-themed baby ape cartoons for around £150 a pop. Willian, Jack Wilshire and Ashley Cole tweeted their approval, but have since deleted their online endorsements. In the meantime, the NFTs that used trademarked imagery, like the Premier League trophy, have been withdrawn, and the value of the NFTs is close to zero.

Football's love affair with NFTs is over for now, but its relationship with another form of digital chicanery – cryptocurrency

– is in full bloom. In 2022, for example, Spurs were partnered with Libertex, who would help you mine crypto for yourself. AstroPay, Burnley's sponsors, would let you buy stuff with cyrpto if you found any. Alternatively, you could trade it on the apps of Chelsea's WhaleFin or Brentford's CoinJar. Crypto exchanges which ran their own currencies were also available: Dogecoin at Watford, Tezos at Manchester United, PEAKDEFI at West Ham and Bitci.com at Wolves. If you had any crypto-currency left, Southampton's gambling partner, Sportsbet.io, would let you lose it with them.

Useful as all this advertising has been for ensnaring people in cryptocurrency, nothing comes close to the pernicious engineer-ing of the Socios scheme – now the official 'fan token partner' of Arsenal, Aston Villa, Crystal Palace, Everton, Leeds, Manchester City and Tottenham Hotspur.[17] In this unpleasantly parasitic relationship, Socios pay the club a large signing-on fee and a percentage, probably around 50 per cent, of their sales of fan tokens. These are offered to the public, but obviously aimed at the club's fan base. Purchases can only be made with Socios's own cryptocurrency – Chiliz – which fans must first acquire with real money. In return, the purchaser gets an NFT token and the opportunity to participate in polls on whatever minor and inconsequential issue the company and the club can agree upon: the contents of which player's toilet bag would you like to see posted to Instagram, or which of three hackneyed motivational slogans would you like put up in the dressing room? Beyond the crushing banality of such gestures, West Ham supporters were morally outraged when the club first signed up to Socios in 2019. The Supporters' Trust mounted a 'Don't Pay to Have Your Say' campaign, arguing that 'the undemocratic nature of buying a say and paying for influence is completely unaccept-able' and forced the club to cancel the deal.[18] Others have not been as vocal or as fortunate. The tokens themselves are not, Socios and the clubs assure everyone, speculative assets, although the language of their launch has been cut and pasted from every other crypto scheme and the Socios app offers a trading option and real-time price reports. This is just as well, as the value of the tokens has collapsed, with no reason to think that it will ever increase. Indeed, if one looks at the small print, token holders will find that they only have any access to the polls and other 'unique experiences' on offer as long as Socios has a relationship with the club. Once that ends, well, you just have a digital keepsake of the club's indifference to you. On the other hand, perhaps, in time, the token will appreciate in value as a historical artefact of football clubs' complicity in these shameless scams.

20.

The Queen Is Dead

Football, the Monarch and Memorialisation

In recent years, West Ham games have been preceded by tracks from the Clash, the Jam and the Cockney Rejects, but on 8 September 2022, before their Europa Conference League game against Bucharest's FCSB, it was strictly classical music. The teams lined up to play with their club badges covered by a black silhouette. Most extraordinary of all, the relentless digital advertising boards were turned off. The only image shown on the big screen that evening was that of the now late Queen Elizabeth II handing the World Cup trophy to West Ham and England captain Bobby Moore in July 1966. Before the kick-off the crowd gave a lusty, impromptu rendition of 'God Save the Queen' and then watched the home side win 3–1. Most members of the football world would follow West Ham's reverential and nostalgic tone, but not all. That evening FC Zurich and Arsenal held a minute's silence at half time, the restless home fans booing after thirty seconds, the away fans mustering a chorus of the national anthem. In Dublin, Shamrock Rovers fans sang 'Lizzie's in a Box' to the tune of KC and the Sunshine Band's 'Give It Up'. Similarly, in Edinburgh, when Hearts and İstanbul Başakşehir came out of the tunnel at half time with black armbands and stood for a minute's silence and the national anthem, both were interrupted by parts of the crowd.

Victoria's death in 1901, Edward VII's in 1910 and George V's in 1936 had all prompted debates over whether sport should continue during the period of official mourning. Some sports stopped entirely, but football continued and games were only postponed if they fell on the day of the funeral itself, or in London during the few days beforehand. George VI's passing in 1952 once again saw rugby, hockey and cricket close down, while football – the day of the funeral aside – continued. Games were often preceded by the singing of 'Abide with Me' followed by the national anthem. Impromptu black armbands were worn by players and supporters, but none of these acts were universal, nor was their absence considered problematic. Seventy years later, much of this was reversed: cricket, rugby and golf all continued without pause prior to the funeral, but football stopped and aggressively policed itself. Games at every level of the league pyramid, of all genders and ages across the UK, were cancelled for the weekend after the Queen's death, and dissent of almost any kind was not tolerated.

Permissible dissent was typified by former England players and football pundits Gary Neville and Peter Crouch, who raged against the authorities, arguing that surely full stadiums, black armbands and singing the national anthem was a better and more appropriate send-off for Her Majesty? Less oleaginous views were actively repressed. When fellow former player and pundit Trevor Sinclair tweeted, 'Racism was outlawed in the 1960s and its been allowed to thrive so why should black and brown mourn!! #queen', he found himself attacked online, and suspended from media work until he had deleted the tweet and made a grovelling apology. One Preston North End supporter asked a club chat group, 'Will I be ejected from the stadium if I boo during a minutes silence for the death of the queen?' He then responded to a comment on his post, writing, 'What about if I do a Nazi salute in her honour?', in reference to a real film of the Queen as a child making Nazi salutes with her father, mother and sister. For this he was banned from the club for life.[1] The biggest football story of the long period of official mourning was David Beckham, who was lauded for not jumping the enormous queue to walk past the Queen's coffin. All games were cancelled for the day of the funeral itself. Sheffield International announced that their Sheffield & District Fair Play League game against Byron House, called off due to the funeral, would be played as a friendly and were widely censured as well as promised draconian punishment by Sheffield FA, who thought them 'disrespectful' and 'despicable'. No such punishment was forthcoming for the two private schools, Rossall and Eton College, who played not one but two games on the day that the FA had called a stop to the grassroots game.[2] Thus, football has acquired the gravitas once reserved for the games of the upper classes, and that has allowed it to define the norms of popular patriotic mourning; but, as the differential treatment of Sheffield and Eton suggests, it has acquired their hypocrisy, too.

When football did return the week after the Queen's funeral, the Premier League mandated a minute's silence, the national anthem, blank advertising screens and applause in the seventieth minute. England complied, but open dissent simmered in the Celtic periphery. The national anthem was loudly booed at Wrexham before their game against Dagenham and Redbridge.[3] Fans of Dundee United, a club that began life as Dundee Hibernian, reprised the 'Lizzie's in a Box' song in their game against Rangers at Ibrox. Celtic fans had dealt with Prince Philip's death in 2021 by launching fireworks from the graveyard that sits at the back of Celtic Park and breaking the minute's silence.[4] This time around, they displayed banners at their midweek game in Poland reading 'Fuck the Crown'. At an away game at St Mirren they outfoxed their hosts, who had opted for a minute's applause rather than a minute's silence to try to prevent the inevitable booing, by singing their hearts out and applauding through many choruses of 'If you hate the royal family clap your hands'.[5]

What accounts for this reversal? When did the 'patriotic' middle-class sports become indifferent to royal mourning, and when did football start policing the boundaries of deference? The Queen had served as the patron of the Football Association for many years, but this was true of literally hundreds of sporting organisations, and she had in any case passed the role on to Prince William a decade earlier. She had certainly presented a dozen or so FA Cups and a World Cup, but it was obvious that her real sporting passion was reserved for horse racing. The 1966 World Cup Final was enough to inscribe her into the popular folk history of football, but the scale and form of the game's response grew out of a series of deeper and interconnected changes over the previous quarter of a century. First, football established a symbolic relationship with death through the commemoration of its own tragedies. While this led to the first acts of collective mourning and observed minutes of silence in the game, it also created a space in which football's tribalism and capacity for emotional cruelty could be showcased in the form of tragedy chanting. More recently, this kind of relationship to the past has been balanced out by the nostalgic, even elegiac celebration of the greats, the holding of minutes of silence on their passing and their immortalisation in the form of statues, which are now present at the majority of league stadiums. While both of these phenomena were focused on football's own mortality, they have been supplemented by acts of remembrance for the dead beyond the stadium, securing the game as a place in which public respect is demonstrated, historical moments are marked and collective narratives and norms are created. The most important of these, and the one that has brought football into a close and deferential relationship with some of the most conservative forces in the country, has been its embrace of the Royal British Legion, the military and the poppy.

313

The presence of statuary is the most obvious indicator of football's commemorative relationship with its own past. Prior to the 1990s there were almost no statues of players or coaches in British football, just a bust of Herbert Chapman hidden away in Highbury's marble halls and a small bronze of England and Swindon Town striker Harold Fleming inside the club's offices. In 1987 Stanley Matthews appeared in the shopping centre of his home town, Hanley, but not at any of the grounds where he had played. The first statue to actually be placed in a public space outside a football stadium did not arrive until 1991, when Newcastle United put Jackie Milburn in front of St James' Park. A handful of old 'giants' followed through the 1990s – Matt Busby at Old Trafford, Bill Shankly at Anfield, Billy Wright at Molineux, for example – but since the millennium numbers have exploded, with more than fifty new statues commissioned in the 2000s, another fifty between 2010 and 2020, and more to come. The most recent crop includes a small number of contemporaries, but football remains, overwhelmingly, in the key of nostalgia. Most common have been the local heroes, club legends and trusty servants like John Atyeo at Bristol City and George Cohen at Fulham. Chairmen – Dave Whelan at Wigan, Jack Hayward at Wolves – were also rewarded for their troubles. Attempts to redress the almost complete absence of players of colour (Thierry Henry aside) and the total absence of women saw commissions for a statue of Walter Tull at Northampton Town, the West Bromwich trio of Brendon Batson, Laurie Cunningham and Cyrille Regis in Sandwell shopping centre, and Lily Parr at the National Football Museum in Manchester. One club, though, stands out in the scale of its patronage and perhaps its rush to refashion the meaning of its history. Manchester City had installed a sculpture of 1950s goalkeeper Bert Trautmann in 2003, but made up for lost time, unveiling the stars of the club's new hegemony – David Silva, Vincent Kompany and Sergio Agüero – and for the legacy fans they added a triad of Colin Bell, Francis Lee and Mike Summerbee.

The aesthetic of all these sculptures is remarkably narrow. Standard-issue cast bronzes, a majority have been commissioned from just a few contemporary sculptors, most of whom specialise in conservative memorials. Some are just poorly executed – Waltham Forest Council commissioned a bronze of Harry Kane, local boy and then Tottenham player, but perhaps because it was such a dreadful likeness, kept it hidden in a municipal warehouse. Even where the likeness is good, most of these works lack a sense of movement or energy. David Silva and Middlesbrough's George Camsell, poised mid-dribble, are the exceptions rather than the rule. None of this really matters, though, because since the universal adoption of the smartphone, they exist not to be looked at, but to appear as props in innumerable selfies.

Statues aside, British football crowds are not unfamiliar with death, but they have had a very troubled relationship with its remembrance. In 1946, thirty-three people died in a crush on the terraces of Bolton Wanderers' Burnden Park, an early indicator of the perilous state of the country's Victorian football infrastructure and its careless crowd management. The game was played out while the bodies were removed from the terraces, and no minute of silence was held across English football for the dead. The victims of the 1958 Munich air disaster, including eight players and three other members of Manchester United's staff, were at least acknowledged in English football's first public displays of grieving. Scotland would prove more reticent. There had been warning signs at Rangers' ground, where crushes on the infamous Stairway 13 had resulted in two deaths in 1961 and multiple serious injuries in 1967 and 1969, but they went unheeded. In 1971, at the end of an Old Firm game, 66 Rangers fans were killed and more than 200 injured in the crush on the same stairway. Ibrox was subsequently rebuilt, a small plaque commemorated the disaster, but Rangers did not hold a minute's silence before a game until 2011.

Official acts of remembrance may have been thin on the ground, but football crowds performed their own. What has come to be called tragedy chanting – malicious songs that reference these calamities – has been with us for some time. Opponents of Manchester United, especially Liverpool fans in the 1970s and 1980s, would mime the flight of an aeroplane, simply chant 'Munich' or, most cruelly, they would sing, 'Who's that dying on the runway? Who's that dying in the snow? It's Matt Busby and his boys making such a fucking noise cos they can't get their aeroplane to go.' Opponents of Rangers were equally vicious, singing, 'Who's that lying on the stairwell? Who's that lying on the floor? Sixty-six Huns in scarves and flares/Lookin' fucked up oan the stairs ... and they'll no be goan tae Ibrox anymore.' The next wave of disasters – the Bradford fire and the Heysel disaster in 1985 – also attracted this kind of treatment. Bradford have got off relatively lightly. Blackpool apologised to them when they played Billy Joel's 'We Didn't Start the Fire' over the stadium's speakers before a game at Bloomfield Road, and small groups of fans, at Newport and Rochdale for example, have been heard singing 'Bradford's on fire'.[6] Heysel saw thirty-nine Juventus fans, fleeing a charge by Liverpool supporters across the terraces, crushed to death by a collapsing wall they were jammed against. This desperate moment has mainly been used as a stick to beat Liverpool with. Opposing fans have mocked the chant, 'Li-ver-pool, Li-ver-pool', by reproducing its rhythms as, 'Mur-der-ers, Mur-der-ers'. In every corner of the country, crowds have used Liverpool's culpability at Heysel to undermine the club's experience of the Hillsborough disaster, suggesting, like the tabloid press in 1989, that the blame lay with them, not the police: 'Always the victims, it's never your fault.'

None of this has gone away. At a Carling Cup game in 2011 between Leeds and Manchester United the home fans sang the Munich song, and the away fans responded by unfurling a banner that read 'Istanbul', a reference to the fatal stabbings of Leeds fans Chris Loftus and Kevin Speight before the 2000 UEFA Cup semi-final with Galatasaray. Then, to the tune of Monty Python's

'Always Look on the Bright Side of Life', United fans sang, 'Always look out for Turks carrying knives.' In 2012 Liverpool fans got onto the pitch at Anfield during a game against United and mimed aeroplanes to the away fans, who, of course, went into their whole repertoire of anti-scouse and Hillsborough songs. In fact, over the last decade the frequency and viciousness of tragedy chanting has appeared to increase. In 2016 a minute's silence at Ibrox was broken by noise from the crowd. This was initially blamed on Celtic fans supposedly shouting, 'I hope you die,' but it transpired that it had actually been a cry of 'fuck the Pope' from a Rangers fan who could no longer contain his bile. Celtic fans, silent on the day, have not stayed so. The accumulating tit-for-tat toxicity of Old Firm games saw graffiti appear around Ibrox before the same fixture in 2023 – reading 'HaHa66' and 'too many survived' – while Celtic fans booed that day's minute's silence. In 2016 police had to dismantle a large banner hung above Junction 5 of the M62 motorway between Manchester and Liverpool that read 'Manchester United scum 58'. While in 2023 a German flag bearing an aeroplane and the number 58 was hung on the Shankly Gates at Anfield before the game with Manchester United.[7]

Reprehensible as this might be, Liverpool have been on the receiving end of a great deal more, and not just from United fans. Consider just the recent history. Manchester City supporters sang the Hillsborough songs at Anfield in 2022 and at the Etihad in 2023. The same year, sixteen Chelsea fans were booted out of Anfield for doing the same, and another was arrested for chanting at Stamford Bridge later in the year. Three Arsenal fans were banned from football for chanting during their third-round FA Cup tie against Liverpool, as were two more Chelsea supporters at Wembley for the 2024 League Cup final. Tragedy chanting has also acquired its own repertoire of mime. A Spurs fan who had acted out Liverpool fans pushing their own, suggesting that they were culpable for their own deaths, was banned from the club's stadium. In a widely shared clip, one

United fan, at the end of their victorious quarter-final clash with Liverpool in the 2024 FA Cup, was seen in a state of delirious celebration placing his splayed hand over his face as if it were the wire cage that had asphyxiated so many Liverpool fans at Hillsborough. Certainly, in the chat rooms there are many, probably a majority of supporters who abhor the chants; but there are plenty who cleave to the justificatory logic of tit-for-tat abuse. The FA, the Premier League and the clubs have been setting up all kinds of task forces and committees to try to tackle the problem. The charitable foundations at Liverpool and Manchester United have been funding education programmes among their fans, but there is little cause, so far, to suggest that any of this is working. The bereaved and the traumatised have been left to suck it up, or as in the case of Stephen Kelly, who lost a brother at Hillsborough, to walk away: 'I don't go to the match now or listen on the radio or watch on TV. You can hear the chants there. I've lost my love for it and that's sad because those chanters have done that – the majority were probably not even born when Hillsborough happened.'[8]

Alongside the viciousness of tragedy chanting, British football has slowly developed a more formal mode of remembrance for its dead. Minutes of silence were held across football on the passing of Bobby Moore in 1993 and Sir Matt Busby in 1994; George Best and Sir Bobby Robson were accorded the same respects. At a more parochial level, the deaths of much-loved local players and coaches were increasingly marked at their home grounds, and in a strange instance of grief inflation, the passing of their relatives – Glenn Hoddle's father at Spurs, Frank Lampard's mum at Chelsea – was also noted. However, in the last quarter of a century football grounds have become places in which other deaths are marked. The template for these wider public remembrances was set by the silences held after Princess Diana and Dodi Fayed's deaths in 1997, 9/11, the murder of Ken Bigley by Islamists, the 2004 Pacific tsunami and the London terror attacks of 2005. This created a framework in which certain kinds of public figures, terrorist attacks and natural disasters were allocated a slot. Consistency, though, has not been football's strong suit. Public figures whose passing has been noted in Britain's stadiums have included Pope John Paul II, though not his successors, the Queen Mother but also cult radio DJ John Peel, and, perhaps most remarkably, Nelson Mandela but not Margaret Thatcher. Dave Whelan and John Madejski, owners of Wigan Athletic and Reading respectively and both Conservative Party donors, called for a minute's silence to mark her passing, but they were almost entirely alone. Thatcher's well-known dislike for the game and its fans meant that there was little love lost between them. Liverpool and Everton fans had, as her death approached, been singing, to the tune of 'She's a Jolly Good Fellow', 'We're gonna have a party when Maggie Thatcher dies'; and at the games played after her death had been announced, banners were raised saying, 'Ding Dong the Witch is Dead,' 'You took our milk, but you never took our pride,' and, with reference to Hillsborough, 'You didn't care when you lied. We didn't care when you died.' She received a state funeral, but the only silence held for her in football was at Finchley and Wingate, a club in the seventh tier in her old North London constituency.

More recently, the football authorities have deemed the 130 deaths from the Bataclan theatre attack of 2015 sufficiently serious to warrant a minute's silence and the wearing of black armbands across the leagues. So too the Manchester Arena and London Bridge attacks of 2017, which saw black armbands worn at the promotion play-offs and a minute's silence and wreath-laying at the FA Cup final. However, in 2019, the murderous attack on a mosque in Christchurch that saw fifty-one fatalities was not considered of a similar calibre, let alone the innumerable and more deadly suicide bombings in Afghanistan, Pakistan and Egypt.

Individuals thought important enough to merit league-wide acts of remembrance include Cyrille Regis and commentator

John Motson, both of whom were widely loved and respected, neither of which can be said of the Thai billionaire and owner of Leicester City, Vichai Srivaddhanaprabha. Surprising, then, that his demise in a helicopter accident, albeit at the King Power Stadium, should be marked by a minute's silence, but not that of other 'venerated' recently deceased but more penurious owners, like Wolverhampton's Jack Hayward. In 2023 the Premier League mandated a minute's silence for an earthquake in Morocco and devastating floods in Libya – both worthy of note, for sure – but chose not to mark the equally awful floods that had been sweeping through southern Africa or the considerably more disastrous Turkish earthquake that year.

There was never any doubt that the Queen's death would be marked by football, but the scale of football's official response – closer to the obsequious gravitas of the BBC – was a product of this now established culture of remembrance and the game's recent alignment with the norms of the bastions of loyalism and deference – the British Legion, the British military and the right-wing press. The relationship has not always been so close. At the beginning of the First World War, cricket, rugby and hockey closed down for the duration of the conflict. Professional football, however, carried on. Until 1916 the British military remained a volunteer force, but it had few means to directly engage with the young working-class men they required. In the absence of conscription they turned to football clubs, whose stadiums served as highly effective recruitment centres, many producing the 'pals' battalions in which an increasing number of players and supporters of a single club would serve and be slaughtered together. Useful as this was to the military, conservatives increasingly railed against the failure of enough professional players to sign up, seeing a lack of patriotism in the sport and, by association, among the working classes. The clamour was so loud that the 1915 FA Cup final was the last professional game played for almost four years. In the aftermath of the war Armistice Day was first established as a national day of mourning in 1919, and in 1921 the poppy was first used as a symbol of remembrance and an instrument of fund-raising for veterans. Public commemorations and silences, however, were confined to the Cenotaph, local war memorials and civic spaces, not football grounds. In 1927 the hymn 'Abide with Me' – one deeply resonant of the war years – was sung for the first time before the FA Cup final and military marching bands were present, but there were no formal minutes of silence or poppy sales at matches, a situation that did not change following the Second World War.

Perhaps the most important barrier to football's deeper involvement with remembrance was the fact that professional football was simply not played on a Sunday until 1974, and for the next couple of decades only rarely. In 1995, as part of the fiftieth anniversary of the end of the Second World War, national commemorations began to take place on both Armistice Day (11 November) and Remembrance Sunday, held on the nearest weekend to this. At the same time, at the behest of the broadcasters, more games were being played on a Sunday. This created a lot more slots in the football calendar for games that fell under the rubric of remembrance. The changes coincided with the death of Princess Diana, which shifted the public's appetite for and expectations of acts of public mourning, and a recognition at the Royal British Legion that the centrality of military acts of remembrance, indeed the whole remembrance show, was waning. A few years later the military and the then Labour government were also worried by the seeming lack of support for the disastrous operations in Iraq and Afghanistan they were engaged in. Prime Minister Tony Blair was very clear about the need not merely for supporting, appreciating and remembering the armed forces, but for acquiescing to their deployment: 'The armed forces want public opinion not just behind them but behind their mission.'[9] The Chief of the Defence Staff, General Jock Stirrup, was even more blunt: 'Support for our servicemen and women is indivisible from support for the mission.'[10] In this context, the British Legion, the right-wing press, the military and parts of the political class steadily ratcheted up the pressure on institutions of all kinds to foreground the military and the poppy in acts of remembrance, and football was in their sights.

One example of the increasing expectation, indeed requirement, of public figures to wear poppies came in 2001 when Sven-Göran Eriksson, on his first day as England manager, was, to his surprise, told to wear one.[11] Since then, they have become effectively compulsory for presenters, pundits, officials and coaches. In 2003 Leicester City were the first club to put a poppy on their shirt over the remembrance weekend, closely followed by Hearts, Norwich and West Bromwich. Emboldened by these initiatives, the Royal British Legion began in 2008 to campaign for clubs to play with poppies on their shirts at remembrance events. The following year, the *Daily Mail*, noting that fifteen of the Premier League clubs had planned to play with poppies, mounted a vituperative campaign against the other five. All five caved in, and in 2010 every single Premier League club played in shirts with poppies. The teams of the EFL and the SPL soon followed suit, even Celtic, though widespread fan protest and pressure would see them abandon the poppy the following season.

Attention then switched to the international game. In 2011 the FA had planned for England to play a friendly against Spain with a poppy on their shirt, before FIFA ruled that it was a political symbol and therefore impermissible. Prime Minister David Cameron frothed at the mouth, arguing that it was 'absurd and outrageous to claim wearing a poppy is a political act'.[12] Two members of the far-right group the English Defence League staged their own protest, climbing on top of FIFA's headquarters in Zurich, unveiling a banner stating: 'English Defence League. How dare FIFA disrespect our war dead and wounded. Support our troops.'[13] The FA, unable to move FIFA, went into poppy overdrive. It announced that Fabio Capello's squad would break off from training at Wembley to stand at the centre circle for a two-minute silence to mark Remembrance Day. They were also issued with special warm-up sweatshirts featuring poppies. Wreathes were laid in the centre circle, and poppies were on sale inside and outside the stadium. There were no further friendlies in early November for the next few years, but the remembrance police were still keeping tabs. When, during Euro 2016, a trip by the squad to a Battle of the Somme memorial in France was cancelled on the advice of Dave Reddin, the FA's head of performance services, the *Daily Mail* dug up a veteran's great grandson: 'It is an absolute joke that they haven't been able to pay their respects. It is 100 years since the Somme, it is the British Army's bloodiest battle and they can't give up three hours.'[14] The same voices went into overdrive that November, when again FIFA refused permission for England, Scotland and Wales to wear poppies on their shirts. The teams played with poppy armbands and FIFA fined them. In 2017 a compromise was reached, FIFA accepting that Armistice Day was an event of national significance – and thus somehow not political – and that poppies could be worn if a team's opponents consented. In so doing FIFA colluded with the British Legion, the armed forces and their political and media supporters in the effort to render invisible the politics of the poppy and the uncritical support for British militarism and foreign policy it has nurtured. It has become the norm in football grounds to hear that we are giving thanks for the service of all military personnel that have died protecting our freedoms and values, not merely in the world wars, but in Northern Ireland, Malaya, Aden, Kenya, Suez, Iraq, Afghanistan and every other colonial and post-colonial conflict that Britain has engaged in. One might try to claim that these acts of violence were in some sense equivalent to the defeat of fascism, but if that is the case it is hard to think of a more extreme politicisation of an 'event of national significance'.

In the years since the Brexit referendum the poppy and the armed forces have entirely colonised football's act of remembrance. Consider, for example, the order of service at West Ham in 2017 before their league game against Liverpool. Music was provided by the Royal Air Force Air Cadets band, and Trevor Brooking read the John McCrae poem 'In Flanders Fields'. The players, coming onto the pitch, were met by a guard of honour combining members of the Royal British Legion and current servicemen. The programme notes cheerily informed the public that club captain Mark Noble had not only delivered free match tickets to their base, but had received a 'a tour of the barracks and shown a display of the weaponry'.[15] Wreaths were laid in the centre circle by West Ham's chairman David Gold, Liverpool's CEO Peter Moore, the Mayor of Newham and a West Ham fan whose lower right leg had been amputated after serving in Afghanistan. Then 'The Last Post' was played before the minute's silence and, as the programme gushed, it was 'complimented [sic] by supporters in the East Stand creating an awe-inspiring Remembrance mosaic'. If that wasn't enough, a replica Spitfire had been installed outside the ground for the occasion. Rangers and Hearts have allowed actual army artillery pieces inside their grounds and used them to announce the minute's silence. A more DIY version of the phenomenon was seen in 2021 when a large military vehicle decorated with poppies parked outside a pub in the east end of the Glasgow, where hundreds of Rangers fans had assembled before the game.[16]

There was, mercifully, no military hardware at the Army Fun Zone outside Notts County's Meadow Lane when the club hosted a women's match between the British Army and the Bundeswehr, but a giant dartboard and inflatable slides were considered suitable. In this respect, the greatest achievement of the new rituals in football was to so drain the act of remembrance of any tangible connection to the real suffering and devastation caused by military violence that it turned into a festival of unimaginable kitsch. As Miguel Delaney, chief football writer at the *Independent*, observed in 2019: 'At Arsenal last week, the entrance to the media room featured a metal outline of a World War One soldier, before you were "treated" to a huge white cake adorned with pastry poppies ... Southampton had a huge flag featuring more and more poppies, getting bigger and bigger. Liverpool had a similar effect on their corner flags.'[17] In 2017 Leicester City had a man dressed in black with a giant foam poppy for a face. Tranmere Rovers went one better and created a mascot that was just one huge waddling poppy, with pantomime black shoes poking out. The usual club mascots barely did any better when it came to preserving the dignity of the occasion. Swansea's Cyril the Swan bowed its elongated head, but only at the cost of its beak bayoneting its stomach, and no amount of low bows and hands behind backs could disguise the demented rictus grin of Southend's Sammy the Shrimp. A similar gravitas was delivered by clubs' Remembrance Day strips, Hartlepool United opting for a Spitfire theme and Millwall actually playing in camouflage. These interventions suggest that, despite Bolton's military third kit embroidered with the words 'lest we forget', this is precisely what has happened.

Remembrance weekend has not been the end of the matter, as football has forged deeper connections with the military. At Lincoln City the music from the film *The Dam Busters* precedes every game, honouring the locally based RAF squadrons that during the Second World War dropped bouncing bombs on German hydroelectric dams. Shrewsbury Town have been celebrating Armed Forces Day for over a decade, and in 2023 astronaut Colonel Tim Peake landed a military helicopter in the centre circle and delivered the match ball. The EFL has, along with many of its clubs, signed the Armed Forces Covenant, as part of a British Legion campaign that seeks to mobilise support from civil society for veterans. Perhaps in a society that actually did look after its veterans – who are more likely to suffer poverty, homelessness, ill health and mental breakdown than their civilian peers – we might not need to rely on five-a-side games at Norwich and Millwall to keep body and soul together.

In the absence of any real covenant between the British state and its soldiers, football's small veteran programmes are sticking plasters. Resistance or critique to this pitiful state of affairs has been almost entirely absent. Celtic fans, in particular the Green Brigade, have been the only visible opponents, famously erecting a banner in 2010 at Celtic Park that read, 'Your deeds would shame all the devils in Hell. Ireland, Iraq, Afghanistan. No bloodstained poppy on our Hoops.' Since then, Celtic have ceased to wear the poppy on their shirts, while the Green Brigade, in less poetic mode, have been singing at games scheduled over the remembrance weekend, 'You can stick your fucking poppy up your arse.' Among the players, only two have resisted the tide. Manchester United's Serbian defender Nemanja Matić said the poppy reminded him of NATO's bombing of his hometown Vrelo, and he was broadly left in peace. However, in 2012, James McClean, then playing for Sunderland and hailing from the republican heartlands of Derry, was treated very differently. Polite, concise, but firm, McClean made it clear that he had no intention to disrespect the fallen and their families. He patiently explained that were the acts of remembrance confined to the dead of the world wars he would have no problem participating; but having grown up in a place where the British Army were accused of murdering civilians in the Bloody Sunday killings of 1972 and had served effectively as an army of occupation, it was simply impossible for him to wear the poppy. His reward for this was a decade of booing in stadiums, abuse and death threats on social media, and bullets in the post.[18]

Eight months after the Queen's death, the coronation of King Charles III seemed to confuse rather than enthuse British football. Football Twitter was shocked to find the UEFA Champions League chorus being played in Westminster Abbey as the monarch was anointed, until it became more widely known that the UEFA tune was an adaptation of Handel's 'Zadok the Priest' – composed in 1727 for King George II and performed at the coronation of every British monarch since. The national anthem was given an outing at the games played that weekend, but rarely sung as more than a dutiful dirge. Celtic fans, as ever, were at the forefront of dissent, displaying the banner 'Fuck the King. Crown the Champions' at their game against Hearts, while on the big day itself they sang, 'You can shove your coronation up your arse.' At their game with Brentford, Liverpool fans booed the national anthem and chanted, 'Kenny is our King' and 'Fuck the Royal Family, feed the poor'.[19] Perhaps the loudest chorus of all came from James McClean, now playing for Wrexham, enjoying their return to the Football League and acknowledging the love from the fans who sang, to the tune of Abba's 'Voulez-Vous', 'James McClean (a-ha)/Running down the wing (a-ha)/Makes the Wrexham sing (a-ha)/And he hates the fucking King.'[20] There was plenty of abuse on social media, but McClean was unrepentant, posting a video of himself singing along with the crowds: 'Do I make any apologies for doing so? Absolutely not.' It is probably just as well that he wasn't singing this on the streets of London, where protesting members of anti-monarchist group Republic were brusquely dealt with by the police. That said, the House of Windsor can survive these small outbreaks of football republicanism. Honoured or disdained, their relationship with football has made them appear an ever-more irreplaceable part of the furniture.

21.

Qatar 2022 and All That

Political Football on a Global Stage

The presence of the Middle East in world football, above all the fossil-fuel monarchies of the Gulf, has been increasing for two decades. The UAE bought Manchester City in 2008, a Qatari state investment fund bought PSG in 2011 and Saudi Arabia's sovereign wealth fund bought Newcastle United in 2021. All three countries hosted major regional football tournaments and lavished their parastatal sponsorships across the world game. Between mid-November and mid-December 2022, Qatar would sit at the very centre of that world, and football in Britain, like everywhere else, would come to a halt and take note. The Qatar 2022 World Cup, impossible to play in the heat of a Gulf summer, had been switched to the winter, the entire calendar of world football rearranged by FIFA to accommodate it.

From the moment Qatar, against most people's expectations, won the bid in 2010, it proved to be the most politicised World Cup ever. In Britain and northern Europe, the build-up to the tournament was dominated not by discussion of teams' form or the break-out stars to come, but by issues of migrant workers, women's and LGBT rights in Qatar, and the availability of alcohol. In fact, the fate of migrant workers in Qatar would hold the headlines for almost a decade after investigations by the

Guardian and human rights organisations first argued that between 5,000 and 6,000 of them would perish in the twelve years between Qatar being awarded the tournament and staging it. Debates over these numbers raged; the organisers claimed that deaths on narrowly defined World Cup projects numbered in just the dozens. Either way, Western audiences become familiar with the facts: Qatar's migrant work force laboured under enormous debts owed to unscrupulous recruitment agencies; were subject to excruciatingly bad and dangerous work conditions; faced pathological levels of heat while working in the Gulf sun; were subject to appalling living circumstances; and toiled under the kafala system, itself a legacy of the British Empire, in which their employers had the right to withhold their passports, prevent them changing job and ultimately to expel them from the country. The Qataris responded to the pressure first with a set of very limited internal reforms, and then in 2017 the proposal to work with the UN's International Labour Organization (ILO) and effectively dismantle the kafala system, replacing it with a state-bureaucratic rather than personal system of migrant control, as well as improving and monitoring living and working conditions. Trade union membership, however, would remain illegal.

Not surprisingly, in the year leading up to the tournament, polls suggested that a significant majority of Britons disapproved of Qatar staging the tournament, and a small number thought that England should boycott the event. Both the FA and Gareth Southgate argued that engagement was a better tactic than withdrawal, and the boycott movement was restricted to a small number of pubs and venues that refused to show the games on television and a small number of fans who declared that they personally would not be watching the tournament. As coverage of Qatar increased, the public was exposed to troubling reports of the country's treatment of women, the repressive control of journalists and the illegality of homosexuality. Disquiet among the broadcasters was sufficient for the BBC, unlike at any World Cup before, to choose to run a thirty-minute explainer on these issues in preference to showing the tournament's opening ceremony, while Alan Shearer, a man who had guarded his political views closely, called on air for FIFA and Qatar, in line with a proposal from Amnesty International, to compensate workers and their families.

However, once the tournament had actually started, the issue of migrant workers effectively disappeared from the conversation, and the main bone of contention in the British and much of the European press became Qatar's treatment of LGBT fans and symbols. Prior to the tournament, both FIFA and the Qataris had attempted to walk a very narrow line in which, on the one hand, they claimed that the World Cup was open to all and the safety and security of everyone in Qatar was guaranteed, while on the other hand asking that visitors 'respect the local culture' – a culture in which obvious displays of physical affection, both heterosexual and homosexual, were frowned upon, and gay Qataris were shamed, vilified and imprisoned. In the run-up to the tournament, the venerable LGBT campaigner Peter Tatchell staged a one-man protest in Qatar before being seen off the premises.[1] Foreign Secretary James Cleverly, to considerable criticism, gave his tacit approval to this accommodation when he told the Foreign Affairs select committee before his departure to the tournament, 'When British nationals travel overseas, they should respect the laws of their host country. Genuinely, my question is, for those gay fans who want to go watch the football, what advice realistically should I give other than the advice I believe will keep them safe?'[2] To which Gary Lineker shot back on Twitter, 'Whatever you do, don't do anything Gay. Is that the message?' The Secretary General of the Supreme Committee for Delivery and Legacy, the grandiose name for the organising committee, pointed out that when England had last staged the World Cup, homosexuality was also illegal. But Britain and its football cultures had changed a lot since 1966. Indeed, the significantly bigger and more self-confident presence of the LGBT community in football was perhaps the main reason that these issues displaced coverage of the fate of migrant workers.

This may well have come as a surprise to casual observers of the game. The tragic death of Justin Fashanu, who was outed by the *Sun* in 1990 and took his own life in 1998, weighed heavily over British football. It remained the case that no professional male footballer had come out while still playing, until seventeen-year-old Jake Daniels, signed to Blackpool's academy, did so in 2022. As late as 2016 a British parliamentary inquiry into homophobia in sport could argue: 'Despite the significant change in society's attitudes to homosexuality in the last 30 years, there is little reflection of this progress being seen in football.'[3] Leading LGBT advocacy group Stonewall claimed that 72 per cent of English football fans regularly witnessed homophobic abuse, and that a fifth of them would be 'embarrassed' if their favourite player came out.[4] However, academic research, deploying methodologically sounder surveys, found that 93 per cent of fans had no objection to an openly gay player being contracted to the team they supported, most believing that clubs, agents and governing bodies were truly responsible for the problem. Equally importantly, these studies found that three-quarters of LGBT fans felt 'safe' attending matches and that previous feelings of intimidation and anxiety had dissipated in recent years.[5]

This quiet transformation was driven, in part, by the wider progressive changes in British attitudes to sexuality in the twenty-first century, but a series of initiatives within the game had also moved the dial. The Gay Football Supporters Network (GFSN), founded in the 1990s, had steadily grown, such that registered LGBT supporters' groups could, by 2022, be found at almost every Premier League ground and those of the leading Scottish clubs – as well as at many smaller teams. The GFSN football league, which provides a safe space for playing the game, could look back on almost twenty years of growth and the emergence of dozens of inclusive LGBT grassroots clubs like Leftfooters, Stonewall FC and Village Manchester. Club banners and insignia, combined with the rainbow flag, flown by supporters' groups like the Gay Gooners, Villa and Proud, and at Ipswich the Rainbow Tractors, had become regular and visible features of the football landscape, so quotidian that they were barely noticed. In 2013 Stonewall had launched its Rainbow Laces campaign, encouraging players and fans to wear them for two weeks of the season in support of LGBT rights. There was, of course, plenty of opposition to this kind of initiative. Clubs that added rainbow flags to their social-media profiles would record thousands of homophobic comments, as did EA Sports when it introduced a rainbow shirt as an option for teams in *FIFA 17*. At the same time, it had become apparent that the women's game had long been an inclusive and safe space for LGBT players and fans, while in the men's game the cause had gained some very high-profile allies from among the players, not least Liverpool captain Jordan Henderson. When one gay Liverpool fan thanked him for wearing rainbow laces in 2020, he replied on Twitter: 'You'll never walk alone Keith. If wearing the #RainbowLaces armband helps even just one person then it's progress. Everyone is welcome at Liverpool Football Club. Hope you enjoyed the game tonight. #YNWA.'[6]

With similar debates going on across Europe, football associations who had supported LGBT inclusivity in the past were feeling real political pressure to act. Consequently, seven of the qualifying nations (Belgium, Denmark, England, France, Germany, Netherlands and Wales) had agreed that their team captains would wear 'One Love' armbands in their opening games. FIFA had initially stayed silent on their plans, but in the days before the tournament began, and under considerable pressure from the Qataris, announced that they would be issuing a range of 'good cause' armbands for team captains to wear instead, and behind closed doors let it be known, in no uncertain terms, that should players take to the field wearing anything else, they would be issued with yellow cards and fined. The Europeans backed down, though a modicum of protest continued. BBC pundit Alex Scott reported from the England–Iran game wearing a One Love armband. The Danes went on to play one game in a specially commissioned all-black kit in remembrance of the migrant workers who had died to build the World Cup infrastructure, and the Germans would line up for a pre-match team photograph with their hands over their mouths, protesting what they saw as an infringement of their right to free speech. David Beckham, who since his appearance in the gay lifestyle magazine *Attitude* had been English football's longest-standing LGBT icon, was serving as an ambassador for the World Cup at the cut price rate of just £10 million, and remained silent on the matter.

The Qataris could not control what foreign teams and broadcasters did or said, but they proved determined to control what could be shown and seen inside their stadiums. Alexander Backer, chair of Stonewall FC, said, 'I never felt my physical safety was threatened, but all the stuff with [rainbow] flags, it was clear the Qatari organisers wanted you to conform with their view of an appropriate way of life'. Another fan, one of hundreds reporting the policing of insignia, recalled, 'I brought out an England flag with rainbow colours on and I've got T-shirts with the same – I had problems with both. The T-shirt they finally let that in, the flag was confiscated twice within the stadiums. The final time I didn't get it back.'[7]

Tricky as it was to get a rainbow flag or bucket hat into a Qatari stadium, those who wanted to acknowledge the recent uprising in Iran would find the task much harder. Through the autumn of 2022 demonstrations in Iran protesting the imposition of the hijab and other restrictions on women turned violent. The religious police cracked down hard on street protest, specifically targeting young women, wounding some and arresting many. After 22-year-old Mahsa Amini died in police custody, the situation exploded into a nation-wide protest drawing on a much bigger constituency than just the youth of the big cities where it had begun. The Iranian players had given tacit support to the protest by refusing to sing the national anthem before friendlies, and even stayed silent in Qatar before their opening game against England. However, intense pressure from Tehran, and veiled threats to their families back home, saw them grudgingly mouth the words thereafter. Many Iranian fans living in Qatar or from the wider diaspora made the journey to support the team and brought with them T-shirts and flags bearing the uprising's slogan, 'Women. Life. Freedom', as well as Pahlavi-era Iranian flags. Given the intimacy of the relationship between Tehran and Doha, these items were policed in an even more draconian fashion than rainbow T-shirts, with both Qatari security and a strangely large number of pro-government Iranian fans confiscating them, and often intimidating or even attacking their bearers. Some turned to writing the words on their bodies and showing them off in the stands – but even here the Qataris were alert enough to make those they caught scrub the words from their skin.[8]

Wales were going to their first World Cup since 1958, and it was evident that something more than just playing football was at stake. The previous year, the chief executive of the FAW, Noel Mooney, had said, in language reminiscent of the nineteenth-century founders of the GAA or the interwar workers' sports movement, rather than that of a contemporary football administrator: 'We're not just a football association. We are a movement.' Wales' preparations for the tournament suggested as much. Mooney argued, 'What is very important to us is creativity, the arts, the Welsh language.' Thus, the FAW chose not to spend money on the huge public screens and beer gardens that had accompanied Euro 2016, not that the Welsh weather in December would have been terribly accommodating of such a strategy, but chose instead to support Welsh football events, mainly in grassroots settings, foregrounding language, culture and music. Once again, music would form a key component of Wales' football odyssey. In the run-up to Qatar 2022, the FAW, the players and the Welsh crowd embraced Dafydd Iwan and his 1960s folk protest song 'Yma o Hyd'. Iwan was a longstanding Welsh nationalist and activist, a former president of Plaid Cymru who had been arrested during the Welsh-language protests and sit-ins of the 1960s. Echoing the final lines of the national anthem, 'may the old language endure', the song was a joyful celebration of Welsh resilience and resistance: 'Despite everyone and everything we're still here.' The song had, at times, been taken up by rugby fans in Llanelli and football crowds at both Swansea City and Wrexham, then it began to be heard at Wales' football games. The players requested that Iwan perform the song live before the kick-off of their penultimate qualifying game for the World Cup, against Austria, and they went on to win it 2–1. The coach, Rob Page, revealed, 'We played it every day before training and on the coach.' Iwan was back for the final and decisive qualifier against Ukraine in Cardiff, singing with the crowd before the game, and with the crowd and the squad on the pitch afterwards. In an extraordinary moment of popular national imagining and remembrance, the FAW then commissioned a remix of the song for the World Cup, layering Welsh crowds over Iwan's voice in a film montage of football, coal mine closures, Welsh-language protests and the flooding of the Tryweryn valley, in which the Welsh village of Capel Celyn was sacrificed in 1965 to build a reservoir for northern England. In keeping with Wales' new diversity, and for those of less traditional musical tastes, Sage Todz, a Black Welsh rapper, made and released his own bilingual version of the song.

The Welsh squad was announced by Rob Page, near his childhood home, at Tylorstown Welfare Hall, the last remaining miners' institute in the area, in a mood closer to a school fete than the usual aseptic press conference. Page stood next to a giant bucket hat in Welsh colours, the fashion accessory of choice for the Red Wall. In circulation for some time, but first popularised at Euro 2016, even Mark Drakeford, the otherwise rather colourless Welsh First Minister, was wearing one for Euro 2020, tweeting a shot of himself watching Wales versus Turkey. By 2022, players were wearing them on the pitch, the FAW had installed giant hat sculptures in the central squares of Cardiff, Swansea and other cities, and the wider public embraced them: 'Bucket hats are everywhere in Wales … schoolyards, city centre squares and even in hardware shops hanging incongruously above paint pots and tools.'[9] Football and the national team were no longer a minority pursuit, but had arrived at the centre of Welsh popular culture. Laura McAllister told the BBC, 'It was always an oddity to be a football fan and now it's so main-stream.' Richard Grigg, one of just eleven fans that famously travelled to see Wales play Georgia in Tbilisi in 1994 and get thrashed 5–0, noted the deeper transformation in the football nation: 'There is a culture to it now … It's much more nation-alistic, there's much more use of the Welsh language in songs and more people speak Welsh.' The actor Michael Sheen was called in to offer the squad a speech before going to Qatar, but it was much closer to a twenty-first-century bardic poem: 'A storm, a red storm, is coming to the gates of Qatar/It sparkles and crackles with the spirit of '58 and Jimmy Murphy's boys.'[10]

The contingent of fans that made it to Qatar made their presence felt in 'hotels that rose from the desert but were decked out like a primary school in Llanelli on St David's Day'.[11] Dafydd Iwan played a short set to hundreds of supporters inside one of those hotels, and the Welsh government paid for a giant bucket hat to be installed in central Doha, with the message: 'Wales is a nation that is home to acts of kindness.' There was to be no reprise of the glories of Euro 2016, however. Wales managed a 1–1 draw in their opening game against the USA where, in the final minutes of the match, Gareth Bale won and then scored a penalty to equalise. Then they lost 2–0 to Iran, and were soundly beaten 3–0 by England in their final game. Wales were going home, but not to recrimination or with an air of real disappointment. On the contrary, there was enormous pride that they had been there at all. As one supporter put it: 'Our children's generation will not assume that being a plucky loser is their preordained place in the order of things. They can do and be whatever they want. Not just in football, but in any field they choose.'

Good as Bale's equaliser had been, for many nationalists the highlight of the tournament was defender Ben Davies's press conference where, for the first time on television, a player for the national team spoke in Welsh. He got the standard Twitter trolling – 'Ben Davies loser speaking Welsh' – but he also got a lot of support. Davies was articulate in his defence: 'The language is important to me, I don't need to explain to anyone how important it is to speak Welsh.'[12] It was becoming increasingly important to the FAW, who had long insisted on referring to the national team as Cymru at home but were now contemplating the same for the rest of the world. Turkey had recently decreed that their national teams should be referred to in their Turkish form – Türkiye – so why not Cymru? A small change, perhaps, but the Welsh language needed every bit of help it could get. As of 2022, only about 20 per cent of the country spoke Welsh as a first language. The Welsh government was aiming for a million Welsh speakers by 2030, and the advance of Welsh-language education and television was helping them edge towards that target. However, in the northern and western heartlands of the language, limited economic opportunities were driving a significant number of young Welsh speakers away, to be replaced by incoming English-speaking retirees. This is a longstanding problem which Welsh football has struggled to address; Wales' first consciously Welsh-language football club, Y Glannau St Asaph, was founded back in the mid-1990s; but it wasn't joined by a second until the creation of Yr Wyddgrug in the North East Wales Championship in 2023. Clubs in North Wales complained that they were, despite the FAW's commitment to bilingualism, forced to conduct disciplinary hearings and other administrative matters in English, or to pay for translators themselves. When Talysarn FC, in Gwynedd, went public with these complaints, the bitterness of the backlash, though entirely par for the course, was a measure of how difficult the struggle for linguistic equality had been: 'I'm sure you can all speak English up there so quit moaning about having to have a translator, it's pathetic. Welsh is an awful dying language and I'm Welsh. I don't want it forced down my throat by you or Plaid Cymru.'[13] Ben Davies and the FAW might have disagreed, but they were going to need more than a World Cup appearance to take on this level of venom.

It was a small and rather unusual English football nation that actually went to Qatar. The enormous cost of attending the tournament, the mid-winter timing and the impact of the cost of living crisis breaking over the country all helped keep numbers down, but perhaps the single most important factor was Qatar's policy on alcohol. Drinking in public was not permitted, and being drunk in public was also an offence. FIFA sponsors Budweiser would be allowed to sell beer in the fan zones near to the stadiums after 6.30 p.m., and, of course, for those who could afford it, alcohol was available in hospitality suites at the games and in the bars and restaurants of Doha's five-star hotels. In the week before the tournament, under considerable pressure from the Qatari government, it was agreed that beer would not be available around the stadiums and would be restricted to just a few of the more distant fan zones. Given the central place of drinking, preferably excessive drinking in public spaces, among England's core travelling support, it is little wonder that most of them gave Qatar a miss. Ecuadorian fans, at their game, may have chanted, 'We want beer,' but there was no movement on the issue. Of course, some England fans did make the journey, and certainly found a variety of ways to consume alcohol, but for the first time since records began, not a single English or Welsh fan was arrested during a World Cup tournament. The Qataris could be forgiven for a modicum of smugness on seeing that in Tenerife, where considerable numbers of English and Welsh fans had headed for a spot of winter sun and football, drunken fighting broke out in the streets during their group-stage clash.[14]

In their search for a modicum of 'normality' at a very abnormal World Cup, parts of the press gave a lot of space to 'World Cup Guy', whose craggy, middle-aged face, wreathed in joy, went viral on social media. Andy Milne, a Mancunian who had attended every England World Cup campaign for two decades, was a reassuringly old-school version of the football nation.[15] By the same token, an equally rubicund gentleman in an England kit was a hit on social media when an Israeli journalist asked him if 'football is coming home?' He replied, 'Course it is, yeah … but … more importantly … Free Palestine!' and proceeded to celebrate with a group of Arab fans.[16] Under these circumstances there was room for a more ethnically diverse England support than usual. In particular, many supporters with South Asian roots had family and business connections in Qatar, where the Indian community had been a significant migrant presence for almost half a century. Mohamed Suleiman from Bolton reported with some surprise that there were so many faces like his own around: 'I think English fan culture is changing … It's becoming more diverse. More welcoming. And you can definitely see it in Qatar.'[17] Back home, a survey revealed that two-thirds of the country, including the majority of minorities, thought the team a better source of national unity and pride than the flag. The nation was more divided on the matter of Crusader costumes. For some time now, fans had been supporting England in costumes of chain mail and St George flag tabards, a look that appeared, in England at any rate, part *Monty Python and the Holy Grail*, part English Defence League fancy-dress party. In Qatar it appeared to be a reference to the holy wars of the eleventh to thirteenth centuries, when European feudal armies conquered substantial parts of the Middle East, laying waste to Islamic shrines and populations alike. Not surprisingly, two fans equipped with plastic swords were prevented from attending England's opening game. The tabloids tried to work themselves and their readers into a froth, but one wonders what would happen to Qataris who tried to attend Wembley dressed as Saladin, bearing scimitars and wearing moon and crescent tabards?

In the round of sixteen, England showed their best form, sweeping aside African champions Senegal 3–0, but in the quarter-finals the defending champions and seeming favourites for the tournament France beat them 2–1. Late in the game Harry Kane had the chance to take it to extra time, but uncharacteristically missed his penalty. In contrast to earlier World Cups, and the penalty misses at Euro 2020, there was no outpouring of bile for either Southgate or the team. It just wasn't going to be England's World Cup. A nation that had just lived through the turmoil that had seen three prime ministers in as many months, near economic meltdown after the Truss government's disastrous mini-budget and an unprecedented cost of living crisis didn't seem to have any anger or energy left.

In fact, it wasn't going to be France's World Cup either, or Europe's or the global north's. The 2022 World Cup belonged to the global south. Of course, this was a matter of hosting and location, but even in South Africa in 2010 the stadiums had been overwhelmingly full of white people, both South Africans and travellers from Europe and North America. So too in Brazil in 2014 where, despite half of the population identifying as Afro Brazilian, one reporter thought, 'If I didn't know any better I would think I was in Kansas.'[18] In Qatar the reverse was true. Qataris themselves were a major presence, men dressed in their pristine white thobes and women in black abayas, creating an entirely different aesthetic from the unironed masculinity and drab colour palette that predominates in Europe. Saudis, who came in their tens of thousands across the border, mixed replica national team shirts and traditional robes, and they were supplemented by other faces from across the Gulf – Emiratis, Kuwaitis and Bahrainis. Qatar's huge migrant populations from Algeria, Egypt, Lebanon and Palestine were well represented, not least at Morocco's games, which drew huge support right across the region and ignited street celebrations from Tunis to Islamabad. Qatar's significant populations of middle-class Indian and Pakistani descent were an important segment of the crowd, and they were joined, especially in the expensive hospitality suites, by India's new football-loving middle and upper classes, who were just a short flight away. That said, barely any of the nearly 2 million migrant workers from South Asia, Nepal, Bhutan and the Philippines were present.

Demographics aside, the politics of the tournament showed a political tilt to the global south. Qatar itself proved more than a match for FIFA, forcing the previously unchallengeable over-lords of the World Cup to adopt their line on the presence of rainbow insignia and alcohol. While this may have gone down badly in the global north, it went down very well in those many other parts of the world where the criminalisation of both alcohol and homosexuality were still the norm. The same constituencies nodded their heads when the Qataris condemned European critiques of both country and tournament as barely disguised racism and Islamophobia.

On the pitch this shift was registered by the two biggest stories of the tournament, Morocco and Argentina. Pan-Arab and pan-African solidarities were on proud display in Qatar and across the Middle East. They had already been evoked by Tunisia's post-colonial rebuke to France, beating their B-team though departing after the group stage; but it was Morocco's remarkable march to the semi-final that drew the biggest crowds and provided the most intense celebrations. They combined visiting Moroccans, Qatar's significant Moroccan migrant worker population and the hundreds of thousands of Egyptians, Jordanians and Lebanese who live and work in Qatar. They were joined by huge crowds in Morocco itself, across the Arab world, among the Moroccan diaspora in Europe and, perhaps more intensely than anywhere, by Palestinians, whose flag and cause were a very visible part of the Moroccan team's celebrations and the subject of many of the crowd's songs. The Qatari security were altogether more relaxed about the presence of these flags compared with the many others that had been flown during the tournament.

Argentinians, unburdened by any of the political concerns that kept fan numbers from the global north so low, arrived in force. By the quarter-finals, they literally filled every stadium the team played in and brought a vivacity and energy that stood in stark contrast to European contingents, which had mostly been small and relatively restrained; a contrast exemplified by the tiny strip of Dutch orange in an ocean of Argentinean sky blue at their quarter-final. They also had the better story. France had ended Morocco's dreams by beating them in the semi-final and now stood to defend the title they had won in 2018, a feat not achieved since Brazil won the 1958 and 1962 World Cups. Argentina had inexplicably lost their opening game to Saudi Arabia, but, led by Lionel Messi, had dragged themselves back into the tournament. Messi had already lost one final with the national team in 2014, and now, in what was surely his last opportunity to win the World Cup, stood on the threshold of divinity. The teams played what was truly one of the great, if not the greatest World Cup final of all time: 2–2 at full time, 3–3 at the end of extra time, Argentina having won the game twice only for France twice to find a way to pull it back. Third time round, in the penalty shoot-out, Argentina won it again. The Emir of Qatar, before handing the trophy to Lionel Messi, placed a bisht – a traditional ceremonial robe and a marker of honour – on his shoulders. Messi and Argentina had the World Cup, but Qatar was the biggest winner of all.

Given the criticism in Britain of Qatar's limited media freedoms, lack of political opposition, treatment of migrants and its heavy-handed control of the World Cup, the strike at *Match of the Day* in March 2023 made an interesting coda. Host Gary

Lineker had earlier tweeted his criticism of the government's Illegal Migration Bill, particularly the language that was used to demonise migrants – reminiscent, he rightly thought, of Germany in the 1930s. The noise from the *Daily Mail* and the Tory backbenches was deafening. Whether Lineker was right or not was immaterial, rather the logic was that a person paid by public monies was not permitted to criticise government policy, the kind of truncation of human rights they know all about in Doha. The BBC stood Lineker down. In response, fellow pundits Ian Wright and Alan Shearer announced that, in solidarity, they would not be appearing either. The entire body of commentators came out on strike too, and 200,000 people signed an online petition calling for Lineker's reinstatement. Having failed to secure the rights to the Premier League's world feed with commentary, the BBC was forced to air a very scanty *Match of the Day* with just edited games and no commentary. A few Tories, like Scott Benton, MP for Blackpool South, tried to make the best of it, claiming on social media that it was 'the best episode ever', a turn of phrase that suggested he had never seen the show. Most found it unwatchable. The BBC caved in, Lineker was allowed back on, subject to innumerable new protocols, and the chair of the BBC, who it transpired had facilitated a loan to the Prime Minister prior to his appointment, resigned. As to the demonisation of migrants, the government didn't seem too put out by Lineker's criticism. That summer, Home Office minister Robert Jenrick deemed that the Mickey Mouse murals at a children's asylum-seeker reception centre were too welcoming and had them painted over.

22.

Power Games

English Football and the Middle East

A Middle Eastern presence in English football is not entirely new. It can be traced back as far as 1911, when the young Egyptian striker Hussein Hegazi, bound for Cambridge University, stopped off to play first for Dulwich Hamlet and then scored a goal for Fulham in a try-out game against Stockport. A decade later his compatriot Tewfik Abdullah played for both Derby Country and Cowdenbeath. More recently, the Premier League and the Championship have begun to import players from the region, most notably Liverpool's Egyptian star Mo Salah, but he is just one of dozens of North Africans who have played in the league since the 2010s. A better measure, though, of the shifting balance of power in the world is that the Middle East's biggest impact on contemporary English football is not on the pitch, but off it, as sponsors and owners. Emirates airline has been the biggest presence, first as Chelsea's shirt sponsors then at Arsenal, whose stadium is now synonymous with them. In recent social-media posts the club has claimed that the values of the club and the airline are synonymous too. The FA Cup, picked up by the airline in 2015, may be going the same way.

Middle Eastern ownership began eclectically. In 1977 Sam Hammam, a Lebanese businessman who had made his money in construction and property in the Gulf, left Beirut when it became engulfed by civil war. He settled in Wimbledon because he loved tennis, but became interested in football and bought the local club two years later, taking the non-league side all the way to the Premier League before selling up in 1997. Unable to keep away, he owned Cardiff City between 2000 and 2006. In 1997 the Egyptian businessman Mohamed Al-Fayed bought Fulham for £6.25 million as one component of his ultimately unsuccessful multi-pronged strategy to crack the British establishment and get himself a British passport. Under Al-Fayed, Fulham rose from the third level of English football to become Premier League regulars. They also played in Europe and, perhaps less surprisingly, remain the only club to have had a sculpture of Michael Jackson installed outside their ground. By the time he sold the club in 2013 to US-Pakistani car-parts billionaire Shahid Khan, Al-Fayed had dropped another £187 million, but most of that was covered by the near quarter of a billion dollars he received for the sale.

Some of the more recent Middle Eastern interventions have followed a similarly eclectic path. In 2013 Prince Abdullah bin Mosaad Al Saud, a senior Saudi royal and at one point in charge of the country's ministry of sport, bought 50 per cent of Sheffield United. After a protracted legal battle with his co-owner, Kevin McCabe, he took 100 per cent ownership in 2019. He spent much of the next five years watching Sheffield United get promoted and relegated from the Premier League while trying to sell the club on. Meantime, the Al-Qadi family from Jordan, who made their money in banking, purchased Bristol Rovers in 2016. They have gone on to sell a majority stake to a Kuwait businessman, Hussain AlSaeed, while parking Rovers in their natural position – somewhere in the bottom third of League One before overseeing negotiation to League Two in 2025. The Moroccan businessman Abdallah Lemsagam was co-owner of Oldham Athletic for a tempestuous four years between 2018 and 2022 that saw him embroiled in a series of bitter conflicts with the fans, and the club fell out of the Football League for the first time in 115 years. Egyptian billionaire Nassef Sawiris was one half of the consortium that bought 45 per cent of Aston Villa in 2018, while Saudi entrepreneur Nawaf Al Shammari is part-owner of Sutton United on the southern fringes of London, who were relegated to the national league in 2024; both appear to be no more than trophy assets. In these cases Middle Eastern owners are driven by the same mix of motivations as other foreign investors – personal ambition, conspicuous consumption, personal ego trips for the terminally bored. However, at Manchester City and Newcastle United something else has been at stake: power.

Power was certainly part of the reason that the deposed and exiled Thai Prime Minister Thaksin Shinawatra bought Manchester City in 2006, using the club to maintain his profile at home. In 2008, after his wife had been convicted in absentia of corruption charges in Thailand and his foreign assets were frozen, the Premier League deemed him no longer a fit and proper person to own the club. Thus, when Sheikh Mansour, a member of the Abu Dhabi royal family, came along as a prospective buyer, a quick 'no questions asked' sale was facilitated.[1] The new regime was initially fronted by Sulaiman Al-Fahim, a garrulous and clownish TV star from the UAE, but he was soon replaced by the altogether more serious and accomplished Khaldoon Al Mubarak. Manchester City continue to maintain the fiction that the club is the personal property of Sheik Mansour, operating at arm's length from the state institutions of the UAE and its power elite. It is, nonetheless, a fiction. It is worth recapitulating the multiple state offices occupied by City's 'owner' and its chairman.

Sheikh Mansour is the fifth of nineteen sons of the ruling Sheikh Zayed, and one of the six sons of his favoured wife; two of his full brothers are the UAE's foreign minister and president – the country's de facto ruler. Well placed in the upper echelons of UAE politics when the club was purchased in 2008, Sheikh Mansour is now the country's deputy vice president, deputy prime minister, and chairs two of the country's huge sovereign wealth funds, the Central Bank and the Abu Dhabi National Oil Company (ADNOC). Little wonder, then, that in fifteen years he has only visited Manchester once, and seen City play only twice. Khaldoon Al Mubarak sits on all the key strategic committees of the UAE state – its Executive Council, the Supreme Council for Financial and Economic Affairs, and the Executive Affairs Authority. He is also the CEO of the sovereign investment fund Mubadala, and still finds space in his diary to chair the state's nuclear energy and aluminium corporations. Manchester City is, in short, a state project and an instrument of global soft power. As Garry Cook, then CEO of the club, said with admirable candour when the UAE was first contemplating buying City, 'If you're developing your nation and you're looking to be on the global stage, we are your proxy brand for the nation.'[2] Al Mubarak was equally explicit, saying the purpose of the club was: 'Telling the world ... the true essence of who Abu Dhabi is'.[3] What the true essence of the UAE actually is, is another matter; but it would certainly include its unambiguously autocratic character and terrible record of human rights abuses.[4]

The UAE have been nothing if not meticulous and ambitious in their transformation of Manchester City. Beneficiaries of an incredible deal with the local council, who own the stadium, City pay a peppercorn rent while having full control over capital works and stadium revenues. Originally, the City of Manchester Stadium seated 48,000; it has mutated into the Etihad and will, by 2026, seat 62,000 people, including many more sky boxes with premium ticket prices, all conjoined to new luxury hotels. A huge swathe of east Manchester has, at the cost of £200 million, been converted into the Etihad Campus, complete with sixteen full-size pitches, training and medical facilities, hotels, dormitories, and a 7,000-seater stadium for the women's team. All are, in the club's own mantra, 'Best in class'. The club has also become the centre of a now thirteen-team global City Football Group, whose identikit sky-blue teams range from

New York to Montevideo, from Girona to Yokohama. Abu Dhabi has also used its presence in Manchester to secure extraordinarily favourable terms for buying and building on public land. Hailed as exemplary redevelopments by City and the council, the Manchester Life project's ownership has been transferred offshore to Jersey, and almost no revenue from rents, sales or tax has accrued to the city. Affordable housing is, as ever, the bare minimum, and barely affordable.[5]

While this element of the project has received relatively little attention, and almost none in the local Manchester press, the football has been captivating and diverting. In the first six years of Emirati ownership City helped break the old sporting order, winning the Premier League twice and, alongside Chelsea and Leicester, deposing Arsenal and Manchester United. In the years since the arrival of Pep Guardiola in 2016, they have created a new order in which they have been unambiguously dominant. The ground for this had long been laid. The senior management of the club had been drawn from among Guardiola's peers at Barcelona. Half a billion pounds had been spent in the transfer market on players that suited what they knew would be his style of play. A period of transition was built into the plan, allowing for a disappointing first season in which the team finished just third in the table while they were adapting to Guardiola's model. Since then, City have won six Premier League titles. Between 2018 and 2024 they won thirteen of the twenty-eight competitions, domestic and European, that they participated in, including four League Cups, two FA Cups and the Champions League. In that time they have had, on average, two-thirds of the possession in all the games that they played. Although not alone in favouring a game of control, possession and passing, or being a team drilled to compress space off the ball and create it on the ball, Guardiola's Manchester City were without peer in England. To some it has been a cold and calculating style of play, the rough, turbulent edge of the game sacrificed to efficiency, but it has been devastatingly effective.

In the years since the UAE acquired City, its annual income has grown from just over £100 million in 2008 to more than £700 million in 2024, taking them from the twentieth-richest club in the world to being second only to Real Madrid. Partly, this can be explained by the expansion of the Etihad and the near full crowds it enjoyed, the rise in media income for the Premier League and for most of the era the Champions League, and the bonuses that come with winning so many competitions. But the really decisive shift came in commercial income from sponsorships. Between 2010 and 2020, City raked in £1.7 billion; more than Liverpool, Arsenal and Chelsea, who had long ago acquired the global fan bases and global commercial appeal that might justify such significant commercial investments. Fifty-six per cent of those sponsorships came from companies based in the UAE or from companies with significant UAE ownership and connections, like South Korean tyre manufacturers Nexen. Silver Lake, an American investment fund, provided a useful £389 million in funds when they bought 10 per cent of City Group in 2019. A few months later, and entirely coincidently, the UAE's Mubadala sovereign fund invested $2 billion in Silver Lake.[6]

In 2013, UEFA's Financial Fair Play (FFP) regulations came into force: capping permitted losses at a club to £45 million a year, checking accounting practices and requiring fair market valuations of sponsorship deals. While a dozen clubs were found to have fallen foul of the regulations, the balance sheets of PSG and Manchester City raised so many red flags that independent audits were required. Both clubs were found to have massively exceeded permissible losses, and PSG's deal with the Qatar Tourism Authority was found to be, by any rational calculation, worth just a fraction of what it had paid. PSG contested all of this and then did a deal with UEFA, in which they took a €60 million hit and a reduction in the size of their Champions League squad as a little rap on the knuckles. City's response was far more combative. Simon Cliff, then City's chief legal officer, said of his boss, 'Khaldoon [Al Mubarak] says he would rather spend £30 million on the best 50 lawyers in the world and sue them for the next 10 years than agree a financial penalty.'[7] Auditors PwC not only found enormous losses, but a trail of sponsorship deals that were not actually signed by the companies involved and fair valuations of those deals that were almost half of what City had received. Again, City cut a deal and took the same punishment as PSG.

That might have been the end of the matter, but in 2016 and 2018 the whistleblowing website Football Leaks, in collaboration with *Der Spiegel*, released a cache of emails between City's executives that threw new light on the club's sponsorship and accounting practices.[8] Enough light for UEFA to relaunch its investigations into City, including some of the sponsorship deals first examined in 2014, as well as its handling of player image rights and off-book payments to staff. The most incriminating exchange suggested that of the £67.5 million coming from Etihad Airways, the company was paying only £8 million, the balance being paid by Sheikh Mansour's company Abu Dhabi United Group (ADUG); though this, it appeared, was just one of many hidden subsidies from the UAE to the club. Similar chicanery in City's deals with other sponsors was uncovered, while the $30 million sale of the squad's image rights to a marketing agency was, in effect, funded by the UAE. In February 2020 UEFA found City in breach of FFP regulations, fined them €30 million and banned them from the Champions League for two seasons. UEFA described the club's behaviour as 'a sophisticated, thoughtful, and fundamental attempt to circumvent or violate the financial fair play rules'.[9] This was not, however, the judgement of the Court for the Arbitration of Sport (CAS), where City challenged UEFA's rulings. Created by the major sporting federations, including UEFA, CAS was a tribunal system designed to ensure that these kinds of cases did not end up in national and criminal courts. Many critics of the system have suggested that CAS has an inbuilt bias towards federations over any other litigants, but on this occasion it made a number of rulings that shifted the balance of legal power in the case decisively towards City.[10] In particular, CAS permitted City executives to offer evidence in the case, and placed this above the evidence of the leaked emails. In addition, it ruled that many of UEFA's charges fell outside the permissible time period for this kind of legal action. Consequently, CAS ruled that City's only provable failings were its refusal to actively cooperate with UEFA's investigation, and so its punishment was reduced to just a fine.

The success of the UAE's football project, as well as that of Qatar, did not go unnoticed in the rest of the Gulf, above all in Saudi Arabia. In 2017 the Kingdom published its Vision 2030, setting out the plan for a diversified and modernised Saudi economy after fossil fuels. Like its smaller neighbours, the Saudis saw sport and entertainment as a central element of this economy and an enormously powerful instrument in reshaping global perceptions of the country. Since then, Saudi companies have amassed an unparalleled global network of sports sponsorships – more than 300 in over 20 different sports – turned the world of golf upside down by the creation of an alternative circuit to the PGA, and massively invested in staging boxing and esports.[11] It was in this context that in April 2020 a consortium made up of PCP Capital Partners – the vehicle for intermediary Amanda Staveley – billionaire property developers the Reuben Brothers and the Public Investment Fund of Saudi Arabia (PIF) offered Mike Ashley £300 million for Newcastle United and its debts.

Opposition to the deal came from a variety of human rights organisations, notably Amnesty International, who highlighted the country's terrible record on women's rights, LGBT rights, the treatment of migrant workers and press freedoms, not least the barbaric murder and dismemberment of regime critic Jamal Khashoggi by Saudi agents in the country's Turkish consulate.[12] But the most consequential objection came from beIN Sports, the global broadcaster owned by the Qatari state and holder of the Premier League's media rights for the Middle East and North Africa. Since 2017, Saudi Arabia had been orchestrating a boycott of Qatar – motivated by their opposing views on regional diplomacy and relationship with Iran and the Muslim Brotherhood – which had not only seen it close land and air routes to its neighbour, but also block beIN Sport's feed to the Kingdom. Just for good measure, they had then pirated the feed and rebroadcast it as a 'Saudi' channel, beOUT Sports. It appears that, for the Premier League, murder is one thing, but pirating expensive media rights is another. The League's decision on Saudi ownership of Newcastle – a process that usually took days – was still unresolved by late June, at which point the bid was withdrawn. It later transpired that the Saudis had failed to fill in the details on the Premier League form required for the 'owners and directors test'. The Premier League went on to announce that the bid would have been blocked, as they did not believe that PIF was a sufficiently separate entity from the Saudi government. Newcastle United Supporters Trust and eighty disappointed MPs lobbied chief executive Richard Masters to make the Premier League's reasoning more transparent. Newcastle United countered the ruling, saying they had 'overwhelming evidence and legal opinions that PIF is independent and autonomous of the Saudi Arabian government',[13] and took out two legal actions against the Premier League: the first, an arbitration that would contest the League's claim that PIF was not independent of the Saudi government, and a second at the Competition Appeal Tribunal, alleging that the Premier League's refusal to allow the takeover was a non-competitive practice.[14] Both sides were saved from spending any more money on their expensive legal teams when, in early October, Saudi Arabia announced that they had lifted the ban on beIN Sports and had filled in the blanks on the Premier League application form. Miraculously, the very next day, the takeover of Newcastle United was officially confirmed, as the Premier League had now 'received legacy binding assurances that the Kingdom of Saudi Arabia will not control Newcastle United'.[15] Legally binding they might have been, but they cannot have been rooted in any realistic understanding of the way in which political power operated in the country.

In 2017 Mohammed bin Salman (now abbreviated to MBS) was made Crown Prince by King Salman bin Abdulaziz, and was thus both next in line to the throne and the most powerful person in government. His first move was to corral and then incarcerate a significant slice of the country's royal house and aristocratic elite in the Ritz Carlton Hotel in Riyadh. There they were told, in no uncertain terms, that they would be relinquishing their state offices, political influence and much of the money and shareholdings they had accumulated over the last few decades. Almost a trillion dollars' worth of assets were taken from them, and much of this was then allocated to PIF, run by Newcastle United's new chairman, Yasir Al-Rumayyan. In a region noted for the centralisation of its state institutions, the concentration of power among a very small number of actors, and the highly personalised relationships between royalty and their subjects, Saudi Arabia now outstripped is neighbours. All significant opposition to MBS had been removed, all alternative viewpoints inside and outside the regime had been closed down, and all senior state offices and institutions reported directly to him; a kind of personalised absolutism closer to Louis XIV's France than any more bureaucratised modern dictatorship. PIF, for example, notionally autonomous, in fact reported to the Council of Economic and Development Affairs, chaired by MBS, while it was clear that Al-Rumayyan's position at the fund was entirely in the gift of the Crown Prince. Documents revealed as part of a court case in Canada in 2021 made it clear that rather than mere oversight, MBS was exercising direct control over Al-Rumayyan and PIF's key decision-making processes.[16] In 2019, Al-Rumayyan was made the chair of Saudi Aramco, the national oil company, and the single most important economic institution in the country; one which directly funded most of the country's public expenditure, as well as supplying innumerable sinecures for the ruling elite. The idea that the Crown Prince would consider the institution and its leadership in any sense insulated from his personal command or the central organs of the Saudi state is simply risible. The same could be said of the government's denial that it had been involved at any point in the takeover talks. It would later emerge that trade minister Lord Grimstone had been involved in a long conversation with MBS's office and the Premier League as the sale of Newcastle progressed.[17]

The other Premier League clubs remained hostile to the new owners. Gary Hoffman, chair of the board and a leading figure in getting the deal over the line, was in effect forced to resign. The clubs also voted for tighter financial controls over and closer scrutiny of new sponsorship deals. The fan base was divided. A very small minority appeared to be against the takeover and have since organised themselves as NUFC Fans Against Sportswashing. The majority, however, were either quietly or noisily pleased, appearing at St James' Park in fancy-dress versions of Arabian headwear. It is hardly surprising. Mike Ashley's reign at Newcastle had been, like his retail empire, a mean, cheapskate operation. Refusing to lose any more money than he had already lost on acquiring the club, its infrastructure was run down, its staffing levels were bare bones, often employed on zero-hour contracts with appalling wages. The players did better but never enough to field a competitive or even entertaining team, and twice they were poor enough to be relegated. The city itself, barely recovered from the long deindustrialisation of the late twentieth century, was stripped bare by a decade of twenty-first century austerity and left with the lowest life expectancy and wages of the English regions. The new owners, by contrast, paid the living wage, treated their staff well, repaired the training ground, rebuilt the club's community outreach and invested in the women's team. At the same time Saudi Arabia's appalling record of human rights transgressions and domestic political repression continued unabated, but in Newcastle, at least, the city's MPs, newspapers and local councillors have been mute; still hoping, no doubt, for the oft promised but as yet undelivered wave of Saudi investment in the city.[18] Eddie Howe, the coach installed by the Saudis, has proved, in the face of questioning on these issues, to be a master of dissimulation.[19] Progress on the pitch was slow, with just a single season back in the Champions League in the first three seasons of Saudi ownership. PIF found that UEFA and the Premier League's financial rules, which now restrict how much money they can lose, meant that they could not repeat City's astronomical growth during the first six years of Emirati ownership. Saudi sponsors and partners have been racing to St James' Park, and the club's second kit now looks remarkably like that of the Saudi national team, but in the wake of PSG and City's past transgressions the rules governing these deals are much tighter and the scrutiny much greater. It was, nonetheless, enough for Newcastle to win the League Cup in 2025, their first domestic trophy since the 1950s; now the club not only pay the living wage, but the wages of sin too.

In Manchester and Abu Dhabi, they have also been enjoying them. One particular source of satisfaction for the latter must be the way in which so much of City's fan base has been effectively recruited to the sportswashing cause. City's fan forums have been bursting with rationalisations of the UAE's largesse and attacks on journalists and publications that have dared to criticise the project. In addition, there has been a lot of revelling in how all of City's critics have been thwarted and a great deal of energy expended in attempting to delegitimise any opposition.[20] Another source of satisfaction has been all the winning. The 2022–23 season culminated with Manchester City's seventh Premier League title win under Emirati ownership and, finally, a Champions League title that completed, alongside the FA Cup, a historic treble. It was not just the numbers, but the manner of the victory that was so resonant. With the arrival of Norwegian striker Erling Haaland, City had assembled the most expensive and best paid squad in English football, playing unstoppable football. Arsenal, revived by Mikel Arteta, who had served his managerial apprenticeship under Guardiola at City, led the league for much of the year. But the master brought City back and sent them on a long unbeaten run that would take them to the top of the table, a place they would not relinquish. Little wonder, then, that the rest of the clubs should have been so supportive of the Premier League's own efforts to investigate City's finances. In March 2023, after almost four years of preparation, the Premier League announced it was appointing an independent tribunal to investigate City on 115 transgressions of the League's rules; in effect, an even more detailed and comprehensive version of the charge sheet pursued by UEFA.[21] This time, however, there would be no recourse to CAS, the full cache of leaked emails was to be deployed, no time limitations would be permitted, no executives would be giving evidence and a Premier League legal budget would be deployed that matched City KC for KC.

That battle would have to wait. First there was Europe to deal with. City might have bested UEFA, but they had come up short in the Champions League and even been humiliated by Real Madrid the previous year. In 2023, however, there was a sharp reversal of fortunes, as City dispatched them from the competition in a 4–0 victory in Manchester. Even the shy Sheikh Mansour and his brother Mohamed bin Zayed, the president of the UAE, showed up for the final in Istanbul to see City beat Internazionale by a single goal. Perhaps the biggest victory of all, though, came in their game against Bayern Munich in the quarter-finals of the competition. Bayern's travelling fans unfurled a banner reading, 'Glazers, Sheikh Mansour – All Autocrats Out. Football belongs to the people,' to which the City fans responded by singing, 'Sheikh Mansour, My Lord, Sheikh Mansour'.[22] As of 2024, the six Premier League titles in seven years was a marker of hegemony, but no clearer statement of the Gulf's suzerainty over English football could be imagined than that chant.

23.

Playing Against the Clock

Football and the Climate Crisis

The climate crisis has been creeping up on British football for more than a decade now. The country's changing weather patterns have brought more rain more often, and more frequent and extreme climatic events. Consequently, by 2014 the average grassroots pitch in England was losing five weeks' play per season to the weather, and a third of all pitches were losing between two and three months of play.[1] The professional game, despite possessing considerably better drainage, was not unaffected: twenty Football League fixtures were cancelled in the 2015–16 season due to appalling weather. In December 2015 the game got a glimpse of the future when the torrential downpours accompanying Storm Desmond saw Carlisle United's Brunton Park under a couple of metres of water and the club forced out of the stadium for seven weeks, at considerable financial cost.[2]

In February 2020 the future began to arrive. Storm Jorge swept across southern England with such ferocity that five matches were cancelled across League One, League Two and the National League, just before Covid and the national lockdown postponed everything. Two years later, in February 2022, Storm Eunice brought weather bad enough to force a whole weekend of professional fixtures to be cancelled and flooding that submerged lower-league grounds at Belper Town in Derbyshire, Barton Rovers in Bedfordshire and Tadcaster Albion in North Yorkshire. Potters Bar in Hertfordshire had their stand tipped over and smashed by the high winds. Eunice was just one of a series of storms that winter to wreak havoc on grassroots football. Research from the Climate Coalition estimated that 62,500 amateur matches were now cancelled or delayed by weather impacts every year, primarily heavy rainfall, which translated, on average, to around five cancellations or postponements per club in England. In Wales, this figure rose to seven games a season.[3] The FA, though, seemed to think that the matter had got even worse. In evidence presented to the Culture, Media and Sport select committee, the chair of the FA, Debbie Hewitt, thought that 'we have something like 120,000 games a season cancelled because the pitches are not playable'.[4]

It was an equally bad year in 2023. In January freezing weather saw more than sixty games cancelled across every men's league below the Premier League and in the Women's Super League and Championship too. Earlier on that winter, Motherwell's game against St Mirren had been called off after Fir Park's frozen pipes had cracked, flooding the stadium for almost a week. Extreme cold and snow also saw a Rangers versus Ross Country game abandoned, not because of the state of the pitch at Ibrox but because the collapse of the region's transport systems had made attendance virtually impossible. In the autumn a rain storm over East London during West Ham United's game against TSC Backa Topola in the European Conference League was so intense that much of the crowd retreated from the stands to the concourses, only to find them awash with water. A few weeks later, Storm Babet shut down all but two fixtures in the top flight of Scottish football, with even greater disruptions further down the pyramid. An official at Stenhousemuir put their cancellation that weekend into context: 'We had our first flooding event in 2021 that impacted inside our stadium. The volumes of rainfall overwhelmed the drains in the roads outside and it caused significant damage inside the club. It happened a second time a few weeks later ... This seems to be happening on a more regular basis.'[5]

Stenhousemuir were not alone in thinking that these problems were coming round more often. Worsbrough Bridge Athletic in South Yorkshire announced that their pitch had flooded for the sixth consecutive year, while a survey of English football spectators and players found that 40 per cent had experienced extreme weather at football matches over the previous year.[6] Northern Ireland was no different, with Annagh United seeing their ground disappear under more than a metre of water after the River Bann broke its banks.

The following year, 2024, opened with Storm Henk, which left Banbury United and the Powerleague five-a-side hub in Nottingham six feet underwater.[7] The brief return of freezing temperatures saw a weekend in January in which a quarter of League One and more than half of League Two and National League matches could not be played. When it wasn't freezing, it kept raining through one of the wettest winters on record. Altrincham, who had spent considerable money on drainage and mitigation, still had a game with Dorking postponed four times. An official from Whitby Town, flooded again that season, described the impact of these cancellations as a 'slow death' and an inexorable fate: 'It seems clear that extreme weather conditions will continue to impact football over the coming seasons ... It's something now that's becoming more and more apparent every year – the pitch can't cope with the weather.'[8]

Premier League clubs have, so far, largely avoided postponements and cancellations. Their facilities, and especially their expensively drained and heated pitches, have been able to withstand extreme rain and cold much more effectively than the lower leagues, but their climate risks are rising. In 2022 a flash rainstorm saw Fulham's club shop flooded, an event that will be increasingly likely over the next twenty-five years, for all of

Craven Cottage sits right on the bank of the Thames. At the peak of Storm Henk, Nottingham Forest's City Ground was just inches away from being flooded by the swollen waters of the River Trent, which runs behind the Trent End stand.

These events, concerning as they appear, are a mere prologue to the deluge that is to come. In 2020 the Rapid Transition Alliance report 'Playing Against the Clock' looked at the predictions for levels of precipitation and sea-level rises around all of the ninety-two English league stadiums, and found that by 2050 a quarter would be facing very serious risks of annual flooding.[9] In the cases of Scunthorpe, Grimsby Town and Southampton, they might actually be underwater. Even where stadiums are likely to be spared, the flooding around them will make access impossible. Middlesbrough and Doncaster Rovers, for example, might want to consider investing in a flotilla of small boats to ferry supporters across their sodden neighbourhoods. Zurich Insurance repeated this exercise in 2023 and added in the risks faced by clubs from windstorms and drought, for Britain's wetter winters will also be more stormy and are likely to alternate with serious summer heatwaves.[10] They found that over a third of England's league clubs will be facing serious annual climate-related risks by 2050. The usual suspects – Grimsby Town, Hull City, Doncaster Rovers – are still in great danger of flooding, but they have been joined as high-risk grounds by Leicester City, Lincoln City, Newport County and Norwich City. In February 2022 the winter winds that swept the Netherlands were of sufficient power to tear the roof off second-tier side Den Haag's stadium, in the Hague. The Atlantic windstorms heading for Lancashire and Cumbria are likely to do the same over the next couple of decades, most especially at Morecambe, Barrow, Fleetwood Town, Burnley and Preston North End. They at least will be spared the water shortages that are likely to affect Norwich City, Ipswich Town, Colchester United, Plymouth Argyle and Exeter City. It is notable that despite the wide coverage afforded to both of these reports, not a single club has directly commented on them, nor appears to have made any public statement about their preparations for these eventualities.

Football is certainly threatened by the climate crisis, but to what extent is the game actually responsible for the problem? How much carbon does football actually emit? A comprehensive and accurate answer to this question awaits, but we can make some reasonable estimates. Consider the size of the football economy: the Premier League's annual turnover is approximately £6 billion. Add in the English Football League, at around £1 billion, the Scottish, Welsh and Northern Irish leagues, as well as the women's game and the national football associations, and we are, in total, at £7.5 billion. To this we should add the turnover of grassroots football, from lower leagues to five-a-side hubs, the sales and emissions of the sportswear industry dependent upon the game, as well as the betting and broadcasting sectors whose own energy use at server farms is not inconsiderable. Given all that, £10 billion would not be an overestimate for a broadly defined football sector. That is around 0.5 per cent of UK GDP. Football is clearly less carbon-intensive per economic unit than some activities, like concrete and steel production, but probably more carbon-intensive than others, as the industry generates such big transport emissions. If football's emissions per unit GDP are in line with the average for the economy as a whole, then 0.5 per cent of the UK's annual emissions of 426 million tonnes of CO2e translates into about 2.2 million tonnes for football. This estimate is supported, if not confirmed, by thinking about the maths from the bottom up: consider Liverpool's calculation of the club's carbon footprint in 2019, among the most comprehensive yet done in the Premier League.[11] Total emissions were around 0.125 million tonnes CO2e, which is around 5 per cent of the estimate of football's emissions as a whole. This may seem a lot for one club, but given the extraordinary economic inequality of the industry and the fact that Liverpool's turnover, now touching half a billion, is around 5 per cent of the total turnover of the football sector, it is probably about right. Football's carbon footprint, at half a per cent of the UK's total, may not sound like a lot, but it is more than the entire annual emissions of many small countries, like Djibouti or the Maldives.

How is football generating so much carbon? Taking Liverpool's calculations as a starting point, just 1 per cent of emissions come from the direct use of gas and electricity. Employee travel, including flying the squad around, adds another couple of percentage points. Catering and internet use take us to 10 per cent. Supporters travelling to the match, in a season truncated by Covid, accounted for a further 10 per cent, an unusually low figure for a club. In recent years it has climbed closer to 20 per cent. Carbon generated in the club's many supply chains added another 10 per cent, leaving merchandising – above all, kit sales – as responsible for over half the club's emissions. The balance between these components varies according to the size and commercial reach of clubs, with smaller clubs than Liverpool selling far fewer shirts, and so fan travel takes up a much bigger slice of their overall emissions, closer to half their totals.

Football's response to the challenge of decarbonisation has been very uneven. For a decade, Forest Green Rovers have been at the vanguard. Dale Vince, owner of the renewable energy company Ecotricity, bought the club in 2010 and committed it to zero carbon emissions. He also made its catering vegan and its pitch organic, not to mention steering them from the seventh level to League One in 2022. Alongside adverts for Quorn and CBD products, and messages of support from the novelist Jilly Cooper, Extinction Rebellion banners were hung at the stadium. On match days the digital boards keep spectators informed of how much carbon dioxide has been released into the atmosphere since kick-off. Planning permission has been given to build a new carbon-zero stadium, the first in England to be made of wood for more than a century. The club was also, alongside the IOC and FIFA, one of the original signatories of the UN's Sport for Climate Action Framework, a voluntary agreement among sports organisations to become carbon zero by 2040 and to advocate for climate action among their fans and partners. Since the framework's creation in 2018, the FA, the Premier League and the EFL have signed up, but only eight other English clubs have joined Forest Green – Arsenal, Bristol City, Liverpool, Millwall, Oxford United, Southampton, Spurs and Wolverhampton Wanderers – and none in Scotland, Wales or Northern Ireland. There has been a flurry of policy documents, sustainability strategies, slogans and photo opportunities from these clubs, and a terrible silence from the vast majority of others. Easy wins, for what are in effect medium-sized companies with money to invest, have included switching to green energy suppliers and LED lighting, or more ambitiously generating their own power, like Arsenal have done by building an array of solar panels on the roof of the Emirates. Club electric vehicles, installing EV chargers, water recycling and reusable cups have followed. The EFL launched a Green Football weekend in 2022, while the Premier League has promised to include minimum environmental criteria in its club-licensing plans, though the Conservative government declined to include such measures in the work of the planned independent football regulator. All of this has, so far, been relatively painless and inexpensive, but tackling emissions from food, transport and sportswear is proving rather harder, each area illuminating different elements of the contested politics of climate change.

Until recently, the only fruit and vegetables to be found at a British football stadium, soggy chips and rat burger onions aside, were on the pitch. The vicious racist trope of throwing bananas at Black players was a regular feature of the 1970s and 1980s. Struggling Southampton coach Ian Branfoot was struck by a tangerine in 1994 shortly before his sacking. Graham Taylor, on his return to Watford after his impossible sojourn with England, was assailed by flying turnips. Chelsea fans, for almost two decades, threw bunches of celery on to the pitch, a totemic reference to a lewd music-hall chant. Despite the stricter policing of fruit and vegetables, celery included, in 2018 a Spurs fan was banned for life for throwing a banana at the feet of Arsenal striker Pierre-Emerick Aubameyang, while Aston Villa manager Steve Bruce was hit by a cabbage. But in keeping with the new environmental thinking at some clubs, football has turned from throwing to growing. Graham Potter drew on this shift metaphorically, comparing his own team-building efforts at Brighton to his father's work on the allotment: 'He would always start off doing a lot of digging, a lot of heavy work, with not too much to show for it … eventually he would start to see things coming through and he would have some vegetables. But it takes time.'[12] Brighton have yet to create an actual allotment, but carefully tended vegetable gardens can now be found at the training grounds of Aston Villa – where a young academy prospect, Jack Grealish, was photographed harvesting carrots – Liverpool, Norwich City, Tottenham Hotspur and Wolverhampton Wanderers, all of them supplying their club's canteens. During the Covid lockdown, when already swollen waiting lists for allotments grew much longer, Tottenham's Eric Dier turned his own back garden over to horticulture and let in the cameras.

If the arrival of the vegetable garden and allotment in British football is, in part, a throwback to an older era of working-class life, then the arrival of veganism, vegetarianism and plant-based foods is a distinctly modern element in football's food culture. Stanley Matthews was the only vegetarian in the English game in the 1940s and 1950s, and he was deemed a little odd for that reason. Neil Robinson, through his long years at Swansea and Grimsby, was the sole vegetarian of the 1970s and 1980s. Inside and around the grounds the standard menu at British football remained meat pies and pasties, boiled burgers, and hot dogs made from mechanically recovered meat. While this remains the norm outside many football grounds, a process of change has been underway inside. In the executive suites and restaurants, still meat heavy, vegetarian and vegan options have been creeping in, while on the concourses meatless options, beyond chips and a Mars bar, have been appearing. At one level this shift corresponds to the small but definite rise in the number of people eating vegetarian (10 per cent) and vegan diets (2–3 per cent) among the general population, but there has also been a conscious push in this direction. Forest Green Rovers became a vegan club in 2017, serving only plant-based foods in the stadium and expecting staff and players to eat vegan too. In the closing minutes of the game that secured promotion from the National League to the Football League that year, BBC Gloucestershire's Bob Hunt goaded the unreformed meat eaters of the EFL: 'Let me tell you this – Cheltenham, Swindon, Newport – you are going to eat hummus next season, because Forest Green Rovers are in the Football League!' More recently, Forest Green have been joined as vegan clubs by Newark & Sherwood United, who play in the ninth-tier United Counties League Premier Division North, and Bristol grassroots team Kale Madrid.

Not everyone in football has been entirely comfortable with these changes. Away fans at Forest Green and Newark have regularly chanted, 'You can shove your vegan pasty/burger up your arse.' Walsall fans chided a Forest Green player who lay injured on their pitch with, 'You dirty vegan bastard', and followed this up to the tune of Lally Stott's 1971 pop classic 'Chirpy Chirpy, Cheep Cheep' with, 'Where's your burger gone?' By contrast, Duncan Ferguson, the ex-Everton hard man and no one's idea of a vegan, seemed after his first day as Forest Green's new coach very happy with the food on offer, and promised to eat his first vegan burger when he won his first game. At the same time he quipped, 'The food here is really good. Remember, I've been in Barlinnie,' in reference to the six weeks he spent in prison having been found guilty of assault for headbutting Raith Rovers defender John McStay while playing for Rangers in

1994.[13] The *Sun*, never happier then when policing inconsistencies in the behaviour of environmentalists, drooled over the story that the Forest Green squad had ordered a huge takeaway after their game with Mansfield consisting of a dozen fish suppers and a dozen rounds of chicken and chips. Confronted with this, the club informed the *Sun* that time after the game was not club time and the players were free to eat what they wanted.[14]

Resistant as parts of football might be to plant-based food, the game also has a growing number of serious adherents. Football players who have switched to a vegan diet include Chris Smalling, Héctor Bellerín, Fabian Delph, Jack Wilshire and Karen Carney. Jermain Defoe and Sergio Agüero have also dabbled, and all have said that their rate of injury recovery improved. Most surprising of all was Graeme Souness's conversion to a vegan diet, though he insisted that this was for reasons of animal welfare rather than sporting performance or climate action. Vegan or not, plant-based food companies have been eager to enlist football players at the clubs they sponsor, like Quorn – Liverpool's tortuously named Official Sustainable Protein Partner – whose adverts featured Jordan Henderson, Alex Oxlade-Chamberlain and Xherdan Shaqiri discussing the merits of athletes going dairy-free. Even Cheddar AFC, where, according to captain Kieran Webster, 'cheese is in the player's blood,' had a season sponsored by a Cheddar-style non-dairy alternative, Cheddarton.[15] All that said, culinary culture-war warriors should rest easy. It remains the case that there is no shortage of meat products, whose provenance it would be best not to inquire into too deeply, at British football grounds.

Transport emissions in football highlight two bigger problems in environmental policymaking: the seeming untouchability of rich people's carbon-intense lifestyles, and the huge structural barriers to sustainable consumption for the rest of the population. Flying is, by some way, the most problematic mode of transport. Flying in small private jets is even more polluting, producing per passenger mile more than forty times the carbon emissions of train and coach journeys. Elite football players and club staff use them a lot. In the absence of much of a high-speed rail network in Europe, flying is the only realistic option for many European games, but the number of domestic flights is large and growing. In 2023 BBC Sport reported that Premier League teams had taken eighty-one flights in connection with a sample of just a hundred matches played in the first two months of the year. The average duration of these flights was just forty-two minutes, with some lasting less than half an hour. Over 80 per cent of these journeys could have been accomplished in under four and a half hours by electric coach, producing a fraction of the emissions.[16] It's not just the Premier League, either. Wrexham, for example, taking their cue from their Hollywood owners, took sixteen domestic flights over the 2022–23 National League season. Clubs have defended the practice, citing convenience, of course, but also the need for players to have more time for recovery and rest in a busy schedule. At the same time, sports doctors have argued that flying in pressurised cabins makes inflammation and swelling much worse, and seems to have a bad effect on athletes' hamstrings. Undeterred, Premier League clubs are flying their squads further and further, as pre-season tours in Asia and North America become longer, not to mention mid-season warm-weather breaks in the Middle East and the private jets chartered to fly, on occasion, a single player to expedite a transfer. A small number of clubs – including Forest Green Rovers, Swindon Town and Bristol Rovers – signed up to a sustainable transport pledge, agreeing not to take domestic flights. However, the frequent flyers have yet to even accept there might be a problem, or that they can do anything about it. Steve Cooper, then manager of Nottingham Forest, responded to criticism of the twenty-minute flight his team took to Blackpool by saying, 'Whether it is right or wrong, I think it is pretty normal … to fly distances like that.'[17] While this kind of reckless consumption is the norm for the rich, the famous and the powerful, it is hard to see how football will be reaching carbon zero any time soon, and even harder to imagine how it might meaningfully advocate for change elsewhere.

Football is certainly struggling to persuade its fans to shift their travel habits in a more sustainable direction. The last comprehensive survey on fan travel, published in 2013, found that for home fans, 6 per cent walked to the stadium and just 1 per cent took their bike. Forty per cent took the car, and a third of those were car-sharing.[18] A small majority came by train, tram, bus or coach. For Premier League clubs in London, where public transport is good and parking expensive, only a fifth of their fans arrived by car. Outside the Premier League, fans of smaller clubs in smaller towns, and clubs with significant rural and suburban hinterlands, were more car dependent than the average. At National League clubs and in grassroots football, where access to public transport is much sparser, car journeys make up more than two-thirds of the total.

Since these studies were conducted, the survey evidence has been much more fragmented, but from club-level studies, a number of trends, all in keeping with wider changes in the transport sector, can be discerned. The number of foreign fans and tourists who attend football matches has increased from 9,000 in 2011 to more than 1.5 million in 2019, and that has meant a lot more flying.[19] Car use is up, even in London. In 2023 Spurs, for example, reported that 40 per cent of their supporters were now arriving by car and the numbers using public transport had declined. The Covid pandemic saw public transport use drop precipitously, but the slow decay of the system over the last decade has also been at work. Reduced timetables, soaring ticket prices and limited capacity have all taken their toll on football fans. Even for those prepared to brave the vagaries of British public transport, the scheduling of games for the benefit of television audiences, especially early on a Sunday and a Saturday, and late on a Friday or Monday, makes it impossibly inconvenient and expensive for away fans to use it.

Clubs have responded unevenly to these issues, some subsidising bespoke minibus services and chartering coaches, but they are not making much of a dent in car use. Manchester City have established the most comprehensive and sustainable package of match-day travel for their fans, launching an electric bus service on eight different routes, bringing supporters from across the Greater Manchester area. A magnificent gesture, for sure, but one unrepeatable for the vast majority of clubs, and testament to just how threadbare the nation's bus services have become. Cycling numbers have barely shifted, but then cyclists have been very poorly served by football. The space devoted to the squad's and the directors' car parks at most grounds would be enough to store a whole stand's worth of cyclists, so the few that have been taking their bike have had to make do with unsecured corners of stadiums or lampposts in the streets around them. Brentford, Spurs and Arsenal are among the very few that have invested in proper, secure bike parking. This is good news for the intrepid, and could be easily repeated across the country's stadiums, but until the road network that gets people there is considerably more bike-friendly than at present, it is hard to imagine White Hart Lane or the Emirates swarming with the volume of bike traffic arriving at Danish or Dutch stadiums. However powerful football might be, it is operating within a transport infrastructure that has privileged high-carbon private car use for over half a century, underinvested in public transport, virtually ignored cyclists and pedestrians, and placed no limits on aviation. Football can, as they say, have a go, but politically and economically it is out of its league.

Football is also locked into a problematic relationship with the fashion industry. Globally, the clothing and textile industries are responsible for an estimated 10 per cent of carbon emissions. Over the last decade, the world, but especially the global north, has been buying more and more clothing, wearing it for a shorter amount of time, and disposing of it in ever-more irresponsible ways. Sportswear in general and football in particular have been no different. Nearly all football shirts are made of polyester, itself made of oil. It is, for manufacturers, a fabulously flexible and useful material, but for the environment it is a disaster. Its processing requires enormous amounts of energy and water, and its capacity for recycling and safe disposal is very poor. It is effectively non-biodegradable, and what breakdown does occur in landfill results in the release of dangerous microfibres. Incineration of polyester avoids the former but pollutes the soil and air with a range of toxic chemicals. Forest Green Rovers played for a season in shirts made from bamboo and coffee grounds, but for the moment polyester is king.

According to UEFA, 60 per cent of the apparel that clubs purchase is never used.[20] When sponsors change, old branded shirts cannot be given away, so they are dumped or burnt. Recycling shirts is possible, but made much more expensive and complicated by bad design, mixing other fibres with polyester and the addition of personalised names and numbers. Manchester City and Puma, anticipating the EU's circular economy directives, have taken control of much more of their garments' life cycles, actively encouraging fans to return their old shirts to the Etihad Stadium, from where they can be entirely recycled into new shirts. Perhaps, for the bigger clubs at least, this will become the new norm, but for the moment recycling is not an option for most, resale and reuse markets are in their infancy, and so the vast majority of shirts make their way to the charity sector or to landfill. Even those that do go to the charity sector don't necessarily get used again, with much of the donations being sold to clothing and textile traders in Africa, and much of that ends up being burnt on the fringes of Ghanaian cities. Given all of these problems, the simplest way to reduce football's environmental impact might be to make and sell fewer kits. However, with big clubs relying on merchandising for 10 to 20 per cent of their income, and the sportswear industry driven by its own relentless profit imperatives, clubs and companies are aiming to increase their sales every year. The release of new designs every season is the main engine for this growth, but clubs are also releasing more third kits and even, like Arsenal, fourth kits. In this context, Brentford's plan to keep the same kit for two seasons was an act of rare commercial restraint – one that few other clubs have chosen to repeat.

Despite the vocal resistance to veganism in some quarters of British football culture, and a wider backlash against green initiatives from the populist right, surveys of football supporters suggest that there is a large majority in favour of change. A UK-based survey of 1,400 supporters revealed that over 90 per cent agreed on the importance of protecting the environment and fighting climate change.[21] Another found that two-thirds of fans were disappointed that their clubs were not prioritising environmental sustainability.[22] A survey of Wolverhampton Wanderers supporters, not necessarily the most fertile territory for green politics, found that 85 per cent of them cared about environmental sustainability and 70 per cent thought Wolves had a responsibility to raise awareness of climate change.[23] This consensus among the football-going public perhaps explains why the small number of active climate sceptics and deniers in the game have struggled to be heard or taken seriously. David Icke, in a previous life Hereford's goalkeeper and a BBC sports presenter, long ago mutated into a professional conspiracy theorist, arguing that climate change was an elite globalist hoax, but he has had few peers among contemporary footballers. Matt Le Tissier has certainly offered sneers and scepticism, but saved his best work for Covid and vaccines. Lee Dixon has kept very quiet on the topic since he faced an outcry after commentating on Arsenal against Manchester United in late summer 2022. Struggling to understand why so few modern goalkeepers wore caps in the sunshine, he told co-commentator Peter Drury, 'Goalies used to wear caps when it was sunny. And now we've got global warming, allegedly, and all that.'[24] More elaborate thoughts came from David Cotterill, who played for Birmingham City and Wales, and had been busy on Twitter writing of the unprecedented temperatures of July 2022: 'These heatwaves in Europe are nothing new, they've been happening for many decades. But now, they have an agenda to push. Your car drive to work is to blame. So we must ban petrol/diesel engines and get driving that Tesla that we can limit and control.'[25] Yet, even in these febrile times, he got no traction.

Football climate activists are not too thick on the ground either, but they are certainly more numerous. Dull sustainability reports aside, the most visible statement from a club has been Reading's, who, while sinking under their own debts, played the 2022–23 season in a recycled plastic shirt, sporting climate stripes on its arms – a graphic that illustrates the increasingly warm average global temperatures of the last few hundred years by means of blue (below average) and red (above average) lines. Among individual footballers, foreign and retired players have been the most outspoken. Mathieu Flamini, who played for Arsenal and Crystal Palace, co-founded a multi-billion dollar company that sustainably mass-produces industrial hydrocarbon substitutes, and has been calling for more footballers to take up climate activism. Héctor Bellerín, in addition to his vegan advocacy, invested in 10 per cent of Forest Green Rovers and, when football returned after the first Covid lockdown, pledged to fund the planting of 3,000 trees in the Amazon for every game Arsenal won till the end of the season. In 2021 Kai Havertz, then at Chelsea, spoke out on the issue when his home town in western Germany was inundated by floods. Michael Doughty, a Swindon Town legend, retired, founded carbon-zero sportswear company Hylo and works as his old club's sustainability officer, while Peter Crouch and Gary Lineker have been quietly signing petitions and tweeting their support for climate action.

Current players have been more cautious, and in the case of Leeds' Patrick Bamford rather cryptic. When asked about the meaning of his trademark goal celebration, he said, 'The Z celebration is actually a lightning bolt symbol. It's supposed to be a bolt for the planet, so it's kind of raising awareness for climate change and obviously there's a lot that needs to be done so I'm trying to help everyone learn about that.'[26] Brentford's captain Ben Mee and Wycombe's David Wheeler, the only player in British football with an MSc in environmental management, have been more straightforward in their statements. Mee offset the carbon emissions of his transfer from Burnley to Brentford, while Wheeler was the first player to sign up with Football for Future – England's first football and environment advocacy group – stating, 'I believe climate change is the most significant threat to our way of life and the biggest issue of our time.' In the women's game, climate activists include Lotte Wubben-Moy of Arsenal and Katie Rood, a New Zealander who played at Southampton and Hearts. Calling out the Women's Super League for taking money from Barclays, while detailing the bank's record on funding fossil-fuel projects, Rood also wrestled with the argument that keeps so many in football quiet: 'I am using my career to fight for the defining issue of our generation: tackling climate change. Call me a hypocrite if you like – I would accept another call-up from New Zealand with all the travel involved – but nobody is perfect and that charge won't stop me from using my platform to encourage positive change.'[27]

The balance of forces in football parallels the wider politics of climate action. Climate deniers and populist sceptics are on the retreat. Activism and awareness are growing among the young. Football's mainstream has acknowledged the reality of the climate crisis but is still coming to terms with the scale of the task in front of it, not least the recognition that they are working with food, transport and manufacturing systems that are entirely unsuited to the task. As with the installation of heat pumps or the purchase of electric cars, only a small and wealthier vanguard has begun to take action, while the poor do not have the resources to make changes even if they want to. Above all, the football industry is still in thrall to conventional economic thinking, to the idea that one can aim for ever-expanding levels of income and consumption, and meet the extraordinary environmental targets required to keep the planet habitable. Consequently, for all the good deeds, the game has proved incapable of acting with the speed and decisiveness that the moment demands. In the absence of meaningful change from the mainstream, parts of the climate movement have shifted from lobbying to direct and disruptive action. The Premier League has showcased both of these dimensions of the politics of the climate crisis: the greenwash of the Spurs–Chelsea carbon neutral Game Zero in September 2021 and the despairing, polarising spectacle of Just Stop Oil's pitch invasions.

Game Zero, played at Tottenham's stadium, was the biggest public intervention by a Premier League club in the climate debate. It was also well-meaning, with teams travelling by electric coach and plant-based options dominating the game's menu. However, given the decision not to include flights taken by foreign fans in its carbon audit and the ineffectiveness of the carbon offsets that made the carbon-zero sums work, it was, in the end, specious. Indeed, nearly all carbon-zero claims in football fail this test, for it has become clear that the global carbon-credit market, allowing emitters to invest in renewable-energy schemes, carbon capture and reforestation, is broken, and most of the schemes it relies upon have been ineffective at best, entirely bogus at worst.

It is precisely this kind of greenwashing across government and society that has driven the climate movement down more radical paths. Just Stop Oil made football matches one of their earliest targets for disruptive protest. In March 2022 activists invaded the pitch at six Premier League games, most successfully at Arsenal and Everton, where they also managed to lock themselves on to the goalposts. Football was divided on how to take this. The Premier League promised the introduction of special sprint stewards to catch future invasions. Most of the interventions were met by plenty of booing and online rage, but BBC commentator Gary Lineker was speaking for a constituency that was beginning to think not just about today's game, or even the rest of the season, but about the seasons to come. He tweeted, 'You approve of this young man's methods or not, he's right, his future is perilous,' and no amount of sprint stewards can protect him or the game from that.[28] Football, like every other element of our society, has some very difficult questions to answer and choices to make.

Conclusion

'There's Always Next Season'

Football and the Politics of Hope, 2024–25

'We've made quite a bit of history over the last four or five years – not all of it good'

Gareth Southgate

I

Speaking on the eve of England's quarter-final game against France at the Qatar 2022 World Cup, Gareth Southgate was reviewing his own tenure as manager, but he could have been speaking of the nation as a whole for the last decade and half.[1] If the final weeks of Rishi Sunak's government and the first year of Keir Starmer's were anything to go by, then the elision of football and the state of this troubled land is set to continue.

On 22 May 2024, standing in a relentless downpour outside 10 Downing Street, Rishi Sunak called a general election for 4 July – a few days after what appeared to be the most likely date for England playing a round of sixteen match in the upcoming European Championship in Germany. Tory strategists hoped the newly invigorated England under Southgate might provide a feel-good boost. However, the experience of two of Sunak's predecessors – Harold Wilson in 1970 and David Cameron in 2016 – who had both fought national campaigns while an international football tournament was in progress, suggested this might have been over-optimistic. Wilson himself thought the most likely last-minute factors in his government's defeat in the general election were the announcement of a poor set of balance of trade figures and the dreadful weather on polling day itself. By contrast, Secretary of State for Local Government Tony Crosland thought that England's defeat in their World Cup quarter-final game against West Germany just a few days before the vote counted against the Labour government. He went as far as to argue that Labour had lost due to 'a mix of party complacency and the disgruntled *Match of the Day* millions'. Denis Howell, the Minister for Sport, agreed: 'The moment goalkeeper Bonetti made his third and final hash of it on the Sunday, everything simultaneously began to go wrong for Labour for the following Thursday.'[2] On the other hand, it would be hard to argue that Cameron's defeat in the Brexit referendum can be laid at the door of a faltering England performance in the early rounds of Euro 2016, even if the two campaigns – England's and Remain's – had uncanny parallels: not least that both seemed undermined by Russian influence, be it state-sponsored hooligans attacking England fans in France or state-sponsored internet trolls manipulating social media. Perhaps the most that can be said is that football narratives can set the tone and shape the meaning of other events; but tone matters.

Sunak was spared a calamitous football defeat or scenes of public disorder at the Euros, but as the election unfolded football made him seem awkward and out of touch. An early encounter with Welsh voters saw him ask, 'So, are you looking forward to all the football?', a question met with embarrassed silence given that Wales had not qualified for the Euros.[3] His dribbling and refereeing skills, shown off at Chesham United, were unlikely to have endeared himself any further to the football nation. His evident discomfort on the pitch was perhaps to be expected, given his aspirations off it; Tory peer Lord Finkelstein revealed to the electorate: 'Rishi told me that when he was a kid, it was his dream to be a director at Southampton.' Which is, of course, fair enough, but was hardly the material out of which a normalised and accessible version of Sunak could be fashioned.[4]

To Sunak's right, Nigel Farage and the Reform party eschewed football-themed set pieces, preferring to pick the occasional fight. The release of England's new tournament strip in March 2024 provided the perfect opportunity. Unremarkable in every way, the shirts featured a small St George flag on the back of the neck, but in tones of purple and pink. Lee Anderson, now running as a Reform candidate, went into performative over-drive, decrying it as 'namby-pamby, pearl-clutching, hand-wringing nonsense'. Harry Redknapp thought it 'an abso-lute disgrace'. In a now familiar move to protect his right flank, Keir Starmer offered more temperate but equally conservative commentary: 'The St George's flag doesn't need to be changed … we need to be proud of it. So I think they should just recon-sider this and change it back.'[5] What no one managed to mention was that UKIP in particular, but not alone, had shamelessly reinterpreted the Union Jack for their own purposes. In fact, UKIP had turned it purple, with a yellow party badge added, in a design that made the flag look like the wrapper of cheap supermarket bread, while the Tories, having removed any dangerous off-brand scrap of red from the flag, put it in shades of blue all over their lecterns and pamphlets. While busy making fatuous arguments about flags, none of these politicians had anything to say about the fact that the shirt was retailing at the extortionate price of £124. More concerning for Farage was the right of travelling England fans that summer to keep singing the 'German Bombers' song to their hosts. Speaking on LBC, he said, 'It's very important that young men are not men, they shouldn't drink beer, they shouldn't have fun, they shouldn't chant, no no, we are to live in a modern puritan world. Is it any wonder that so many young Gen Z-ers are now supporting me … because they're being told not to be young lads.'[6]

If Farage saw football as a space in which his politics of male grievance and victimhood could be amplified and his militarist nostalgia indulged, Keir Starmer perceived it as a place in which communitarian values still endured and a more progressive version of English national identity might be mobilised.[7] More than any other leader of a political party in recent political history, Starmer has built his political persona and electoral campaigning around football: introducing himself, again and again, as the son of a toolmaker, a regular five-a-side player and an Arsenal season-ticket holder of long standing.[8] Remarkably, in the four short years since he had become leader of the Labour Party, Starmer had made speeches and attended events at, among others: Accrington Stanley, Carlisle United, Ilkeston Town, Norwich City, Port Vale and Wycombe Wanderers, not to mention a dozen Premier League grounds; and had claimed to have taken advice on leadership from Gareth Southgate and Arsène Wenger. His 2024 ground-hopping general election campaign began at Gillingham's Priestfield Stadium; the party's manifesto was launched in Crewe and was followed by a speech at Crewe Alexandra. En route to polling day, similar events – a speech to an invited audience – were held at a succession of small clubs in marginal constituencies, including: Halesowen Town, Worcester City, Aldershot, Bristol Rovers, Northampton Town and Grimsby. In a first for British politics, Starmer gave election interviews to football podcasts: the *Guardian Weekly*, where he fended off any suggestion that a Labour government might contemplate radical change – dismissing the notion of a 10 per cent levy on the transfer market to fund the grassroots, or any idea that states should be prohibited from owning clubs – and then with Gary Neville, with whom he traded anodyne bromides.[9]

This kind of caution was the leitmotif of Labour's campaign – dubbed the 'Ming vase strategy' – as the party sought to gingerly get its precious lead in the polls over the election-day line. Something similar was going on for Southgate's England, who, while carrying the weight of considerable expectation and seemingly equipped with a remarkable array of attacking talent, played at Euro 2024 in a state of cautious torpor. A narrow win against Serbia and tepid draws with Denmark and Slovenia got the team through to the knock-out stages, but generated enough bile among some England fans for Southgate to be jeered off the pitch, ducking the beer cups coming his way.[10] Danny Baker's intemperate outburst can stand proxy for one strand of the wider mood: 'To be fair Southgate has really turned this England side around. Last match we were dull and hopeless. Now we're hopeless and dull. Over Promoted Weird Beard has stunk up another fixture.'[11] Similar responses could be found on social media and heard on a hundred punditry shows. There would have been a lot more of that if Slovakia had held on to their 1–0 lead in the round of sixteen, but England were saved by injury-time goals from Harry Kane and Jude Bellingham.

Scotland's journey through the Euros was over before the election, but the fans still threw the party that should have happened in 2021, when the last Covid restrictions put a lid on the national fervour that accompanied the men's team's appearance at Euro 2020, their first international tournament since 1998. Estimates varied, but somewhere between 150,000 and 200,000 Scots, around 5 per cent of the adult population and most of them ticketless, made the trip to Germany. They had, given how poorly Scotland performed, a sensational booze-drenched carnival. It was a bigger, louder performance of the Scottish nation than ever, but not one bound in any way to the cause of independence. Indeed, it came at a moment when the SNP and the wider nationalist movement were at their lowest ebb for over a decade; a fact confirmed by the SNP's collapse at the polls soon after. In the later stages of the tournament, with Scotland long departed, only the *National*, perhaps the most pro-independence outlet in the country, made the case for 'Anyone but England'. On the eve of the final their headline implored the Spanish to win, reminding that nation of their English tourists and migrants: 'They drink all your beer. They make a mess of your plazas. They eat fried breakfasts all day instead of your wonderful food. They retire in your towns and sponge off your public services.' But such was the criticism from all quarters that they were forced into an apology and a retraction.[12]

The Labour Party, like England, had not fought an entertaining campaign. It had none of the swelling inevitability of Blair's landslide in 1997, yet four days after the Slovakia game the general election delivered an unparalleled victory for their unimaginative restraint. Despite only winning 34 per cent of the popular vote, the geographic concentration of those voters and the widespread practice of tactical voting gave Labour 411 seats – an overall majority of over 170. Whereas before the election 55 English League clubs sat in Labour constituencies and 37 in Tory ones, the new electoral map was entirely red but for a single club – Bromley, where the club had only just made it into the League and Tory candidate Peter Fortune had won by a mere 302 votes.[13] In addition, there were four football seats for independent left candidates, some of them previously expelled from the Labour Party, who now represented Arsenal, Aston Villa, Leicester City and Blackburn Rovers.

For a moment, the prospect flickered that such a comprehensive victory would yield a bolder and more decisive government than its tepid prospectus offered; a glimmer of hope that Labour in power would, in some sense, raise their collective game. The message from Germany on that front was not entirely encouraging. England squeezed past Switzerland on penalties in their quarter-final; looked a little more promising and bold for the 2–1 victory over the Netherlands in the semi-final, but didn't quite have the class or the verve to beat Spain in the final itself. A few days later, Southgate stood down as England coach with his term of office explicitly compared to Starmer's victory and his time in power to come. Jonathan Freedland in the *Guardian* cast him as the 'proto-Starmer – a welcome island of national stability surrounded by rolling political chaos', while Jason Burt in the *Telegraph* thought he had 'made the impossible job possible'. On the other hand, despite Southgate being the most successful England men's coach since Alf Ramsey, the angry brigade thought good riddance. Splenetic right-wing contrarian Mick Hume, for example, suggested the fans had 'hurled metaphorical pints at Southgate for squandering another chance to make history, and fervently hoped we had seen the back of him and his soul-destroying brand of football'.[14]

Whatever had happened on the pitch, it became clear that Southgate's legacy of tolerance, inclusivity and anti-racism was far from universally embedded in the country. Just a few weeks after the Euros ended, a terrible and murderous attack on children at a dance class in Southport near Liverpool was deliberately misrepresented and manipulated on social media by the far right. This ignited a series of violent riots, near pogroms, that turned their fury on mosques and hotels and hostels housing refugees in some of England's poorest towns and neighbourhoods. While race riots in Oldham and elsewhere in the 2000s and EDL marches in the 2010s had attracted a significant number of football casuals and firms, there were only scattered reports of football shirts in 2024. In Sunderland a number of the people attacking a mosque and the home of Filipino nurses were seen in club strip, while in Blackpool the *Lead* reported: 'Punks – in town for the annual Rebellion festival – squared off against men in football shirts, separated only by police.'[15] Much more representative, certainly more widely reported, were those who showed up to post-riot clean-ups in club colours. Jonathan Wilson, reporting for the *Guardian* from Sunderland, wrote, 'On the following morning, as dozens of people gathered in the centre of Sunderland to help with the clear-up, it was striking how many were in football shirts. One man, wearing a white 1996–97 away shirt, told the BBC how he felt the riots "misrepresented the city and the club".'[16]

It is extraordinary, though now not surprising, that at such a pivotal moment in the nation's narrative, politicians, commentators and the general public should be reaching for football analogies to grasp its meaning. Was a football coach an augury of political competence and stability to come, or a warning of the dangers of an over-cautious and defensive programme for government? Were football supporters a redoubt of the worst kind of nativism and racism, or the core of an active and inclusive civil society? Whatever the answers to these questions, and the many others that football has offered to us over the last decade, their presence in popular and political culture confirmed that the game had become a central metaphorical space in which this country has addressed itself.

II

What country, then, had we become? In the realm of football, in makes no sense to talk of a UK or British game; the long-standing devolution of the game to the four nations had long demonstrated the cultural and social division of the United Kingdom into its four constituent nations. In the last decade and a half, the already uneasy compact between them has frayed. The Celtic peripheries have become ever more marginal to English football, while the national teams of Wales and Scotland have carried a rising tide of national pride and at times a call for independence. Northern Irish football remains caught in the force field of its internal divisions and competing national identities. Even England, long a proxy for Britishness, has become a space in which a new English secessionism has been articulated. It is, perhaps, too glib to suggest that the course of the 2024–25 Premier League season tracked the political shift in the country, though the new dominance of Liverpool in red over the now diminished and crisis-ridden Manchester City in blue suggested as much. In the end, despite the leftist bent of Liverpool's local fan base and fan culture, the sense of collective relief that City's run of four league titles in a row would not be extended, and even the cup victories for Crystal Palace, Newcastle and Tottenham, English football is not a convincing herald of a new age of social equality. Perhaps the most powerful analogy of the kind of country we have become can be found at the bottom rather than the top of the football pyramid.

In 1968, in a very different Britain, the journalist and screenwriter Arthur Hopcraft, in his celebrated survey of the game *The Football Man*, argued: 'The point about football is that it is not just a sport that people take to like cricket or tennis or long distance running. It is inherent in the people. It is built into the urban psyche, as much a common experience to our children as uncles and school. It is not a phenomenon; it is an everyday matter.'[17] More than half a century later, in this regard at least, nothing much has changed. Football continues to have a hold over the emotions and the imagination that other sports simply cannot match. In fact, its presence in British sporting life is more dominant and encompassing than in Hopcraft's time, built not only into the urban psyche, but the suburban, small and new-town psyches too, its ubiquity comparable not just to uncles and schools, but now to aunts too and the digital worlds we spend so much time inside. Beyond the commercial circus and spectacle of professional football, it remains an everyday matter. The eleven-a-side game may have shrunk and street football been driven to the point of extinction, but more people are playing more kinds of football than ever, and more people are volunteering to organise it. New clubs and new constituencies, from new refugees in Glasgow to new mothers in Manchester, are reshaping and renewing the organised landscape of the game. Its absence during the Covid lockdowns made clearer than ever Hopcraft's claim that: 'Its sudden withdrawal from the people would bring deeper disconsolation than to deprive them of television.'

The everyday is not always edifying: the lamentable state of the country's playing fields reflects the terrible state of the public realm after more than a decade of austerity; the treatment of referees in grassroots football points to a pervasive decline in our trust in authority and our capacity for civility; the commercial pressures at work in the youth game and the casualty rate of the academy system are testament to the aggression and avarice of a ruthlessly competitive economic and educational system. On the other hand, much of the time, football reinforces families and friendships, and builds deeper networks of social capital that combine conviviality, solidarity and local self-help. As fans' support of food banks, and the reaction of clubs, large and small, to Covid demonstrated, football is intensely communitarian. At their most generous, the norms of football culture recognise that a team is only as good as its weakest link; that a level playing field really should be the normal basis of human interaction; that success is the product of collective effort, but that, in any case, process and participation count for more than victory. The importance of these values, embodied in playing and supporting the game, has become even more apparent as the institutions of social democratic Britain, from trade unions to what remains of the welfare state, have been pulverised by austerity, stagnation and the chaos of the last decade.

If the everyday culture of football is testament to an enduring localism and the egalitarian and collaborative strands of our society, the business practices of the professional game reflect an economy that is globalised, deeply unequal and viciously self-interested. In the last decade, the already significant gap between the rich and the rest in football and British society has simply got larger. Project Big Picture and the European Super League experiment demonstrate that the rich are still not satisfied with their cut and are prepared to destroy the current status quo if it is to their benefit. By the same token, even when thwarted, they are not prepared to establish a more equitable distribution of resources within the institutions that do exist, as the unresolved standoff between the Premier League and the EFL over solidarity payments makes clear. At the same time, while proclaiming the economic virtues of their rule, they have in fact been racking up ever greater levels of debt and have failed to make the game, or clubs at any rate, profitable; though, like the wider economy, football lawyers, accountants and intermediaries like agents have been making a killing. The globalisation of ownership in English football has continued apace. In the first half of the 2024–25 season, Everton and its debts were finally sold to the venture capital firm the Friedkin Group, making American owners a majority in the Premier League. They are an ever increasing presence in the lower leagues too, where Sheffield United were sold by their Saudi owners to a group of American businessmen and Norwich City were purchased by American billionaire Mark Attanasio from Delia Smith and her husband – now, like ceremonial royal figureheads, denuded of power but made Life Presidents. Well intentioned as they all no doubt are, the recent behaviour of their peers continues to demonstrate what actually happens when social and communal assets like football clubs are owned by billionaires, hedge funds, private equity and nation states. Manchester City fought the Premier League tooth and nail over its regulation of associated party transactions, winning a number of court cases that make it harder to regulate the flood of money coming into clubs from sponsors linked to their owners. Many clubs have continued to raise ticket prices, squeeze out concessionary places for children and elders, and all to make more space for one-off, casual and tourist fans who will pay considerably more for their seats and spend considerably more at the club shop.

Most egregious of all, and proof that native oligarchs are every bit as toxic as their foreign peers, has been Jim Ratcliffe's short reign at Manchester United. Having purchased a quarter of the club from the Glazers for over a billion pounds, he has found himself in charge of an institution deeply in debt, with large and continuing interest payments on its loans, and whose fixed assets – the training ground and Old Trafford – have been left to rot for almost two decades. The response has been a series of petty cuts. Hundreds of lower-paid staff have been made redundant. Those that remain have seen their Christmas bonus evaporate, their access to the club canteen curtailed, while stewards who were once allocated a £50 steward-of-the-match prize will just have to make do with the minimum wage. Along the way, the club's official historian has been sent on his way, the budget of the club's charitable foundation cut, while the new regime has attempted to move on Matt Busby's family, who have been occupying expensive premium seats for some decades. Of course, none of this comes even close to recouping the money that Ratcliffe shamelessly wasted on recruiting and firing Dan Ashworth as the club's director of football or dispensing with Erik ten Hag as coach – moves that cost United, along with appointing new manager Ruben Amorim, more than £20 million. While this kind of ruthless cost-cutting and executive largesse has proved successful in making money out of Ineos – Ratcliffe's hydrocarbon empire – it is not going to do so at Manchester United. The billionaires and the hedge funds can fantasise all they like about making English football profitable, but as the last decade has proved, even inside the world's richest football league and under conditions of increasingly tight financial regulation, football clubs lose money, and they will continue to do so, for the real currencies in circulation are vanity, status, celebrity, influence and power.

Through all of this the English FA has been a mere bystander. The repeated attempts to reform its structure and democratise its governance in the 2000s have ceased, a measure perhaps of its marginality. It has had almost nothing to say about Project Big Picture or the European Super League, nor did it possess the moral authority or practical means to do anything about them. It has failed to be a broker in the struggles between the Premier League and the EFL. It has made no contribution to UEFA's attempts to regulate European football, and it has ceded control of the nascent women's professional game to the clubs. It has attempted to lead change with initiatives like its diversity code, but as with its efforts to improve safeguarding and the treatment of referees, it has had only the most limited impact on the professional game. Its stewardship of the national teams and the grassroots game make it what Walter Bagehot, the Victorian theorist of the British constitution, called the *dignified* parts of the British polity, 'those which excite and preserve the reverence of the population', in contrast to 'the *efficient* parts – those by which it, in fact, works and rules'. The Premier League, and to a lesser extent the Football League, have fulfilled these functions, and nowhere more so than in the realm of politics, where it has been a very active and efficient lobbyist, not least through offering 'hospitality packages' to the House of Commons. In the three years running up to the election they had entertained a third of the cabinet, more than sixty MPs in total, two-thirds of them from the Labour Party. Already under fire for accepting donors' money for clothes and spectacles, Prime Minister Starmer, it was revealed, had also accepted a lot of football hospitality: more than £35,000 worth of football tickets during the previous parliament, though they were gifts in accordance with parliamentary rules.[18] As the legislation to establish the independent football regulator ground its way through parliament, Tory peers in the House of Lords – including Baroness Brady, vice-chair of West Ham United, and Lord Pannick, the KC of choice for Manchester City – were busy crafting dozens of amendments seeking to dilute and diminish its already limited powers.[19]

It is worth recalling that the process that led to this legislation was triggered by the massive fan protests that accompanied the formation of the European Super League in 2021; a fact that demonstrates the power and capacity of fans to politically organise and the high regard in which fandom is now apparently held. However, like so many of the spontaneous uprisings and outbursts of political protest, not only in Britain but across the world, that marked the 2010s – from the Occupy movement to the Arab Spring and the Brazilian street protests of 2013 – the impulse for change has been managed, mainstreamed and eventually extinguished. The possibility of real structural transformations has always been ruled out, not least in the football regulator debate, where efforts to encourage social ownership of clubs, to make human rights issues a stronger part of the owners' test, to shift more of the game's money to the grassroots and to include environmental sustainability as part of club licensing systems, have all been thwarted. Far-right populists have, as yet, failed to sustain a significant presence in the game beyond the EDL's shithousery and Reform's culture-war spats over the England team; but the sense that the system is broken and that the mainstream left and right will not – or cannot – change the status quo has been an important driver of their popularity. In fact, the realm of contemporary football offers a number of clues to the sources of the new populist politics: the rise of tribalism and the role of social media; the recasting of politics as fandom; the discontents of the post-industrial working class and its intersection with identity politics.

Football fandom has, of course, always been intensely partisan. There was no golden age of comradely amity among supporters, but there was less solipsism. There were once plenty of fans who would go to see Everton one week and Liverpool the next, the same in other two-club cities like Bristol and Nottingham, fans who saw their tribe as all of football rather than just one team. Clubs that are currently 'fierce rivals' like Crystal Palace and Brighton, or Southampton and Portsmouth, can only actually trace their animosity back a few decades. Since then, the irrational monomania of Nick Hornby's *Fever Pitch* has become, despite the author's self-deprecation and scepticism, in effect, the contemporary standard of authentic support. This can be turned inwards, as the online rage towards players and coaches and their 'unacceptable performances' suggests, but for the most part it is directed outwards. The long-held bias of

many supporters towards their own club when it came to referees or official sanctions has been magnified many times over by
social media, as fans share and cluster around the same narratives and viewpoints on WhatsApp groups and Reddit. The new
fan-led YouTube channels, like Arsenal TV and Redmen TV,
have given voice to, and left unchallenged, the most intransigent
of opinions. The hyperemotional state of the terraces has been
prolonged all week as injustices are endlessly replayed and
dissected. The confrontational snark of match-day chants and
banter is repeated and finessed on X and Facebook. Owners,
coaches and players are, if the team is doing okay, given a free
pass, be it a petrostate's human rights transgressions or a
centre-forward facing multiple accusations of sexual assault. It
is a landscape of performative emotion and identity within
which shared conceptions of truth are harder to sustain, in
which neutral expert authority is deemed impossible and
conspiracy theory flourishes; precisely the conditions under
which right-wing populism has been nurtured. For populists, a
more successful tactic, rather than attempting to mobilise
supporters directly, has been to take this model of fandom and
apply it directly to politics.[20] James Meek, accounting in the
London Review of Books for the rise of Jacob Rees-Mogg –
from back-bench curio to cabinet minister – argued: 'His career
shows how much like sport British politics has become, where
politicians have fans and supporters, rather than voters who are
swayed by their arguments or troubled by their extra-parlia-
mentary activities. If you don't support the Rees-Mogg team,
you have no time for him anyway; you're not going to hate him
more. If you're a fan, it isn't so important that he should take
personal responsibility for making the country better or that he
should be morally consistent. What matters is that he lands
telling blows on the other team.'[21]

Football, which, despite the demographic transformation of
its crowds, remains a public space in which a version of industrial working-class masculinity is still the norm and is, in some

sense, publicly revered as authentic, is an obvious place for populists to operate. Their core constituencies – older, traditional conservative voters, declining regions and small towns, working-class voters receptive to their anti-immigrant and aggressive nationalist pitch – are a key component of the game's crowds. Across all these social divisions they have been attracting more support from men than from women, and the grievances of the 'average' working man are essential grist to their mill; in particular, anti-racism and feminism, conflated as 'woke', have been cast, alongside migrants, as the causes of their immiseration rather than the devastating impact of globally mobile capital and new technologies. No wonder, then, that Nigel Farage should want to preserve the right of England fans to atavistically taunt their German peers or that Joey Barton should see the arrival of women pundits and commentators as the beginning of the end for the 'straight white man' in football. Though both were roundly condemned, they also tapped in to a real and significant segment of feeling within a football culture where racism and misogyny are often close to the surface. Interestingly, neither man seemed to see a problem with the wholesale sell-off of national assets to foreign owners or ticket-pricing policies that exclude their constituency.

While they continue to make gains among the wider electorate by pursuing these strategies, they are, I suspect, in football at any rate, fighting a losing battle. In fifty or a hundred years, if anyone is still writing about the history of football in Britain, it will not be Brexit or Covid or the disaster capitalism of club owners that stands out as the most remarkable change, but the irreversible feminisation of the game that has been under way. It is hard to underestimate the significance of this. In its original upper-class Victorian incarnation and in its working-class industrial pomp, football has been an overwhelmingly masculine space that has both symbolised and contributed to the exclusion of women from the public sphere. Toxic masculinity and the sexist backlash it sustains are not about to disappear, but it is hard to imagine that they will be able to slow, let alone roll back the explosive growth of women in the men's game and of the women's game itself. The same can, I think, be said for the racist attitudes that remain present in football and in its institutions, and which would in other circumstances offer a promising space for right-wing populists to operate. The now huge presence of players of colour, both foreign and domestic, in the grassroots game, the professional game and the national teams of Britain is a constant rebuke to notions of white nativism and exclusionary forms of nationalism; anti-migrant sentiments are much harder to mobilise when supporters are cheering them on in such numbers. Indeed, a case could be made, as responses to the England team taking a knee suggest, that while football retains a core of old-school racism, it has also nurtured a quieter but more widespread anti-racism among its constituency. What remains to be seen is whether this can be mobilised to break the deep and structural racism of the game and its institutions. Football, like the rest of our society, has furnished innumerable political resources for right-wing populism, but retains within it key obstacles and challenges to its advance.

Climate denial is another card that the far right likes to play. Again in some ways, football is making that a harder trick to pull off too. In May 2024, in driving rain, Arsenal beat a dismal Manchester United 1–0 at Old Trafford. The downpour was so heavy and the state of the stadium's roofs so poor that waterfalls tumbled down onto the stands and cascaded down the steps to the pitch, while water seeped into Arsenal's dressing room.[22] Flash-flooding in September engulfed Telford FC's pitch, and the rains were so relentless in London that, after a major flood, a massive sinkhole opened up in the pitch at AFC Wimbledon, closing the stadium for weeks.[23] Storm Bert, that November, sent extreme winds across the west of the country, tearing the roof off Newquay AFC's stands and forcing the postponement of Blackburn's game with Portsmouth. In early

December 2024, Storm Darragh was even more fearsome: threatening to rip the scoreboard panels off the wall of Notts County's Meadow Lane; forcing the cancellation of the Merseyside derby; damaging the roof at Swansea's ground; destroying the roof at non-league Sawbridgeworth Town FC in Hertfordshire; and flooding Everton's new stadium, then still under construction at Bramley-Moore Dock. And 2025 began in a similar fashion. On New Year's Day, Wigan Athletic's match against Huddersfield Town was postponed due to severe flooding in the surrounding area, so bad that it would have been impossible for the crowd to get to the stadium.[24] A few weeks later, the fearsome gales of Storm Eowyn swept across Scotland, damaging big stadiums (Celtic Park and Ibrox) and small grounds (Arbroath and Greenock Morton) alike.[25]

Football, of course, survived these blows. Roofs were repaired, pitches were drained, rearranged fixtures were played. Yet the cost of fixing the problems is mounting, the cost of insurance premiums is rising, and there is only more extreme weather to come. Eventually, these costs and complications will start to corrode the financial and infrastructural fabric of the football nation, both at grassroots and the top of the game. There is an optimistic take on this scenario. Football, in fact, offers a powerful space for effective climate action. It remains, despite everything, a place in which people really do think that collective action works – the *sine qua non* of a response to the climate crisis. At its very heart, football believes that no cause is truly lost till the final whistle is blown; that last-minute turnarounds and comeback miracles really are possible. These are rare and precious cultural resources. Were football to truly tackle its own carbon footprint it would be well placed to make the case for the bigger and broader changes we must all make if we want to keep the game sustainable and the planet habitable. More likely, perhaps, is that the spectacle will continue to dazzle rather than illuminate; the professional game will continue to seek ever-higher revenues and more fossil-fuel sponsorship, driving higher levels of consumption and requiring the burning of more and more carbon. While elite football remains wedded to an uncontrollable arms race of over-spending and the relentless commercialisation and growth this demands, and while it is owned by individuals and institutions that have no regard for our common future, it is quixotic to think otherwise. Perhaps, then, the most salient truth that the game will have offered us is confirmation of Fredric Jameson's speculation, one that haunts our times, that, 'It is easier to imagine the end of the world than the end of capitalism.'

Acknowledgements

Love and thanks for conversation and comment to Mark Burnham, Martin Calladine, Rob Colls, Jo Czutkowna, Paul Darby, Miguel Delaney, Nick Fishwick, John Foot, Dick Holt, Martin Johnes, David Kynaston, Hugh McDonald and Tom Webb. As ever, my Pitzer College students for hearing it all first time around, and to Dodi Tapaya, Professor Davina and Andre Wakefield for making the stay possible. Publishing love to Steve Burdett for saving my blushes and cleaning me up; Joel Simons for taking me on and seeing me through; and Sally Holloway for doing the deal.

Notes

Preface

1. See for example: Cruse, M., 'Everton embroiled in "perfect storm" of trouble, warns Toffee Blues contributor', *MerseySportLive*, 10 April 2024, https://merseysportlive.co.uk/2024/04/10/everton-embroiled-in-perfect-storm-of-trouble-its-killing-us/; Murray, E., '"It's a perfect storm": Rodgers says critics not giving Celtic leeway in Europe', *Guardian*, 22 October 2024, https://www.theguardian.com/football/2024/oct/22/brendan-rodgers-celtic-critics-europe-champions-league-atalanta

2. Storey, D., 'English football is in a state of emergency – decisions taken now will impact the next generation', *Independent*, 25 September 2020, https://inews.co.uk/sport/football/english-football-is-in-a-state-of-emergency-the-decisions-taken-now-will-impact-the-next-generation-659631

Introduction: 'Let the Soap Opera Begin!'

1. 'Premier League: "Let the soap opera begin", says CEO Richard Masters', BBC Sport, 22 August 2022, https://www.bbc.co.uk/sport/av/football/62399536

2. 'FOOTBALL ON THE SMALL SCREEN – UNITED!', beyondthelastman.com, 5 November 2019, https://beyondthelastman.com/2019/11/05/football-on-the-small-screen-united/

3. 'Which football matches have featured TV show spoilers?', *Guardian*, 13 November 2019, https://www.theguardian.com/ football/2019/nov/13/which-football-matches-have-featured-tv-show-spoilers

4. 'EastEnders 1–0 Barcelona', BBC Sport, 4 April 2020, http://news. bbc.co.uk/sport1/hi/funny_old_game/1260552.stm

5. Data from late 2023.

6. 'Leicester could be a champion of globalisation thanks to Premier League success', University of Leicester, 17 May 2016, https://le.ac. uk/news/2016/may/leicester-could-be-a-2018champion-of-globalisation2019-thanks-to-premier-league-success

1. 'We're All Leaving Europe!'

1. Taylor, M. (2004), 'Sutcliffe, Charles Edward (1864–1939)', *Oxford Dictionary of National Biography* (online ed.), Oxford University Press.

2. Quoted in Glanville, B., 'The great Chelsea surrender', *The Times*, 17 April 2005, https://www.thetimes.com/travel/destinations/ europe-travel/the-great-chelsea-surrender-pz008ngvs85

3. Quoted in Spencer, P., 'When Three Beat Six: The Common Market Match', byfarthegreatestteam.com, February 2018, https://www. byfarthegreatestteam.com/posts/three-beat-six-common-market-match/

4. Spurling, J., 'Getting into Europe: The 1973 Common Market Match', *When Saturday Comes*, 2016, https://www.wsc.co.uk/ stories/getting-into-europe-the-1973-common-market-match/

5. Millichip cited in Thorpe, M., 'How English clubs clawed their way back into Europe', *Guardian*, 25 March 2020, https://www. theguardian.com/football/2000/mar/25/sport.uefa

6. Brown, G., 'Gordon Brown says "we need to lead Europe, not leave it – just ask Leicester City"', *Mirror*, 10 May 2016, https://www. mirror.co.uk/news/uk-news/gordon-brown-says-we-need-7940337

7. The whole song can be heard here: 'Britain's Coming Home: Ukip supporter puts new lyrics to Three Lions song – video', *Guardian*, 24 February 2016, https://www.theguardian.com/politics/video/ 2016/feb/24/britains-coming-home-ukip-supporter-puts-new-lyrics-to-three-lions-song-video

8. Balls, E., 'Unlike Euro 2016, EU referendum only gives us one chance to get it right so vote Remain', *Mirror*, 14 June 2016,

https://www.mirror.co.uk/news/uk-news/unlike-euro-2016-eu-referendum-8182469

9. Cadwalladr, C., 'Vote Leave faces scrutiny over £50m football contest', *Guardian*, 20 May 2018, https://www.theguardian.com/politics/2018/may/20/vote-leave-scrutiny-facebook-data-football-contest-brexit

10. Press Association, 'Karren Brady warns Brexit would have "devastating" effect on British clubs' *Guardian*, 29 January 2016, https://www.theguardian.com/football/2016/jan/29/karren-brady-warns-brexit-british-clubs

11. PA Sport, 'Premier League chief Scudamore backs Remain in EU referendum', ESPN, 20 June 2016, https://www.espn.co.uk/football/story/_/id/37475905/premier-league-chief-richard-scudamore-backs-remain-eu-referendum

12. Britain Stronger in Europe, 'EU Referendum Press Releases: Britain Stronger in Europe – Sporting Figures Back Remain', 2016, viewed at https://www.ukpol.co.uk/eu-referendum-press-releases-britain-stronger-in-europe-sporting-figures-back-remain

13. 'EU referendum: Ex-footballer David Beckham backs Remain', BBC News, 21 June 2016, https://www.bbc.co.uk/news/uk-politics-eu-referendum-36584685

14. Ferdinand, R., 'Why the EU referendum has made me want to vote for the first time', *Standard*, 21 June 2016, https://www.standard.co.uk/comment/comment/rio-ferdinand-why-the-eu-referendum-has-made-me-want-to-vote-for-the-first-time-a3277121.html

15. Campbell, S. 'Come on you Brexiteers! Former England captain Sol Campbell kicks out: A vote to Leave would boost British football', *Mail on Sunday*, 3 April 2016, https://www.dailymail.co.uk/debate/article-3520982/Come-Brexiteers-Former-England-captain-Sol-Campbell-kicks-vote-Leave-boost-British-football.html

16. Churchill, D., 'David James and John Barnes: Brexit would boost home-grown English football talent', *Standard*, 2016, https://www.standard.co.uk/news/uk/david-james-and-john-barnes-brexit-would-boost-homegrown-english-football-talent-a3262991.html

17. @Carra23, Twitter, 24 June 2016, https://x.com/Carra23/status/746223946937176064

18. 'Foreign players "shocked" by Brexit at Euro 2016', *news24*, 2016, https://www.news24.com/sport/soccer/euro2016/foreign-players-shocked-by-brexit-at-euro-2016-20160624

19. Fifield, D., 'Roy Hodgson quits as England manager after humiliating defeat by Iceland', *Guardian*, 27 June 2016, https://

www.theguardian.com/football/2016/jun/27/roy-hodgson-facing-end-england-manager-iceland-euro-2016

20. In 2021, when coach at West Brom, Allardyce was ruing the new post-Brexit system: 'I have found three players already who were capable of coming here and they're not allowed. It's a shame. Due to the new regulations in terms of the permit they were unable to come to this country, whereas [previously] they would have done.' See, Evans, G., 'Football manager who voted Leave complains about not being able to sign players because of Brexit', *Indy100*, 4 January 2021, https://www.indy100.com/sport/sam-allardyce-brexit-west-brom-transfers-b1781990

21. 'Neil Warnock on Brexit: I cannot wait to get out of the EU!', @ HaytersTV, YouTube, 13 January 2019, https://www.youtube.com/watch?v=Oh-1cc4w5VE

22. Innes, R., 'Graeme Souness reveals he voted for Brexit during this season's most bizarre bit of football punditry', *Mirror*, 19 April 2017, https://www.mirror.co.uk/sport/row-zed/graeme-souness-reveals-voted-brexit-10253585

23. Read, J., 'Football veteran Jamie Carragher backs People's Vote warning UK faces "relegation" after Brexit', *New European*, 8 October 2019, https://www.theneweuropean.co.uk/brexit-news-liverpool-football-jamie-carragher-on-people-s-vote-58752; MacInnes, P., 'Hand of clod? Brexit and Theresa May divide England's 1986 World Cup squad', *Guardian*, 13 December 2018, https://www.theguardian.com/football/2018/dec/13/hand-of-clod-brexit-and-theresa-may-divide-englands-1986-world-cup-squad

24. Beech, S., '"Born in the UK, You'll never sing that" – Ipswich Town fans taunt Luton Town with racist chants & Johnson's Brexit policies', *London Economic*, 15 August 2019, https://www.thelondoneconomic.com/sport/football/born-in-the-uk-youll-never-sing-that-ipswich-town-fans-taunt-luton-town-with-racist-chants-johnsons-brexit-policies-156380/

25. Khomami, N., 'Want to know how Brexit will work? Play Football Manager', *Guardian*, 8 October 2016, https://www.theguardian.com/technology/2016/oct/18/want-to-know-how-brexit-will-work-play-football-manager; Baraniuk, C., 'Brexit simulated in new Football Manager game', BBC News, 18 October 2016, https://www.bbc.co.uk/news/technology-37692481

26. Maher, C., 'How a video game is getting its players to rethink Brexit', *Washington Post*, 10 September 2019, https://www.

washingtonpost.com/video-games/2019/09/10/how-video-
game-is-getting-its-players-rethink-brexit/
27. 'How To Remove Brexit And Work Permits In Football Manager',
FM Projects, YouTube, 19 April 2024, https://www.youtube.com/
watch?v=gFuqfojqg14

2. Uneven Playing Fields

1. 'Football marks the boundary between England's winners and
losers', *Economist*, 29 February 2020, https://www.economist.com/
game-theory/2020/02/29/football-marks-the-boundary-between-
englands-winners-and-losers
2. Ibid.
3. The Blair years may have seen rising inequality, but riding on a
wider global boom they contained a short moment of rising
prosperity, and just enough regulation and redistribution – from
expanding public services to tax credits and the minimum wage –
to justify its compromises. For an equally short moment between
2014 and 2018, the Premier League finally managed to make so
much money and enact a modicum of collective restraint that even
though wages and transfers continued to soar, more than half the
clubs would break even and the league as a whole was actually in
profit. This short interregnum was a matter of both good fortune
and external pressure. Although Sky had increased their payments
over the previous ten years, they had not felt serious pressure from
small competitors like NTL or Setanta. Now, with the arrival of
British Telecom, in the guise of BT Sport, bidding for the rights for
2013–16, they faced a serious opponent with considerably deeper
pockets. Consequently, the value of the League's domestic rights
almost doubled overnight. At the precise moment that these funds
began to rush into Premier League clubs, they were faced by a
stricter degree of regulation; first by UEFA, and then by the Premier
League itself. UEFA, under President Michel Platini, had been
worrying about the financial sustainability of European football
and the impact of the new oligarchs since 2009. By 2014, English
clubs that played in Europe were subject to the Financial Fair Play
regulations they had introduced, requiring strict audits, and limits
on how much a club could lose and how much money new owners
could pump into them. The Premier League, initially much more
reluctant to think about similar measures, had been sufficiently
unnerved by the collapse and bankruptcy of Portsmouth in 2009

and the catastrophic levels of loss being made by many of its clubs to bring in its own Profit and Sustainability Rules (PSR) in 2013. For the next two seasons, significant limits were placed on how much of the new TV money clubs could spend on wages. Thinking longer term, clubs were also limited to a maximum loss of £105 million over any three-year period. It was hardly a command and control economy, but for five years there was just enough pressure and scrutiny, and more than enough new money, to bring the league's wages to income ratio down to 60 per cent, for the collective losses to be staunched, and the rise of its cumulative debt slowed down.

4. Swiss Ramble, 'Would You Invest In The Premier League?', Substack, 26 August 2024, https://swissramble.substack.com/p/would-you-invest-in-the-premier-league

5. Ibid.

6. Fair Game, 'NEW FAIR GAME STUDY REVEALS OVER HALF OF TOP 92 CLUBS ARE "TECHNICALLY INSOLVENT"', https://www.fairgameuk.org/press-releases/half-of-clubs-technically-insolvent

7. Jolly, R., 'The "PSR six" and a new loophole Premier League transfer causing outrage', *Independent*, 3 June 2024, https://www.independent.co.uk/sport/football/premier-league-psr-everton-nottingham-forest-chelsea-b2572708.html

8. See, for example, Chelsea's sale of two hotels to a company closely linked to its owners: Steinberg, J., 'Chelsea's £76.5m hotel deals raise questions over PSR compliance', *Guardian*, 19 April 2024, https://www.theguardian.com/football/2024/apr/19/chelseas-765m-hotel-deals-raise-questions-over-psr-compliance

9. 'Is the Premier League Becoming Less Competitive?', Raumdata Football, 8 July 2020, https://raumdatafootball.com/2020/07/08/is-the-premier-league-becoming-less-competitive/

3. Football's Dirty Secret

1. The lip reader's testimony in court regarding Terry's words can be seen here: Davies, C., 'John Terry case: racist abuse or sarcastic banter?', *Guardian*, 9 July 2012, https://www.theguardian.com/football/2012/jul/09/john-terry-case-racist-language; for a report of the acquittal in the criminal trial: 'John Terry cleared of racism against Anton Ferdinand', BBC News, 13 July 2012, https://www.bbc.co.uk/news/uk-england-london-18827915; for details of the FA

investigation and ban: 'John Terry defence "improbable, implausible and contrived"', BBC Sport, 5 October 2012, https://www.bbc.co.uk/sport/football/19842795

2. The Suarez–Evra encounter is recounted in painful detail here: 'Extracts from the FA report on the Luis Suárez Patrice Evra racism case', *Guardian*, 1 January 2012, https://www.theguardian.com/football/2012/jan/01/fa-report-luis-suarez-patrice-evra; it is clear that while the precise translation of Suarez's words is open to debate, they all carry racist connotations.

3. 'John Terry Verdict: FA Finds Chelsea Captain Guilty Over Racism Charge', *Guardian*, 27 September 2012, https://www.theguardian.com/football/2012/Sep/John-terry-verdict-chelsea-guilty

4. Cleland, J. and Cashmore, E. (2013), 'Fans, Racism and British Football in the Twenty-First Century: The Existence of a "Colour-Blind" Ideology', *Journal of Ethnic and Migration Studies*, 40(4), pp. 638–54. doi: 10.1080/1369183X.2013.777524

5. The details of the texts were published in the *Daily Mail* here: Lawton, M., 'Malky Mackay and Iain Moody investigated by FA over "sexist, racist and homophobic" text messages during time at Cardiff', *Mail*, 20 August 2014, https://www.dailymail.co.uk/sport/football/article-2730307/Malky-Mackay-Iain-Moody-investigated-FA-sexist-racist-homophobic-text-messages-time-Cardiff.html; on the FA ruling: McGowan, A., 'FA's decision on Malky Mackay texts sends "shocking message"', BBC Sport, 17 July 2015, https://www.bbc.co.uk/sport/football/33572770

6. Quinn, B., 'Hate crimes double in five years in England and Wales', *Guardian*, 15 October 2020, https://www.theguardian.com/society/2019/oct/15/hate-crimes-double-england-wales

7. 'Reporting Statistics', Kick it Out, 2024, https://www.kickitout.org/reporting-statistics

8. @sterling7, Instagram, 9 December 2018, https://www.instagram.com/sterling7/p/BrKYvF3gH9e/?img_index=1

9. Fifield, D., 'Chelsea fans barred from game after "bomber" chants against Mohamed Salah', *Guardian*, 11 April 2019, https://www.theguardian.com/football/2019/apr/11/chelsea-fans-barred-bomber-chants-mo-salah; PA Media, 'West Ham "appalled" by footage of fans singing antisemitic song on flight', *Guardian*, 5 November 2021, https://www.theguardian.com/football/2021/nov/05/west-ham-left-appalled-by-footage-of-fans-singing-antisemitic-song

10. Hughes, G., 'Sky Data poll: Nine in 10 football fans have witnessed racism', Sky News, 11 February 2019, https://news.sky.com/story/

sky-data-poll-90-of-football-fans-have-witnessed-racism-at-a-game-11631891; Sridhar, S., 'Racist abuse will not deter me, says Kilmarnock boss Alex Dyer', *Independent*, 31 December 2020, https://www.independent.co.uk/sport/football/scottish/kilmarnock-manager-alex-dyer-racist-abuse-b1780755.html

11. Ingle, S., 'Sophie Jones quits football after racial abuse ban and Sheffield United exit', *Guardian*, 20 March 2019, https://www.theguardian.com/football/2019/mar/20/sophie-jones-sheffield-united-tottenham-renee-hector

12. 'Racism "creeping back" in Scottish football, says Kevin Harper', BBC Sport, 16 October 2019, https://www.bbc.co.uk/sport/football/50066351

13. Fletcher, A., 'Racism in football: "Problems still exist at grassroots level"', BBC Sport, 16 November 2012, https://www.bbc.co.uk/sport/football/20365922

14. Cohen, S., 'Discrimination in football "like wild west" at grassroots level', *Guardian*, 24 July 2019, https://www.theguardian.com/football/2019/jul/24/reports-of-discrimination-in-football-rise-by-a-third-show-new-figures-kick-it-out-racism

15. 'Racism pushes youth football coach to verge of quitting', BBC News, 10 December 2018, https://www.bbc.co.uk/news/uk-england-leeds-46507244

16. Scott, S. 'Exclusive: 79% of Asian grassroots football players subjected to racist abuse', ITV News, 1 April 2019, https://www.itv.com/news/2019-04-01/exclusive-79-of-black-and-asian-grassroots-football-players-subjected-to-racist-abuse

17. 'Child footballers "frequently racially abused", report states', BBC News, 2 September 2019, https://www.bbc.co.uk/news/uk-england-leicestershire-49525172

18. 'Wythenshawe Town manager James Kinsey suspended over "racism" walk-off', Sky Sports, 9 April 2019, https://www.skysports.com/football/news/11095/11688986/wythenshawe-town-manager-james-kinsey-suspended-over-racism-walk-off

19. Steinberg, J., 'From parks to Premier League: the shocking scale of racism in English football', Guardian, 12 April 2019, https://www.theguardian.com/football/2019/apr/12/racism-english-football-parks-premier-league-special-investigation

20. 'Mark Sampson, former England Women coach, apologises to Aluko and Spence', *Guardian*, 21 January 2019, https://www.theguardian.com/football/2019/jan/21/mark-sampson-england-women-apologies-eni-aluko-drew-spence

21. Digital, Culture, Media and Sport Committee, Oral evidence: Sport Governance, HC 320, 18 October 2017, https://committees. parliament.uk/oralevidence/7044/pdf/

22. Ingle, S., 'Peter Beardsley barred from football for seven months over racist language', *Guardian*, 19 September 2019, https://www. theguardian.com/football/2019/sep/19/ peter-beardsley-banned-football-seven-months-racist-language

23. Hunter, A., 'Former Crawley manager John Yems has ban for racism extended to three years', *Guardian*, 19 April 2023, https:// www.theguardian.com/football/2023/apr/19/john-yems-racism-ban-extended-to-three-years-former-crawley-manager-fa-appeal

24. Belam, M., 'Alan Sugar under fire over "racist" Senegal World Cup team tweet', *Guardian*, 20 June 2018, https://www.theguardian. com/uk-news/2018/jun/20/lord-sugar-under-fire-over-racist-senegal-world-cup-team-tweet

25. Brewin, J., 'Former Norwich sporting director denounced for "callous" remarks about black footballers', *Guardian*, 24 March 2024, https://www.theguardian.com/football/2024/mar/24/ former-norwich-sporting-director-denounced-for-callous-remarks-about-black-footballers

26. Fisher, F., 'BBC pundit taken off air after criticism of Derby's "young black lads"', *Guardian*, 16 February 2024, https://www. theguardian.com/football/2020/feb/16/bbc-pundits-derby-young-black-lads-sparks-call-for-action-craig-ramage-max-lowe-kick-it-out

27. Storey, D., 'Fans' phallic obsession with their own teams' players is racist – and also extremely weird', *Independent*, 22 November 2019, https://inews.co.uk/sport/football/football-opinion/ divock-origi-romelu-lukaku-bambo-diaby-ivan-toney-yerry-mina-racist-fan-chants-penis-size-kick-it-out-366063

28. Campbell, P. I., & Bebb, L. (2020), 'He is like a gazelle (when he runs)': (re)constructing race and nation in match-day commentary at the men's 2018 FIFA World Cup', *Sport in Society*, 25(1), pp. 144–62.

29. Nakrani, S., 'Groundbreaking report reveals racial bias in English football commentary', *Guardian*, 29 June 2020, https://www. theguardian.com/football/2020/jun/29/groundbreaking-report-reveals-racial-bias-in-english-football-commentary; the full report 'Racial Bias in Football Commentary (Study): The Pace and Power Effect' can be read here: https://runrepeat.com/racial-bias-study-soccer

30. Campbell, P.I. and Maloney, M., 2022. 'White digital footballers can't jump': (re)constructions of race in FIFA 20', *Soccer & Society*, 23(8), pp. 894–908.

31. 'DFLA vs FLAF: The football lads tackling extremism', BBC News, 21 July 2019, https://www.bbc.co.uk/news/av/stories-49050323

32. Hitchenor, T., 'Premier League players to boycott social media in protest at racist abuse', *Guardian*, 18 April 2019, https://www.theguardian.com/football/2019/apr/18/premier-league-players-boycott-social-media-protest-racial-abuse

33. Bate, A., 'Meet Punjabi Wolves, the fans' group bringing culture and noise to Molineux', *Guardian*, 15 December 2015, https://www.theguardian.com/football/when-saturday-comes-blog/2015/dec/15/punjabi-wolves-fans-group-culture-molineux

34. Famurema, J., '"Football should be an extended family": the fans turning the tide on racism', *Guardian*, 12 September 2020, https://www.theguardian.com/football/2020/sep/12/football-should-be-an-extended-family-the-fans-turning-the-tide-on-racism

35. Ibid.

36. Gayle, H., 'Why I showed the red card to an MBE', *Guardian*, 15 August 2016, https://www.theguardian.com/commentisfree/2016/aug/15/howard-gayle-mbe-liverpool-first-black-footballer

37. Nakrani, S., 'Stan Collymore: "The thing white men hate most is outspoken black men"', *Guardian*, 10 June 2018, https://www.theguardian.com/football/2018/jun/10/stan-collymore-the-thing-white-men-hate-the-most-is-outspoken-black-men

38. 'Rio Ferdinand: We've become complacent with racism … FIFA and UEFA have let us down by failing to eradicate it from football', *Mail Online*, 22 February 2015, https://www.dailymail.co.uk/sport/football/article-2963763/Rio-Ferdinand-ve-complacent-racism-FIFA-UEFA-let-failing-eradicate-football.html

39. BBC Sport, 'Raheem Sterling: FA shows support after gun tattoo row', BBC Sport, 29 May 2018, https://www.bbc.co.uk/sport/football/44289119

40. Sterling, R., 'Raheem Sterling: I don't want the next generation to suffer like me', *The Times*, 23 April 2019, https://www.thetimes.com/sport/football/article/raheem-sterling-i-dont-want-the-next-generation-to-suffer-like-me-5ng7tpqkq

41. Gibson, O., 'Les Ferdinand says entrenched racism curbs opportunities for BME coaches', *Guardian*, 18 March 2019, https://

www.theguardian.com/football/2015/mar/18/les-ferdinand-entrenched-racism-curbs-opportunities-bme-coaches

4. Duty of Care

1. Riach, J., 'Revealed: Premier League clubs charge up to £600 for children to be mascots', *Guardian*, 18 December 2018, https://www.theguardian.com/football/2014/dec/18/premier-league-clubs-charge-600-children-mascots

2. 'Craig Bellamy apologises after Cardiff bullying investigation', Sky Sports News, 25 October 2019, https://www.skysports.com/football/news/11704/11844962/craig-bellamy-apologises-after-cardiff-city-bullying-investigation; Taylor, L., 'Peter Beardsley seeks "new challenge" after leaving role at Newcastle', *Guardian*, 6 March 2019, https://www.theguardian.com/football/2019/mar/06/peter-beardsley-newcastle

3. Ingle, S., 'Peter Beardsley barred from football for seven months over racist language', *Guardian*, 19 September 2019, https://www.theguardian.com/football/2019/sep/19/peter-beardsley-banned-football-seven-months-racist-language

4. Taylor, D., 'Graham Rix and Gwyn Williams accused of racism and bullying while at Chelsea', *Guardian*, 12 January 2019, https://www.theguardian.com/football/2018/jan/12/graham-rix-gwyn-williams-accused-racism-bullying-chelsea

5. PA Media, 'Chelsea settle a High Court case brought by four former youth team players over alleged historical racist abuse', Sky Sports News, 7 February 2022, https://www.skysports.com/football/news/11095/12535416/chelsea-settle-a-high-court-case-brought-by-four-former-youth-team-players-over-alleged-historical-racist-abuse

6. Premier Skills Academy, 'Are academies restricting creativity?', https://www.premierskillsacademy.com/news/20-are-academies-restricting-creativity

7. Cunningham, S., '97% of Premier League academy players never play a minute in top flight, new analysis reveals', *iNews*, 7 January 2022, https://inews.co.uk/sport/football/premier-league-academy-players-figures-appearances-numbers-1387302

8. Calvin, Michael (2017), *No Hunger in Paradise: The Players. The Journey. The Dream*, Random House.

9. McGlinchey, T.R., Saward, C., Healy, L.C. and Sarkar, M. (2022), '"From everything to nothing in a split second": Elite youth

players' experiences of release from professional football academies', *Frontiers in Sports and Active Living*, 4, p. 941482.

10. Blakelock, D., Chen, M. and Prescott, T. (2019), 'Coping and psychological distress in elite adolescent soccer players following professional academy deselection', *Journal of Sport Behavior*, 41(1).

11. McGinty-Minister, K.L., Champ, F.M., Eubank, M.E., Littlewood, M.A. and Whitehead, A. (2023), 'Stakeholder Conceptualizations of mental health and mental illness in English Premier League football academies', *Managing Sport and Leisure*, pp. 1–20.

12. Calvin, 2017.

13. Conn, D., 'Child abuse in sport and the progress made towards eradicating it', *Guardian*, 29 December 2016, https://www.theguardian.com/football/2016/dec/29/fa-child-protection-work-celia-brackenridge

14. BBC News, 'Chelsea FC "paid me £50,000 over abuse"', BBC News, 2 September 2016, https://www.bbc.co.uk/news/uk-38179882

15. 'Dispatches Soccer's Foul Play Repaired', YouTube, 3 December 2016, https://www.youtube.com/watch?v=fB7mbQwhn2k

16. Alexander, K., Stafford, A. and Lewis, R. (2011), 'The experiences of children participating in organised sport in the UK', London, NSPCC, https://www.pure.ed.ac.uk/ws/files/7971883/experiences_children_sport_main_report_wdf85014.pdf

17. Morris, S., 'Damning report reveals Southampton FC's 70s and 80s sexual abuse failures', *Guardian*, 26 November 2016, https://www.theguardian.com/football/2021/nov/26/southampton-historical-sexual-abuse-failures-revealed-in-damning-report-bob-higgins-barnados

18. Taylor, D., 'Andy Woodward: "It was the softer, weaker boys he targeted"', *Guardian*, 16 November 2016, https://www.theguardian.com/football/2016/nov/16/andy-woodward

19. Conn, D., '"You can't carry it": the victims of football's darkest scandal on the power of speaking out', *Guardian*, 21 March 2021, https://www.theguardian.com/football/2021/mar/21/you-cant-carry-it-how-the-victims-of-footballs-darkest-scandal-found-peace-by-speaking-out

5. 'You Must be Joking, Ref'

1. Nakrani, S., '"Love-hate mentality" led to Premier League manager changes, says Lampard', *Guardian*, 25 April 2023, https://www.

theguardian.com/football/2023/apr/25/love-hate-mentality-has-led-to-manager-changes-says-frank-lampard

2. Jackson, B., 'Jermaine Jenas apologises after posting criticism about referee Rob Jones', BBC Sport, 25 September 2023, https://www.bbc.co.uk/sport/football/66914216

3. Lewis, J. (1906), 'The much abused referee', *The Book of Football: A Complete History and Record of the Association and Rugby Games*, pp. 263–64, The Amalgamated Press Ltd.

4. Webb, T. (2016), 'Knight of the Whistle': WP Harper and the Impact of the Media on an Association Football Referee. *The International Journal of the History of Sport*, 33(3), pp. 306–24.

5. Ungoed-Thomas, J., 'Elite football in England has 40 referees – all white. Why don't black officials get top jobs?', *Guardian*, 20 November 2021, https://www.theguardian.com/world/2021/nov/20/elite-football-in-england-has-40-referees-all-white-why-dont-black-officials-get-top-jobs

6. Ungoed-Thomas, J., 'New racism scandal rocks English football', *Observer*, 20 November 2021, https://www.theguardian.com/world/2021/nov/20/new-racism-scandal-rocks-english-football

7. Press Association, 'Notts County owner rips into "scandalous" John Sheridan', *Guardian*, 14 March 2017, https://www.theguardian.com/football/2017/mar/14/notts-county-owner-alan-hardy-rips-into-scandalous-former-manager-john-sheridan

8. Talk Sport, '"It's part of the game" – John Terry defends Chelsea reaction to Zlatan Ibrahimovic challenge', Talk Sport, 12 March 2015, https://talksport.com/football/252602/its-part-game-john-terry-defends-chelsea-reaction-zlatan-ibrahimovic-challenge-150312139497/

9. Cleland, J., O'Gorman, J. and Webb, T. (2018), 'Respect? An investigation into the experience of referees in association football', *International Review for the Sociology of Sport*, 53(8), pp. 960–74.

10. Press Association, 'Schoolgirl football referee asks parents to stop verbal abuse', *Guardian*, 7 September 2015, https://www.theguardian.com/uk-news/2015/sep/07/schoolgirl-football-ref-asks-parents-to-stop-verbal-abuse

11. Keogh, F., 'Referee abuse: Hundreds tell of safety fears at grassroots level', BBC Sport, 14 February 2023, https://www.bbc.co.uk/sport/football/64584541

12. BBC News, 'Parents' abuse at Surrey football matches "could kill"', BBC News, 24 February 2016, https://www.bbc.co.uk/news/uk-england-35649165

13. Rendell, S. and Short, M., 'Referee abuse: FA issued 380 bans for grassroots match official attacks last season', *BBC Sport*, 11 October 2022, https://www.bbc.co.uk/sport/football/61425471

14. Izzard, B., 'Liverpool County FA lack support for grassroots officials, says referee', *Metrosportlive*, 21 November 2022, https://merseysportlive.co.uk/2022/11/21/liverpool-county-fa-lack-support-for-grassroots-officials-says-referee/

15. Ref Chat, 'Northumberland Football League – statement about continuing misconduc', Ref Chat, 14 November 2023, https://refchat.co.uk/threads/northumberland-football-league-statement-about-continuing-misconduct.22747/

16. Taylor, J. (1976), *Jack Taylor – World Soccer Referee*, Pelham Books.

17. Tate, J., 'Footballers need to show referees some respect – we are in short supply', *Guardian*, 13 January 2022, https://www.theguardian.com/football/when-saturday-comes-blog/2022/jan/13/footballers-need-to-show-referees-some-respect-we-are-in-short-supply

18. Pavitt, M., '"I've had knives pulled on me. I've had death threats … and it's getting WORSE": Grassroots referees share their harrowing experiences as Mail Sport launches campaign to stop the abuse', *Daily Mail*, 21 November 2023, https://www.dailymail.co.uk/sport/football/article-12776551/Grassroots-referees-share-harrowing-experiences-Mail-Sport-launches-campaign-stop-abuse.html

19. Keogh, 2023.

20. Buckingham, P. et al., '"The only thing that hasn't happened yet is a referee getting murdered"', *Athletic*, 30 March 2023, https://www.nytimes.com/athletic/4360302/2023/03/30/investigation-grassroots-referees-abuse/

21. See FSA, 'National Supporters Survey 2017: more results', FSA, 3 August 2017, https://thefsa.org.uk/news/national-supporters-survey-2017-more-results/

22. Change.org, 'BAN ANTHONY TAYLOR FROM OFFICIATING CHELSEA GAMES', https://www.change.org/p/ban-anthony-taylor-from-officiating-chelsea-games

23. MacInnes, P., 'VAR given thumbs down by fans for Premier League study', *Guardian*, 2 June 2021, https://www.theguardian.com/football/2021/jun/02/var-given-thumbs-down-by-fans-for-premier-league-study

24. Taylor, 1976.

6. Goodbye, Great Britain

1. Pearce, D., 'Out of touch and out of pocket – how the WRU has been surpassed by the FAW', *nation.cymru*, 28 March 2022, https://nation.cymru/opinion/out-of-touch-and-out-of-pocket-how-the-wru-has-been-surpassed-by-the-faw/

2. Owens, D., 'One night in Toulouse – when Welsh football and music collided beautifully', *nation.cymru*, 16 June 2021, https://nation.cymru/culture/one-night-in-toulouse-when-welsh-football-and-music-collided-beautifully/

3. James, E., 'For Wales fans, the Qatar World Cup is bleak and brilliant all at once', *Guardian*, 24 November 2022, https://www.theguardian.com/football/blog/2022/nov/24/for-wales-fans-the-qatar-world-cup-is-bleak-and-brilliant-all-at-once

4. Cross, T., 'The hope doesn't kill you', *Medium*, 1 July 2017, https://medium.com/@tristandross/the-hope-doesnt-kill-you-fefb53183738

5. Hamman, S., 'Welsh people must be united', *Walesonline*, 2 December 2003, https://www.walesonline.co.uk/sport/football/football-news/welsh-people-must-be-united-2456389

6. Gordon, G., 'Northern Ireland football: Sporting identity is a game of two halves', BBC News, 8 October 2015, https://www.bbc.co.uk/news/uk-northern-ireland-34480101

7. Hargie, O. et al. (2015), 'Social Exclusion and Sport in Northern Ireland', Ulster University, https://niopa.qub.ac.uk/bitstream/NIOPA/1446/1/social-exclusion-and-sport-in-ni-exec-summary.pdf

8. Walker, M., 'Christmas on the Irish border: How one of Brexit's biggest issues is playing out in football', *Independent*, 21 December 2017, https://www.independent.co.uk/sport/football/news/brexit-irish-border-how-one-of-biggest-issues-is-playing-out-warrenpoint-town-a8123261.html

9. 'Joe Gorman: Historical sectarian tweet was "grave error of judgement"', BBC Sport, 13 January 2022, https://www.bbc.co.uk/sport/football/59987746; Bradfield, P., 'Coalisland Athletic: IFA investigates video of pro-IRA chanting on team bus', *NewsLetter*, 3 May 2022, https://www.newsletter.co.uk/news/politics/coalisland-athletic-ifa-investigates-video-of-pro-ira-chanting-on-team-bus-3678573

10. Power, J., '"We hate Catholics" chant by Northern Ireland fans condemned by IFA', *Irish Times*, 26 March 2019, https://www.irishtimes.com/news/social-affairs/we-hate-catholics-chant-by-northern-ireland-fans-condemned-by-ifa-1.3839210

11. 'Youths targeted at football match in north Belfast being treated as sectarian hate crime say PSNI', *Belfast Telegraph*, 4 September 2021, https://www.belfasttelegraph.co.uk/news/northern-ireland/youths-targeted-at-football-match-in-north-belfast-being-treated-as-sectarian-hate-crime-say-psni/40818615.html

12. Reid, K., 'Crumlin Star FC allege "torrent of sectarian abuse" directed at women and children during Islandmagee FC match', *Belfast Telegraph*, 5 February 2023, https://www.belfasttelegraph.co.uk/sport/football/crumlin-star-fc-allege-torrent-of-sectarian-abuse-directed-at-women-and-children-during-islandmagee-fc-match/162904339.html

13. McKeown, G., 'DUP MLA criticised after saying Cliftonville "got what they deserved" for anthem protest', *Irish News*, 7 May 2018, https://www.irishnews.com/news/northernirelandnews/2018/05/07/news/dup-mla-criticised-after-saying-cliftonville-got-what-they-deserved-for-anthem-protest-1323100/

14. @JamieBrysonCPNI, Twitter/X, 5 May 2018, https://x.com/JamieBrysonCPNI/status/992787949631700992

15. 'Michelle O'Neill has attended first Northern Ireland game at Windsor Park', BBC News, 27 February 2024, https://www.bbc.co.uk/news/uk-northern-ireland-68418130

16. 'Linfield to investigate Carrick claim of "vile" sectarian abuse during game with Linfield', BBC Sport, 7 March 2020, https://www.bbc.co.uk/sport/football/51785659

17. 'Portadown FC: Bans and suspended sentences for rioters', BBC News, 15 January 2020, https://www.bbc.co.uk/news/uk-northern-ireland-51127953

18. Moore, S., 'Coleraine football hoods team up with West Ham firm ahead of final with Cliftonville', *Sunday World*, 13 March 2022, https://www.sundayworld.com/news/northern-ireland-news/coleraine-football-hoods-team-up-with-west-ham-firm-ahead-of-final-with-cliftonville/41439782.html

19. Moore, S., 'Sectarian Coleraine FC yobs linked to West Ham firm out to wreak havoc at Cliftonville cup tie', *Sunday World*, 1 February 2023, https://www.sundayworld.com/news/northern-ireland-news/sectarian-coleraine-fc-yobs-linked-to-west-ham-firm-out-to-wreak-havoc-at-cliftonville-cup-tie/1021261454.html

20. 'Euro 2028: NI Supporters' Group questions legacy for football after Casement chosen as host stadium', BBC Sport, 10 October 2023, https://www.bbc.co.uk/sport/football/67068561

21. Murray, E., 'Scottish football told to innovate or risk ills turning terminal', *Guardian*, 18 December 2010, https://www.theguardian.com/football/2010/dec/18/scottish-football-review-henry-mcleish

22. Quoted in Wilson, R. (2012), *Inside the Divide: One City, Two Teams ... The Old Firm*, Canongate, pp. 200–1.

23. Williams, D.J., Neville, F.G., House, K. and Donnelly, P.D. (2013), 'Association between old firm football matches and reported domestic (violence) incidents in Strathclyde, Scotland', *Sage Open*, 3(3).

24. Lavalette, M. and Mooney, G. (2013), 'The Scottish state and the criminalisation of football fans: Michael Lavalette and Gerry Mooney consider football fandom and the "ultras" phenomenon', *Criminal Justice Matters*, 93(1), pp. 22–4; Atkinson, C. (2022), '"Football fans are not thugs": communication and the future of fan engagement in the policing of Scottish football', *Policing and Society*, 32(4), pp. 472–88; Atkinson, C., McBride, M. and Moore, A. (2021), 'Pitched! Informants and the covert policing of football fans in Scotland', *Policing and Society*, 31(7), pp. 863–77; Hamilton-Smith, N., McBride, M. and Atkinson, C. (2021), 'Lights, camera, provocation? Exploring experiences of surveillance in the policing of Scottish football', *Policing and Society*, 31(2), pp. 179–94.

25. Burnett, A. (2024), '"Brigate Verde ... a terrible beauty is born": an exploratory examination of the social leadership of the Green Brigade', *Soccer & Society*, 25(4–6), pp. 603–17.

26. 'Scottish independence: Alan Hansen leads group of football figures urging "patriotic Scots" to vote No', *Standard*, 6 September 2014, https://www.standard.co.uk/news/uk/scottish-independence-alan-hansen-leads-group-of-football-figures-urging-patriotic-scots-to-vote-no-9716221.html

27. Walker, A., '"HARROWING": Football commentator Archie Macpherson reveals Scottish independence referendum abuse was worse than anything experienced at Old Firm games', *Scottish Sun*, 2019, https://www.thescottishsun.co.uk/news/4749340/celtic-rangers-commentator-abuse-scottish-independence-worse-archie-macpherson/

28. Green, C., 'Scottish independence: Accusations of intimidation and violence fly in from supporters of both sides', *Independent*, 2 September 2014, https://www.independent.co.uk/news/uk/scottish-independence/scottish-independence-accusations-of-intimidation-and-violence-fly-in-from-supporters-of-both-sides-9704743.html

29. Whigham, S. and May, A. (2017), '"Sport for Yes?" The role of sporting issues in pro-independence political discourse during the Scottish independence referendum campaign', *International Journal of Sport Policy and Politics*, 9(3), pp. 557–72; Whigham, S., Kelly, J. and Bairner, A. (2021), 'Politics and football fandom in post-"indyref" Scotland: nationalism, unionism and stereotypes of the "Old Firm"', *British Politics*, 16(4), pp. 414–35.

30. Another attempt to break the deadlock has been the arrival of new, often foreign owners at the clubs that might plausibly challenge the Old Firm's hegemony. Aberdeen were bought by US-based Scottish businessman Dave Cormack, whose tenure has been marked by a succession of poor managerial choices and footballing decline. In 2019 Hibs were taken over by Peruvian-born American Ron Gordon and managed just one third-place league finish before his death in 2023. Dundee United were bought by American fossil-fuel magnate Mark Ogren, whose return on his £10 million investment and six managerial appointments in his first five years was to see the team promoted to the SPFL and qualify for Europe, only to then get relegated. Dundee were purchased by Texan duo Tim Keyes and John Nelms in 2013 and for about the same money they have had three promotions, two relegations and eight managers, and have never looked like challengers for the title.

31. 'How Uri Geller Became Chairman of North Berwick Team "The Lambies", A View From The Terrace', BBC Scotland, YouTube, 8 March 2023, https://www.youtube.com/watch?v=RhUgaM5pASQ

7. Which England Will Turn Up?

1. '"Fat Sam out" – West Ham fans hold up anti Sam Allardyce banner during West Brom loss', *Standard*, 26 April 2014, https://www.standard.co.uk/sport/fat-sam-out-west-ham-fans-hold-up-anti-sam-allardyce-banner-during-west-brom-loss-9292008.html; Fifield, D., 'Chelsea's Jose Mourinho says West Ham played "19th-century" football', *Guardian*, 30 January 2014, https://www.theguardian.com/football/2014/jan/30/jose-mourinho-19th-century-football-west-ham-allardyce.

2. 'Sam Allardyce, England Manager for Sale – Undercover Tapes', Daily Motion, https://www.dailymotion.com/video/x4uu14l

3. Ronay, B., 'Gareth Southgate: no star power, no magic bullet, but a man for the times', *Guardian*, 30 November 2016, https://www.

theguardian.com/football/2016/nov/30/gareth-southgate-england-manager-man-for-the-times

4. 'England seal World Cup place – but don't expect a long stay in Russia', *Week*, 6 October 2017, https://theweek.com/football/88841/england-seal-world-cup-place-but-don-t-expect-a-long-stay-in-russia

5. Kelner, M., 'Danny Rose opens up about depression after tragedy and tough year at Spurs', *Guardian*, 6 June 2018, https://www.theguardian.com/football/2018/jun/06/danny-rose-tells-family-not-travel-world-cup-player-racism-fears-abuse-england-football-team

6. Taylor, D., 'England delirium has Gareth Southgate and his tyros dreaming big', *Guardian*, 8 July 2018, https://www.theguardian.com/football/2018/jul/08/england-gareth-southgate-semi-final

7. Putin's performance can be seen at 'Even Putin knows it's coming home', @Joe, YouTube, 4 July 2018, https://www.youtube.com/watch?v=tZIH7WFA6WM

8. '#GarethSouthgateWould – England's manager takes social media by storm', BBC Sport, 4 July 2018, https://www.bbc.co.uk/sport/football/44718387

9. Taylor, D., 'England delirium has Gareth Southgate and his tyros dreaming big', *Guardian*, 2018.

10. BBC News, 'Stage actors rage at audience members watching World Cup on phones', BBC News, 5 July 2018, https://www.bbc.co.uk/news/entertainment-arts-44722812

11. 'English identity open to all, regardless of race, finds poll – and Three Lions is the symbol that unites us', British Futures, 9 June 2021, https://www.britishfuture.org/english-identity-open-football-unites/

12. Hundai, S., 'England may have lost but it gave us a sense of unity our political leaders have failed to do', *Open Democracy*, 17 July 2018, https://www.opendemocracy.net/en/opendemocracyuk/england-may-have-lost-but-it-gave-us-sense-of-unity-our-political-leaders-have-faile/

13. Evans, N., 'Millions of England fans to pull a sickie today after World Cup clash – and it'll cost us £500million', *Mirror*, 4 July 2018, https://www.mirror.co.uk/news/uk-news/millions-brits-pull-sickie-today-12850307

14. Fifield, D., 'England team "have created their own history", says Gareth Southgate', *Guardian*, 2018, https://www.theguardian.com/football/2018/jul/03/england-have-created-their-own-history-gareth-southgate-world-cup

15. Quoted in D. Winner (2024), *Excerpts from a New England*, Pitch Publishing, pp. 72–73.

8. From Lockdown to Meltdown

1. 'Dele Alli: Tottenham midfielder apologises for coronavirus "joke"', BBC Sport, 10 February 2020, https://www.bbc.co.uk/sport/football/51441898
2. Health and Social Care, and Science and Technology Committees, Coronavirus: Lessons Learned to Data, October 2021, p. 34, https://publications.parliament.uk/pa/cm5802/cmselect/cmsctech/92/9207.htm
3. Richards, D., 'Football Manager and My Mental Health', Gaming Respawn, 28 November 2020, https://gamingrespawn.com/features/51895/football-manager-and-my-mental-health/
4. Crawford, G., Fenton, A., Chadwick, S. and Lawrence, S. (2022), '"All Avatars Aren't We": Football and the experience of football-themed digital content during a global pandemic', *International Review for the Sociology of Sport*, 57(4), pp. 515–31.
5. 'Paul Scholes lockdown party claims prompt police visit', BBC News, 3 August 2020, https://www.bbc.co.uk/news/uk-england-manchester-53635942
6. McLaughlin, C., 'Coronavirus: "Hundreds" of five-a-side footballers flouting lockdown', BBC News, 1 July 2020, https://www.bbc.co.uk/news/uk-scotland-53247096
7. 'A lockdown football match took place on a golf course', *The Golf Business*, 19 November 2020, https://thegolfbusiness.co.uk/2020/11/a-lockdown-football-match-took-place-on-a-golf-course/
8. Parker, N., '"WE'VE BEEN RUMBLED": Football fans caught breaking Leicester lockdown after loudly cheering in Nottingham pub when Jamie Vardy scored', *Sun*, 5 July 2020, https://www.thesun.co.uk/news/12039295/football-fans-caught-breaking-leicester-lockdown/; Earnshaw, T., 'Football fans caught watching Leeds United game inside Dewsbury pub', *Dewsbury Reporter*, 25 February 2021, https://www.dewsburyreporter.co.uk/news/crime/football-fans-caught-watching-leeds-united-game-inside-dewsbury-pub-3147013
9. For example: 'Covid: "Horrified" police break up football match', BBC News, 23 February 2021, https://www.bbc.co.uk/news/uk-england-derbyshire-56161301; Meikle, B, 'FOOTIE FINE Lockdown Scotland: Two fined for flouting coronavirus rules with

11-a-side football match in Edinburgh', *Scottish Sun*, 21 February 2021, https://www.thescottishsun.co.uk/news/6717223/lockdown-scotland-fined-covid-rules-edinburgh-football/; Houston, S., 'Football pitches sealed-off as adults flout law and play organised matches', *Daily Record*, 4 February 2021, https://www.dailyrecord.co.uk/authors/paisley-daily-express/football-pitches-sealed-adults-flout-23440783

10. Rashford, M., 'Why I don't stick to football', *Spectator*, https://www.spectator.co.uk/article/why-i-dont-stick-to-football/

11. Ambrose, T., 'Tory MP who accused Marcus Rashford of "playing politics" has second job', *Guardian*, 11 November 2021, https://www.theguardian.com/politics/2021/nov/11/tory-mp-who-accused-marcus-rashford-of-playing-politics-has-second-job

12. Davies, C., 'Planes, trains and football games: Jonathan Van-Tam's best analogies', *Guardian*, 13 January 2022, https://www.theguardian.com/world/2022/jan/13/football-planes-and-trains-jonathan-van-tam-best-analogies

13. Haidt, J. (2024), *The Anxious Generation: How the Great Rewiring of Childhood Is Causing an Epidemic of Mental Illness*, Random House.

14. NHS England, 'Mental Health of Children and Young People in England 2022 – wave 3 follow up to the 2017 survey', https://digital.nhs.uk/data-and-information/publications/statistical/mental-health-of-children-and-young-people-in-england/2022-follow-up-to-the-2017-survey

15. Ames, N., 'Number of footballers with depression symptoms doubles during shutdown', *Guardian*, 20 April 2020, https://www.theguardian.com/football/2020/apr/20/number-of-footballers-with-depression-symptoms-doubles-during-shutdown-survey-fifpro-coronavirus

16. Cited in Sky Sports, 'Percentage of footballers reporting depression symptoms doubles, FIFPRO study finds', Sky Sports, 22 April 2020, https://www.skysports.com/football/news/11095/11975983/percentage-of-footballers-reporting-depression-symptoms-doubles-fifpro-study-finds

17. Kay, O., 'The tragedy of Jeremy Wisten and the lessons football has to learn', *Athletic*, 28 October 2020, https://www.nytimes.com/athletic/2161141/2020/10/27/jeremy-wisten-manchester-city/

18. 'Football's suicide secret', YouTube, 10 July 2013, https://www.youtube.com/watch?v=j4-DW65nn6g

19. Fisher, B., 'PFA study reveals 22% of members depressed or considered self-harm', *Guardian*, 19 May 2020, https://www.theguardian.com/football/2020/may/19/22-of-footballers-depressed-or-considered-self-harm-during-pandemic
20. Wood, S., Harrison, L.K. and Kucharska, J. (2017), 'Male professional footballers' experiences of mental health difficulties and help-seeking', *The Physician and Sportsmedicine*, 45(2), pp. 120–8.
21. Ibid.
22. 'Mental health problems in football', Fifpro, 7 February 2020, https://fifpro.org/en/supporting-players/health-and-performance/mental-health/mental-health-problems
23. Wood, S., Harrison, L.K. and Kucharska, J., 2017.
24. Grounds, B., 'Fabian Delph: Forgotten man answering Everton's midfield conundrum ahead of Manchester City return', Sky Sports, 21 November 2021, https://www.skysports.com/football/news/11096/12471548/fabian-delph-forgotten-man-answering-evertons-midfield-conundrum-ahead-of-manchester-city-return
25. Vidgen, B. et al., 'Tracking abuse on Twitter against football players in the 2021–22 Premier League Season', Alan Turing Institute, 2022, https://www.turing.ac.uk/news/publications/tracking-abuse-twitter-against-football-players-2021-22-premier-league-season
26. @MarcusRashford, Twitter/X, 25 April 2024, https://x.com/marcusrashford/status/1783641291965820954
27. Bradshaw, J., 'Dele Alli: Sleeping pill addiction "widespread" in football, says psychotherapist', BBC Sport, 14 July 2023, https://www.bbc.co.uk/sport/football/66199285; PA Media, 'Addiction to sleeping tablets a big problem in football, says Ryan Cresswell', *Guardian*, 10 August 2022, https://www.theguardian.com/football/2022/aug/10/addiction-to-sleeping-tablets-a-big-problem-in-football-says-ryan-cresswell
28. Carosella, V., 'Depression, Anxiety, Suicide: Mental Health Issues Plaguing Football', *Forbes*, 2 November 2023, https://www.forbes.com/sites/vitascarosella/2023/11/02/depression-anxiety-suicide-mental-health-issues-plaguing-football/
29. Sky Sports, 'Steven Reid: Coping with anxiety and panic attacks as a Premier League player and why I want to help others', *Sky Sports*, 20 July 2022, https://www.skysports.com/football/news/11095/12654532/steven-reid-coping-with-anxiety-and-panic-attacks-as-a-premier-league-player-and-why-i-want-to-help-others; Sordell, M.,

'Ex footballer, Marvin Sordell, on how he overcame his darkest days', BBC One, https://www.bbc.co.uk/programmes/articles/4BVYxcP5Bmd8mPNgrj2sCq4/ex-footballer-marvin-sordell-on-how-he-overcame-his-darkest-days

30. 'West Ham's Michail Antonio reveals he is having therapy after "disliking football"', *Telegraph*, 16 May 2024, https://www.telegraph.co.uk/football/2024/05/16/west-ham-michail-antonio-therapy-disliking-football/

31. Carmody, S. et al. (2022), 'Health conditions among retired professional footballers: a scoping review', *BMJ Open Sport & Exercise Medicine* 8(2), e001196, https://bmjopensem.bmj.com/content/8/2/e001196

32. Gernon, A. (2016), *Retired: What Happens to Footballers When the Game's Up*, Pitch Publishing.

33. Morris, S., 'Heading the ball killed striker', *Guardian*, 12 November 2022, https://www.theguardian.com/uk/2002/nov/12/football.stevenmorris; 'Football and dementia: Alan Jarvis' death "caused by heading balls"', BBC News, 15 October 2020, https://www.bbc.co.uk/news/uk-wales-54561861

34. Gernon, (2016).

35. Conn, D., 'Footballers who once earned millions face penury over tax demands', *Guardian*, 23 January 2015, https://www.theguardian.com/football/2015/jan/23/footballers-tax-demands-hmrc

36. Tracey, D., 'Premier League's Shocking Manager History: 13 Managers Sacked in 2022/23 – Who's Next to Go?', olbg, 30 September 2023, https://www.olbg.com/blogs/football-manager-length-service

37. Calvin, M., *State of Play: Under the Skin of the Modern Game*, Arrow Books, 2019

38. Ibid.

39. Whitehead, J., '"Frightening stress" of management: An unprecedented invincible season is on', *Athletic*, 10 May 2024, https://www.nytimes.com/athletic/5484705/2024/05/10/the-athletic-fc-frightening-stress-of-management-an-unprecedented-invincible-season-is-on/#

40. Calvin, 2017.

9. Taking the Knee

1. Baker, M., 'Former Bristol City and Fulham defender Liam Rosenior backs toppling of Edward Colston statue', *Bristol Post*, 8 June 2020, https://www.bristolpost.co.uk/sport/football/football-news/former-bristol-city-fulham-midfielder-4203320; @rioferdy5, Instagram, 6 June 2020, https://www.instagram.com/rioferdy5/p/CBGjuqIjdtO/?img_index=1; 'George Floyd death: Aston Villa's Tyrone Mings joins Black Lives Matter protest in Birmingham', BBC Sport, 5 June 2020, https://www.bbc.co.uk/sport/52938082

2. 'Black Lives Matter: Cenotaph protesters "protect" war memorial', BBC News, 13 June 2020, https://www.bbc.co.uk/news/uk-england-bristol-53034357

3. 'Burnley "ashamed and embarrassed" by banner flown above Etihad Stadium during Man City game', BBC Sport, 23 June 2020, https://www.bbc.co.uk/sport/football/53145201

4. Unwin, W., 'FA and EFL condemn Millwall fans for booing as players take a knee', *Guardian*, 5 December 2020, https://www.theguardian.com/football/2020/dec/05/returning-fans-boo-as-millwall-and-derby-take-the-knee; https://www.businessinsider.com/colchester-robbie-cowling-refund-tickets-fans-who-boo-taking-knee-2020-12

5. MacInnes, P., 'FA chairman Greg Clarke apologises after using the term "coloured"', *Guardian*, 10 November 2020, https://www.theguardian.com/football/2020/nov/10/fa-chairman-greg-clarke-forced-to-apologise-after-using-the-term-coloured

6. Ingle, S., 'Wilfried Zaha declares he will stop taking a knee and instead "stand tall"', *Guardian*, 18 February 2021, https://www.theguardian.com/football/2021/feb/18/wilfried-zaha-declares-he-will-stop-taking-a-knee-crystal-palace

7. 'Reporting Statistics, 2023/24', Kick It Out, https://www.kickitout.org/reporting-statistics

8. Frame, N., 'Racist Leeds United fan told to "get a new hobby" after 10-year football ban', *Yorkshire Evening Post*, 16 July 2023, https://www.yorkshireeveningpost.co.uk/news/crime/racist-leeds-united-fan-told-to-get-a-new-hobby-after-10-year-football-ban-4219565

9. 'Sheffield man sentenced for racist gesture at footballer Kasey Palmer', BBC News, 20 May 2024, https://www.bbc.co.uk/news/uk-england-south-yorkshire-69038897; Parker, S., 'Alleged racist incident stops Bantams game with Wimbledon', *Telegraph and*

Argus, 3 February 2024, https://www.thetelegraphandargus.co.uk/sport/sportlatest/24095748.alleged-racist-incident-stops-bantams-game-wimbledon/; 'Juninho Bacuna: Fan arrested on suspicion of racially abusing Birmingham City midfielder', BBC Sport, 7 February 2024, https://www.bbc.co.uk/sport/football/68230635

10. Brewin, J., 'Ivan Toney reveals racist abuse on social media after Brentford win', *Guardian*, 15 October 2022, https://www.theguardian.com/football/2022/oct/15/ivan-toney-reveals-racist-abuse-on-instagram-after-brentford-win

11. Ibbertson, C., 'One in four ethnic minority football fans have been racially abused on social media', YouGov, 25 August 2021, https://yougov.co.uk/sport/articles/37732-ethnic-minority-football-fans-racism-social-media

12. Wolstenholme, L., 'Online hate: South Asian fans on facing "firing squad of racist abuse"', BBC News, 1 March 2024, https://www.bbc.co.uk/news/newsbeat-68085784

13. Halle-Richards, S., 'Far-right nationalist group linked to banner flown over Etihad stadium during Man City match – as residents also voice concern over "terrifying" similar leaflets they've had through the door', *Manchester Evening News*, 11 April 2022, https://www.manchestereveningnews.co.uk/news/greater-manchester-news/far-right-nationalist-group-linked-23654543

14. Brown, M., '"Serious disrepute": Grimsby Town fans react after Boris Johnson wears club's hat', *Guardian*, 7 December 2023, https://www.theguardian.com/uk-news/2023/dec/07/boris-johnson-brought-grimsby-into-disrepute-by-wearing-towns-football-club-hat

15. 'Jacob Rees-Mogg recites John Barnes' World in Motion rap in the House of Commons', SkySports News, YouTube, 8 July 2021, https://www.youtube.com/watch?v=d9shjGM5Dm8

16. Mail, H., 'What Liz Truss said about Leeds United legend Don Revie as PM equals Brian Clough', *Yorkshire Evening Post*, 20 October 2022, https://www.yorkshireeveningpost.co.uk/sport/football/leeds-united/what-liz-truss-said-about-leeds-united-legend-don-revie-as-pm-equals-brian-clough-3887934

17. Burrows, B., 'Russell Martin has "no interest" as Rishi Sunak watches Southampton win', *Athletic*, 29 December 2023, https://www.nytimes.com/athletic/5168765/2023/12/29/rishi-sunak-southampton-russell-martin/

18. Syzmanski, S., *Black Representation in English Professional Football: A Statistical Analysis*, Black Footballers Partnership,

2022, https://api.blackfootballerspartnership.com/wp-content/uploads/2022/02/BFP-Stefan-Szymanski-16th-Feb.pdf

19. Howell, A., 'Les Ferdinand: FA diversity code "made no difference" in helping black players get jobs in football', BBC Sport, 19 October 2022, https://www.bbc.co.uk/sport/football/63307161

20. Syzmanski, 2023.

21. 'Football management for black former players is "all snakes and no ladders"', BBC Sport, 19 March 2024, https://www.bbc.co.uk/sport/football/68584776

22. Steinberg, J., 'From parks to Premier League: the shocking scale of racism in English football', *Guardian*, 12 April 2019, https://www.theguardian.com/football/2019/apr/12/racism-english-football-parks-premier-league-special-investigation

23. Ibid.

10. The Silence of the Stands

1. Baldwin, A., 'Play your part, health minister tells Premier League stars', Reuters, 3 April 2020, https://www.reuters.com/article/sports/play-your-part-health-minister-tells-premier-league-stars-idUSKBN21K2AN/

2. 'Danny Rose Part 1 – The Lockdown Tactics', The Lockdown tactics, YouTube, 19 May 2020, https://www.youtube.com/watch?v=zTZb-5qiiaE

3. 'Premier League players are being treated like "lab rats" and "guinea pigs", Danny Rose claims', *Independent*, 19 May 2020, https://www.independent.co.uk/sport/football/premier-league/danny-rose-newcastle-united-lab-rats-guinea-pigs-coronavirus-tests-a9522596.html

4. Allen, B., 'Meet the man who plays crowd noise sounds on a drum machine for Sky Sports Football', *GQ*, 10 July 2020, https://www.gq-magazine.co.uk/sport/article/artificial-crowd-noises

5. Leitner, M.C. and Richlan, F. (2021), 'No fans–no pressure: referees in professional football during the COVID-19 pandemic', *Frontiers in Sports and Active Living*, 3, p. 720488; McCarrick, D., Bilalic, M., Neave, N. and Wolfson, S. (2021), 'Home advantage during the COVID-19 pandemic: Analyses of European football leagues', *Psychology of Sport and Exercise*, 56, p. 102013; Tilp, M. and Thaller, S. (2020), 'Covid-19 has turned home advantage into home disadvantage in the German Soccer Bundesliga', *Frontiers in Sports and Active Living*, 2, p. 593499;

Leitner, M.C., Daumann, F., Follert, F. and Richlan, F. (2023), 'The cauldron has cooled down: a systematic literature review on home advantage in football during the COVID-19 pandemic from a socio-economic and psychological perspective', *Management Review Quarterly*, 73(2), pp. 605–33.

6. Caselli, M., Falco, P. and Mattera, G. (2023), 'When the stadium goes silent: How crowds affect the performance of discriminated groups', *Journal of Labor Economics*, 41(2), pp. 431–51.

7. 'Leeds police officers injured as fans leave piles of rubbish', BBC News, 20 July 2020, https://www.bbc.co.uk/news/uk-england-leeds-53470116

8. Cited in FSA, 'The return of fans and what it means', FSA, 3 December 2020, https://thefsa.org.uk/news/the-return-of-fans-and-what-it-means/

9. 'Rangers crowds march on Glasgow city centre after title win', BBC News, 21 May 2021, https://www.bbc.co.uk/news/uk-scotland-glasgow-west-57127094

10. Campbell, P., '"I won't be as passionate as before": how sports fans changed in lockdown', *Guardian*, 5 June 2020, https://www.theguardian.com/sport/2020/jun/05/passionate-how-lockdown-has-changed-sports-fans-football

11. Hampson, A., '"Like missing a tooth": Football fans revel in return to stadiums as national lockdown ends', *Independent*, 3 December 2020, https://www.independent.co.uk/sport/football/fans-return-stadiums-tickets-b1765576.html

12. 'Fans return: "It was like being with family"', BBC Sport, 24 August 2021, https://www.bbc.co.uk/sport/articles/cl0qxkp0lweo

13. 'Crowds return to football: Your stories from a new season with full stadiums', BBC Sport, 24 August 2021, https://www.bbc.co.uk/sport/football/58231102

14. Ibid.

11. A Crisis of Confidence

1. Cited in Evans, T., 'Football on the front line in the Covid culture war', *Independent*, 23 December 2021, https://www.independent.co.uk/sport/football/covid-jurgen-klopp-liverpool-le-tissier-b1981230.html

2. Beer, T., 'Conspiracy Blames Christian Eriksen's Collapse On Covid Vaccine – But He Hasn't Even Been Vaccinated', *Forbes*, 14 June 2021, https://www.forbes.com/sites/tommybeer/2021/06/14/

conspiracy-blames-christian-eriksens-collapse-to-covid-vaccine-but-he-hasnt-even-been-vaccinated/

3. Badshah, N., 'Anti-vaxxers serving "legal papers" to Alan Shearer go to wrong address', *Guardian*, 23 December 2021, https://www.theguardian.com/uk-news/2021/dec/23/anti-vaccine-protesters-alan-shearer-booster-jab-wrong-address

4. Video at Press Association, 'Watch Jurgen Klopp's powerful message on vaccines in full', *This is Anfield*, 3 October 2021, https://www.thisisanfield.com/2021/10/watch-jurgen-klopps-powerful-message-on-vaccines-in-full/

5. Keane, D., 'Sajid Javid "disappointed" as several England footballers "refuse to take Covid vaccine"', *Independent*, 2021, https://www.independent.co.uk/sport/football/sajid-javid-england-footballers-vaccine-b1931157.html

6. Hughes, M., 'Football's vaccine crisis: Two thirds of top-flight players are not jabbed … Stars are polluting dressing rooms spouting Covid anti-vaxx theories about Bill Gates, infertility and using VITAMINS!', *Daily Mail*, 1 October 2021, https://www.dailymail.co.uk/sport/football/article-10047239/SPECIAL-REPORT-Footballs-vaccine-problem-laid-bare-two-thirds-flight-stars-not-jabbed.html

7. Long, D., 'West Ham's Matt Jones offers an insight into nutrition at a Premier League club', SkySports, 1 October 2022, https://www.skysports.com/football/news/11685/12705213/west-hams-matt-jones-offers-an-insight-into-nutrition-at-a-premier-league-club

8. Pearce, J., '"We have so much information about our players, we know them inside out" – Liverpool's head of nutrition Mona Nemmer', *Athletic*, 15 October 2021, https://www.nytimes.com/athletic/2889580/2021/10/14/we-have-so-much-information-about-our-players-we-know-them-inside-out-liverpool-head-of-nutrition-mona-nemmer/

9. Long, 2022.

10. See the well-argued Cox, M., 'Has the impact of analytics on modern football been overstated?', *Athletic*, 11 September 2024, https://www.nytimes.com/athletic/5756088/2024/09/11/how-has-data-changed-football/

11. Carter, N. (2007), 'Metatarsals and magic sponges: English football and the development of sports medicine', *Journal of Sport History*, 34(1), pp. 53–73; Carter, N. (2009), 'Mixing Business with Leisure? The Football Club Doctor, Sports Medicine and the Voluntary Tradition', *Sport in History*, 29(1), 69–91; Carter, N. (2010), 'The

rise and fall of the magic sponge: medicine and the transformation of the football trainer', *Social History of Medicine*, 23(2), pp. 261–79.

12. Carter, 2010.
13. Bishop, C., 'How Much Every Premier League Club Has Spent on Injured Players' Wages', givemesport, 26 November 2024, https://www.givemesport.com/premier-league-clubs-most-wages-on-injured-players/
14. 'Last season saw record highs of 4,123 injuries and €732.02 million in costs incurred', Howden Group, 14 October 2023, https://www.howdengroupholdings.com/reports/2023-24-mens-european-football-injury-index; McKenna, J., 'The Cost of Premier League Injuries, 2023–24', analyticsfc.co.uk, 18 July 2024, https://analyticsfc.co.uk/blog/2024/07/18/the-cost-of-injuries-in-the-premier-league-2023-2024/
15. Ralston, W., '"The Silicon Valley of turf": how the UK's pursuit of the perfect pitch changed football', *Guardian*, 15 June 2021, https://www.theguardian.com/football/2021/jun/15/silicon-valley-of-turf-uk-perfect-football-pitch
16. Williams, G., 'In Focus: ADI – Trends in Stadium Technology', *FCBusiness*, https://fcbusiness.co.uk/news/in-focus-adi-trends-in-stadium-technology/
17. Nispel, M., 'The immersive content coming to football stadiums', *Broadcastnow*, 14 May 2024, https://www.broadcastnow.co.uk/tech-innovation/the-immersive-content-coming-to-football-stadiums/5193383.article
18. Ibid.

12. Football's Shock Doctrine

1. Klein, N. (2007), *The Shock Doctrine: The Rise of Disaster Capitalism*, Penguin.
2. McInnes, P., 'Project Big Picture: leading clubs' plan to reshape game sparks anger', *Guardian*, 11 October 2020, https://www.theguardian.com/football/2020/oct/11/project-big-picture-premier-league-and-efl-plan-radical-reform-to-avoid-crisis
3. 'Project Big Picture: Premier League chief Richard Masters says there is "no beef" with EFL over failed proposals', Sky Sports, 14 October 2020, https://www.skysports.com/football/news/11095/12104174/project-big-picture-premier-league-chief-richard-masters-says-there-is-no-beef-with-efl-over-failed-proposals

4. Lowe, S., 'Real Madrid's Florentino Pérez claims Super League is here to "save football"', *Guardian*, 20 April 2021, https://www.theguardian.com/football/2021/apr/20/real-madrid-florentino-perez-claims-super-league-is-here-to-save-football

5. 'Fans boo Real Madrid players on arrival in Cádiz amid ESL fallout', *Euronews*, 21 April 2021, https://www.euronews.com/video/2021/04/21/fans-boo-real-madrid-players-on-arrival-in-cadiz-amid-esl-fallout

6. Tondo, L. et al., 'European Super League faces scorn across continent', *Guardian*, 19 April 2021, https://www.theguardian.com/football/2021/apr/19/european-super-league-the-death-of-football-say-fans-in-italy

7. Deleted Twitter account: Allen, A., 'FOOTBALL AT WAR', Arseblog, 20 April 2021, https://arseblog.com/2021/04/football-at-war/

8. Hytner, D., '"Champions League: earn it" – Leeds leave shirts in Liverpool dressing room', *Guardian*, 19 April 2021, https://www.theguardian.com/football/2021/apr/19/leeds-put-champions-league-earn-it-t-shirts-in-liverpool-dressing-room

9. Lewis, T., 'The week English football fans bit back against the billionaire owners', *Observer*, 24 April 2021, https://www.theguardian.com/football/2021/apr/24/the-week-english-football-fans-bit-back-against-super-league-the-billionaire-owners

10. Hunter, A., 'Liverpool's Jürgen Klopp and James Milner critical of Super League plans', *Guardian*, 19 April 2021, https://www.theguardian.com/football/2021/apr/19/liverpools-jurgen-klopp-unimpressed-by-european-super-league-plans

11. Ibbetson, C., 'Snap poll: football fans overwhelmingly reject European Super League', YouGov, 19 April 2021, https://yougov.co.uk/sport/articles/35361-snap-poll-football-fans-overwhelmingly-reject-euro

12. Dawes, O., 'John McGinn thinks Liverpool should have a new name after Super League confirmation', HITC, 19 April 2021, https://www.hitc.com/john-mcginn-thinks-liverpool-should-have-a-new-name-after-super-league-confirmation/

13. Premier League, 'Premier League and The FA joint statement', Premier League, 9 June 2021, https://www.premierleague.com/news/2167982

14. Wallace, S., 'Europe's elite suffer sport's most astounding humiliation – and wounds will take a long time to heal', *Telegraph*, 20 April 2021, https://www.telegraph.co.uk/football/2021/04/20/europes-elite-suffer-sports-astounding-humiliation-will-take/

15. Burnham, A., 'After the Super League fiasco, we have one last chance to reclaim English football', *Guardian*, 22 April 2021, https://www.theguardian.com/commentisfree/2021/apr/22/ reclaiming-football-european-super-league-fiasco

13. 'Let's Go Fucking Mental!'

1. Morris, S., 'Football thriving in Wales as Bale and co raise Euro 2020 hopes', *Guardian*, 25 June 2021, https://www.theguardian. com/uk-news/2021/jun/25/football-thriving-in-wales-as-bale-and-co-raise-euro-2020-hopes
2. Mansfield, M., 'The football fans whose goal is independence', *nation.cymru*, 8 December 2019, https://nation.cymru/news/ the-football-fans-whose-goal-is-independence/
3. 'OBON: Official Video to OBON DAY 2021 Song/Anthem', OBON, YouTube, 17 March 2021, https://www.youtube.com/ watch?v=-KAWylrnlvA; 'Welsh Gov slaps down Westminster plan for children in Wales to celebrate "One Britain One Nation Day"', *nation.cymru*, 22 June 2021, https://nation.cymru/news/welsh-gov-slaps-down-westminster-plan-for-children-in-wales-to-celebrate-one-britain-one-nation-day/
4. Massie, A., 'Scots Have Outgrown the Auld Enemy Rivalry', *The Times*, 17 June 2021, https://www.thetimes.com/article/ scots-have-outgrown-the-auld-enemy-rivalry-6b56g6pt3
5. Hassan, G., 'Scotland is back on the international stage', Gerry Hassan, 9 June 2021, https://gerryhassan.com/blog/ scotland-is-back-on-the-international-stage/
6. Walker, A., 'At England vs. Scotland, it's party over politics', *Politico*, 19 June 2021, https://www.politico.eu/article/ scotland-england-euro-football-match-independence-politics/
7. Monteith, B., 'Euro 2020: Why it's time for Scotland fans to ditch Anyone but England for good', *Scotsman*, 12 July 2021, https:// www.scotsman.com/news/opinion/columnists/ brian-monteith-how-scottish-schadenfreude-shames-us-3303970
8. Brooks, L., 'Anyone but England? Scots and Welsh warm to likeable team but not the hype', *Guardian*, 10 July 2021, https://www. theguardian.com/football/2021/jul/10/anyone-but-england-scots-and-welsh-warm-to-likable-team-but-not-the-hype
9. Ibid.
10. Paton, E., 'ANYONE BUT ENGLAND: Two thirds of Scotland fans WON'T be supporting England in their quest for Euro 2020 glory,

SunSport poll reveals', *Scottish Sun*, 3 July 2021, https://www.thescottishsun.co.uk/sport/football/7347681/scotland-fans-england-euro-2020-poll/

11. Daisley, S., '"Anyone But England" is a sad reflection of Scottish society', *Spectator*, 11 July 2021, https://www.spectator.co.uk/article/anyone-but-england-is-a-sad-reflection-of-scottish-society/

12. Anderson, Lee, Facebook, 3 June 2021, https://www.facebook.com/story.php?story_fbid=38089453125387458&id=1267260966707205&p=30&_rdr

13. Longhi, Marco, Facebook, 3 June 2021, https://www.facebook.com/MarcoLonghi4DN/posts/john-i-have-news-for-you-fans-are-not-racist-labour-are-so-out-of-touch-fans-jus/619448282784210/

14. Southgate, G., 'Dear England', *Players' Tribune*, 8 June 2021, https://www.theplayerstribune.com/posts/dear-england-gareth-southgate-euros-soccer

15. O'Flynn, P., 'Boris's cunning has allowed him to share in England's Euro 2020 glory', *Spectator*, 10 July 2021, https://www.spectator.co.uk/article/boris-s-cunning-has-allowed-him-to-share-in-england-s-euro-2020-glory/

16. Braidwood, J., 'England manager Gareth Southgate is "everything a leader should be", says Gary Neville', *Independent*, 7 July 2021, https://www.independent.co.uk/sport/football/england-euro-2020-gareth-southgate-neville-b1880092.html

17. Christenson, M., '"He is nine years old" – more Danes tell of being abused by England fans', *Observer*, 10 July 2021, https://www.theguardian.com/football/2021/jul/10/he-is-nine-years-old-more-danes-tell-of-being-abused-by-england-fans

18. @tyronemings Twitter/X, 12 July 2021, https://x.com/tyronemings/status/1414655312074784785

19. 'The Baroness Casey Review: An independent Review of events surrounding the UEFA Euro 2020 Final "Euro Sunday" at Wembley', p. 6, https://www.thefa.com/news/2021/dec/03/baroness-casey-review-uefa-euro-2020-final-20210312

20. Ingle, S., 'Violent England fans an embarrassment to the team and not welcome, says FA', *Guardian*, 5 June 2019, https://www.theguardian.com/football/2019/jun/05/england-fans-baton-charged-portugese-police-nations-league-porto

21. Casey Report, p. 29.

22. Ibid., p. 31.

23. Ibid., p. 37.

24. Ibid., p. 42.

25. Ibid., p. 42.
26. Ibid., p. 44.
27. Ibid., p. 47.
28. Ibid., p. 51.
29. Ibid., p. 51.

14. Poetry in Motion

1. 'The World of Gazza!! exhibition: the life and times of Paul Gascoigne – in pictures', *Guardian*, 18 May 2023, https://www.theguardian.com/football/gallery/2023/may/18/the-world-of-gazza-exhibition-the-life-and-times-of-paul-gascoigne-in-pictures
2. @Alan_Measles, Twitter/X, 10 July 2018, https://x.com/Alan_Measles/status/1016744893488750594
3. Sherwood, H., 'Carol Ann Duffy writes poem paying tribute to England's female footballers', *Guardian*, 29 November 2023, https://www.theguardian.com/books/2023/nov/29/carol-ann-duffy-poem-tribute-to-england-female-footballers-lionesses-we-see-you
4. See Bolasie and Wright-Phillips here: 'Lord of the Mics 6 – Bradley Wright-Phillips v Yannick Bolasie (2014)', Grime Music HQ, Daily Motion, 2014, https://www.dailymotion.com/video/x4a2kd0; and Palmer here: 'Cole Palmer dancing to Clarks by Vybz Kartel', YouTube, 13 July 2023, https://www.youtube.com/watch?v=aq5KWUo6iCo
5. See the excellent overview, Burdsey, D. and Doyle, J. (2022), 'Football and the sounds of the Black Atlantic', *European Journal of Cultural Studies*, 25(2), pp. 533–50.
6. 'Fans return: "I went back to the home of football"', BBC Sport, 24 August 2021, https://www.bbc.co.uk/sport/articles/c5n6wl700z0o

15. The Fall of the Roman Empire

1. Sky News, 'Ukraine invasion: Chelsea manager Thomas Tuchel criticises own fans for chanting for Abramovich during minute's applause', Sky News, 6 March 2023, https://news.sky.com/story/ukraine-invasion-chelsea-manager-thomas-tuchel-criticises-own-fans-for-chanting-for-abramovich-during-minutes-applause-12559126
2. Everton has subsequently been sold to the American private equity Friedkin group.

3. Topham, G. 'British rail is nationalised all over again – by foreign states', *Observer*, 1 April 2017, https://www.theguardian.com/business/2017/apr/01/british-rail-franchises-foreign-owners-subsidy; on the water industry, see, Leach, A. et al., 'England's water: the world's piggy bank', *Guardian*, 30 November 2022, https://www.theguardian.com/environment/ng-interactive/2022/nov/30/englands-water-the-worlds-piggy-bank

4. D'Urso, J., 'The EFL club owned by a convicted fraudster', *Athletic*, 6 March 2024, https://www.nytimes.com/athletic/5310045/2024/03/06/fleetwood-town-andy-pilley-investigation/

5. The background on Morecambe's owners can be read here: 'Supercars, missing millions and fit and proper people', The Ugly Game, 2 September 2022, https://theuglygame.wordpress.com/2022/09/02/supercars-missing-millions-and-fit-and-proper-people/; Ailwyn, A., 'Worcester Warriors: the inside story of a rugby club's collapse', *Guardian*, 5 October 2022, https://www.theguardian.com/sport/2022/oct/05/worcester-warriors-the-inside-story-of-a-rugby-clubs-demise

6. House of Commons, Digital, Culture, Media and Sport Committee, 'Current issues in rugby union', House of Commons, 2023, https://publications.parliament.uk/pa/cm5803/cmselect/cmcumeds/1018/report.html

7. Slater, M., 'From Disney to delivering Portsmouth's promotion, the Eisners have a Premier League plan', *Athletic*, 2 May 2024, https://www.nytimes.com/athletic/5457859/2024/05/02/portsmouth-promoted-eisners-disney/#

8. Froston, N., 'Gillingham's U.S. takeover has brought real and rapid change – "English clubs are special"', *Athletic*, 23 September 2023, https://www.nytimes.com/athletic/4874103/2023/09/22/gillingham-us-takeover-galinson/

9. 'New Huddersfield Town owner Kevin Nagle admits he "barely" knew club existed', ITV News, 27 June 2023, https://www.itv.com/news/calendar/2023-06-27/towns-new-owner-barely-new-huddersfield-existed#

10. 'The US millionaires investing in lower-league clubs', BBC Sport, 23 April 2021, https://www.bbc.co.uk/sport/football/56674024

11. @berkebakay, Twitter/X, 1 May 2023, https://x.com/berkebakay/status/1653142848387301376

12. Paul, O., 'Sunderland owner Stewart Donald blames "abusive" fans for scaring off would-be buyers and says he's "desperate" to sell', *Sun*, 2020, https://www.thesun.co.uk/sport/12151908/

sunderland-owner-stewart-donald-blames-abusive-fans-for-scaring-off-would-be-buyers-and-says-hes-desperate-to-sell/

13. Buckingham, P., 'Acun Ilicali, the Turkish TV millionaire with dreams of helping Hull City roar again', *Athletic*, 25 January 2022, https://www.nytimes.com/athletic/3080158/2022/01/20/acun-ilicali-the-turkish-tv-millionaire-with-dreams-of-helping-hull-city-roar-again/

14. 'Notts County owner Hardy facing FA investigation over intimate picture', *Guardian*, 27 January 2019, https://www.theguardian.com/football/2019/jan/27/notts-county-owner-hardy-apologises-for-posting-intimate-picture-online

15. See, Hanton, A., (2024) Vassal State: 'How America Runs Britain', London: Swift Press.

16. Birmingham were bought in 2009 by Hong Kong developer Carson Yeung, and in 2011 won the League Cup, were relegated from the Premier League and they have not been back since. Yeung's money dried up and his presence diminished, until finally in 2014 he was arrested on money-laundering charges at home, sentenced to six years in prison and disappeared altogether. The club then was sold on to Chinese businessman Paul Suen's Birmingham Sports Holdings, who racked up more debt, watched the ageing stadium decline, broke the EFL's profitability rules and saw nine points deducted from the club, and bankrolled season after season of relegation struggles. Cardiff were purchased by Malaysian tycoon Vincent Tan, who alienated himself from the fan base by changing the club's shirts from blue to red – a much more popular, lucky colour back home, but not perhaps the hue for a side widely known by their nickname the Bluebirds. Years of fan protest eventually saw the club return to its original colours. Since then, Tan has pioneered the awkward football-oligarch style with the now blue shirt tucked into his tightly belted suit trousers. Nearly £200 million later, and with just two seasons in the Premier League, he has been trying to find someone to take the club off his hands and cut his losses, but there don't seem to be many takers for the price he would like. Blackburn Rovers were purchased in 2010 by the Indian industrial chicken conglomerate Venky's, under whose ownership the club have spent much of their time languishing in mid-table Championship mediocrity. QPR had a rotating cast of owners including Malaysian airline entrepreneur Tony Fernandes, Indian billionaire Lakshmi Mittal, and now Malaysian majority owner Ruben Gnanalingam, but have just three seasons in the

Premier League to show for hundreds of millions of pounds spent. The £39 million paid by Vichai Srivaddhanaprabha for Leicester City in 2010 proved a rather better investment. Around £100 million was enough to get the club back into the Premier League, and then to actually win it in 2016. Whatever his original intentions, he was by 2016 a romantic believer, telling the Leicester fans, 'Our spirit exists because of the love we share for each other and the energy it helps to create, both on and off the pitch.' We all need love, but there were other reasons for owning the club too. Vichai made his fortune by staying close to politics and securing the monopoly of duty-free shops at Thailand's booming airports. The real prize, then, was influence and kudos at home, where Vichai was able to present the team and the Premier League trophy to the King of Thailand. It was, no doubt, this example that led first to Thai businessman Sumrith 'Tiger' Thanakarnjanasuth buying Oxford United in 2018, and then in 2021 selling it on to Indonesian oligarchs Anindya Bakrie and Erick Thohir. The former is the scion of one of Indonesia's biggest conglomerates, whose father ran for president in 2014 and who has expanded the family firm to create one of the country's largest media groups. The latter, also a son of one of Indonesia's richest corporate families, served as President Widodo's re-election campaign manager and as a cabinet minister, when not running the Indonesian football federation. That men of such considerable wealth and power, and who in Thohir's case have been part-owner of Inter Milan, should think a club in the third level of English football worth their time and money is simply remarkable. The most recent addition to the field, and a measure of the hegemonic position of English football in global popular culture, came from the sale of Wycombe Wanderers, owned by New Orleans sports investor and Republican political hopeful Rob Couhig, to the Georgian billionaire Mikhail Lomtadze, who made his money owning Kazakhstan's most important finance app.

16. The Return of the Repressed

1. Burrows, T., 'Dissent in the Premier League: Who are the worst offenders?', *Athletic*, 18 February 2024, https://www.nytimes.com/athletic/5271973/2024/02/14/premier-league-dissent-yellow-cards/
2. Home Office, 'Football-related arrests and banning orders, England and Wales: 2021 to 2022 season', https://www.gov.uk/government/

statistics/football-related-arrests-and-banning-orders-england-and-wales-2021-to-2022-season

3. MacInnes, P., 'The rise of disorder at football: why is it happening and what can be done?', *Guardian*, 18 February 2022, https://www.theguardian.com/football/2022/feb/18/the-shocking-rise-of-disorder-at-matches

4. Adams, R., '"Bubble" of post-pandemic bad behaviour among pupils predicted to peak', *Guardian*, 25 August 2024, https://www.theguardian.com/education/article/2024/aug/25/bubble-of-post-pandemic-bad-behaviour-among-pupils-predicted-to-peak

5. Pearson, G. (2024), *An Ethnography of English Football Fans: Cans, Cops and Carnivals*, Manchester University Press.

6. MacInnes, 2022.

7. Buckingham, P. et al., 'Special report: The "flagrant" use of cocaine at football grounds', *Athletic*, 19 May 2022, https://www.nytimes.com/athletic/2973547/2021/11/24/special-report-the-flagrant-use-of-cocaine-at-football-grounds/

8. Newson, M. (2021), 'High and highly bonded: Fused football fans who use cocaine are most likely to be aggressive toward rivals', *International Journal of Drug Policy*, 93, p. 103263.

9. Stott, C., Pearson, G. and West, O. (2020), 'Enabling an evidence-based approach to policing football in the UK, *Policing*, 14(4), pp. 977–94; Pearson, G. and Stott, C. (2022), *A New Agenda for Football Crowd Management: Reforming Legal and Policing Responses to Risk*, Springer Nature.

10. Stott et al., 2020.

11. Ibid.

12. 'Bristol City fans receive police payout over "false imprisonment"', BBC News, 25 September 2019, https://www.bbc.co.uk/news/uk-england-bristol-49824108

13. The FSA, 'Wrexham fans challenge new police powers ... and win', FSA, 18 January 2017, https://thefsa.org.uk/news/wrexham-fans-challenge-new-police-powers-and-win/

14. 'Football police chief says cocaine a "contributing factor" to increased disorder', BBC Sport, 8 February 2022, https://www.bbc.co.uk/sport/football/60300610

15. 'A high court judge has ruled that Owen Oyston and his son Karl, the owners of Blackpool football club, must pay £31m to the minority shareholder Valeri Belokon for his shares after operating an "illegitimate stripping" of the club following promotion to the Premier League in 2010', from Conn, D., 'Oystons ordered to buy

out Blackpool shareholder for £31m after losing court battle' *Guardian*, 6 November 2017, https://www.theguardian.com/ football/2017/nov/06/oystons-blackpool-ordered-pay-shareholder-high-court-valeri-belokon

16. Turner, M. and Lee Ludvigsen, J.A. (2024), 'Safety and security battles: Unpacking the players and arenas of the Safe Standing movement in English football (1989–2022), *Sociological Research Online*, 29(2), pp. 454–71; Turner, M. (2023), *The Safe Standing Movement in Football: Fan Networks, Tactics, and Mobilisations*, Taylor & Francis.

17. Quoted in Turner, M. (2021), 'The Safe Standing movement: Vectors in the post-Hillsborough timescape of English football', *The Sociological Review*, 69(2), pp. 348–64.

18. Ibid.

19. 'Fan-Led Review of Football Governance: securing the game's future', 2021, https://www.gov.uk/government/publications/fan-led-review-of-football-governance-securing-the-games-future/fan-led-review-of-football-governance-securing-the-games-future

20. 'Leeds: Chief executive Angus Kinnear says some review calls "Maoist"', BBC Sport, 1 December 2021, https://www.bbc.co.uk/sport/football/59481154

21. 'Football risks killing the golden goose, warns Aston Villa's Christian Purslow', *Independent*, 25 November 2021, https://www.independent.co.uk/sport/football/premier-league-tracey-crouch-christian-purslow-aston-villa-graham-potter-b1964367.html

22. Parish, S., 'Why we must not hand over the running of football in this country to the government', *Sunday Times*, 27 November 2021, https://www.thetimes.com/sport/football/article/steve-parish-why-we-must-not-hand-over-the-running-of-football-in-this-country-to-the-government-bwcjlmlz7

23. Gray, J., 'Premier League accused of trying to delay fan-led review', *theIpaper*, 28 March 2023, https://inews.co.uk/sport/football/premier-league-delay-fan-led-review-mp-tracey-crouch-2239261

24. A new player in the field, Fair Game was formed in 2021. It was an alliance of over thirty clubs, some fan-owned, some in private hands, but all of whom were ready to sign up to a serious agenda of change in the governance of the game. They welcomed the review but lobbied relentlessly for much stricter forms of audit, licensing and directors test, as well as more power for the regulator and a more encompassing model of good governance within the sport. Its reports on these matters and detailed policy proposals

were superior to anything produced by government itself, let alone the Premier League, while its huge network of sympathetic MPs helped ensure there was no backsliding by the DCMS. See: https://www.fairgameuk.org/

25. Rookwood, J. and Hoey, P. (2024), 'From the Anfield wrap to boss night and the Paris protests: Football, politics, identity and the cultural evolution of fan media and supporter activism in Liverpool', *International Journal of the Sociology of Leisure*, 7(1), pp. 83–107.

17. Alternative England

1. Liew, J., 'Euro 2024 diary: polyester, parkrun and how England squad might vote', *Observer*, 7 July 2024, https://www.theguardian.com/football/article/2024/jul/07/euro-2024-diary-germany-england-berlin-leipzig. A measure of the wholesomeness of the occasion was the fact that on Wembley Way a woman returned my bank card to me after it had fallen on the pavement; had that happened at the men's game I have little doubt the card would have been heading for Tesco and a contactless purchase of fags and lager.

2. Cooke, R., 'Women and girl's football on the rise, according to FA', Sky Sports, 7 March 2018, https://www.skysports.com/football/news/12040/11279988/women-and-girls-football-on-the-rise-according-to-fa; 'Women's and Girls' Football Sees Record Growth in a Historic Four Years for the Game', FA, 27 September 2024, https://www.thefa.com/news/2024/sep/27/women-and-girls-stratgy-progress-inspiring-positive-change-20242709

3. 'Sport England Active Lives survey says 100,000 more girls playing football', BBC Sport, 8 December 2022, https://www.bbc.co.uk/sport/63904046

4. Wrack, S. (2021), 'Estate of Mind: The Making of Emma Hayes', in Atyeo, C. (ed.), *Football, She Wrote: An Anthology of Women's Writing on the Game*, Floodlit Dreams

5. Women in Sport (2018), 'Where Are All the Women? Shining a light on the visibility of women's sport in the media', Women in Sport, 2018, https://womeninsport.org/wp-content/uploads/2018/10/2018-Where-are-all-the-Women.pdf

6. Williams, J., Pope, S. and Cleland, J. (2023), '"Genuinely in love with the game": football fan experiences and perceptions of women's football in England', *Sport in Society*, 26(2), pp. 285–301; Pope, S., Williams, J. and Cleland, J. (2022), 'Men's football fandom

and the performance of progressive and misogynistic masculinities in a "new age" of UK women's sport', *Sociology*, 56(4), pp. 730–48.

7. Patrick, P., 'Why is the BBC's women's football coverage so patronising?', *Spectator*, 4 July 2022, https://www.spectator.co.uk/article/why-is-the-bbc-s-coverage-of-women-s-football-so-patronising/

8. Young, T., 'Am I allowed to make fun of women's football?', *Spectator*, 12 August 2023, https://www.spectator.co.uk/article/am-i-allowed-to-make-fun-of-womens-football/

9. Unwin, W., 'Taking my daughter to her first WSL game reminded me of the joy football can bring', *Guardian*, 4 October 2024, https://www.theguardian.com/football/2024/oct/04/taking-my-daughter-to-her-first-wsl-game-reminded-me-of-the-joy-football-can-bring

10. Williams, Pope and Cleland, 2023.

11. 'Clothing' in Dunn, C. (2023), *Woman Up: Pitches, Pay and Periods*, Hero Press

12. Sawyer, M., 'A different goal: how women's football is changing the beautiful game', *Observer*, 8 September 2024, https://www.theguardian.com/football/article/2024/sep/08/a-different-goal-how-womens-football-is-changing-the-beautiful-game

13. Wrack, S., 'Survey finds 82% of female players experience pain wearing football boots', *Guardian*, 27 June 2024, https://www.theguardian.com/football/2023/jun/27/female-players-pain-wearing-football-boots-european-club-association-study

14. House of Commons Women and Equalities Committee (2024), *Health barriers for girls and women in sport*, Third Report of Session 2023–24, https://committees.parliament.uk/publications/43602/documents/216689/default/

15. Dunn, 2023, p. 94.

16. Wade, P., 'How the period conversation is gaining momentum in football', *Independent*, 4 April 2023, https://www.independent.co.uk/life-style/health-and-families/lionesses-nike-beth-mead-australia-new-zealandb2313874.html

17. Dunn, 2023.

18. House of Commons Women and Equalities Committee, 2024.

19. 'Opening weekend brings record audiences', Premier League, 16 August 2023, https://www.premierleague.com/news/3636215

20. *Women at the Match*, FSA, 2021, https://thefsa.org.uk/wp-content/uploads/2021/11/Women-at-the-Match-report.pdf

21. Lynam, D., 'London 2012 Olympics: unbelievable effort from the BBC but where was Gary Lineker?', *Telegraph*, 11 August 2021, https://www.telegraph.co.uk/sport/olympics/9467064/London-2012-Olympics-unbelievable-effort-from-the-BBC-but-where-was-Gary-Lineker.html

22. MacInnes, P., 'Keegan asked to "keep his opinions to himself" on female football pundits', *Guardian*, 5 October 2023, https://www.theguardian.com/football/2023/oct/05/kevin-keegan-asked-to-keep-his-opinions-to-himself-on-female-football-pundits

23. @Joey7Barton, Twitter/X, 9 December 2023, https://x.com/Joey7Barton/status/1733427897937940956

24. 'Joey Barton: Emma Hayes says women are used to "systemic misogyny" following comments', BBC Sport, 8 December 2023, https://www.bbc.co.uk/sport/football/67659547

25. Williams, D.J., Neville, F.G., House, K. and Donnelly, P.D. (2013), 'Association between old firm football matches and reported domestic (violence) incidents in Strathclyde, Scotland', *Sage Open*, 3(3), pp. 1–7.

26. Kirby, S., Francis, B. and O'Flaherty, R. (2014), 'Can the FIFA world cup football (soccer) tournament be associated with an increase in domestic abuse?', *Journal of Research in Crime and Delinquency*, 51(3), pp. 259–76.

27. Ivandić, R., Kirchmaier, T., Saeidi, Y. and Blas, N.T. (2024), 'Football, alcohol, and domestic abuse', *Journal of Public Economics*, 230.

28. Sandhu, S., 'Euro 2020: Domestic abuse spikes in England with 400 extra cases reported during football tournament', *theIpaper*, 13 July 2021, https://inews.co.uk/news/uk/euro-2020-domestic-abuse-england-increase-cases-during-football-tournament-1100995

29. Trendl, A., Stewart, M., and Mullett, T. (2021), 'The role of alcohol in the link between national football (soccer) tournaments and domestic abuse – Evidence from England', *Social Science & Medicine*, 268, pp. 1–9.

30. Brooks-Hay, O. and Lombard, N. (2018), '"Home game": domestic abuse and football', *Journal of Gender-based Violence*, 2(1), pp. 93–108.

31. Taylor, D., 'Antony and Player X: Football's blurred priorities when it comes to accusations of offences against women', *Athletic*, 9 September 2023, https://www.nytimes.com/athletic/4845536/2023/09/09/antony-player-x-manchester-united/

32. Conn, D., 'Richard Scudamore's emails expose two-man board in need of overhaul', *Guardian*, 18 May 2018, https://www.the

guardian.com/football/2014/may/18/richard-scudamore-sexist-
emails-premier-league-review

33. Kuper, S., 'Women in football fail to score top jobs off the pitch',
Financial Times, 22 July 2023, https://www.ft.com/content/
64aa2382-c1ba-404d-8c30-31fe86f8076e

34. Gill, A., 'Football's gender problem: from the pitch to the
boardroom, women are still being blocked from the top jobs', *The
Conversation*, 7 January 2019, https://theconversation.com/
footballs-gender-problem-from-the-pitch-to-the-boardroom-
women-are-still-being-blocked-from-the-top-jobs-106905; Bryan,
A., Pope, S. and Rankin-Wright, A.J. (2021), 'On the periphery:
Examining women's exclusion from core leadership roles in the
"extremely gendered" organization of men's club football in
England', *Gender & Society*, 35(6), pp. 940–70.

35. Garry, T., 'Data shows 89% of women in football industry
experience discrimination', *Guardian*, 19 June 2024, https://www.
theguardian.com/football/article/2024/jun/19/women-in-football-
discrimination-survey

36. 'Women's Super League Finances 2022/23', Swiss Ramble,
Substack, 22 July 2024, https://swissramble.substack.com/p/
womens-super-league-finances-202223

18. Playing for a Pittance

1. Magowan, A., 'Premier League & cost of living: How many clubs
pay real living wage?', BBC Sport, 26 September 2022, https://
www.bbc.co.uk/sport/football/62996172

2. Fitzpatrick, D. and Hoey, P. (2022), 'From fanzines to foodbanks:
Football fan activism in the age of anti-politics', *International
Review for the Sociology of Sport*, 57(8), pp. 1234–52.

3. See inter alia, Blackpool FC, 'Winter Warm Hubs Update',
blackpoolfc.co.uk, 3 February 2023, https://www.blackpoolfc.co.
uk/news/2023/february/03/winter-warm-hubs-update/; 'Manchester
United open Old Trafford cafe as warm hub', BBC News, 7
December 2022, https://www.bbc.co.uk/news/uk-england-
manchester-63886540

4. Utilita (2022), 'Price to Play Report: A study revealing the impact
of the cost of living crisis on participation levels in grassroots
football', https://static1.squarespace.com/static/
60955bae0b22356355d4afb0/t/62824f1de4eee0617c9a1296/
1652707105008/Utilita+Price+to+Play+Report+-+May+2022.pdf

5. Slack, T. et al., 'Cost of living crisis: "Biggest threat to non-league football since WW2"', BBC News, 20 October 2022, https://www.bbc.co.uk/news/uk-england-63243195

6. Brown, H., 'Almost a third of Scottish parents say cost of living will impact ability to afford football for children, according to report', *Scotsman*, 17 May 2022, https://www.scotsman.com/health/almost-a-third-of-scottish-parents-say-cost-of-living-will-impact-ability-to-afford-football-for-children-according-to-report-3696219

7. 'The FA – Written Evidence', Committees, UK Parliament, 21 January 2021, https://committees.parliament.uk/writtenevidence/22277/html/

8. PA Sport, 'Wayne Rooney is last of the "street footballers" – David Moyes', *ESPN*, 11 May 2018, https://www.espn.co.uk/football/story/_/id/37553864/wayne-rooney-last-street-footballers-david-moyes

9. Murray, E., 'Pitches, coaches and iPads: what are the reasons for Scotland's talent decline?', *Guardian*, 9 November 2016, https://www.theguardian.com/football/2016/nov/09/scotland-talent-decline-kenny-dalglish-england-wembley

10. Department of Transport, 'Vehicle licensing statistics: July to September 2023', 12 December 2023, https://www.gov.uk/government/statistics/vehicle-licensing-statistics-july-to-september-2023

11. 'Only one in four children play out regularly on their street compared to almost three-quarters of their grandparents generation', Save the Children, 5 August 2022, https://www.savethechildren.org.uk/news/media-centre/press-releases/children-today-62-percent-less-likely-to-play-outside-than-their

12. Carrington, D., 'Three-quarters of UK children spend less time outdoors than prison inmates – survey', *Guardian*, 25 March 2016, https://www.theguardian.com/environment/2016/mar/25/three-quarters-of-uk-children-spend-less-time-outdoors-than-prison-inmates-survey

13. Walker, M., 'As English football's longest-serving academy director retires, he leaves behind a much-changed game', *Independent*, 28 April 2017, https://www.independent.co.uk/sport/football/premier-league/middlesbrough-dave-parnaby-academy-youth-players-manchester-city-relegation-a7708396.html

14. Ekpoudom, A., 'How south London became a talent factory for Black British footballers', *Guardian*, 31 March 2022, https://www.

theguardian.com/football/2022/mar/31/south-london-crucible-for-black-british-footballers

15. Cited in Lovett, S. 'The Nation's Game – life at the bottom of the pyramid: Part 2, Out with the old and in with the new?', *Independent*, 27 March 2018, https://www.independent.co.uk/sport/football/news/nations-game-grassroots-football-pyramid-premier-league-football-association-why-decline-participation-fa-a8274141.html

16. Walker, M., 'A shot in time: At its peak, London's Hackney Marshes was home to a staggering 120 pitches', *Daily Mail*, 8 October 2017, https://www.dailymail.co.uk/sport/football/article-4961024/A-shot-time-Hackney-Marshes-home-120-pitches.html

17. Department of Education, 'Register of decisions of playing field land disposals', 7 Feb 2025, https://www.gov.uk/government/publications/school-land-decisions-about-disposals/decisions-on-the-disposal-of-school-land#approved-applications; Doward, J., 'As British teams conquer Europe, cuts force sale of 710 local football pitches', *Guardian*, 2 June 2019, https://www.theguardian.com/society/2019/jun/02/tory-cuts-force-sale-710-local-football-pitches

18. Griffiths, I., 'Welsh football: Grassroots clubs frustrated by poor facilities', BBC News, 16 June 2022, https://www.bbc.co.uk/news/uk-wales-61812386

19. Lovett, S., 'The Nation's Game – life at the bottom of the pyramid: Part 6, The government struggles hindering grassroots football', *Independent*, 30 March 2018, https://www.independent.co.uk/sport/football/news/nation-s-game-grassroots-football-premier-league-fa-government-councils-newcastle-united-a8281741.html

20. Fahey, J. (2022), *Futsal: The Indoor Game that Is Revolutionizing World Soccer*, Melville House.

21. Bailey, L., 'Still in the game: The rapid rise of walking football – in pictures', *Guardian*, 18 August 2023, https://www.theguardian.com/football/gallery/2023/aug/18/still-in-the-game-the-rapid-rise-of-walking-football-in-pictures

22. Cole, S., 'What happened to MyFootballClub – the club where fans decided everything?', *Guardian*, 26 October 2017, https://www.theguardian.com/football/2017/oct/26/what-happened-to-myfootballclub-ebbsfleet-united

23. Fenn, A., 'Hashtag United have conquered YouTube and non-league is next: behind the scenes of a phenomenon', *FourFourTwo*, 16 November 2018, https://www.fourfourtwo.com/features/hashtag-

united-have-conquered-youtube-and-non-league-next-behind-scenes-a-phenomenon

24. Quadri, M., 'How SE Dons Became the Sunday League Club That Took on the World', *Versus*, 18 November 2020, https://www.versus.uk.com/articles/how-se-dons-became-the-sunday-league-club-that-took-on-the-world

25. Aqlan, M., 'A Refugee No Longer', *Players' Tribune*, 30 July 2020, https://www.theplayerstribune.com/articles/homeless-world-cup-mujahed-aqlan

26. 'How football helped the survivors of Glasgow hotel knife attack', BBC News, 14 July 2021, https://www.bbc.com/news/av/uk-scotland-57841539

27. Marsh, D., 'Changing Lives FC: Inside the initiative transforming lives of UK's migrants and refugees', *Mirror*, 16 December 2022, https://www.mirror.co.uk/sport/football/news/changinglives-migrant-refugee-football-team-28729748

28. Aarons, E., 'Middlesbrough give refugees football kit and feeling of belonging', *Guardian*, 12 April 2018, https://www.theguardian.com/football/2018/apr/12/middlesbrough-refugees-football-community

29. Kendall-Rayner, P., 'First refugee football team set to make debut in the Liverpool County Premier League this weekend', *Liverpoolworld*, 2 September 2021, https://www.liverpoolworld.uk/news/first-refugee-football-team-set-to-make-debut-in-the-liverpool-county-premier-league-3368841

30. Ames, N., 'How Hackney Wick FC became a safe haven from gangs and knife crime', *Guardian*, 17 August 2021, https://www.theguardian.com/football/2021/aug/17/how-hackney-wick-fc-became-a-safe-haven-from-gangs-and-knife

31. Taylor, R., 'I founded Grenfell Athletic Football Club as a way to heal our local community', *Metro*, 4 September 2021, https://metro.co.uk/2021/09/04/i-founded-grenfell-athletic-fc-as-a-way-to-heal-our-local-community-15155896/

32. Foster, R., 'Grenfell Athletic: the football club uniting a community hit by tragedy', *Guardian*, 15 March 2022, https://www.theguardian.com/football/2022/mar/15/grenfell-athletic-the-football-club-uniting-a-community-hit-by-tragedy; Hadgu, B., 'The Grenfell Memorial Cup Brought a Neglected Community Together Through the Beautiful Game', *Versus*, 30 May 2022, https://www.versus.uk.com/articles/the-grenfell-memorial-cup-brought-a-neglected-community-together-through-the-beautiful-game

33. PA Sport, 'Martin Glenn defends possible Wembley sale and says it makes economic sense', Sky Sports, 30 May 2018, https://www.skysports.com/football/news/11095/11389284/martin-glenn-defends-possible-wembley-sale-and-says-it-makes-economic-sense

19. When the Fun Stops

1. Purves, R.I., Critchlow, N., Morgan, A., Stead, M. and Dobbie, F. (2020), 'Examining the frequency and nature of gambling marketing in televised broadcasts of professional sporting events in the United Kingdom', *Public Health*, 184, pp. 71–8, https://www.sciencedirect.com/science/article/pii/S0033350620300512

2. Torrance, J., Heath, C., Andrade, M. and Newall, P. (2023), 'Gambling, cryptocurrency, and financial trading app marketing in English Premier League football: A frequency analysis of in-game logos', *Journal of Behavioral Addictions*, 12(4), pp. 972–82.

3. Rossi, R. et al. (2024), 'Gambling Marketing and the Premier League: The Continued Failure of Industry Self-Regulation', University of Bristol, 2024, https://www.bristol.ac.uk/media-library/sites/business-school/documents/Premier_League_Report_2024.pdf

4. Djohari, N., Weston, G., Cassidy, R. and Kulas-Reid, I. (2021), 'The visibility of gambling sponsorship in football related products marketed directly to children', *Soccer & Society*, 22(7), pp. 769–77.

5. Davies, R., 'UK gambling addiction much worse than thought, says survey', *Guardian*, 19 May 2020, https://www.theguardian.com/uk-news/2020/may/19/uk-gambling-addiction-yougov-research

6. Public Health England, 'Gambling-related harms: evidence review', 2019, https://www.gov.uk/government/publications/gambling-related-harms-evidence-review

7. Brewin, J., '"Stop promoting them": victims call for football to end tragic link with gambling', *Guardian*, 14 October 2022, https://www.theguardian.com/football/2022/oct/14/stop-promoting-them-victims-call-for-football-to-end-tragic-link-with-gambling

8. Seddon, S., 'Gambling addiction clinics "full of young men in football shirts"', *Metro*, 23 November 2022, https://metro.co.uk/2022/11/23/gambling-addiction-clinics-full-of-young-men-in-football-shirts-17812331/

9. Gambling with Lives, 'Addictive Gambling Products, GwL, 2020', Gambling with Lives, 2020, https://www.gamblingwithlives.org/research/addictive-gambling-products/

10. Gambling Commission, 'Understanding why people gamble and typologies', Gambling Commission, 2024, https://www.gamblingcommission.gov.uk/statistics-and-research/publication/understanding-why-people-gamble-and-typologies

11. Grimes, J., 'I was addicted to betting on football – a ban on ads on the front of shirts is nowhere near enough', *Guardian*, 14 April 2023, https://www.theguardian.com/commentisfree/2023/apr/14/football-gambling-betting-shirts-ban-ads-addiction

12. UNODC, 'Global Report on Corruption in Sport', chapter 9, 2022, https://www.unodc.org/documents/corruption/Publications/2022/Global_Report_on_Corruption_in_Sport_Chapter_9.pdf

13. Auclair, P., 'The trillion-dollar gambling game', *Josimar*, 12 August 2021, https://josimarfootball.com/2021/08/12/the-trillion-dollar-gambling-game/

14. Cited in Auclair, P., 'Gambling with lives', *Josimar*, 31 January 2022, https://josimarfootball.com/2022/01/31/gambling-with-lives/

15. Kerr, J. et al., '8Xbet's British Exit', *Josimar*, 3 January 2025, https://josimarfootball.com/2025/01/03/8xbets-british-exit/

16. D'Urso, J., 'Losing three months' wages in Paul Pogba crypto scheme: "The main reason we invested was him"', *Athletic*, 1 March 2023, https://www.nytimes.com/athletic/4138359/2023/03/01/paul-pogba-crypto-scheme/; Rushden, M., 'Cryptodragons' den: what is Paul Pogba selling and should we be wary?', *Guardian*, 18 November 2021, https://www.theguardian.com/football/blog/2021/nov/18/here-be-cryptodragons-what-is-paul-pogba-selling-and-should-we-be-wary

17. The entire sorry story of football's relationship with crypto and NFTs is brilliantly covered in Calladine, M. (2024), *No Questions Asked: How Football Joined the Crypto Con*, Quality Books.

18. FSA, 'West Ham end controversial blockchain partnership', FSA, 1 July 2020, https://thefsa.org.uk/news/west-ham-end-controversial-blockchain-partnership/

20. The Queen is Dead

1. Ingle, S., 'Preston ban football fan for life for derogatory tweet about the royal family', *Guardian*, 13 September 2022, https://www.theguardian.com/football/2022/sep/13/preston-ban-football-fan-for-life-for-derogatory-tweet-about-the-royal-family

2. Rumsby, B., 'Eton College condemned for ignoring FA's ban on football after Queen's death', *Telegraph*, 12 September 2022,

https://www.telegraph.co.uk/football/2022/09/11/eton-college-ignores-fas-ban-football-queens-death/

3. Stubbings, D., 'Wrexham AFC condemns fans after "small number" boo one-minute silence for the Queen', *Shropshire Star*, 14 September 2022, https://www.shropshirestar.com/news/royal-family/2022/09/14/wrexham-afc-condemns-fans-after-small-number-boo-one-minute-silence-for-the-queen/

4. Cassidy, R., 'Fireworks set off at Celtic Park during silence for Prince Philip as cops launch probe', *Daily Record*, 11 April 2021, https://www.dailyrecord.co.uk/news/scottish-news/fireworks-set-celtic-park-during-23893146

5. 'Celtic Fans – If you hate the Royal Family clap your hands', Celtic Fans, YouTube, 18 September 2022, https://www.youtube.com/watch?v=_odneR-kl6A

6. Press Association, 'Blackpool play We Didn't Start the Fire by Billy Joel during Bradford match', *Guardian*, 27 February 2016, https://www.theguardian.com/football/2016/feb/27/blackpool-we-didnt-start-the-fire-billy-joel-bradford-city; 'Bradford City complain to FA over fire chants at Newport County', Sky Sports, 25 February 2020, https://www.skysports.com/football/news/11750/11942338/bradford-city-complain-to-fa-over-fire-chants-at-newport-county

7. Fitzsimmons, F., 'Police remove offensive banner referencing Munich Air Disaster from M62', *Liverpool Echo*, 17 October 2016, https://www.liverpoolecho.co.uk/news/liverpool-news/police-remove-offensive-banner-referencing-12039464

8. Mitten, A., '"Please stop singing about Hillsborough and Munich"', *Athletic*, 22 August 2022, https://www.nytimes.com/athletic/3526057/2022/08/22/united-liverpool-munich-hillsborough/

9. Cited in Dixon, P. (2018), *Warrior Nation: War, Militarisation and British Democracy*, Forceswatch, p. 16.

10. Ibid.

11. Angelsey, S., '"It was a huge job, but beautiful. It is, and it was for me, every day": When Sven-Goran Eriksson came to England and won hearts and minds', *FourFourTwo*, 26 August 2024, https://www.fourfourtwo.com/features/when-sven-came-england-and-braved-xenophobic-storm

12. 'David Cameron calls Fifa's England poppy ban "absurd"', BBC News, 9 November 2011, https://www.bbc.co.uk/news/newsbeat-15652356

13. Press Association, 'EDL stages roof-top protest at Fifa headquarters over poppy ban', *Guardian*, 2011, https://www.theguardian.com/football/2011/nov/09/edl-roof-top-fifa-poppy

14. Gysin, C., 'Fury of war dead's families after England footballers are banned from visiting Somme memorial during Euro 2016 because three-hour trip would be "too draining"', *Daily Mail*, 8 June 2016, https://www.dailymail.co.uk/news/article-3630411/Fury-war-dead-s-families-England-footballers-banned-visiting-Somme-memorial-Euro-2016-three-hour-trip-draining.html

15. 'Captain Noble honours local Servicemen', whufc.com, 3 November 2017, https://www.whufc.com/news/articles/2017/november/03-november/captain-noble-honours-local-servicemen

16. 'Bristol Bar: Tank parked outside Glasgow pub for Remembrance Sunday', *Glasgow Times*, 14 November 2021, https://www.glasgowtimes.co.uk/news/19716168.bristol-bar-tank-parked-outside-glasgow-pub-remembrance-sunday/#

17. Delaney, M., 'The time has come for football to start asking some difficult questions about remembrance', *Independent*, 11 November 2019, https://www.independent.co.uk/sport/football/news/poppy-armistice-day-2019-remembrance-a9198001.html

18. McClean's experience is very well covered in Kay, O., 'James McClean, Wrexham's new signing who suffers "more abuse than any other in England"', *Athletic*, 19 July 2023, https://www.nytimes.com/athletic/4618457/2023/06/19/james-mcclean-the-footballer-who-suffers-more-abuse-than-any-other-in-england/

19. Kenny-Jones, P., 'The four new coronation chants Liverpool fans sung during victory over Brentford' (video), Empire of the Kop, 7 May 2023, https://www.empireofthekop.com/2023/05/07/four-coronation-chants-liverpool/

20. 'James McClean: Wrexham player "makes no apology" over anti-monarchy song', BBC Sport, 16 April 2024, https://www.bbc.co.uk/sport/football/68829125

21. Qatar 2022 and All That

1. Batty, D., 'Peter Tatchell stopped in Qatar while staging LGBT+ rights protest', *Guardian*, 25 October 2022, https://www.theguardian.com/uk-news/2022/oct/25/peter-tatchell-qatar-doha-lgbt-rights-protest

2. House of Commons, Foreign Affairs Committee, 'Oral evidence', 8 May 2018, https://committees.parliament.uk/oralevidence/7929/html/; 'Foreign and Commonwealth Office's preparations for the 2018 World Cup in Russia', Committees, UK Parliament, 8 and 9 May 2018, https://committees.parliament.uk/work/2842/the-foreign-and-commonwealth-office-s-preparations-for-the-world-cup-inquiry/

3. House of Commons, Culture, Media and Sport Committee, 'Homophobia in Sport', 2017, https://publications.parliament.uk/pa/cm201617/cmselect/cmcumeds/113/113.pdf

4. 'Stonewall: "Homophobic views still prevalent in sport"', PFA, 21 September 2016, https://www.thepfa.com/news/2016/9/21/stonewall-homophobic-views-still-prevalent-in-sport

5. Letts, D. and Magrath, R. (2022), 'English Football, Sexuality, and Homophobia: Gay Fans' Perspectives on Governance and Visibility', in Coombs, D. and Osborne, A. (eds), *Routledge Handbook of Sport Fans and Fandom*, Routledge, pp. 192–203, https://pure.solent.ac.uk/ws/portalfiles/portal/32338231/2022_Handbook_of_Sports_Fandom_Letts_and_Magrath.pdf

6. @JHenderson, Twitter/x 6 December 2020, https://x.com/JHenderson/status/1335713994498334729

7. Both these quotes from Lucas, K., '"It was clear they wanted you to conform": What being in Qatar was like for England fans', *theIpaper*, 19 September 2022, https://inews.co.uk/sport/football/world-cup-2022-what-qatar-like-england-fans-2035873?srsltid=AfmBOorf7FTYATnrf5c0ng0Rs1qCl-HgQpaJ3OSocxPB0ClaEJL5Ma9U

8. MacInnes, P., 'Iran supporters continue World Cup protests on tense evening in Qatar', *Guardian*, 29 November 2022, https://www.theguardian.com/football/2022/nov/29/protests-around-iran-at-world-cup-continue-but-security-take-a-step-back

9. Pritchard, D., 'World Cup 2022: Wales fans' rise from counterculture to mainstream', BBC Sport, 18 November 2022, https://www.bbc.co.uk/sport/football/63506860

10. Sheen's performance can be seen at 'Michael Sheen gives rousing speech to Welsh national team: "That's the blood of Wales"', *Guardian Sport*, YouTube, 28 September 2022, https://www.youtube.com/watch?v=Ek43TZJhUGc

11. James, E., 'For Wales fans, the Qatar World Cup is bleak and brilliant all at once', *Guardian*, 24 November 2022, https://www.theguardian.com/football/blog/2022/nov/24/for-wales-fans-the-qatar-world-cup-is-bleak-and-brilliant-all-at-once

12. '"Welsh language fight will always be there": Footballer Ben Davies on how he deals with online hate', ITV News, 3 February 2023, https://www.itv.com/news/wales/2023-02-03/ben-davies-the-welsh-language-fight-will-always-be-there

13. Lewis, T., 'Campaigners back Gwynedd football club trolled over Welsh language stance', *North Wales Live*, 4 August 2023, https://www.dailypost.co.uk/news/north-wales-news/campaigners-back-gwynedd-football-club-27438018

14. 'England vs Wales World Cup Fans Fight Each Other in Tenerife', Daily Motion, https://www.dailymotion.com/video/x8fukv0

15. Grant, J., 'DOPPELGANGER: Who is England superfan Andy Milne? Meet the Steve McClaren lookalike cheering on Euro 2024 national team', *Sun*, 2024, https://www.thesun.co.uk/sport/28796467/andy-milne-england-superfan-euro-2024-national-team-who/

16. See 'England Fan in Qatar: Free Palestine!', In Context, YouTube, 5 December 2022, https://www.youtube.com/watch?v=1Itk7jjsYug

17. Ingle, S., '"Fan culture is changing": England cheered by diverse crowds in Qatar', *Guardian*, 2 December 2022, https://www.theguardian.com/football/2022/dec/02/safe-and-welcoming-england-fan-culture-diversifying-in-qatar

18. Araujo, F., 'The lack of black faces in the crowds shows Brazil is no true rainbow nation', *Guardian*, 1 July 2014, https://www.theguardian.com/commentisfree/2014/jul/01/brazil-black-faces-crowd-rainbow-nation-world-cup

22. Power Games

1. The whole sorry process is well chronicled in Conn, D. (2012), *Richer than God: Manchester City, Modern Football and Growing Up*, Quercus.

2. Ibid.

3. Conn, D., 'From desert skyscrapers to Manchester City's sky blue land of riches', *Guardian*, 18 September 2009, https://www.theguardian.com/football/2009/sep/18/manchester-city-abu-dhabi-mubarak

4. See, for example: 'United Arab Emirates, 2023', Amnesty International, 2023, https://www.amnesty.org/en/location/middle-east-and-north-africa/middle-east/united-arab-emirates/report-united-arab-emirates/; Hassan, T., 'UAE Events of 2023',

Human Rights Watch, 2024, https://www.hrw.org/world-report/2024/country-chapters/united-arab-emirates

5. Goulding, R., Leaver, A. and Silver, J. (2022), 'Manchester offshored: A public interest report on the Manchester Life partnership between Manchester City Council+ The Abu Dhabi United Group'; Goulding, R., Leaver, A. and Silver, J. (2024), 'When the Abu Dhabi United Group Came to Town: Constructing an Organisational Fix for State Capitalism through the Manchester Life Partnership', *Antipode*, 56(3), pp. 896–921.

6. 'Tech-Hungry Mubadala Pours $2B In New Partnership With US-Based Silver Lake', *Forbes*, 20 September 2020, https://www.forbesmiddleeast.com/innovation/technology/mubadala-to-invest-$2b-in-pe-firm-silver-lake

7. 'How Oil Money Distorts Global Football', *Der Spiegel*, 11 February 2018, https://www.spiegel.de/international/world/financial-fair-play-manchester-city-and-psg-pact-with-the-sheikhs-a-1236414.html

8. For overviews and detailed commentary on Football Leaks and the various inquires see: Buschmann, R. and Wulzinger, M. (2018), *Football Leaks: Uncovering the Dirty Deals Behind the Beautiful Game*, Faber & Faber; Delaney, M. (2024), *States of Play: How Sportswashing Took Over Football*, Hachette.

9. 'Manchester City showed "blatant disregard" in Uefa FFP case, but didn't breach FFP says Cas', BBC Sport, 28 July 2020, https://www.bbc.co.uk/sport/football/53571659

10. Goh, C.L. and Anderson, J. (2021), 'Unveiling the Criticisms of the Court of Arbitration for Sport', available at SSRN 3951894.

11. The scale and reach of Saudi sports sponsorship can be seen here: Elsborg, S. and Zidan, K., 'Saudi Arabia's grip on World Sport', Play the Game, 2024, https://www.playthegame.org/media/rxflxlpt/saudi-arabias-grip-on-world-sport.pdf

12. Ingle, S., '"English football will sell itself to anyone": human rights groups condemn Saudi-Newcastle deal', *Guardian*, 7 October 2021, https://www.theguardian.com/football/2021/oct/07/english-football-will-sell-itself-to-anyone-human-rights-groups-on-saudi-newcastle-deal

13. NUFC, 'News. Club statement', 9 September 2020, https://www.newcastleunited.com/en/news/club-statement2

14. Competition Appeals Tribunal, 'St James Holdings Limited v The Football Association Premier League Limited', 22 April 2021,

https://www.catribunal.org.uk/cases/14025721-st-james-holdings-limited

15. Premier League, 'Premier League Statement', 7 October 2021, https://www.premierleague.com/news/2283712

16. Kirchgaesnner, S., 'Revealed: Newcastle chairman's links to Saudi "anti-corruption" drive', *Guardian*, 16 October 2021, https://www.theguardian.com/world/2021/oct/16/revealed-newcastle-chairmans-links-to-saudi-anti-corruption-drive

17. Amin, L. et al., 'Revealed: How Tory minister aided Saudi takeover of Newcastle United', *Open Democracy*, 26 September 2022, https://www.opendemocracy.net/en/dark-money-investigations/saudi-arabia-newcastle-united-takeover-gerry-grimstone/

18. A good survey of what little investment has occurred, as yet, is Whitehead, J., 'Saudi influence in Newcastle: A story of property, prosperity and power', *Athletic*, 6 October 2023, https://www.nytimes.com/athletic/4932881/2023/10/06/newcastle-saudi-city-reubens/

19. See, for example: 'My specialist subject is football. It's what I know and as soon as I deviate from that into an area where I don't feel qualified to have a huge opinion I go into dangerous ground so, at the moment, I prefer to stick to what I believe I know.' Quoted in Taylor, L., 'Howe maintains tunnel vision amid Newcastle human rights questions', *Guardian*, 16 March 2022, https://www.theguardian.com/football/2022/mar/16/eddie-howe-tunnel-vision-newcastle-human-rights-questions

20. Kearns, C., Sinclair, G., Black, J., Doidge, M., Fletcher, T., Kilvington, D., Liston, K., Lynn, T. and Santos, G.L. (2024), '"Best run club in the world": Manchester City fans and the legitimation of sportswashing?', *International Review for the Sociology of Sport*, 59(4), pp. 479–501.

21. A detailed survey of the charges can be seen in Whitehead, J., 'Man City's Premier League charges – exploring what their past cases and evidence reveals', *Athletic*, 31 January 2025, https://www.nytimes.com/athletic/5925048/2025/01/31/manchester-city-premier-league-charges-evidence/?source=emp_shared_article

22. Johnson, I., 'Bayern Munich fans unfurl anti-Glazer and Sheikh Mansour banner vs Man City', *Manchester Evening News*, 12 April 2023, https://www.manchestereveningnews.co.uk/sport/football/football-news/bayern-banner-glazers-sheikh-mansour-26678117

23. Playing Against the Clock

1. 'Alliance survey: bad weather and lack of facility investment is impacting participation figures', SRA, 2014, https://sportandrecreation.org.uk/news/alliance-survey-bad-weather-and-lack-of-facil

2. Welsh, J., 'Carlisle United and their two-year battle to get over Storm Desmond', Planetfootball, 8 February 2018, https://www.planetfootball.com/in-depth/carlisle-united-two-year-battle-get-storm-desmond

3. BASIS, 'Game Changer: The impact of climate change on sports in the UK', 2018, https://static1.squarespace.com/static/58b40fe1be65940cc4889d33/t/5a79bac853450a7495861454/1517927115822/Game+Changer.pdf

4. House of Commons, Digital, Culture, Media and Sport Committee, 'Oral evidence', 28 March 2023, https://committees.parliament.uk/oralevidence/12939/html/

5. Cited in BASIS, 'Game Changer 2: The impact of climate change on sports in the UK', 2023, https://basis.org.uk/wp-content/uploads/2023/11/Game_Changer_2.pdf

6. Ibid. See also 'Storm Henk floods Worsbrough Bridge Athletic's Park Road ground', BBC News, 5 January 2024, https://www.bbc.co.uk/news/uk-england-south-yorkshire-67885656

7. Moldoveanu, R., 'Powerleague Nottingham football pitch almost completely underwater following Storm Henk', *Nottingham Live*, 4 January 2024, https://www.nottinghampost.com/news/local-news/powerleague-nottingham-football-pitch-almost-9013033

8. Jervis, O., 'Whitby Town sound "slow death" warning as non-league clubs combat climate change', *Yorkshire Post*, 7 February 2024, https://www.yorkshirepost.co.uk/sport/football/whitby-town-sound-slow-death-warning-as-non-league-clubs-combat-climate-change-4508006

9. Goldblatt, D., *Playing Against the Clock, Global Sport and the Climate Crisis*, Rapid Transition Alliance, 2020, https://rapidtransition.org/resources/playing-against-the-clock/

10. 'Nearly half of all professional football stadiums put at risk by climate change', Zurich, 9 October 2023, https://www.zurich.co.uk/media-centre/football-and-climate-change

11. 'The Red Way', Liverpool FC, 2021, https://backend.liverpoolfc.com/sites/default/files/2023-03/LFC%20The%20Red%20Way%20V12%20-%20compressed.pdf

12. Hopkinson, T., 'Graham Potter explains why managing Brighton in the Premier League is just like gardening', *Mirror*, 21 February 2021, https://www.mirror.co.uk/sport/football/news/graham-potter-reveals-how-gardening-23528845

13. Kay, O., 'Duncan Ferguson: Vegan burgers, global warming, and putting Forest Green on the map', *Athletic*, 6 February 2023, https://www.nytimes.com/athletic/4156870/2023/02/06/duncan-ferguson-forest-green-rovers-everton/

14. Sales, D., 'HYPOCRITES: Forest Green Rovers branded hypocrites as players caught gobbling chicken, fish and chips despite club's vegan claims', *Sun*, 11 November 2018, https://www.thesun.co.uk/sport/football/7716040/forest-green-rovers-vegan-chicken-fish-chips/

15. Taylor, M., 'Cheddar AFC causes a stir with fresh vegan sponsorship deal – with support of famous England star', *Somerset Live*, 20 August 2023, https://www.somersetlive.co.uk/news/somerset-news/cheddar-afc-causes-stir-fresh-8692079

16. Lockwood, D., 'Premier League domestic flights: BBC Sport research shows 81 flights from 100 games', BBC Sport, 23 March 2023, https://www.bbc.co.uk/sport/football/65017565

17. Mallows, T., 'Nottingham Forest boss Steve Cooper defends flying to Blackpool for FA Cup tie', BBC Sport, 9 January 2023, https://www.bbc.co.uk/sport/football/64208101

18. 'Door to turnstile: Improving travel choices for football fans', Campaign for Better Transport, 2013, https://bettertransport.org.uk/wp-content/uploads/legacy-files/research-files/Door_to_Turnstile_CfBT_FINAL_web.pdf

19. Townsend, M., 'Football joins tourism's premier league as overseas fans flock to games', *Guardian*, 21 October 2012, https://www.theguardian.com/football/2012/oct/21/football-tourism-premier-league

20. 'UEFA Circular Economy Guidelines', UEFA, 2024, https://editorial.uefa.com/resources/0287-19687e946432-280d53c9ac66-1000/uefa_circular_economy_guidelines_low_res.pdf

21. Daddi, T. et al., 'The environmental awareness and behaviour of professional football supporters: an empirical survey', Life Tackle Project, 2020, https://lifetackle.eu/assets/files/LIFE_TACKLE_Report_on_supporters_survey.pdf

22. Dixon, E., 'Two thirds of UK fans believe soccer should be more sustainable', sportspro, 29 November 2024, https://www.sportspro.com/news/football-clubs-sustainability-fans-study-premier-league-efl-november-2024/

23. 'Fan survey feeds One Pack, One Planet project', wolves.co.uk, 27 January 2023, https://www.wolves.co.uk/news/sustainability/20230127-fan-survey-feeds-one-pack-one-planet-project/

24. 'Lee Dixon appears to doubt global warming during Arsenal commentary', *Independent*, 5 September 2022, https://www.independent.co.uk/sport/football/lee-dixon-global-warming-arsenal-commentary-b2159965.html

25. @cotterill-david Twitter/X, 18 July 2022, https://x.com/cotterill_david/status/1549074386237415424

26. Coates, T., 'Patrick Bamford's goal celebration explained as Leeds United striker details lightning bolt move', *Leeds Live*, 2 September 2021, https://www.leeds-live.co.uk/sport/leeds-united/patrick-bamfords-goal-celebration-lightning-21466535

27. Rood, K., 'If women's football cares about the climate crisis it must cut ties with Barclays', *Guardian*, 2 February 2024, https://www.theguardian.com/football/blog/2024/feb/02/womens-football-climate-crisis-cut-ties-barclays-katie-rood

28. @GaryLineker, Twitter/X, 18 March 2022, https://x.com/GaryLineker/status/1504878980213661703

Conclusion: 'There's Always Next Season'

1. Hytner, D., 'Gareth Southgate challenges England to make history against France', *Guardian*, 5 December 2022, https://www.theguardian.com/football/2022/dec/05/gareth-southgate-challenges-england-to-make-history-against-france

2. Howell, D. (1990), *Made in Birmingham: The Memoirs of Denis Howell*, Queen Anne Press. Howell continued, describing an election rally held at a factory the day after the game: 'Roy [Jenkins] was totally bemused that no question concerned either trade figures nor immigration, but solely the football and whether Ramsey or Bonetti was the major culprit. I tried to be good-humoured about my answers, but for the first time I had real doubts and knew the mood was changing fast – and afterwards my wife Brenda came back from canvassing and said: "I don't like the smell of it at all; it's just like 1959 all over again."'

3. 'PM mocked for football blunder on campaign visit', BBC News, 23 May 2024, https://www.bbc.co.uk/news/videos/cgllg7p9nx3o

4. Hughes, S., 'Political football: How soccer has shaped the UK general election', *Athletic*, 3 July 2024, https://www.nytimes.com/athletic/5605430/2024/07/03/uk-general-election-football/

5. Paley, T., 'Keir Starmer calls for England to scrap kit with new St George's Cross design', *Guardian*, 21 March 2024, https://www.theguardian.com/football/2024/mar/21/keir-starmer-calls-for-england-to-scrap-euros-kit-with-new-st-georges-cross-design-football

6. Rigley, S., 'Nigel Farage says Germans need to "get a sense of humour" if football fans sing Ten German Bombers chant', LBC, 13 June 2024, https://www.lbc.co.uk/news/nigel-farage-says-germans-need-to-get-a-sense-of-humour-ten-german-bombers/

7. See 'Keir Starmer: What Football Means to Me', Labour Party, YouTube, 14 June 2023, https://www.youtube.com/watch?v=sudfSPWfr8E

8. Baldwin, T., 'Keir Starmer's football obsession isn't just good politics … it's at the heart of who he is', *Guardian*, 16 June 2024, https://www.theguardian.com/politics/article/2024/jun/16/keir-starmers-football-obsession-isnt-just-good-politics-its-at-the-heart-of-who-he-is

9. Stacey, K., 'Keir Starmer calls for review of late kick-offs at football matches', *Guardian*, 18 June 2024, https://www.theguardian.com/politics/article/2024/jun/18/keir-starmer-review-late-kick-offs-football-matches; 'Gary Neville Meets Sir Keir Starmer', The Overlap, YouTube, 21 June 2024, https://www.youtube.com/watch?v=d93CyN2G_M4

10. Robson, J., 'Cups thrown at England manager Gareth Southgate after a 0–0 draw with Slovenia at Euro 2024', Associated Press, 26 June 2024, https://apnews.com/article/gareth-southgate-england-fans-beer-cups-cd5911cd2d069644562f0b77d7c952ef

11. @prodnose, Twitter/X, 20 June 2024, https://x.com/prodnose/status/1807456983584227337

12. @ScotNational, Twitter/X, 12 July 2024, https://x.com/ScotNational/status/1811857044523131384

13. @OmarChaudhuri, Twitter/X, 5 July 2024, https://x.com/OmarChaudhuri/status/1809250164483264547/photo/1

14. Freedland, J., 'Gareth Southgate has proved that quiet competence can lift a nation – it's a lesson that goes far beyond sport', *Guardian*, 12 July 2024, https://www.theguardian.com/commentisfree/article/2024/jul/12/gareth-southgate-england-football-woke-keir-starmer; Hume, M., 'Did the Southgate-loving soccerati watch the same Euros as us?', *Spiked*, 15 July 2024, https://www.spiked-online.com/2024/07/15/did-the-southgate-loving-soccerati-watch-the-same-euros-as-us/

15. Walker, E., 'Skirmishes and Simmering Tensions as Blackpool Protest in Wake of Southport Attack Takes Place', The Lead, 3 August 2024, https://thelead.uk/skirmishes-and-simmering-tensions-blackpool-protest-wake-southport-attacks-takes-place

16. Wilson, J., 'Sunderland's anti-riot stance shows how football clubs and cities are proudly united', *Guardian*, 10 August 2024, https://www.theguardian.com/football/article/2024/aug/10/sunderlands-anti-riot-stance-football-clubs-cities-proudly-united

17. Hopcraft, A. (2013), *The Football Man: People & Passions in Soccer*, Aurum.

18. Mason, R., 'Keir Starmer's £35k in free tickets puts football regulator plans under scrutiny', *Guardian*, 19 September 2024, https://www.theguardian.com/politics/2024/sep/19/keir-starmers-35k-in-free-tickets-puts-football-regulator-plans-under-scrutiny

19. MacInnes, P., 'Hopes for regulator in the balance as Lords tie up Football Governance Bill', *Guardian*, 14 January 2025, https://www.theguardian.com/football/2025/jan/14/hopes-for-regulator-in-the-balance-as-lords-tie-up-football-governance-bill

20. See Campos, P. (2022), *A Fan's Life: The Agony of Victory and the Thrill of Defeat*, University of Chicago Press, for the US experience of this phenomenon.

21. Meek, J., 'The Two Jacobs', *London Review of Books*, 1 August 2019, https://www.lrb.co.uk/the-paper/v41/n15/james-meek/the-two-jacobs

22. 'State of Old Trafford's disrepair evident as water floods Manchester United's stadium – video', *Guardian*, 13 May 2024, https://www.theguardian.com/football/video/2024/may/13/old-trafford-water-floods-manchester-united-stadium-video

23. Low, H., 'AFC Wimbledon stadium flood "was a matter of time"', BBC News, 8 October 2024, https://www.bbc.co.uk/news/articles/cx2ypg2m9rpo

24. 'Wigan's game against Huddersfield postponed due to flooding', *Independent*, 1 January 2025, https://www.independent.co.uk/sport/wigan-huddersfield-league-one-horse-racing-england-b2672417.html

25. Jones, M., 'Storm Eowyn batters Celtic and Rangers stadiums as roof ripped off and match under threat', *Mirror*, 24 January 2025, https://www.mirror.co.uk/sport/football/news/storm-eowyn-celtic-rangers-ibrox-34548924

Index

Abdullah, Tewfik 344
'Abide with Me' 321
Abraham, Tammy 53
Abramovich, Roman 19, 43, 224, 227, 228, 245
Abu Dhabi National Oil Company (ADNOC) 347
Abu Dhabi royal family 44, 346
Abu Dhabi United Group (ADUG) 350
academy system 71–3, 77–8, 147, 386
Accrington Stanley 231, 247, 380
Adams, Ian 181
Adams, Tony 8, 148
Adarabioyo, Tosin 64
Agnelli, Andrea 189, 190
Agüero, Sergio 17
Alan Turing Institute 150
Alcapone, Dennis:
'World Cup Football' 220–1
Al-Fahim, Sulaiman 234–5, 346
al-Faraj, Ali 235
Al-Fayed, Mohamed 41, 279, 345
Al Mubarak, Khaldoon 346, 347, 350

al-Qadi, Wael 249
Al-Rumayyan, Yasir 353–4
Al Saud, Mosaad 345
Al Shahadat, Malik 295
Al Shammari, Nawaf 346
Alcapone, Dennis 220
All or Nothing (Amazon) 10
Allam, Assem 256
Allardyce, Sam 32, 131–3
Alli, Dele 134, 141, 145, 151
Allison, Sam 83
All-Party Parliamentary Group on Football 258–9
Aluko, Eni 55, 272, 276
Amini, Mahsa 333
Amnesty International 330, 351
Amorim, Ruben 388
Amoruso, Lorenzo 121
Ancelotti, Carlo 145
Anderson, Lee 200, 379
Anderson, Rachel 268
Andrews, Peter 72
Annagh United 360
Annan Athletic 129

anti-fascist/racist groups 52, 59, 393
anti-vaccine movement 174, 175
Antonio, Michail 152
Antonov, Vladimir 235
AONISC (Amalgamation of Northern Ireland Supporters Clubs) 117
Ape Kids Club FC 307
Arab Spring 389
Archibald, Steve 127
Ardiles, Ossie 40
Argentina national team 342
Armed Forces Covenant 325
Armistice Day 320–1, 323
Armitage, Simon 217
Arsenal
Arteta at 356
and Covid 142, 165
FA Cup final (1932) 80
fans 12, 107, 159, 192, 248, 308, 317, 380
green initiatives 364, 370
League title (1931) 37
ownership 229
remembrance 324–5
Wenger at 41, 177

Arteta, Mikel 142, 356
Ashburner, Charles 196
Ashley, Mike 257, 351, 354
Ashton, Luke 303
Ashworth, Dan 388
Asians (British) 54, 157, 159, 293
Assembly, Legislative 112
Astle, Jeff 152
Aston Villa 27, 38, 46, 49, 70, 82, 156, 158, 193, 204, 229, 243, 247, 262, 305, 308, 346, 365, 382
Aston, Ken 81, 97
Athletic 251, 278
Atkinson, Ron 40
Atlético Madrid 141
Attanasio, Mark 387
Atwell, Stuart 96
Atyeo, John 314
Aubameyang, Pierre-Emerick 52, 365
Auld, Bertie 127
AUOB Cymru (All Under One Banner Wales) 197
Aurier, Serge 143

Ba, Demba 19
Backer, Alexander 333
Bacuna, Juninho 159
Bagehot, Walter 389
Bailey, James 7
Bailey, John 285
Bakay, Berke 236
Baker, Danny 381
Bala 104
Baldwin, Rhys 89
Bale, Gareth 104, 105, 336
Ball, Alan 26
Balls, Ed 29
Ballysillan Swifts 112
Balotelli, Mario 214
BAME
    commentators/reporters 58
    fan abuse 53
    online abuse 159
    player abuse 54–5

referees 83–4
supporters/fan groups 60–1, 84
targets (Diversity Code) 162
see also racism
BAME Coaches Association 55, 163
BAME Football Forum 54–5
BAME Referee Support Group 84
Bamford, Patrick 373
Banbury United 360
Bangla Bantams 61–2
Bankas Dnoras 235
Barcelona 177, 189–90, 348
Barclays 281, 374
Barnes, John 8, 62, 161, 221
Barnsley 38, 216, 242, 243
Barr, Jethren 115
Barry, Paul 231
Barton, Joey 249, 276, 392
Barton Rovers 359
Basque football 23
Bastard, Segar 81
Batson, Brendon 62, 314
Bayat, Mogi 238–9
Bayern Munich 27, 28, 177, 183, 191, 356
BBC
    Qatar World Cup coverage 330
    Sports Personality of the Year 273
    women's football coverage 268–9, 270
    see also individual programmes
BBC Wales 142
Beale, Bobby 7
Beardsley, Peter 56, 70
Beaune, Clément 191
Beckham, David 30, 204, 217, 312, 333
Beckham, Victoria 9
beIN Sports 351–2
Belfast Agreement 108, 110, 112, 117, 121

Belfast City 113
Bell, Colin 314
Bellamy, Craig 70, 154
Bellingham, Jude 381
Belper Town 359
Benham, Matthew 229
Benjamin, Andrew 197
Bennell, Barry 75, 76
Bent, Marcus 154
Benton, Scott 343
Berlusconi, Silvio 189
Berylson, John 234
BES Utilities 232
Best, George 178, 286, 318
Beswick, Gary 246
Better Together campaign 127
Bet365 300
Betting and Gaming Council 302
Betway 46, 300
The Big Step (charity) 221, 304
Bigley, Ken 318
bin Abdulaziz, Salman 353
bin Mosaad Al Saud, Prince Abdullah 345
bin Salman, Mohammed 353, 354
bin Zayed, Mohamed 356
Birmingham City 242, 372
BK8 305–6
Black Collective of Media in Sport (BCOMS) 58
Black Footballers Partnership (BFP) 162
Black Lives Matter movement 156, 157, 158
Blackburn Rovers 41, 131, 242, 290, 382
Blackburn United 54
Blackpool 38, 172, 232, 257
BlackRock 229
Blair, Tony 42, 109, 258, 321
Blakeley, Lydia 215

Blantyre United 297
Blatter, Sepp 91
Bloody Sunday 100, 326
Bloom, Tony 229
Boavista 23
Bolasie, Yannick 219
Bolton Wanderers 49, 131, 132, 152, 315
Bonnyrigg Rose 129
Borussia Dortmund 191
Bowery, Jordan 249
Boylett, Mandy 29
Bradford City 38, 61, 237–8
Bradley, Ben 145
Bradshaw, Dave 87
Brady, Karren 30, 165, 389
Brady, Tom 242
Branfoot, Ian 364
Brent Council 210
Brentford 38, 47, 53, 94, 158, 159, 176, 179, 220, 229, 304, 370, 372, 374
Brentwich United 6, 229
Brexit Party 160
Brexit Referendum (2016)
  aftermath 1, 32–6
  build-up 29–32
  hate crime increase after 52, 59
  Leave campaign 2, 30, 31, 34, 40, 79
  Remain campaign 30–1, 378
  voting patterns 38–9, 69, 101
Bridge, Platt 87
Brighouse, Harold: The Game 222
Bright Path investments 242
Brighton and Hove Albion 38, 255–6
Bristol City 156, 231, 254, 314, 364
Bristol, Paul/Thea 230
Bristol Rovers 39, 249, 255–6, 275, 276, 345, 368, 380

British Army 323, 324, 326
British Empire 329
British Future survey 137
British Legion see Royal British Legion
British military 320, 321–2, 325–6
Brooking, Trevor 324
Brown, Gordon 29, 42
Brown, Laurie 181
Brown, Wes 154
Bruce, Kenny 111
Bruce, Steve 131, 365
Brunton Park, Carlisle 358
Bryson, Jamie 113
BT Sport 157
bucket hats 335–6
Budge, Ann 128–9
Buford, Bill: Among the Thugs 217
Bugg, Jake 219
Bugiel, Omar 159
Burnden Park disaster, Bolton (1946) 3, 315
Burnham, Andy 195
Burnley 37, 39, 155, 157, 256, 305, 361
Burrowes, David 191
Burt, Jason 383
Burtenshaw, Norman 81, 82
Burton Albion 231
Bury 49
Busby, Matt 25, 27, 314, 316, 318, 388
Byrne, Ian 284

Cairney, Frank 77
Callaghan, Ian 286
Calvin, Michael 72
Cambridge United 39, 231
Cameron, David 29, 32, 51, 322, 378
Campbell, Sol 31, 63
Campus, Etihad 347
Camsell, George 315
Cantona, Eric 31, 295
Capel Celyn 335
Capello, Fabio 131, 322
Capital Partners 351

Carabao Cup 171, 248
Cardiff City 18, 33, 51, 70, 105, 106–7, 142, 256, 345
Carling Cup 316
Carlisle, Clarke 148, 261
Carlisle United 358, 380
Carneiro, Eva 280
Carney, Karen 281, 367
Carney Report 281
Carr, J.L.: How Steeple Sinderby Wanderers Won the F.A. Cup 218
Carragher, Jamie 32, 34, 191
Carrick Rangers 114
Carson, Michael 77
Carter, Danielle 60
Cartwright, Anthony: Iron Towns 218
Casement Park, Belfast 115, 116–18
Casement, Roger 117
Casey, Baroness 204
Casey Report 204–5, 207
Cash, Matty 247
CASisDEAD 221
Cassidy, Martin 89
Casuals United 59
Cattermole, Lee 84
Caulker, Steven 152
Cavanagh, Edward 82
Cazoo 46
Cech, Petr 32
Ceferin, Aleksander 190
Celtic
  European Cup 26, 27, 28
  fans 28, 114, 119–20, 126, 312, 317, 326, 327
  see also Old Firm
Celtic Boys Club 75–6, 77
Celtic Park, Glasgow 99, 122, 124, 126, 312, 326, 394
Chainrai, Balram 235
Champions League
  club income 46, 120, 194
  and Covid 141–2

English clubs win 17,
  28, 228, 348, 355, 356
expanded 187
final 2022 263–4
game delayed by
  EastEnders 8
music 326
and Super League 189,
  190, 194
UEFA club punishments
  349–50
Changing Lives FC 294
Chansiri, Dejphon 242–3
Chapman, Herbert 314
Charity Shield 187
Charles III, King 326–7
Charlton Athletic 74
Chaudhuri, Omar 38
Cheddar AFC 367
Chelsea
  Champions League 17,
    28, 228
  decline first Euro 25
  fans 19–20, 39, 52, 64,
    94, 96, 192, 227, 228,
    261, 317, 364–5
  Game Zero 375
  Mourinho as manager
    19, 86, 280
  ownership 19, 43,
    227–8, 229
  player contracts 48
  racism at 50, 70
  sale 224, 228
  sexual abuse case 74
  2014–15 League season
    19
Chelsea Charitable
  Foundation 228
Chelsea Supporters'
  Trust 192
Chesham United 378
Chiedozie, John 221
Chiellini, Giorgio 32
China Dili 244–5
China, investment in
  English football 243–5
Chinese Communist
  Party 243
Chinese Super League
  243
The Christmas Truce
  (play) 222

Churchill, Winston 157
City of Manchester
  Stadium 347
  see also Etihad
    Stadium
Clancy, Kevin 85
Clapton Community FC
  296
Clark, Dave 220
Clarke, Greg 131, 157–8,
  188, 279
Clattenburg, Mark 83,
  97
Cleverly, James 330
Cliff, Simon 349–50
Cliftonville FC 111, 113,
  114
climate change/crisis
  activism/direct action
    373–4, 375–6, 394
  carbon emissions of
    football 362–3
  and carbon zero 375
  decarbonisation efforts
    363–4
  greenwashing 375
  pitch flooding 358–61,
    393 394
  predictions 361
  sceptics/deniers 372–3,
    374, 393
  and sportswear 363,
    370–2
  and transport 363–70
  water shortage 361
Climate Coalition 359
Clough, Brian 40
Clowes, David 232
Club Together FC 295
Clyde Greenock Morton
  129
*C'mon Wales: Our Euro
  2016* (BBC Wales) 103
coaching/coaches
  academy system 71–3,
    77–8, 147, 386
  mental health problems
    154–5
  modern *vs* traditional
    287
  opportunities limited
    for Blacks 62, 63,
    162–3

sexual abuse 73–8
touchline behaviour 86,
  246
Coalisland Athletic 111
Coates family 231
cocaine 154, 205, 207,
  251–2
Cohen, George 314
Colchester United 157,
  231, 361
Cole, Ashley 307
Cole, Cheryl 9
Coleman, Chris 103
Coleman, Fitzroy 220
Coleraine Casual Army
  114
Collins, Jamie 105
Collymore, Stan 62
Colston, Edward 156
commentators/pundits
  58, 275, 276–7, 392
Community Shield 187
Competition Appeal
  Tribunal 352
Conservative Party
  austerity 1, 16, 46, 284,
    289, 354, 386
  and Covid 141, 142–3,
    145, 164–5, 170, 171,
    172
  election timing (2024)
    337–8
  football affiliations
    160–1, 261
  homophobia in sport
    inquiry 331
  'hostile environment'
    policy 51
  Illegal Migration Bill
    343
  and independent
    football regulator 195,
    261–3, 364, 389
  One Britain, One
    Nation Day 198
  open to Russian money
    19, 227
  racism summits 56, 60
  sanctions Russian
    oligarchs 224, 228
  on taking the knee 200
  see also Brexit; Scottish
    Conservative Party

Constantine United 293
Conte, Antonio 227, 246
Conway, Paul 242
Cook, Garry 347
Coon, Caroline 215
Cooney, Kyra 271
Cooper, Jilly 363
Cooper, Steve 368
Corinaldi, Delroy 163
Coronation Street 5, 6, 7, 8, 11, 12
cost of living crisis 1, 224, 225, 283, 285, 338
Cotterill, David 372
Couhig, Rob 245
Court for the Arbitration of Sport (CAS) 350–1
Cove Rangers 129
Coventry City 158, 219, 241
Covid pandemic
  and Champions League tie 141–2
  crowds return after 87, 170, 171, 224, 246
  football as metaphor 146
  and mental health decline 146, 147
  mutual help networks 144–5
  national lockdowns 142–3, 170, 171
  and Premier League 46–7, 141, 142, 144, 164–5, 166–9, 170–3, 182, 224
  protocol breaking 143–4, 169, 250
  vaccination programme 171, 174–6
Cowling, Robbie 231
Crawley Town 56, 144, 148
Crerand, Paddy 127
Cresswell, Ryan 151
Crewe Alexandra 75, 76, 231, 380
Crooks, Garth 62, 221
Crosland, Tony 378
Crouch, Peter 311, 373

Crouch, Tracey 261, 263
Crumlin Star 112, 114
cryptocurrency 306, 307–8
Cryptodragons 307
Crystal Palace 31, 38, 53, 158, 160, 220, 229, 248, 250, 256–7, 263, 284, 308, 373, 385, 390
Cucurella, Marc 93
Cummings, Dominic 30
Cunningham, Laurie 314
cycling 370
Cymru 104, 196, 337
see also Wales national team

Dagenham 230
Dai Yongge 244–5
Daily Mail 31, 64, 175, 194, 322, 323, 343
Daily Mirror 29
Daily Record 200
Daily Telegraph 132, 194, 206
Daniels, Jake 331
Danson, Mike 232
data analytics 168–9, 179–80
Davies, Ben 337, 338
Davies, Mims 60
Davies, Pete: *All Played Out* 217
Davis, Keinan 249
Davy, Russell 74
De Bruyne, Kevin 145
Dean, Dixie 286
Dean, Mike 83, 85, 97, 98
Dear England (play) 223–4
Deeney, Troy 53, 157
Defoe, Jermain 367
Dein, David 41
Delaney, Miguel 324
Deller, Jeremy 213, 214
Delph, Fabian 136, 150, 367
Dembélé, Ousmane 179
dementia 152
Demin, Maxim 227

Democratic Football Lads Alliance (DFLA) 59, 159–60
Department for Culture, Media and Sport (DCMS) 157, 233
Der Spiegel 350
Derby County 38, 57, 216, 232, 249, 344
Derry City 110
Diaby, Bambo 57
'Diamond Lights' 218
Diamond, Neil 219
Diana, Princess 318, 321
Díaz, Luis 94
Didcot Town 285
Dier, Eric 365
digital technology 179–80, 182–3
Digne, Lucas 247
Dingley, Hannah 280
Dixon, Lee 372
Dizzee Rascal: 'Shout for England' 218
Docherty, Tommy 181
domestic violence 277
Donald, Stewart 239
Doncaster Rovers 361
Donnelly, John: *The Pass* 222
Doughty, Michael 373
Dowden, Oliver 193
Draghi, Mario 190
Drakeford, Mark 197, 336
drama, football in 221–4
Drury, Peter 372
Duffy, Carol Ann 217
Dulwich Hamlet 284, 344
Dundee Hibernian 312
Dundee United 127, 128, 248, 312
Dunford, Louis 220
Dunk, Lewis 247
Dunn, Pat 217
Dyche, Sean 155
Dyer, Alex 54
Dyke, Emily 86
Dyke, Greg 131
Džeko, Edin 17

Earps, Mary 273
EastEnders (BBC) 6, 7–8, 11, 12
Easter Rising 117
Eastern Senior League 292
Easton Cowboys 215, 295
'Eat Out to Help Out' (Covid) 170
Ebbsfleet United 230, 291
economic crisis (2008) 16, 46
Economist, The 38, 39
Ecotricity 231, 363
Edinburgh City 129
EEC 26–7
Effi, Inih 53
8Xbet 306
Eisner, Michael 235
Ekins, Graham 86
Elizabeth II, Queen 26, 310, 311, 312–13
Elleray, David 81, 83, 94, 97
Ellesmere Port 289
Ellis, David 158
Elšnik. Timi 53
Emmerdale 8, 12
England, Darren 94
England national team
  Euro 1996 133
  Euro 2020 202–4
  Euro 2024 381–3
  new strip (2024) 379
  vs Hungary (1953) 2
  vs Rest of Europe 24, 25
  vs Scotland (2014) 99–100
  World Cup 2018 133–8
  World Cup 2022 340
English Defence League (EDL) 59, 322, 339, 383, 390
English FA *see* Football Association
English Football League (EFL)
  club ownership 230–45, 387

development of 37
gender imbalance of workforce 279–80
Green Football weekend 364
inequality *vs* Premier league 44–6, 48, 49, 281, 386
and Project Big Picture 187
Enke, Robert 148
Enter Shikari 219
Eriksen, Christian 174–5
Eriksson, Sven-Göran 322
Etihad Airways 350
Etihad Campus, Manchester 347
Etihad Stadium, Manchester 160, 270, 317, 347, 349, 371
Eton College 312
Europa Conference League 8, 310
European Championship
  early tournaments 25–6, 28
  1996 28, 100, 133, 135, 142, 223
  2016 29, 30, 51, 32, 103, 104–5, 323, 378
  2020 7, 158, 161, 171, 196–210, 381
  2024 72, 377, 381–3
  2028 116
  Women's (2022) 265
European Conference League 256, 359
European Super League and call for independent regulator 161, 194–5, 389
  formation 188–90
  opposition/cancellation 161, 190–3, 261, 389
  see also Women's European Super League
European Union 1, 2, 20, 29, 31, 32, 39, 40, 69, 101, 108, 109, 110
Evans, Ched 279

Evans, Marcus 242
Evans, Roy 27–8
Everton 27, 47, 96, 188, 220, 227, 229, 250, 286, 308, 319, 375, 387, 390, 394
Evra, Patrice 50
Exeter City 230, 256, 361
Extinction Rebellion 363
Eze, Eberechi 287

FA *see* Football Association
FA Cup 8, 9, 38, 68, 80, 166, 213, 216, 234, 238, 259, 319, 320, 321, 344, 355
Facebook 107, 127–8, 200, 391
'Fanfare for Europe' (1973 festival) 26
Fan-Led Review of Football Governance 261–3
fans/supporters
  disorder, Euro 2020 203, 204–10
  disorder, rise post-Covid 224, 247–52, 255
  fandom in politics 391
  gender makeup of crowds 274
  LGBT groups 331–2
  partisanship 390–1
  and populism 391–2, 393
  protests/campaigns 255–63, 389–90
  and racism *see* racism
  responses to women's game 269–70
  social activism 284, 386
  taking the knee backlash 200–2
  tragedy chanting 313, 316–18
  vegetable throwing 364–5
  see also under individual clubs

Fans Against
  Criminalisation 124,
  127
Fans Against
  Sportswashing 354
Fans Supporting
  Foodbanks 284
Farage, Nigel 160,
  379–80, 392
Faroe Islands 113
Fashanu, Justin 331
fashion industry 370–2
Fatboy Slim 219
Fayed, Dodi 318
FC United 284, 295
Fellowes, Julian: *The
  English Game* 10
Fenway Sports 185
Ferdinand, Anton 50
Ferdinand, Les 62, 63,
  65, 163
Ferdinand, Rio 30, 63,
  156
Ferguson, Alex 17–18,
  86
Ferguson, Barry 127
Ferguson, Duncan 366
Fermino, Roberto 218
Fernandes, Bruno 246
Fiennes, Joseph 223
FIFA 24–5, 92,132, 134,
  142, 322, 323
FIFA (game) 14, 58–9,
  292
FIFPRO surveys 147, 149
Findlay, Alistair 217
Finkelstein, Daniel 261,
  379
First World War 117,
  171–2, 222, 267,
  320–1, 323
Firth, Colin 136
'Fitba Crazy' 148
Flamini, Mathieu 373
Fleetwood Town 232,
  361
Fleming, Harold 314
Floyd, George 156, 157
flying 363, 367–8
Foden, Phil 64
food banks 284, 386
*Football Against the
  Enemy* (Kuper) 217

Football Association (FA)
  'Art and Football'
    exhibition (1953)
    213–14
  ban on women playing
    (1921–72) 267
  Diversity Code 162
  FIFA membership 24
  first woman chair 279
  integration of women's
    game (1993) 266, 268
  lack of reforms 388–9
  patron 313
  racism in 83, 157–8
  response to abuse of
    officials 84–5, 86,
    89–90
  response to racism 54,
    56–7, 59–60
  response to sexual
    abuse scandals 76,
    77–8
  and sale of Wembley
    Stadium 298
  withdrawal from UEFA
    27–8
  and Women's Super
    League 281
Football Association of
  Wales (FAW) 102,
  103–4, 334
Football Foundation 298
Football Lads Alliance
  (FLA) 59
Football Leaks (website)
  350
Football Manager (game)
  34–5, 142, 292
Football Policing Unit
  255
Football Radar 240
Football Supporters'
  Association (FSA) 92,
  188, 255, 258–9, 260,
  261, 263, 331
Football Taskforce (New
  Labour) 43–4, 260
Footballers' Wives (ITV)
  9–10
'Football's Coming
  Home' 135–6
Football's Suicide Secret
  (BBC) 148

Ford, Lucy 275
Forest Green Rovers
  231, 275, 280, 363,
  364, 366, 367, 368,
  371, 373
Fortune, Peter 382
fossil-fuel companies 16
Fosun International 244
Fowler, Arthur 7
Foy, Chris 83
Frank, Thomas 176
Free Palestine campaign
  124, 339
Freedland, Jonathan 382
Freund, Peter 236
Friedkin Group 387
Fry, Stephen 191
Fulham 39, 41, 148, 229,
  279, 298, 314, 345,
  360–1
futsal 290

Gaelic Athletic
  Association (GAA)
  108, 115
Gala Fairydean Rovers
  129
Galinson, Brad 235–6
gambling
  Asian bookmakers
    305–6
  evolution in football
    299
  football advertising
    300–1, 302
  problem gambling
    301–4
  reforms 304
Gambling Act 2005 300
Gambling Commission
  302
Gambling with Lives 303
Game Zero 375
Gascoigne, Paul 143,
  154, 213, 218
Gates, Bill 176, 183
Gay Football Supporters
  Network (GFSN)
  331–2
Gaydamak family 234
Gayle, Howard 62
Geller, Uri 129
Generation Z 146–7

George, Charlie 215
George VI, King 136
Gerrard, Steven 18, 63, 126
Gibson, Steve 230
Giles, Johnny 26
Gillett, George 18, 257
Gillingham 235–6
Ginola, David 8
Girdwood Community Hub 112
Glasgow City 122
Glazer family 18, 185, 188, 387
Glenn, Martin 56, 298
Gnonto, William 57
'God Save the Queen' 99, 108, 112, 199, 310
Gold, David 256, 324
Goldie Lookin Chain 102–3, 219
Goldring, Colin 232–3
golf 311, 351
Gomez, Joe 287
Goodwillie, David 279
Gordon, Douglas
  Tears Are Not Enough 213
  Zidane 214
Gorman, Joe 111
Graham, George 40
Graham, James: Dear England 223–4
Grant, Charles 231
grassroots football
  caged pitches 287–8, 290
  decline and cost of living crisis 284–5
  decline of eleven-a-side/ pitches 288–90
  decline of street football 286–7
  decline of Sunday league 288–9, 293–4
  digital/social media clubs 291
  funding 186–7, 262, 297–8, 367
  inclusiveness 267
  migrant/refugee clubs 293–5

play lost due to weather 358, 359
  rise of referee abuse/ disorder 86–90, 385–6
  socialist/anarchist clubs 295–6
  Sunday league 288–9, 293–4
  walking 290–1
  women's 268
Gravesen, Thomas 154
Grealish, Jack 143, 365
Green Brigade 126–7, 326
Green and White Army 108, 112
Green, Robert 217
greenwashing 375
Greenwood, Mason 279
Greenwood, Ron 221
Grenfell Athletic 297
Grenfell Tower disaster (2017) 225, 297
Griffi, Leigh 114
Griffi, Sandy 81
Grigg, Richard 336
Grigg, Will 109
Grimes, James 302–3
Grimsby Town 160–1, 231, 255, 284, 361
Grimstone, Lord 354
Guardian 76, 133, 271, 380, 383
Guardiola, Pep 176, 177, 178, 183, 192, 348, 356
Guimarães, Bruno 159
Gullit, Ruud 41

Haaland, Erling 356
Hackney Wick 296
Haidt, Jonathan 146
Halesowen Town 380
Hall, John 41
Hammam, Sam 106, 344
Hampden Park, Glasgow 198, 248
Hancock, Matt 164, 165
handball 92
Hansen, Alan 66, 127
Hardaker, Alan 25
Harding, Matthew 227
Hardy, Alan 240

Harper, Kevin 53
Harper, Percy 80
Harrison, Tony: V 216
Hart, Joe 105
Hartlepool United 53, 115, 325
Hashtag United 292
Hassan, Gerry 198
Hassen-Dakhli, Inès 20
hate speech/crimes 51–2, 60
  see also racism
Havertz, Kai 373
Hayes, Emma 277
Hayward, Jack 314, 320
Heaney, Seamus 216
Hearts 125, 127–9, 284, 310, 322, 324
Heath, Eddie 74
Heath, Edward 26
Hector, Renée 53
hedge funds 164, 241, 242, 388
Hegazi, Hussein 344
'Hells Bells' 219
Hemmings, Trevor 231
Henderson, Jordan 192, 332, 367
Hendrie, Lee 153
Henry, John W. 188
Henry, Thierry 29, 221, 314
Her Game Too campaign 275
Hermit, Wallace 55
Hermoso, Jenni 282
Herron, John 111
Heskey, Emile 154
Hewitt, Debbie 279, 359
'Hey Jude' 220
Heysel Stadium disaster (1985) 3, 27, 258, 316
Hibernian 125, 128, 217, 248, 306
Hicks, Tom 18, 257
Hickson, Paul 75
Higgins, Bob 75, 76, 77
Hilborne, Stephanie 273
Hill, Gordon 81, 97
Hill, Ricky 221, 293
Hillsborough Family Support Group 260

Hillsborough Stadium 243
disaster (1989) 3, 18, 160, 258, 259, 316, 318
Hirst, Damien 214
Hobsbawm, Eric 201
Hoddle, Glenn 218, 318
Hodgson, Roy 32, 131, 132, 256, 261
Hoffman, Gary 354
Holgate, Mason 159
Holmes, Duane 53
Holt, Andy 231
Homeless World Cup 145
Hong Kong 229, 235, 245
Hontiveros, Rosa 305
Hooper, Simon 94
Hopcraft, Arthur: *The Football Man* 385
Hornby, Nick: *Fever Pitch* 217, 390
House of Commons Select Committee 56
Howe, Eddie 131, 165, 355
Howell, Denis 378
Howes, Derek 117
Howson, Stephen 293
Huddersfield Town 37, 85, 165, 236, 244, 257, 394
Hudson, Callum 307
Hughes, Richard 165
Hughes, Ted 216
Hull City 153, 239–40, 256, 361
Hull Tigers 256
Hume, Mick 383
Hundal, Sunny 137
Hunt, Bob 366

Ibrox disaster (1971) 3, 315, 316, 317
Iceland 32
Icke, David 372
Ilkeston Town 380
Ilıcalı, Acun 239–40
I'm a Celebrity ... (ITV) 8

'I'm Forever Blowing Bubbles' 220
Independent Football Regulator (IFR) 194–5, 261–3, 364, 389
Infantino, Gianni 92
Inter Milan 19
International Labour Organization (ILO) 329
Ipswich Town 34, 37, 219, 236, 242, 361
Iran protests (2022) 333–4
Irish Cup 113, 114
Irish Football Association (IFA) 108, 111, 113, 114
Islan, Humayun 61
Islandmagee 112
It's Always Sunny in Philadelphia (Netflix) 237
ITV 8, 40, 276
Iwan, Dafydd 335, 336

Jackson, Michael 345
James, David 8, 31, 154
James, Ellis 104
James, Lutel 54
James, Tommy 112
Jameson, Fredric 395
Jarvis, Alan 153
Javid, Sajid 175
Jenas, Jermaine 80
Jennings, Pat 26
Jenrick, Robert 343
'jibbing' 207–8, 251
Joel, Billy 316
Johal, Sarbjot 233
John Paul II, Pope 319
Johnson, Boris 34, 141, 161, 193, 196, 200, 202
Johnson, Brennan 249
Johnson, Gary 74
Jones, Carwyn 105
Jones, Nathan 155
Jones, Sophie 53
Jorgensen, Jeanette 203
JPMorgan Chase 189
Jumpers for Goalposts (play) 222

Junior Cup 112
Just Stop Oil 375
Justice FC 295
Juventus 27, 190, 191

Ka-shing, Li 229
Kaepernick, Colin 157
Kahn, Shahid 298
Kaidi, Tarik 296
Kale Madrid 366
Kamara, Chris 8
Kamara, Hassane 239
Kane, Harry 31, 71, 94, 135, 137, 202, 315, 340, 381
Kano 221
Kaplan, Steve 241
Kapoor, Bhavs 159
Kasanga, Bobby 296
Kavanagh, Chris 246
Keane, Roy 31, 300
Keegan, Kevin 42, 276
Kelly, Chloe 266
Kelly, Dave 284
Kelly, Stephen 318
Kelty Hearts 129
Kensington and Chelsea Council 297
Kent FA 89
Keys and Gray affair 275
Khan, Sadiq 270
Khan, Shahid 345
Khashoggi, Jamal 351
Kick It Out 52, 54, 63, 158
King, Colin 55, 163
King, Gerald 77
Kinnear, Angus 262
Kinsey, James 55
Kitchener, Lord 220
Klein, Naomi 185
Klopp, Jürgen 34, 94, 96, 145, 175, 177–8, 179–80, 246
knee slides 183
Kompany, Vincent 314
Křetínský, Daniel 229
Kroenke, Stan 192
Krul, Tim 145
Kuper, Simon 279
Football Against the Enemy 217

La Liga 167, 190
Labour Party
  election campaign
    (2024) 380–1, 382,
    384
  football affiliations 42,
    202, 389
  Football Taskforce
    43–4, 260
  New Labour and
    football 17–18, 42–4,
    46, 119
  see also Scottish
    Labour; Starmer, Keir
Lai, Guochuan 244
Lambert, Rickie 174
Lamela, Erik 143
Lampard, Frank 63, 79,
    177, 318
Lansdown, Steve 231
Lanzini, Manuel 143
Lasses Against Fascism
    59
LBGT
  and Qatar World Cup
    330–1, 333
  rainbow laces 332
  supporter groups 331–2
Le Tissier, Matt 160,
    174, 175, 372
League Cup 7, 107, 120,
    125, 187, 248, 317,
    355
Leckey, Mark: Fiorucci
    Made Me Hardcore
    214–15
Lee, Chien 242
Lee, Francis 314
Leeds United 27, 38, 57,
    142, 169, 172, 181,
    216, 262, 308, 316
Leicester City 20, 48,
    131, 144, 248, 306,
    320, 322, 325, 361,
    382
Leighton, Jim 127
Lemsagam, Abdallah 345
Lennon, Aaron 151
Lennon, Neil 122
Levien, Jason 241
Lewes FC 295
Lewis, Joe 229
Lewis, John 80, 81

Leyton Orient 155
Liew, Jonathan 265
Lim, Peter 231
Lincoln City 325, 361
Lineker, Gary 222, 330,
    342–3, 373, 375–6
Linfield FC 114
Liverpool
  carbon emissions/action
    362, 364, 365
  Champions League 8,
    28, 141–2, 263–4
  fans 12, 18, 27, 96,107,
    257, 258, 264, 284,
    316, 317, 319, 327,
    332, 384, 390
  Klopp at 96, 175,
    177–8, 179–80, 246
  Northern Ireland moves
    games to 100
  ownership 229
  Premier League title
    (2020) 169
  2013–14 season 18–19
  see also Project Big
    Picture
Livingstone 230, 248
Lloyd Webber, Andrew:
    The Beautiful Game
    222
Lo Celso, Giovani 143
Lockhart, Carla 113
Lofthouse, Nat 286
Loftus, Chris 316
London APSA (All
    People's Sports
    Association) 293
London Bridge attack
    (2017) 59, 319
Longhi, Marco 200
Louis-Dreyfus, Kyril
    239
Lowe brothers 23
Lowe, Rupert 160
Lowry, L. S.: Going to
    the Match 213–14
Lucas, Sarah: Geezer
    215
Lukaku, Romelu 57
Luton Town 73, 172,
    229, 284, 304
Lynam, Des 216, 276
Lyons, Josh 148

MacAnthony, Darragh
    233–4
McCafferty, Jim 77
McClean, James 326, 327
McCoist, Ally 120
McElhenney, Rob 10,
    237
McGinn, Rosie 213
Mackay, Malky 51
Maclean, Rachel 136
McLeish, Henry 119
Macpherson, Archie 127
Macron, Emmanuel 191
Madejski, John 319
Madsen, Imaan 203
Major, John 40, 42
Manchester Arena attack
    (2017) 59, 319
Manchester City
  academy 147
  Champions League
    (2023) 355, 356
  club network 48
  Cup success 220, 238,
    348
  fans 82, 192, 219, 252,
    317, 354, 355, 356
  green initiatives 370,
    371
  Guardiola at 179–80
  income growth 349
  kit 219
  League titles 16–17, 18,
    48–9, 348, 355–7, 384
  ownership, Thai 242,
    346
  ownership, UAE 16–17,
    44, 328, 346–7
  sponsors 45–6, 306,
    349, 350
  sportswashing 354, 355
  stadium sculptures 314
  UEFA regulations
    breached 349–51, 356,
    387
Manchester Life 348
Manchester United
  academy 72
  Beckham on success
    30–1
  Champions League 28
  and cryptocurrency
    307, 308

European Cup quest 25–6
fans 12, 52, 53, 57, 107, 192, 221, 257, 293, 316–17, 318
Ferguson as manager 17–18
medical support 180, 181
ownership 229, 387–8
Premier League dominance 48
sponsors 227, 228
vs Wrexham (2023) 10–11
women's team 270, 271
see also Munich air disaster; Project Big Picture
'Manchester Football Double' 220
Mancini, Roberto 200
Mandarić, Milan 234
Mandela, Nelson 319
Manic Street Preachers 102, 103
Mann, John 54
Mansour, Sheikh 3467, 350, 356
Marber, Patrick 223
Marinakis, Evangelos 142, 229
Marriner, Andre 83
Martin, Russell 161
mascots 67–8, 167, 325
Massey, Sian 275
Massie, Alex 198
Masters, Richard 5, 188, 263, 352
Match of the Day (BBC) 6, 276, 301
strike (2023) 342–3
Matić, Nemanja 326
Matthews, Cerys 102
Matthews, Stanley 314, 365
Maxwell, Robert 256
May, Caz 275
May, Theresa 32, 33–4, 51, 133, 136, 160
MC Zakhar 221
Mee, Ben 374
Meek, James 391

Méïté, Yakou 53
Memorial Stadium, Bristol 249
Mendy, Benjamin 143
mental health
in coaches 154–5
as comedic affliction 148
and Covid 146, 147
crisis 146–7
football as therapy 296–7
in players 146, 147–9, 150, 151–2
Merriman, Huw 191
Messi, Lionel 214, 342
Mic'd Up with Michael Owen 97
Middle East
holy wars 339
presence in English football 15, 17, 225, 229, 328, 344–6
Middlesbrough 38, 133, 230, 249, 361
Milburn, Jackie 314
Miles, Kevin 261
Millichip, Bert 28
Millwall 157, 234
Milne, Andy 339
Milner, James 192
Milton Keynes 231
Mina, Yerry 57
Minds United 296
Mings, Tyrone 156, 204
Moody, Iain 51
Mooney, Noel 290, 334
Moore, Bobby 256, 310, 318
Moore, Darren 163, 215, 243
Moore, Peter 324
Morecambe 232–3, 247, 361
Morfuni, Clem 234
Morris, Mel 232
Morocco national team 341–2
Morton, Greenock 394
Moss, Jon 85
Motherwell 128, 129, 359
Motson, John 320

Mount Pleasant Park FC 295–6
Mourinho, José 19, 86, 132, 143, 280, 301
Moyes, David 127, 145, 165, 221, 256, 286
Munich air disaster (1958) 25, 315, 316, 317
Munoz, Xisco 243
Murphy, Jimmy 336
music and football 102–3, 218–21
Muslim Brotherhood 352
Myers, Ryan 303
MyFootballClub (crowdfunding website) 291

Nagle, Kevin 236
National 200, 381
National Front 59
National League 162, 164, 230, 358, 360, 366, 368
National Lottery 298, 299
Ndombele, Tanguy 143
Ncmmer, Mona 177
Neuer, Manuel 32
Neville, Gary 132, 194, 202–3, 311, 380
New Saints stadium 106
New Salamis FC 293
New York 236, 348
New Zealand 281, 374
Newark & Sherwood United 366
Newcastle United
coach abuse case 75, 77
fans 42, 257, 272
football director 63
injuries 182
Jackie Milburn statue 314
League Cup (2025) 355
mascots 68
ownership, Saudi 328, 346, 351–5
racism at 70
Newcastle United Supporters Trust 352

Newport County 103, 105, 107, 219, 230, 361
Newquay AFC 393
Newry City 114
Newton Heath 257
Neymar Jr 306
NFT (non-fungible tokens) 306–7
Nhadau, Fy 103
Ní Chuilín, Carál 112
Noble, Mark 324
Norgaard, Christian 94
North Berwick 129
North Lancashire and District Football League 288
Northampton Town 53, 80, 148, 249, 314, 380
Northern Ireland
Belfast Agreement 108, 110, 112, 117, 121
Brexit and politics 101, 109–10
sectarianism in football 112–15
stadium upgrades 115–16
2028 Euro bid 115–17
Northern Ireland national team 107–8
fans (Green and White Army) 108
Northern Ireland Premier League 26, 111
Northumberland Youth League 87
Norwich City 57, 77, 161, 215, 322, 361, 365, 380, 387
Nottingham Forest 27, 38, 47, 85, 96, 182, 220, 229, 249, 361, 368
Notts County 53, 84, 219, 237, 240, 324, 393
novels about football 218
NSPCC 75, 76
NUFC Fans Against Sportswashing 354

Nuneaton & District Sunday League 289
Nutmeg (magazine) 129
Nuttall, Paul 160

Ó hOisín, Cathal 107
Oatley, Jacqui 276
Odegaard, Martin 271
Off the Ball (Radio Scotland) 129
Offensive Behaviour and Threatening Communication Act 123
offside 92, 94
Ofili, Chris 214
Okocha, Jay-Jay 132
Old Firm
and domestic violence 277
inequality *vs* Premier clubs 130
and Offensive Behaviour Act 123–4
policing summit 122
Scottish league dominance 119–20, 125–6
sectarian chanting/violence 85, 108, 112, 114, 115, 120–1
see also Ibrox disaster
Old Trafford 192, 314, 387, 393
Oldham Athletic 84, 345
Oldham riots 383
'Olé (We Are England)' 218
Olympiacos 142
'One Britain, One Nation' 198
One Love armbands 332, 333
O'Neill, Michael 31–2
O'Neill, Michelle 113–14
OOF magazine 213, 215
Ormond, George 75
Orwell, George 201
Osman, Danyal 54
osteoarthritis 152
Ottolenghi, Yotam 178
Owen, Michael 97, 307
Owen, Spencer 292

Oxford United 39, 155, 256, 364
Oxlade-Chamberlain, Alex 367
Oyston family 232, 257
Oyston, Owen 257

Pacific Media Group 242
Paddock, Stretford 293
Paddy Power 301
Page, Rob 335
Palmer, Cole 219
Palmer, Kasey 158
Pankhurst, Dale 112
Pannick, Lord 389
Paris Saint-Germain (PSG) 191, 328, 349
Parish, Steve 31, 229, 263
Parnby, Dave 287
Parr, Lily 314
Parreno, Philippe 214
Parry, Rick 188
Partick Thistle 128, 129, 215, 230
Partridge, Pat 81
Patel, Priti 200
Paterson, Don: *Nil Nil* 216
Patrick, Philip 270
Patriotic Alternative 160
PCP Capital Partners 351
Peace, David 218
Peake, Col Tim 325
Peel, John 319
Pell, Harry 247
Pentonville Prison 117
Pérez, Florentino 189
Perry, Grayson: *Football Stands for Everything I Hate* 214
Perryman, Steve 286
Peterborough United 77, 234
Philip, Prince 312
Philippines offshore Gaming Operators (POGO) 305
Phillips, Mark 59
Phoenix FC 295
physiotherapists 180–1
Pick, Frank 213

Pickering, Tony 75
Pickford, William: *How to Referee* 80
Pilley, Andy 232
Pindoria, Davina 159
pitches
  caged 287–8, 290
  fan invasions 248–50, 257, 375
  flooding 358–61
  turf management 182–3
Plaid Cymru 335, 338
plane banners 157, 160, 192
players
  alcohol/drug abuse 148
  British *vs* European 23
  bullying 151
  club success *vs* economic success 38–9
  and cult of youth 66–7
  demanding work schedule 150–1
  gay 331
  injuries 149–50, 151, 180–3
  investment schemes 153–4
  mental-health problems 146, 147–9, 150, 151–2
  numbers playing (UK) 14, 285
  nutrition 177–9
  offences against women 278–9
  pay cut request for (Covid) 164–5
  racism in *see under* racism
  in retirement 152–4
  taking the knee 157, 158, 200–2
  wages 16, 39, 44, 125, 165
  see also under Premier League
PlayZones 298
Plymouth Argyle 361
poetry and football 216–17
Pogba, Paul 53, 307
Police Scotland 123–4

policing football 122, 252–5, 263–4
Poll, Graham 82
Pompey Supporters Trust 235
poppies 313, 321, 322–5
populist politics *vs* football 390, 391–2, 393
Port Vale 230, 249, 380
Portsmouth FC 37, 234–5, 256, 390
Potter, Graham 365
Pour, Ali 111
Powell, Enoch 61
Pozzo, Gino 238, 239
Premier League
  artificial crowds (Covid) 167–8
  and Brexit voting 38–9
  club debt 44, 46–7, 387, 388
  and Covid 46–7, 141, 142, 144, 164–5, 166–9, 170–3, 182, 224
  Elite Player Performance Plan (EPPP) 71
  and European Super League 193–4
  foreign *vs* British ownership (2023–24) 228–9
  foreign players/ managers, early 40–1
  formation 17, 40, 46
  globalisation under New Labour 42–4
  homegrown players limit 44
  impact of crowdless matches (Covid) 168–9
  inequality *vs* EFL 44–6, 48, 49, 281, 386
  misogyny 279
  'No Room for Racism' campaign 60, 157
  player development/ contracts 47–8
  political lobbying 389
  preferential voting rights 188

profit and sustainability rules 46
racism in *see* racism in football
responses to independent regulator 262–3
as richest/most popular league 17
sponsorship 45–6, 227, 228, 300–1, 304, 305–6, 344
tickets sold 14
2011–12 title 16–17
2013–14 season 18–19
2014–15 season 19–20
2015–16 season 20
US as majority owners 387
VAR introduction 79–80, 92
Prescott, John 17
Preston North End 35, 37, 311–12, 361
privatisations 229–30
Pro Evolution (game) 193
Professional Footballers' Association (PFA) 60, 148, 149, 152, 261, 268
Professional Game Match Officials Limited (PGMOL) 94, 96–7
Project Big Picture 185–8, 386, 388
Provan, Davie 127
Public Investment Fund of Saudi Arabia (PIF) 351, 352, 353, 355
Pulis, Tony 215
Punjab United 293
Punjabi Cultural Day 61
Punjabi Forest 61
Punjabi Rams 61
Punjabi Wolves 60–1
Pure Radio Scotland 199
Purslow, Christian 262
Putin, Vladimir 133, 136
pyrotechnics 126, 206, 247, 248

Qatar Investment
  Authority 229
Qatar Tourism Authority
  349
Qatar World Cup 2022
  alcohol restrictions 338,
  341
  BBC coverage 330
  boycott movement 329
  England fans at 338–40
  final 342
  Iranian players/fans at
  334
  LGBT fans at 330–1,
  333
  migrant worker scandal
  328–9
  Moroccan fans at
  341–2
  Qataris/Gulf states at
  340–1
  Welsh fans at 336–7
QPR 17, 63, 242

racism
  Black Lives Matter
  backlash 157–8
  black players speaking
  out 62–5
  in commentary 58
  fans vs players 53–4,
  57–8, 64, 158–9, 364,
  365
  FA's response to post-
  Brexit racism 59–60
  government response
  60
  in grassroots game
  54–5
  increase since Brexit 52,
  59
  managers/coaches
  accused 55–7, 70
  Mann Report 54
  in media 64
  'No Room for Racism'
  campaign 60
  players vs players 53
  Sky Sports survey 52–3
  Radio 5 Live survey 89
Radio Scotland 129
Radio Times (BBC) 6,
  276

Rahic, Edin 237, 238
Railway End Crew 114,
  115
Rainbow Laces
  campaign 332
Raith Rovers 42, 279,
  366
Ramage, Craig 57
Ramsdale, Aaron 248
Ramsey, Aaron 103
Ramsey, Alf 26, 383
Rangers 27, 96, 111,
  119–20, 121, 122,
  125–7, 128, 171, 248,
  306, 315, 324
  see also Old Firm
Ranieri, Claudio 20
Rapid Transition Alliance
  361
Rapid Wien 23
Rapinoe, Megan 270
Rashford, Marcus 145,
  150, 203, 204
Ratcliffe, Jim 387–8
Ravenhill Stadium,
  Belfast 115
Rayner, Angela 191
Reading 244–5, 256, 319
Real Madrid 19, 25, 104,
  189, 190, 214, 263,
  349, 356
Red Lion (play) 222–3
Red Pitch (play) 222–3
Red Wall (Welsh fans)
  104, 335
Redbridge 230
Reddin, Dave 323
Redknapp, Harry 8, 306,
  379
Reedtz brothers 240
Rees-Mogg, Jacob 33,
  161, 391
Ref Support UK 89
referees/officials
  abuse of (grassroots
  game) 86–90
  abuse of (professional
  game) 79–81, 82,
  84–6, 98, 246, 247
  abuse of (social media)
  85
  BAME 83–4
  bodycams 90

conspiracy theories 96
crackdown on dissent
  (2023–24) 246–7
decline in behaviour
  towards, reasons
  85–6
FA response to abuse of
  84–5, 86, 89–90
first female in Premier
  League 276
leaving game 88–9
leniency 85
performance assessment
  95–6
as personalities 97–8
professionalisation of
  82, 83
social class vs players/
  fans 81–3
  see also VAR
REFF (Royal Spanish
  Football Federation)
  190
Reform UK 160, 379,
  390
refugee clubs 294–5
Regis, Cyrille 221, 314,
  319
Reguilón, Sergio 143
Reid, Peter 33
Reid, Steven 152
remembrance
  armbands 310, 311,
  319, 323, 332
  minute's silence 311,
  323
  poppies 313, 321,
  322–5
  strips 325
  statues 314–15
Remembrance Day/
  Sunday 126, 160, 321,
  322–3, 325
Rennie, Uriah 82
Republica Internationale
  295
Reuben Brothers 351
Revie, Don 161, 181
Reynolds, Ryan 10, 237
Rhys, Gruff 103
Rice, Declan 71, 135
Richards, Jazz 104
Richards, Micah 300

Riley, Mike 82
Rising Baller (charity) 151
Riverside Stadium, Middlesbrough 200
Rix, Graham 70
Roberts, Mark 124, 255
Robertson, Andy 307
Robinson, Ben 231
Robinson, Callum 176
Robinson, Karl 155
Robinson, Neil 365
Robinson, Peter 109, 113
Robson, Hal 103, 104
Robson-Kanu, Bobby 318
Romero, Cristian 93
Ronay, Barney 133
Rood, Katie 374
Rooney, Coleen 9
Rooney, Wayne 66, 133, 286
Roper, Frank 74, 78
Rose, Danny 63, 134, 151, 165, 166
Rosenior, Leroy 156
Rotheram, Steve 195
Rotherham United 230, 247
Rous, Stanley 24, 81
Rowlinson, Jakob 215
Royal Air Force 324
Royal British Legion 313, 320, 322, 323, 325
Rubiales, Luis 282
Rugby World Cup 102
Rupp, Stefan 237–8
Russia
  invasion of Ukraine (2022) 1, 47, 224, 228, 283
  presence in English football 227

Sadler, Simon 232
Sage Todz 335
St Albans 219
St George flag 7, 133, 137, 202, 266, 339, 379
St Mirren 128, 129, 216, 312, 359

St Patrick's 112
Saka, Bukayo 203
Salah, Mo 344
Salford United 231
Salmond, Alex 99, 122
Sampson, Mark 55–6
Samuel, Martin 194
San Marino 116
Sancho, Jadon 204, 287
Sarwar, Anas 127
Saudi Arabia
  Newcastle United takeover 328, 346, 351–5
  Vision 2030 351
Savage, Robbie 8
Savile, Jimmy 74
Sawbridgeworth Town 394
Sawiris, Nassef 229, 346
Scadding, Les 230
Scally, Paul 236
Schierenberg, Tai-Shan 215
Schmeichel, Kasper 203
Schmeichel, Peter 8
Scholes, Paul 143
Schön, Helmut 26
Scotland national team
  Euro 2020 198–200
  Euro 2024 381
  underperformance 118–19
  vs England 99–100
  World Cup 1998 118
Scott, Alex 8, 333
Scott, Jill 8
Scott, Mark 121
Scottish Conservative Party 126
Scottish Cup 121, 122, 125, 217, 248
Scottish devolution referendum (1979) 100
Scottish Football Association (SFA) 119
Scottish independence referendum (2014) 29, 99, 126, 127–8
Scottish Labour Party 118, 126, 127

Scottish National Party (SNP) 118, 122–4, 381
Scottish Parliament 118, 124
Scottish Premier League 120, 125, 130, 261
Scottish Review 198
Scottish Sun 199
Scoutable United 294
Scudamore, Richard 30, 279
Scunthorpe 249, 361
Second World War 24, 37, 171, 172, 177, 180, 201, 265, 288, 321, 325
Senator, Asher 221
Shamrock Rovers 310
Shanahan, Carol 230
Shankly, Bill 314
Shaqiri, Xherdan 367
Sharp, Billy 249–50
Shaw, Luke 203, 307
Shearer, Alan 175, 330, 343
Sheen, Michael 336
Sheeran, Ed 219
Sheffield United 165, 229, 249, 279, 345, 387
Sheffield Wednesday 242–3
Sheridan, John 84
Sherwood United 366
Shilton, Peter 33
Shinawatra, Thaksin 242, 346
Short, Ellis 239
Show Racism the Red Card survey 53
Showunmi, Enoch 293
Shrewsbury Town 231, 325
Shrigley, David 215
Silicon Valley 183
Silva, David 314, 315
Silva, Marco 246
Silver Lake (investment fund) 349
Simmons, David 294
Simon, Reuben 83
Sinclair, Trevor 311

Sinderby Wanderers 218
Sinn Féin 101, 107, 110, 112, 113–14, 115
SISU (investment company) 241
Skepta 221
Skripal, Sergei 133, 227
Sky Bet 300–1
Sky Sports 33, 40, 52–3, 167, 174, 184, 275, 300, 301
sleeping pills 151
Smalling, Chris 367
Smith, Arthur: *An Evening with Gary Lineker* 222
Smith, Chris 260
Smith, Delia 30, 215, 230, 387
soap operas
football cameos 8
football references in 7–8
football themed 6–7, 9–10
vs football 5, 9–16
Soccer Saturday 174
Soccer's Foul Play (Channel 4) 75
social inequality 147, 149
social media
abuse 150, 158, 159, 275, 332
digital clubs 292–3
and fandom 390–1
followers, soaps *vs* football 12
and youngsters 86, 146–7
Socios (crypto scheme) 308–9
Somerset FA 90
Sordell, Marvin 152
Souček, Tomáš 85
Souness, Graeme 33, 367
Southampton 75, 76–7, 161, 188, 325, 361, 364, 390
Southampton Saturday Football League 288
Southgate, Gareth 133–8, 176, 199, 200,

201, 203 214, 223, 329, 377, 380, 381
Southport riots (2024) 383
Sparks, Vicki 276
Spartans 129
Spectator 145, 202, 269–70
Speed, Gary 103, 148
Speight, Kevin 316
Spence, Djed 249
Sport for Climate Action Framework (UN) 364
Sport England 267, 288, 298
Sportemon Go 306–7
Sporting Bengal 293
Sporting Khalsa Sikhs 293
Sports Council 75
see also Sport England
sports medicine/science 180–1
sportswashing 354, 355
Srivaddhanaprabha, Vichai 320
stadiums
flooding/storm damage 358–61, 393–4
music at 218–20
re-development 47, 115–16
safety reform 259–61
statues at 314–15
see also pitches
Stamford Bridge 19, 52, 64, 169, 192, 228, 317
Standard Chartered 46
Starmer, Keir 2, 202, 377, 379, 380, 389
Staveley, Amanda 351
Stein, Jock 27
Stelling, Jeff 300
Stenhousemuir 359–60
Sterling, Raheem 52, 64–5
stewards 250, 388
Stewart, Michael 127
Stewart, Paul 76, 78
Stewart, Tony 230
Stirling Albion 129
Stirrup, Gen. Jock 321
Stockwood, Jason 231

Stoke City 39, 155, 232
Stone, Michael 117
Stonewall FC 332
Storey, Daniel 3
Stormont Assembly 110, 113, 115–16
storms (named) 358–61, 393–4
Stormzy 221
Stott, Lally 366
Strapzy, Don 293
Strathclyde Police 121, 122
street football 286–7
Strictly Come Dancing (BBC) 8
Suárez, Luis 50
Sugar, Alan 41, 57
Suleiman, Mohamed 339
Sullivan, David 229, 256
Summerbee, Mike 314
Sun 64, 330, 367
Sunak, Rishi 161, 263, 282, 377, 379
Sunday league 288–9, 293–4
Sunderland 10, 17, 23, 37, 38, 84, 239
Sunderland riots (2024) 383
Sunderland 'Til I Die (Netflix) 10, 239
Super Furry Animals 102, 103
Supporters Direct 258
Supporters' Trust 308
Supreme Council for Financial and Economic Affairs 347
Sutcliffe, Charles 23
Sutton United 346
Swansea City 18, 33, 105, 106, 107, 230, 241, 335
'Sweet Caroline' 219
Swindon Town 155, 234, 314, 368, 373
Szymanski Report 162–3

Tadcaster Albion 359
Tatchell, Peter 330
Taylor, Anthony 83, 94, 96, 247

Taylor, Graham 364
Taylor, Jack 81, 82, 97
Taylor, Neil 104
Taylor Report 258, 259
Taylor, Rupert 297
Tebas, Javier 190
Ted Lasso (Apple TV) 10, 237, 279
Telford 393
ten Hag, Erik 388
Tenerife 339
Tensel, Wesley 176
Terry, John 9, 50–1, 85, 307
Terson, Peter: *Zigger Zagger* 222
Thames Valley Royals 256
Thatcher, Margaret 319
Thomas, Clive 81
Thrasivoulou, Jamie 216
ticket prices 41, 45, 243, 259, 284, 369, 387
Tierney, Paul 96
Tiggs Da Author 221
Times, The 64, 198
Titanic: The Musical 136
'Together Stronger (C'mon Wales)' 103
Toki, Satyam 87
Toney, Ivan 57, 94, 159, 304
Topola, Backa 359
Torbett, Jim 75
Torquay United 230, 275
Toshack, John 103
Total Network Solutions 106
Tottenham Hotspur 20, 27, 57, 94, 215, 229, 249, 261, 308, 365, 385
Townsend, Troy 54
tragedy chanting 313, 316–18
Tranmere Rovers 62, 160, 325
Trautmann, Bert 314
Trinder, Richard 88
Trippier, Kieran 137
Truss, Liz 161, 283
Tuchel, Thomas 246
Tull, Walter 314

Turing, Alan 150
Turner Prize 214
2 Tone Records 219

UAE
  Manchester City ownership 16–17, 44, 346–8
Uddin, Anwar 61
Udinese 238
UEFA
  and European Super League 194
  formation 25
  FA withdraws from 27–8
  FFP financial regulations 349
  see also Champions League; European Championship
UKIP 28, 29, 160, 379
Union Bears 127
Union Jack 101, 113, 120, 379
United! (BBC) 6–7, 13
United Nations (UN) 24, 304, 364
United States
  English club takeovers 10–11, 107, 235–7, 240–2, 257, 368, 387
Unwin, Will 271
Uribe, Mateus 135
Usmanov, Alisher 227

van Dijk, Virgil 94
Van-Tam, Jonathan 146, 176
VAR (Video Assistant Referee)
  correct decisions increased 94
  fan surveys on 92, 94–5
  introduction of 79–80, 92–3
  missed incidents/bad decisions 93–4, 96–7
Vardy, Jamie 134, 144
Vardy, Rebekah 9
VCS (Vulnerable Citizen Support) 296

veganism/vegetarianism 365–7
Vieira, Patrick 250
A View from the Terrace (BBC) 129
Vilda, Jorge 282
Village Manchester 332
Vince, Dale 231, 363
'Vindaloo' 200

Waddingham, Hannah 279
Waddle, Chris 33–4, 218
'Wagatha Christie' affair 9
Wagner, Tom 241
Wales Championship 337
Wales national team (Cymru) 101, 102, 103–5, 196–7, 336–7
Walford Town 7
Walker, Jack 41
Walker, Kyle 143
Walking Football Association 290
Wallace, Sam 194
Wallace, William 200
Wallinger, Mark: *They Think It's All Over … It Is Now* 214
Waltham Forest 315
Ward, Lucy 276
Warnock, Neil 33
Warren, Lee 88
Warrenpoint Town 109
Watford 165, 224, 238–9, 308, 364
Weatherfield County 7
Webb, Howard 83, 85, 97
Webber, Stuart 57
Webster, Kieran 367
Week 134
Welcome to Wrexham (documentary) 10, 237
Weir, Colin 230
Welch, Rebecca 276
Wellens, Richie 155
Welsh football fans (Red Wall) 104, 335–6

and popular music culture 101–2, 335
see also Wales national team; Welsh Premier league
Welsh Football Fans for Independence 197
Welsh independence 197
Welsh, Irvine: *Dead Men's Trousers* 217–18
Welsh language 337–8
Welsh Premier League 105–6
Welsh Rugby Union 102
Wembley Stadium 199, 204, 205, 206, 292, 298
Wenger, Arsène 41, 86, 177, 256, 380
West Bromwich Albion 39, 132, 151, 152, 159, 163, 169, 176, 215, 244, 314, 322
West Ham United 7, 8, 46, 52, 68, 115, 131–2, 177, 178, 229, 249, 256, 284, 301, 308, 323–4
Wheeler, David 374
Whelan, Dave 314, 319
Whitby Town 360
Whittingham, Jason 232
Wigan Athletic 38, 49, 154, 319, 394
Wigan Rose 87
Wilde, Oscar 226
Wiley, Alan 83
William, Prince 191, 282, 313
Williams, Alex 221
Williams, Ashley 104
Williams, Gwyn 70
Williams, Ifor 237
Williams, Roy: *Sing Yer Heart Out for the Lads* 222
Williams, Tyrell 223
Willock, Joe 159
Wilshire, Jack 301, 307, 367
Wilson, Harold 378

Wilson, Jonathan 383
Wimbledon, AFC 230, 231, 393
Windrush generation 220, 293
Windsor Park, Belfast 107, 108, 111, 112, 113, 114, 115, 116
Winkelman, Pete 231
Winstone, Ray 300
Winter, Jeff 83
Wise, Dennis 8
Wisten, Jeremy 147
Wolverhampton Wanderers 6–7, 37, 229, 231, 244, 364, 365, 372
women commentators 276–7, 392
Women and Equalities Committee 272, 274
Women in Football 276, 280
Women's European Championship 2022 217, 224–5, 265–6
Women's FA Cup 2024 271
women's football
Carney Report 281
club inequality 281
crowds 265–6, 271–2
FA ban 267
growth of 266–7
Her Game Too campaign 275
injuries 274
kit 272–3
and media coverage 268–9
and menstruation 273
number of players/ teams (UK) 266–7
responses to rise of 269–70
Women's Super League 15, 164, 266, 270, 281, 359, 374
Women's World Cup 266, 268–9, 281–2
Wood, David 117
Woodward, Andy 76, 78
Worcester City 380

Worcester Warriors 233
World Bank 24
World Cup
1930s 24
1966 2, 313
2010 217
2018 92, 133–8
2022 *see* Qatar World Cup
'The World of Gazza!!' (exhibition) 213
'World in Motion' 161
Worsbrough Bridge Athletic 360
Wrexham 10–11, 106, 107, 237, 255, 312, 327, 335, 368
Wright, Billy 314
Wright, Bradley 219
Wright, Ian 8, 62, 63, 191, 343
Wubben-Moy, Lotte 271, 374
Wycherley, Ronald 231
Wycombe Wanderers 84, 186, 230, 380
Wythenshawe Town 55

X (Twitter) 150, 159
Xi Jinping 243
Xia, Tony 243

Y Glannau St Asaph 337
Yarro, John 295
Yems, John 56
Yeoh, Francis 229
YesCymru 197
'Yma o Hyd' 335
Yorkshire Post 80
'You'll Never Walk Alone' 220
Young, Ashley 53
Young, Toby 270
Yr Wyddgrug 337

Zaha, Wilfried 53, 158, 287
Zayed, Sheikh 346
Zidane (Gordon/ Parreno) 214
Zola, Gianfranco 29
Zurich Insurance 361